Temples of Enterprise:

Creating Economic Order in the Bronze Age Near East

Michael Hudson

©2024 ISLET – Verlag
©2024 Michael Hudson
Set in Baskerville
All rights reserved

www.michael-hudson.com
www.islet-verlag.de

Cover design by Miguel Guerra. It depicts Enmetena's amargi proclamation (Enmetena inscription AO 24414. Louvre, Paris). The depiction is based on Lambert, Maurice, "L'expansion de Lagash au temps d'Entemena," *Rivista Degli Studi Orientali* 47:3.

Index by Ashley Dayman

Typeset by Global University for Sustainability

Hudson, Michael, 1939-
Temples of Enterprise: Creating Economic Order in the Bronze Age Near East

ISBN 978-3-949546-18-1 paperback
ISBN 978-3-949546-19-8 hardback

Contents

Preface	iii
Introduction	1
Summary	9

I Money's Origins: Fiscal Account-Keeping and Credit

1. Origins of Money and Interest: Palatial Credit, not Barter (2020)	19
2. Civic and Temple Origins of Ancient Coinage	49
3. Social vs. "Individualistic" Theories of the Origins of Money and Interest (2004)	71
4. How Interest Rates Were Set, 2500 BC-1000 AD (2000)	91
5. How Clean Slates Restored Order: Circular vs. Linear Time (2002)	119

II Land Tenure: From its Fiscal Origins to Financialization

6. How the Organization of Labor Shaped Civilization's Economic Takeoff (2015)	141
7. Land Tenure: From Fiscal Origins to Financialization (1998)	157
8. Land Monopolization and Taxation from Antiquity to Post-Roman Europe (1998)	179

III Urban Origins, Social Cosmology and Privatization

9. After the Ice Age: Calendar-Keeping and the Archaic Urban Cosmos (2009)	207
10. From Sacred Enclave to Temple to City (1999)	213
11. Entrepreneurs: From the Near Eastern Takeoff to the Roman Collapse (2010)	249
12. Money and Land as Public Utilities	295

Map: Ancient Near East and Mediterranean	303
Subject Index	305
Name Index - People(s)	325
Name Index - Places	331

Preface

The twelve articles collected in this volume describe how the most basic features of Western economic organization – money, markets, land tenure and enterprise – were created in the temples and palaces of the ancient Near East. My perspective on these topics originated in the five international colloquia organized by the Institute for the Study of Long-term Economic Trends (ISLET) with Harvard University's Peabody Museum from 1994 to 2015. When these meetings began, most assyriology, Egyptology and classical studies tended to accept the views of modern economic orthodoxy. Archaic social values were so different from today's views that there was resistance to recognizing the extent to which the Bronze Age economic takeoff, 3500-1200 BC, followed policies radically unlike our own.

That was the case above all with the royal debt cancellations that provided the prototype for the biblical Jubilee Year. Most of the debts being annulled were owed as rents and fees to temple and palace collectors for the advance of land, seeds, animals, and beer from ale houses (literally pubs). These debts were cancelled because they exceeded the agrarian population's ability to pay, and non-payment would have led to a loss of liberty and, in due course, loss of the self-support land that archaic societies allotted in proportion to the ability of its cultivators to provide corvée labor and serve in the military.

Royal debt cancellations were my initial concern in planning these international colloquia. But the fact that most debt obligations were to be paid in grain or silver led to an analysis of money's origins. Its main role was to pay debts and other obligations, typically at harvest time, and also for account-keeping to allocate resources within the temples and palatial economy. Official values were assigned to grain and some other key commodities precisely to standardize debt settlements in what actually was a credit economy. Money did not originate out of on-the-spot barter as long had been believed to be the case. Interest-bearing debt similarly emerged in conjunction with payment of advances to traders or of overdue agrarian debts in Mesopotamia's mixed public/private economies. Fluctuations in supply and demand did not play a role in such debt settlements. The aim was to stabilize and standardize the palatial economy's fiscal relations with the economy at large.

Like peeling away layers of an onion, understanding the institutional context in which archaic societies monetized debts and set interest rates required explaining the organization of land tenure and how the temples and palaces were corporately distinct institutions set apart from the community at large. There has been well-founded criticism among Assyriologists about characterizing these large institutions as "public" in view of their control by the royal family, and given the role played by "private" merchants to whom textiles were consigned for foreign trade or who were advanced land or herds to administer.

But when considering the public/private dichotomy in the context of the Bronze Age Near East, the key is that society's land, labor obligations and the credit and debt system were treated as what today are called public utilities. They were to be managed in a way that preserved economic resilience, not privatized without concern for private self-interest leading to practices that would damage and destabilize the economy.
Land tenure was subject to so many social obligations that it originally was as much public as private. But the personal indebtedness of smallholders was the great lever working to establish patron-client relationships and privatize land tenure. Debt-induced privatization led to widening inequality as debtors had to work off their debts with labor or lose their personal liberty and land rights. Royal Clean Slate overrides reversed this polarization repeatedly over the course of thousands of years.

The economic practices that were created as part of the Near East's social and political system were adopted in a new "privatized" context by Greece and Italy around the 8th century BC. A great discontinuity occurred as palatial economies were replaced by oligarchies, which gained power largely through the dynamics of interest-bearing debt no longer checked by royal Clean Slates. The new non-palatial context for credit and debt led to the major distinguishing economic feature of subsequent Western civilization: what came to be sanctified was the inviolability of debt, not its cancellation; that is, an exponentially increasing debt burden owed to a *rentier* oligarchy. In classical antiquity, creditor oligarchies obtained the land of smallholders and used their resulting wealth to control government and resist popular pressures to cancel debts and redistribute the land such as had occurred in the Near East.

Bronze Age societies could not have survived for long if they had held today's views about the "security of contracts" (headed by creditor claims) and the irreversibility of land transfers from debtors to the wealthy. Today's economic and ideological orthodoxy shies from recognizing what Aristotle stated so clearly over two thousand years ago:

Democracies evolve into oligarchies. Mesopotamia avoided that fate for thousands of years under its regime of "divine kingship."

My main debt for this book is to Carl Lamberg-Karlovsky for inviting me to join the Peabody Museum as a research fellow in 1984, and helping organize the two decades of colloquia from 1994 to 2015 at New York University, Columbia University, the British Museum and ISLET. My co-editors Baruch Levine, Marc Van De Mieroop, Cornelia Wunsch and Piotr Steinkeller selected the participants in these colloquia and co-ordinated their contributions. Five chapters of this book are from these colloquia reconstructing the origins of land tenure and urbanization, money and interest-bearing debt, royal Clean Slate proclamations and the organization of labor.

The initial chapter on the origins of money and interest-bearing debt is reprinted from a recent encyclopedia on money and credit. Chapter 2 on coinage and the last chapter on money and land as public utilities are new. The remaining chapters on land tenure, urban origins and the privatization of enterprise are from scholarly journals and anthologies. I have edited them to avoid repetition among the articles, and have taken the opportunity to improve the language and organization. I have been greatly helped by my copy editor Ashley Dayman, and by my usual team of typesetters in Hong Kong, Kelven Cheung and Jin Peiyun.

The greatest help has come from my wife, Grace Hudson. Her support and protection of my time has enabled me to keep the focus needed to write the articles in this book. I could not have completed these studies without her loving support. This book is appropriately dedicated to her.

Introduction

Every economy in history has required planning. The question is, by whom and in whose interest? How are personal economic interests, property rights and credit and fiscal obligations aligned with overall social balance, growth and resilience?

The Neolithic agricultural revolution's planting, harvesting and specialization of labor required lines of authority, rules for interpersonal relations and forward planning. Bronze Age religion, ideas of social order and authority played a major role in organizing production and exchange. Near Eastern temples and palaces innovated land tenure and its associated labor obligations, weights, measures and money to regularize the production and distribution of crops, handicrafts and basic services.

Mesopotamia in particular had a need to organize foreign trade to obtain metal, stone and other raw materials lacking in the region's rich alluvial soil. Many of the textiles and other handicrafts that it consigned to traders were woven by dependent labor, mainly war widows and orphans employed in temple and palace workshops as a distinct sector of the economy. The role of Mesopotamian temples in developing this specialization of labor and creating rules for monetary exchange and credit for foreign trade explains why they can indeed be called temples of enterprise.

Structuring markets and commercial enterprise hardly could have been innovated by individuals bartering and lending money, cattle or grain to one another on their own. It required a critical social mass and the organizational and planning capacity provided by large institutions, first Mesopotamian temples and then palaces. And social resilience required the economy to be managed as an overall system in order to prevent credit imbalances from destabilizing basic land-tenure relations. Most economic life was conducted by running up credit balances, mainly by cultivators during the crop year and by merchants conducting long-distance trade. Management of this credit frequently obliged rulers to intervene in the economy, doing so in ways consistent with traditional social values.

The social ethic of archaic society was much like that of today's low-surplus communities in viewing large personal wealth as a threat to social balance. That ethic was the reverse of the modern "greed is good" ideology. Early civilization used regulatory oversight to subordinate selfishness and promote overall welfare. Maintaining resilience in an environment subject to crop failures from bad weather, pestilence and warfare required institutionally shaped "market forces" to cope with the strains that resulted from agrarian debt that threatened to lead to permanent bondage and appropriation of land by creditors.

The Bronze Age Near East avoided this fate by rulers proclaiming Clean Slates cancelling debts, liberating debtors from bondage and returning to debtors the self-support land that they had lost. That was how the societies in which interest-bearing debt was first developed addressed the accompanying problem of creditor claims on income and property tending to exceed the ability to pay. And this basically is the problem that has confronted economies ever since. But in contrast to classical antiquity's polarization between creditors and debtors, the disruption of personal liberty and land tenure was kept fairly temporary for thousands of years throughout the Near East by the practice of Clean Slates.

Anachronistic anthropological and economic attempts to explain the Bronze Age takeoff

Today's free-market orthodoxy condemns such government activism as interfering with property rights, "the market" and the "security of contracts." But that regulatory oversight is precisely what maintained social cohesiveness from the third to the mid-first millennia BC. Near Eastern societies were regularly freed from the accumulation of debt – and hence the accumulation of creditor claims – that ended up polarizing classical antiquity, leading ultimately to its decline and fall, and bequeathing Rome's pro-creditor philosophy to modern Western legal systems.

If Mesopotamians had been more considerate of modern historians' attempts to understand the logic that underlay their economic practices, they might have left a treatise explaining what they were thinking when they organized their trade and credit relations in the way they did. They no doubt thought that their path was so obvious as to be self-evident in a world that shared similar social values.

What made Mesopotamia unique, however, was its need for foreign raw materials on a scale much larger than that of any other society of the time, and of the modern tribal enclaves that most anthropologists have studied. The Sumerian commercial trade outreach to obtain these materials led to financial innovations and new property relationships. The initial context for charging interest, for instance, seems not to have been the domestic economy. Rather, the practice appears to have arisen as a means of financing Sumer's long-distance trade in a way that provided the consigner (the palace or temples) with what was deemed to be a fair share of the mercantile gains – doubling the value of the consigned export goods in five years (at the usual commercial interest rate of 20 percent per annum in decimal terms).

Until fairly recently these Near Eastern economic origins were unknown to modern scholarship, much of which attempted (and often still attempts) to skip over the actual economic origins of modern civilization by taking surviving tribal enclaves or even early Greek and Roman practices as proxies for "civilization in its infancy." This approach rests on the Victorian idea of a universal set of stages of development, similar and self-contained for each region. In *The Gift* (1925), Marcel Mauss sought the source of interest charges in gift exchange – "prestation," whose French root means "loan," *prête*. He cited the potlatch ceremonies of the Kwakiutl on Canada's Pacific Coast as an example of one-upmanship with some exchangers expected to reciprocate a present with an "overplus."

But there are no pristine societies in today's world with institutions resembling those of Sumer and Babylonia with their standardized administered prices and rates of interest. Gifts represent floating obligations that do not bear interest or have a specified date on which they must be paid. They do not require a monetary system to precisely quantify exchanges. The reciprocities involved are not specified in advance as a definite proportion of the original gift. If an overplus is involved, it is informal and discretionary, an expression of self-image or perhaps a response to peer pressure, but not interest in the economic sense of the term. In contrast, failure to pay debts does not result simply in losing face; it permits the creditor to proceed with formal foreclosure proceedings, leading to debt bondage and forfeiture of land-rights. And unlike gifts, record-keeping of interest-bearing debt is essential as a basis for pledging collateral in anticipation of legal foreclosure procedures for non-payment.

Charging monetary interest represents a quantum leap beyond tribal practice. The historian Tacitus (*Germania* 26) noted that the tribally organized Germans, whose debts were mainly of the wergild type for legal restitution of damages, were not acquainted with loans at interest. This probably can be taken as applying to European tribal communities generally.

Mesopotamia's main creditors were the temples and palaces, as well as travelling merchants such as the Assyrians in central Anatolia ca. 1900 BC. By the 8th century BC, Syrian and Phoenician traders in the Aegean and Italy were the main creditors in the Mediterranean. But classical

Western antiquity does not offer prototypes helpful in explaining the origins of interest. What ancient Greece and Rome did have were formal debt-collection procedures (the village pound) for wergild type debts. These long predated commercial debts for profit-making commerce or rent-yielding agricultural advances, and their payment rules were part of common law.

After the transmission of interest-bearing debt to the West around the 8th century BC most interest in classical Greece was charged by (and to) outsiders, typically aliens or slaves working for them. Benjamin Nelson[1] (1949) has described that the essence of usury is "otherhood," in contrast to the brotherhood of mutual aid. Gifts typically are reciprocated among equals, and it is deemed ungentlemanly to charge interest to one's social peers. Even as classical Greek society was succumbing to usury from the 6th century BC onward, aristocrats refrained from charging interest on loans to each other via *eranos* societies.

It thus is anachronistic to try and infer how money and the charging of interest originated in Mesopotamia by looking at modern tribal enclaves or classical antiquity. Even more anachronistic is the "economic" approach that imagines the ideological justification for modern free-market economies to be so universal that money and interest-bearing debt must have started out in a way that is consistent with and supports the logic of this ideology.

The Bronze Age Near Eastern mentalité

Few anthropologists or economic historians feel comfortable addressing Mesopotamia's pivotal role in innovating and shaping civilization's most basic economic institutions. Despite the fact that the temples and palaces of Sumer and Babylonia developed the key economic innovations that have led civilization to develop in the way it has, the ancient Near East has not had much influence on modern anthropological thinking, and even less on the economic origin myths of how money and interest evolved out of individuals bartering and competing to see who could become the wealthiest.

As Near Eastern economies grew more differentiated, specialized and capital-intensive labor was concentrated in the temples and palaces. Co-ordinating the distribution of food and raw materials within these large institutions required a uniform standard of valuation for internal use

---

[1] Nelson, Benjamin (1960 [1949]), *The Idea of Usury: From Tribal Brotherhood to Universal Otherhood*, 2nd ed. (Princeton).

and exchange (*i.e.*, money). Rising complexity also required credit arrangements. Most obligations were owed to the palace, via its collectors and merchant-managers to whom rulers consigned foreign trade and the rental of land. The task for rulers was to maintain viability by preventing wealthy individuals in this collector-manager class from maximizing their gains at the expense of social resilience, above all by gaining wealth in ways that reduced cultivators to bondage.

The papers in this book focus on five characteristics that shaped the archaic worldview that underlay its credit practices, money and market exchange, land tenure and the organization of labor and enterprise.

Reciprocity characterizes all anthropological communities. A tradition of mutual aid was necessary for resilience and indeed survival. That included personal obligations and penalties for injury such as archaic Germanic wergild and similar practices throughout Western Europe, with collection procedures for such debts. Obligations of this type were kept within the ability of cultivators to meet under normal circumstances. Also based on reciprocity was the assignment of land tenure as part of a *quid pro quo*, with the holder obliged to provide corvée labor to build public infrastructure and serve in the military. Viable growth required ensuring citizens the means of self-support on their assigned plots, and land was provided in proportion to the holder's ability to provide this corvée labor and military service.

Resilience was achieved by Clean Slates restoring economic balance when it was disturbed by warfare, floods or droughts, or by excessive debt obligations beyond the ability to be paid. An oppressive monarchy or oligarchy could not have survived for long if confronted with internal dissent to unseat the ruler, defection to foreign attackers or widespread flight to other land. Land tenure was viewed as a natural right, not as a commodity to be privatized and financialized. Land was still a public utility, a precondition for labor's freedom of self-support, not yet permitted to become a choke point for landlords to permanently reduce debtors to bondage and gain control of their labor and extract crop rent for themselves. Deprivation of self-support would have led to a flight from the land, in an epoch when labor was the scarcest resource.

Standardization was needed for the account-keeping required for forward planning and resource allocation to organize the distribution of food and other products to the palace and temple staffs and for corvée labor projects on a regular basis. The administrative year was divided into uniform 30-day months and a sexagesimal (60-based) system of fractions was used to denominate weights and measures for monthly allocations.

Money emerged as a byproduct of administered price ratios to quantify payments for transactions between the community and the temples and palaces. The silver shekel-weight's value was set as equal to a "basket" of barley, and as accruing monthly interest of one shekel ($1/60^{th}$) per mina when lent out, most paradigmatically for goods consigned to merchants on credit to trade abroad.

Hierarchy assigned status, and everyone was subject to some higher authority. Children and wives were subject to the male household head, who was subject to the ruler, who himself was subject to the city-temple's patron deities of justice and equity.

However, a problem developed as the palatial bureaucracy and mercantile traders acted in their own self-interest, especially as creditors. Households operated increasingly on credit as communities grew larger and production became specialized. When they could not pay their obligations, the officials did so, thereby establishing creditor claims. These debts accumulated wealth outside of the reciprocity ethic, and resulted in creditors gaining control of labor and the land rights of citizens at the expense of palatial claims.

Rulers were not socialist, but they were not yet protectors of a *rentier* aristocracy as would become the case from imperial Rome to modern times. Their aim was to prevent creditors from permanently prying away the palatial sharecropping rents and corvée labor services of smallholders who had fallen into debt. Rulers resisted this incipient rivalry with creditors by annulling agrarian debts. In addition to maintaining widespread self-support for the citizenry on the land, these Clean Slates protected the palace's fiscal needs and its control of labor service and crop rents.

What was conserved was royal authority. Keeping creditors subject to royal intervention was not a radical act. Just the opposite: It was conservative on the part of Bronze Age monarchies. Their hierarchal authority rested on their success in preserving stable social relations to maintain military strength and economic viability.

Liberty – the Bronze Age version of a free economy – required ongoing intervention from "above" the market. Sumerian amargi, Babylonian *misharum* and cognate royal Clean Slate proclamations restored the "mother condition," an idealized "straight order" as a customary norm in the form of freedom of citizens from debt bondage except on a limited temporary basis to work off their debts. (Only foreigners were slaves, mainly captured mountain girls.) That was a basic element of the archaic social contract. To regularly restore this condition – along with the palace's fiscal revenue – every ruler in Hammurabi's[2] Babylonian dynasty annulled agrarian debts upon taking the throne, and when war, crop failure, outbreak of disease or similar "acts of God" (Enlil, Babylon's Storm God) called for such intervention. That also was the logic by which his laws (ca. 1750 BC) cancelled agrarian debts in such circumstances.

By recognizing that an inability to pay debts on a widespread basis threatened to destroy liberty and destabilize social viability and enable a self-aggrandizing oligarchy to emerge, Bronze Age rulers had a more realistic view of the polarizing dynamics of debt than do modern economists. No archaic ruler anticipated British Prime Minister Margaret Thatcher's neoliberal claim that "there is no such thing as society. There are individual men and women and there are families." There was no thought of creating an economy without government playing any role on the ground that all governments do are "interfere," tax, regulate and bureaucratize. Rather than praising monetary success and wealth, Bronze Age rulers and the philosophy of their communities acted to prevent personal wealth aggrandizement from leading to behavior disturbing social balance. Rulers pledged to follow the precepts of their sun gods of justice and justice goddesses protecting the poor from abuses by the rich.

The policies following from this mentality are what make the Bronze Age so relevant for the modern world. But that mentality and the economic reality it created causes cognitive dissonance on the part of economic historians who subscribe to individualistic anti-government fantasies about the origins of money, land ownership and economic enterprise. A Clean Slate policy of rolling back contractual debt obligations and reversing land transfers from debtors seemed so radical as to be unthinkable for most 20th century observers. Many Assyriologists long doubted that these royal proclamations were more than utopian rhetoric. Today, however, the mainstream of Assyriologists and other historians of the ancient Near East and Biblical lands acknowledge the reality of Clean Slates. Yet economists and scholars in other disciplines mostly resist this history, being unwilling to countenance it even as a possibility. To modern eyes it seems natural to

---

[2] In view of the century-long practice of spelling the name of Babylon's ruler "Hammurabi" instead of the most linguistically correct Hammurapi, I have yielded to the inertia of familiarity created in public discussion. But readers should be aware of the point made by Giorgio Buccellati: "The name is usually rendered 'Hammurabi' but this mixes Amorite (*Hammu* for *ammu* 'the (deified) paternal uncle') and Akkadian (*rabic* 'is great'). One should instead keep the original Amorite also fero the second part: *rapi* 'he heals' (as in Hebrew Raphael for *rapā-El*)." Giorgio Buccellati, *At the Origins of Politics: Formation and Growth of the State in Syro-Mesopotamia* (Milan, in press [2013]):162.

permit free markets for debt – yet that is what Bronze Age rulers resisted for millennia, and it is what ended up polarizing the economies of classical Greece and Rome, ultimately causing the latter's collapse. The problem for Rome was not so much "barbarians at the gates" but the domestic creditor and land-monopolizing oligarchy that weakened society economically from within.

Our epoch's privatization of finance and rising overgrowth of debt is the opposite of the archaic policy of restoring an idealized debt-free distribution of land supporting a free smallholder population. Instead of restoring order by wiping out the debt overhead at the point where it becomes economically oppressive, the modern myth of self-regulating markets has rationalized the polarization of wealth ownership that Western economies have suffered, increasingly so since the 2008 financial crash. It provides no logic for preventing such a result. Despite the widening financial imbalance throughout the Western world, our mainstream economic theory rationalizes and applauds the freedom of wealth to maximize its gains even at the expense of social resilience.

The Western world's spirit is claimed to be one of progress and ongoing economic transformation, including what Joseph Schumpeter characterized as "creative destruction" by ambitious wealth-seekers driving society forward. But the overgrowth of debt leading to financial austerity and economic polarization is seen as an anomaly, not as an inherent and in fact universal feature that flows from the dynamics of interest-bearing debt if left unchecked. It is that feature which Bronze Age societies felt compelled to avoid, and indeed they succeeded in subordinating financial gain-seeking to the objective of sustaining overall economic growth and resilience.

According to today's ideological mainstream, civilization never could have taken off in the way that it did. The assumption is that royal overrides limiting financial gain-seeking would have blocked what today is welcomed as the mainspring of prosperity. But according to the Bronze Age world view, any economy, including our modern economies, could not long survive along a path that concentrates income and wealth in the hands of a wealthy financial and property-owning class while reducing the rest of the economy to debt servitude.

Summary

Money, interest-bearing debt, land tenure and rent originated in the temples and palaces of Mesopotamia and Egypt in the third millennium BC. Recognition of how these large institutions created the basic elements of market exchange and economic enterprise dispels the myth of individuals inventing money and markets simply by bartering and lending with each other without government playing any positive role.

Even more antithetical to mainstream financial mythology is the fact that the archaic structuring of credit was accompanied by royal "restorations of order" that freed realms from an overgrowth of debt. The success of these acts seems anomalous to economic historians who oppose public regulation ("interference in free markets") and focus only on the helpful and productive role of credit. Today's ideological claim that pro-creditor laws are natural and should be universal avoids acknowledging how Bronze Age rulers saved their realms from widespread impoverishment by rolling back debts, and how subsequent economies from classical antiquity to today have failed to protect their increasingly indebted populations.

The Western historical continuum is depicted as originating only in classical Greece and Rome, "free" of royal Clean Slates. Despite five centuries of Greek and Roman revolts advocating debt cancellations and land redistribution, their oligarchies amassed wealth by driving debtors into debt bondage, monopolizing the land and using their economic power to avoid paying taxes, bringing on economic polarization, austerity and a fiscal crisis. That is the fate that Bronze Age rulers managed to avert. But their success in protecting the resilience of debtors (that is, most of the population) instead of creditor claims clashes with modern preconceptions. It is a classic case of cognitive dissonance.

Money and interest as fiscal innovations

The five chapters comprising Part I of this book describe the origins of money in fiscal arrangements innovated by Mesopotamian temples and palaces for paying fees, taxes and other debts. These large institutions monetized designated commodities (a silver shekel set equal to a bushel of grain) for the payment of their fees and advances.

Chapter 1 describes how the Bronze Age temples and palaces of Mesopotamia (3500 to 1200 BC) developed cost-accounting to coordinate the flow of food and raw materials needed to provision labor for public building projects and handicraft workshops. That provisioning required designing weights and measures. Prices for food and raw materials (and fees) were assigned monetary values in silver or grain to keep accounts and denominate fiscal balances. Silver and grain so valued were used for payments to the temples and palaces. These were the first forms of money, whose origin is thus in institutional fiscal arrangements. Weighed pieces of silver were used for thousands of years in the Near East, usually in standardized weights often imprinted with the marks of the temples that produced the silver of specified purity (typically 7/8 pure).

Chapter 2, discussing the civic-temple origins of ancient coinage, describes how civic authorities in Greece and Rome followed the Near Eastern practice of assigning to temples the role of minting monetary metals in standardized amounts and overseeing their quality, with coins being minted by temples starting early in the 6th century BC in Greece and Asia Minor. The innovation of coinage was not transformative, but 19th-century historians believed that it catalyzed the debt struggles that erupted throughout the Mediterranean world around this time. What actually caused the social revolts and long string of political murders from the 5th through 1st centuries BC was the refusal of oligarchies to grant the citizenry's demands for land redistribution and debt cancellation, which Near Eastern rulers had been enacting for some 2500 years.

Today's controversies over whether money and debt relations should be publicly regulated or left "free" and unregulated echo the issues raised in antiquity's creditor/debtor struggles. Chapter 3 focuses on the ideological controversy prompted by individualists (following the 19th-century Austrian Carl Menger) imagining early economies to have operated on barter, without debt or public institutions playing a significant role. Opposing public regulation and money creation, this approach views money merely as a commodity to be bartered, not as owing its value to its acceptance for payment of fees and taxes to civic authorities. Governments are portrayed as acting only in predatory ways, and private creditors only as helping debtors improve their economic position, not as reducing them to clientage, bondage and ultimately to serfdom.

This anti-government mythology echoes the rhetoric of Greek and Roman oligarchies accusing reformers of being "tyrants" for advocating debt cancellation and land redistribution. But it was the Greek tyrants of the 7th and 6th centuries BC who prepared the ground for the Greek democratic takeoff by overthrowing creditor autocracies, liberating debt-slaves and redistributing land. Subsequent oligarchies used the word "tyrant" as a term of invective against popular advocates of debt and land reform.

A feature of the Near Eastern credit and debt innovations was the practice of charging interest. Chapter 4 describes how interest rates throughout antiquity were set for ease of mathematical calculation according to the local system of fractions, not by "economic" factors such as profit rates or productivity. Mesopotamia's silver-interest rate of $1/60^{th}$ per month was based on its sexagesimal measure of 60 shekels per mina. Interest rates in Greece and Rome likewise were guided by a concern for the ease of calculation based on the local system of fractions: $1/10^{th}$ annually in classical Greece, which seems to have adopted the decimal system from Egypt; and $1/12^{th}$ (a troy ounce per pound) per year in Rome, whose duodecimal system evidently was based on the division of the year into twelve months.

These interest rates were not based on productivity, profitability or the ability to pay. Babylonian student exercises show that they recognized that herds, for instance, increased at a slower pace than did the growth of debt balances doubling in five years, to say nothing of agrarian rates typically around 33⅓ percent. Recognizing that debts at these rates frequently could not be paid, Bronze Age social values sanctified their cancellation, in contrast to today's economic ideology endorsing the sanctity of debt.

When the idea of charging interest diffused from the Near East to the West ca. the 8th century BC, its introduction led to a self-expanding growth of interest-bearing debt that soon polarized Western economies between creditors and debtors. By reducing much of the population to bondage, Rome's creditor oligarchy dismantled society's ability to grow or even to defend itself by the time the Empire fell in the 5th century AD.

The most problematic debts were personal obligations owed by cultivators living on the margin of subsistence. Chapter 5 discusses Mesopotamia's royal Clean Slate proclamations that prevented debts from overwhelming the economy's ability to pay. To have let the growing debt burden lead to personal bondage or the transfer of land to creditors on more than a temporary basis would have polarized and impoverished society. To prevent agrarian debts from causing economic strains and violating society's norms of equity, they were forgiven and liberty and self-support land rights were restored. But when the idea of charging interest was introduced to the West, it was not accompanied by this practice of Clean Slates, although centuries of popular revolts from Greece to Rome advocated debt cancellation and land redistribution.

Land tenure as a byproduct of the communal organization of labor

The three chapters of Part II review the evolution of land tenure and the increasing appropriation of land rents by creditors and conquerors. Land always has been the most important form of property. The major dynamic shaping land tenure in the late Neolithic and Early Bronze Age was the organization of labor, the scarcest factor of production in archaic civilization. The land always was there, but irrigating it, and supplying transportation and public infrastructure to distribute its crops required the community's labor. To meet these labor needs, land tenure was allotted with labor obligations to be performed by its holders.

Chapter 6 describes the organization of archaic labor and how land tenure initially was organized as a public utility and allotted in proportion to the holder's obligation to perform two basic archaic tasks: corvée labor and service in the military. Warfare was a constant threat and labor was needed for communal building projects. These labor obligations were civilization's first "tax" obligations. It was to enable citizens to perform them that land tenure rights to self-support land were granted as a basic right of citizenship, being necessary for the economy to survive and grow.

Chapter 7 describes how this communally based land tenure was privatized, largely by creditors prying it away from smallholders. Debt was the great lever working to privatize land tenure. This debt-induced privatization led to widening inequality.

The fantasy about money and interest evolving without any role played by the community, palace or temples finds its analog in myths about how private land ownership originated with private individuals acting on their own. John Locke drew a mythical picture of the ancestors of Britain's landlord class earning rights to the land by clearing and improving it with their own labor. The reality, of course, was that the conquering Norman warrior aristocracy imposed groundrent as hereditary tribute.

But Frederick Engels' *Origin of the Family, Private Property and the State* (1884) also was anachronistic in viewing chieftains and powerful families as organizing the state to protect their monopolization of land. That is indeed what happened under classical antiquity's oligarchies, but civilization's initial property formalities hardly could have originated in this way. Down to the mid-first millennium BC labor remained the scarce resource. There was plenty of land. What was needed was labor to work it. Populations were able to obtain land tenure rights by joining communities in need of their labor power. Without such rights, families would have settled elsewhere.

Most archaic communities created land tenure rights by common law, implicitly based on mutual aid and communal seasonal labor. They could not afford the domineering behavior of private wealth accumulation exploiting the labor of others by extracting land rent and interest. That would have led populations to flee or revolt.

Engels' view of how powerful families monopolized the land is much like economic desert-island models explaining land rent as a result of the first settlers blocking off land for themselves. The basic imagery is that of Daniel Defoe's *Robinson Crusoe* (1719). Assume a desert island (the favorite venue for much economic theorizing), and suppose that the first settler (or settlers) claimed ownership of all the land as their own personal property. One day a man, Friday, lands on the island, perhaps as a shipwrecked sailor. He needs access to land in order to survive. But Crusoe says: "The land is mine. I discovered it. You have to work for me, paying rent with your labor." Friday becomes his slave.

That is basically what Engels had his archaic chieftains and leading families do. But one might just as well imagine Friday arriving on the island (or archaic families arriving in communities) and demanding that Crusoe pay *him* to participate in Crusoe's own work to create a crop yield. Or, he could have fought Crusoe, or sided with new arrivals to obtain the land – or made a raft and sailed away in search of new land.

In reality, of course, civilization could not have begun on a desert island. Economic organization requires a critical mass. Labor had a strong hand to play, including by removing selfish chieftains who monopolized the land (overthrown most notably by the Greek reformer-tyrants) or defecting to attackers, or simply running away. Rome's foundation myth depicts its origins as a refuge for runaways, growing as its kings provided newcomers with plots of land in the hilly land by the Tiber.

Chapter 8 outlines the stages of land tenure, taxation and privatization. First came self-support land tenure together with the "tax," initially in the form of labor obligations attached to those land-tenure rights enabling families to support themselves and perform the labor services attached to these rights. But by the end of antiquity the largest landowners became an aristocracy able to evade taxation. That collapsed the fiscal budget, and with it Rome's monetary standard. It was at that endpoint that silver ceased to be "money" and became merely a commodity to be bartered.

Urbanization, temples and commercial enterprise

Part III describes the origins of urbanization in Mesopotamia and how ritual centers developed as gathering places or trading venues before cities emerged in the modern sense of the term.

Chapter 9 reviews Alexander Marshack's description of how such centers emerged already in the Ice Age as meeting places, much like classical amphictyonic centers for tribal divisions to come together at seasonal intervals. Calendrical cosmology was the essential key to the earliest gathering places. Widely dispersed hunter-gatherers developed luni-solar calendars to calculate just when to congregate in their ceremonial centers for gift exchange, marriages and other interaction.

Chapter 10 discusses the sanctification of such sites as public spaces set apart from tribal territory. An urban cosmology developed, centered on a temple, with typically four gates reflecting the seasons, and often ceremonial constructions to celebrate the New Year, equinoxes or solstices. These public centers became year-round cities whose population was private as well as sacred, with developing public administrative functions.

Archaic cities were centered around their temples, and those of Sumer, with their workshops producing handicrafts for export, were the first centers of enterprise. Greek and Italian temples were not the entrepreneurial centers that their Sumerian predecessors had been, but in addition to minting the coinage of their cities and overseeing weights and measures, they promoted an ethic warning against hubris and wealth addiction ("silver-love"). Some Greek cities hosted seasonal regional games, acting as neutral zones sanctifying travel for attendees in what seems to have been an age-old tradition associating religious festivals with seasonal trade entrepots. Medieval European fairs evolved out of this tradition.

Chapter 11 summarizes the evolution of commercial enterprise, starting with its origins in Bronze Age palaces and temples organizing foreign trade and specialized handicraft production in temple workshops. Temples and palaces were the major early creditors, with the first interest-bearing credit probably owed by Sumerian traders who were provided with textiles and other handicrafts produced by the temple labor force to be exchanged for foreign raw materials. Interest on such advances of temple handicrafts, denominated in silver, provided these institutions with an assured share of the merchant's trading profit. Private investors (including royal officials) adopted the contractual practices and credit terms pioneered by the temples as they came to act independently for their own enrichment. But borrowing almost never was undertaken to invest in workshops or other tangible means of production. Roman commerce and banking ended up administered largely by slaves or freedmen as the oligarchy deemed trade and moneylending to be unworthy pursuits.

Chapter 12 reviews the *longue durée* from the Bronze Age to the modern world. Bronze Age economic policy is alien to modern attitudes; in many ways it is the reverse. Modern "free market" ideology advocates the sanctity of contractual creditor rights, and disparages centralized public planning. Financial centers have become societies' major planners, acting in the interest of creditors, not that of the indebted economy at large. Money and credit creation have been increasingly privatized, and the land's rent has become increasingly untaxed, no longer the fiscal base that it was in the Bronze Age. The modern economic ethic opposes redistributive debt cancellations and public appropriation of privatized property.

The long historical continuum of Western civilization has inverted the guiding mutual aid and equity ethic and spirit of society's origins. Personal gain-seeking no longer is subordinated to the commonweal. It has broken "free" of regulation, above all in the sphere of debt financing.

Modern economic orthodoxy does not acknowledge the logic that guided Near Eastern Clean Slates: a recognition that economies do not naturally tend toward equilibrium, much less equality or broad-based prosperity. If left unregulated and "free" for creditors, economies tend to polarize, because the growth of financial claims on wealth and income tend to exceed the ability to pay. That tendency would have reduced many Bronze Age cultivators to irreversible bondage if rulers had not been empowered to restore balance and solvency by intervening from "above" the market and cancelling predatory debts. The Near Eastern takeoff would have been stifled in its cradle under today's idea of "free markets."

Western democracies have not used public power to keep debt in check, but have polarized into financial oligarchies, whose actions are adverse to broad economic welfare. Today's economic polarization is still primarily financial, now resulting from corporate and public debt as well as personal debt. As in antiquity, the only way to restore economic balance is to write down debts. But in contrast to Bronze Age kingship, no central authority in today's Western economies is prepared to do this. The royal Bronze Age proclamations citing the ruler's obedience to the gods and the sanctity of their debt cancellations demonstrate that there is indeed an alternative to today's sanctity of debts being paid at the cost of destabilizing economic and social order.

I
Money's Origins:
Fiscal Account-Keeping and Credit

1

Origins of Money and Interest: Palatial Credit, not Barter*

Neolithic and Bronze Age economies operated mainly on credit. Because of the time gap between planting and harvesting, few monetary payments were made at the time of purchase. When Babylonians went to the public alehouse, they did not pay by carrying grain around in their pockets. They ran up a tab to be settled at harvest time on the threshing floor. The ale women who ran these "pubs" then paid most of this grain to the palace for the consignments that had been advanced to them during the crop year. If the crops failed, rulers cancelled the debts to save debtors from forfeiting their means of support to creditors. That prevented a creditor oligarchy from emerging.

The origins of money and interest are grounded in these credit arrangements and the fiscal practices innovated by Sumerian temples and palaces ca. 3000 BC. These large institutions employed weavers and other craft personnel, fed them with crops grown either on palace or temple land, and supplied them with wool from temple and palace herds managed by entrepreneurs or shepherds. The economy was primarily agrarian, but required foreign trade to obtain metal, stone and other materials not locally available. Textiles and handicrafts were the major export goods.

The scale on which the large institutions operated required forward planning to schedule and track the flow of food and raw materials through their fields and workshops. Calculating budgets and tallying the resulting surpluses or shortfalls for managing cropland and herds, brewing and selling beer, baking bread and producing handicrafts for use within these institutions (and for local or long-distance trade) required a means of denominating and co-measuring these flows.

---

* The initial version of this paper was published as "Origins of Money and Interest: Palatial Credit, not Barter," in S. Battilossi, Y. Cassis, and K. Yago, eds., *Handbook of the History of Money and Currency* (Springer, 2020):45-65. I have augmented it here to comment on the political implications of monetary origin scenarios, and reorganized part of the discussion to dovetail into the papers that follow.

Palace scribes and accountants developed monetary units as an administrative tool, assigning standardized values to key commodities for forward planning and resource allocation, for collection of land rent and other transactions with the rest of the economy, and for trade consignments to be settled in silver at the end of each seafaring or caravan cycle. Textiles and other products were consigned to traders to obtain silver, copper and other raw materials, while land and professional functions or enterprises were consigned to entrepreneurs to manage in exchange for a stipulated revenue. A grid of administered prices was created, set in round numbers for ease of computation and account-keeping.

Renger (1979 and 1984), Bongenaar (2000) and Garfinkle (2004 and 2012) describe this administrative system, and the papers in Hudson and Wunsch (2004) survey account-keeping and monetization of the Mesopotamian and Egyptian economies from the inception of written accounts in the late fourth millennium BC to the Neo-Babylonian period (7th-6th centuries BC). Grain was designated as a *unit of account* to calculate values and co-measure labor time and land yields for resource allocation, and also the *means of payment* for taxes and fees in the agricultural and handicraft sphere. Silver served as the money-of-account and also the means of payment for mercantile enterprise and the financing of trade ventures. Throughout antiquity the temples were in charge of refining silver, and regulating weights, measures and purity standards in general.

To value disparate commodities and facilitate these functions for grain and silver, a bimonetary system was created by setting the shekel-weight of silver (8 grams) as equal to a gur "quart" of grain. Acceptability of grain and silver for settling fees, taxes, rents and other official debt balances catalyzed their use as money throughout the economy.

No such commensurability is found in "primitive money." Philip Greirson (1977:19-21, endorsed by Goodhart 1998) seeks the origins of what has come to be called "state money" in wergild payments for personal injury. But like dowries or bride-price, such fines were denominated in customary market baskets that might include animals or slave girls, items of clothing and jewelry, not a particular commodity. They were pre-monetary and special-purpose.

Likewise, the "spit money" and kindred food money cited by Laum (1924:27-29 and 158-159) was pre-monetary in character, not a common denominator to value disparate commodities. Laum was a follower of Knapp's State Theory of money, but saw the archaic state as a religious cult, not as playing a commercial role. In his view the valuation of goods finds its origins "in the cult, not in commerce (which knows no basis for typology, but remains purely individualistic)." Donations of sacrificial animals defined status, but did not provide a standardized economic and monetary unit. Early fines and contributions were levied without reference to a standardized commodity. That innovation occurred in Mesopotamia early in the third millennium BC.

Origins of money in the palatial economies of Mesopotamia

Van De Mieroop (2004:49) describes the challenge to ancient accountants as being to record not merely "a single transfer, but the combination of a multitude of transfers into a summary. When information piles up and is not synthesized, it becomes useless: a good bureaucrat needs to be able to compress data. The summary account requires that the scribe combine information from various records." In contrast to the grain and silver that served as dual measures of value to evaluate Mesopotamian production and distribution, no monetary common denominators are found in Mycenaean Linear B accounting ca. 1400-1200 BC. Tribute lists and records of deliveries from agricultural centers and workshops were "in kind," with no indication of money as either a measure of value or a general means of payment. Finley (1981:198) cites Ventris and Chadwick (1956:113) to the effect that "they 'have not been able to identify any payment in silver or gold for services rendered,' and that there is no evidence 'of anything approaching currency. Every commodity is listed separately, and there is never any sign of equivalence between one unit and another.'"

Mesopotamia's palaces and temples designated grain and silver as reference points to co-measure the wide range of transactions within their own institutions and with the rest of the economy for grain, textiles, beer, boat transport and the performance of ritual services. Establishing a set of price equivalencies enabled values to be assigned and payments to be made in terms of any commodity listed on the price schedule. Englund (2004:38) cites copper, wool and sesame oil as also being assigned values in an overall price grid, and mutually convertible with grain, silver or each other: "The concept of value equivalency was a secure element in Babylonian accounting by at least the time of the sales contracts of the ED IIIa (Fara) period, ca. 2600 BC."

Cripps (2017) has reviewed the prices for silver, grain and other commodities and found that administrative barley:silver price ratios among Sumerian cities "vary considerably with both the geographic origin of a text and the administrative context in which these ratios occur, whether or not we understand them as prices or equivalents." However, these variations are administered, independently of supply and demand. "The value of barley relative to silver arguably varies for quite other reasons than those of abundance or shortage due to natural events, or because of changes in the market and therefore the demand for and supply of one or the other of these commodities." (See Englund 2012 for a general discussion.)

The 1:1 shekel/gur ratio enabled income and expense statistics to be expressed in terms of a common denominator to administer prices and fees, taxes and other debts owed to the large institutions. Grain could be used as a substitute for silver at a stipulated exchange rate for payments to the large institutions. But a bumper crop causing lower prices in the economy outside the large institutions did not disturb the official fiscal flow in what today are called "constant prices."

To provide a standard of value and serve as the means of payment, grain and silver had to be measured or weighed in standardized units. And to facilitate calculation for resource allocation within the large institutions, these units were based on the administrative calendar created to allocate resources on a regular monthly basis. That required replacing lunar months of varying length with standardized 30-day months (Englund 1988). Each monthly unit of grain was measured in volumetric gur units divided into 60^{ths}, apparently for standardizing consumption by the workforce twice daily during each administrative month. Lambert (1960) describes how Babylonian accounts translated these food rations into labor time for each category of labor – males, females and children.

This sexagesimal system of fractional divisions enabled the large institutions to calculate the rations needed to produce textiles or bricks, build public structures or dig canals during any given period of time. Weights for silver and other metals followed suit, by dividing the mina into 60 shekels. The rate of interest on commercial advances denominated in silver was set in the simplest sexagesimal way: $1/60^{th}$ per month (the decimalized equivalent being 20 percent per year), doubling the principal in five years (60 months). This standardized rate was adopted by the economy at large.

Money and prices

By the end of the third millennium the large institutions were stating the value of foreign trade and other enterprise in terms of silver, which emerged as the "money of the world." Gold was used in less public contexts, such as for capital investment in Assyria's foreign trade ventures after 2000 BC. Its price vis-à-vis silver varied from city to city and from period to period. But attempts to link price changes to variations in the money supply at that time would be anachronistic. "Money" simply took the form of commodities that were acceptable to temples and palaces for payment. These large institutions gave monetary value to wheat, wool and other key products by accepting them at guaranteed prices as payment for taxes and fees.

Monetary values had to be stable in order for producers to plan ahead and minimize the risk of disruptive shifts in prices that might impair the ability to pay fees and other debts. Official price equivalencies thus served as an adjunct to fiscal arrangements. §51 and gap §t (sometimes read as §96) of Hammurabi's laws (ca. 1750 BC) specified that any citizen who owed barley or silver to a *tamkarum* merchant (including palace collectors) could pay in goods of equivalent value, *e.g.*, in grain, sesame or some other basic commodity on the official price grid (Roth 1997:91 and 97).

This ruling presumably was important for agricultural entrepreneurs and herd managers who borrowed from the well-to-do. But most of all, along with §§48-50 of Hammurabi's laws, rulings that stabilized the grain/silver exchange rate "are all meant to give a weak debtor (a small farmer or tenant) some legal protection and help," and are "'given teeth' by stipulating that if [the creditor] takes more he will forfeit 'everything he gave,' that is, his original claim" (Veenhof 2010:286-287). Babylonian debtors thus were saved from being harmed at harvest time when payments were due and grain prices were at their seasonal low against silver in the market economy outside of the large institutions. The palace's exchange-rate guarantee enabled cultivators who owed fees, taxes and other debts denominated in silver to pay in barley without having to sell it for silver.

What was called a "silver" debt thus did not mean that actual silver had to be paid, but simply that the interest rate was 20 percent. If creditors actually wanted silver, they would have had to convert their grain at a low market price at harvest time when crops were plentiful. For debtors, the effect was much like modern farmers signing "forward" contracts so as not to get whipsawed by shifting market prices. Deliveries to the palace's collectors were stabilized, minimizing the effect of price fluctuations outside of the palatial sector, such as outside the city gates in the quay area along the Euphrates.

There was little thought of preventing prices from varying for transactions that did not involve the large institutions. Prices for grain rose sharply in times of droughts, floods or war, as when a crop failure obliged Ur to buy grain from the upstream town of Isin at the end of the

Ur III empire ca. 2022 BC. These price shifts were the result of scarcity resulting from natural causes, not monetary phenomena.

Monetary drains were avoided in such cases by royal "restorations of order" (Sumerian amargi, Babylonian *andurarum*) cancelling agrarian debts because circumstances made them unpayable. To maintain economic balance in the face of arrears that constantly mounted up, new rulers also proclaimed these Clean Slates upon taking the throne. No payments were required from personal debtors, whose obligations were cancelled (although commercial debts were left in place). The details are spelled out in greatest detail ca. 1645 BC in Ammisaduqa's edict §§17-18 (translated in Pritchard 1985).

Despite variation in market prices for transactions outside of the large institutions, Babylonia's bimonetary standard had no Gresham's Law of "cheap" or "bad" money driving out good money. Grain did not drive out silver. Paying official debts in grain at harvest time was part of a stable long-term relationship. Likewise, Babylonian wool prices varied in response to market conditions, but remained fixed by royal fiat for 150 years for debt payments owed to the palace and its collectors. Early "money" was simply the official price schedule for paying debts to the large institutions. (The effect was similar to the U.S. "parity pricing" support of farm prices after the 1930s.) There was no creation of fiat money by temples and palaces to spend into the economy and cause monetary inflation.

Rulers promoted prosperity by providing vegetable oil and other consumer goods at relatively low prices, with what seems to have been an element of idealism. Around 1930 BC, §1 of the laws of Eshnunna (north of Ur, on the Tigris River) was typical in announcing the official rate of 300 cups of barley (60 silas) for 1 shekel of silver, or 3 silas of fine oil, 12 silas of regular oil, 15 silas of lard, 360 shekels (=6 minas) of wool, 2 gur of salt, 3 minas of raw copper or 2 minas of wrought (*i.e.*, refined) copper (Roth 1997:59). These low prices governing official payments were not achieved by reducing the money supply but were, in effect, fiscal subsidies.

The two ideologies of monetary origins

The root of the word *numismatics* (the study or collection of coins) is *nomos*, "law" or "custom." Aristotle wrote (*Ethics*, 1133) that money "is called *nomisma* (customary currency), because it does not exist by nature but *nomos*." It is "accepted by agreement (which is why it is called *nomisma*, customary currency)." Government aims in supplying money always have been primarily legal and fiscal, giving value to money by accepting it in payment of taxes, fees or other payments owed to the government. It is not necessary for such payments to be backed by silver or gold.

For modern times, the policy implication of this "state theory" (that money is created and given value by laws enacted by governments) is that governments can monetize their spending by fiat money – and, as Aristotle added (*Pol.* 1257b10-12), "it is in our power to change the value of money and make it useless." Governments do not have to borrow from banks and bondholders when they run deficits.

Georg Friedrich Knapp's *State Theory of Money* (1924 [1905]) described how money was given value by its fiscal role: the state's willingness to accept it in payment of taxes. Innes (1913 and 1914) added an important dimension by describing the origins of money in paying debts. That linked money to the credit process, not to commodity exchange as such. (Wray 2004 reviews the historiography of early money and reprints Innes's articles.) Karl Polanyi (1944 and 1957) led a school emphasizing that "redistributive" economies with administered price equivalencies took precedence over market exchange setting prices by supply and demand (Hudson 2020). Renger (1979 and 1984) has elaborated the administrative character of Mesopotamia's palatial economies.

These varieties of the State Theory of money (also called chartalism) downplay the role of personal and purely commercial gain-seeking that dominated most earlier views of money's origins. Elaborating what Adam Smith described as an instinct among individuals to "truck and barter," Carl Menger (1892 [1871]) put forth the classical version of the commodity theory of how money originated. Without making any reference to paying taxes or other debts to public authorities, he speculated that money was an outgrowth of barter among individual producers and consumers. According to this view, a preference for metal emerged as the most desirable medium for such trade, thanks to its ability to serve three major functions, best performed by metal:

(1) a compact and uniform store of value in which to save purchasing power, compressing value (savings) into a relatively small space, and not spoiling (unlike grain);

(2) a convenient means of payment, divisible into standardized fractional weight units (assuming that their degree of purity or alloy is attested); and

(3) a measure of value, as a widely acceptable commodity, like silver or gold, against which to measure prices for other products.

The commodity or barter theory depicts metallic money as emerging simply as a commodity preferred by Neolithic producers, traders and wealthy savers when bartering crops and handicrafts amongst themselves. In this origin myth, bullion became the measure of value and means of payment without palace or temple oversight, thanks to the fact that individuals could save it and lend it out at interest. So money doubled as capital – provided by individuals, not public agencies. And payment of debt plays no role in the above three "hard-money" functions.

The politics of monetary origin scenarios

Bankers, bondholders and wealthy investors favor scenarios of how money might have originated without governments playing any role. They want to retain control of the credit system with money that is just a commodity, asset or security in short supply, held mainly by the well-to-do. Public spending is to be financed by borrowing this money from private creditors, not by governments creating their own money.

Charles Goodhart (1998:411) has shown that the metallist "hard money" barter theory does not even apply to modern times. It is a reaction against the trend of public regulation and money creation in the 19th and early 20th centuries. To highlight its politically partisan motivation, he points out that the eurozone was created without a central bank to monetize more than marginal deficits for EU governments. That has left Europe's supply of credit to commercial banks. Contrary to the policy implications of the State Theory of money, Europe's central-bank credit is created only to supply backing for private bank credit creation (or to buy financial securities to support their price level, benefiting the economy's wealthiest financial layer and the valuation of bank deposits and other financial assets), not for governments to spend directly into the economy at large for public purposes and social-economic support.

This pro-creditor approach has turned the prehistory of money into an arena in which free-market economists fight with advocates of public regulation over whether the public or private sector should be dominant, and whether governments should create their own money or leave credit in private hands. Differing views regarding the origins of money thus have different policy implications in the modern-day debate over whether money should be public or private, whether or not it should be backed by public fiat, and whether debt-collection laws should favor creditors or debtors.

Governing authorities are absent from the barter theory's origin myth, because recognizing the public sector's role as provider and recipient of money highlights the public aim of maintaining economic stability and preventing price and debt disturbances that impair resilience for society at large. The acts by Bronze Age rulers to protect debtors are depicted as "interference" with contracts (a euphemism for making creditor rights dominant), not a policy to protect long-term economic growth by minimizing debt defaults, austerity and economic polarization.

Shortcomings of the barter theory of monetary origins

The long-dominant college textbook by Paul Samuelson (1973:274-275) summarizes the logic of the barter theory taught to generations of economics students:

> Inconvenient as barter obviously is, it represents a great step forward from a state of self-sufficiency in which every man had to be a jack-of-all-trades and master of none. ... If we were to construct history along hypothetical, logical lines, we should naturally follow the age of barter by the age of commodity money.

But individuals were not jacks of all trades. By the Early Bronze Age, specialized labor was set corporately apart in Mesopotamian and Egyptian temples and palaces. Ignoring credit arrangements and excluding any reference to palaces or temples in catalyzing the Near Eastern inception of monetization, Samuelson tries to ground his speculation in ostensibly empirical evidence by turning to pseudo-anthropology:

> Historically, a great variety of commodities has served at one time or another as a medium of exchange: ... tobacco, leather and hides, furs, olive oil, beer or spirits, slaves or wives ... huge rocks and landmarks, and cigarette butts. The age of commodity money gives way to the age of paper money ... Finally, along with the age of paper money, there is the age of bank money, or bank checking deposits.

Depicting commodity money as primordial and natural, this view sees the direction of history as culminating in today's commercial banking. It puts credit at the *end* of the Barter-Money-Credit sequence, not at the beginning. But neither prehistorians nor anthropologists have provided supporting evidence for this barter theory. "No example of a barter economy, pure and simple, has ever been described, let alone the emergence from it of money," anthropologist Caroline Humphrey (1985:48) has emphasized, stating that "all available ethnography suggests that there never has been such a thing" (cited in Graeber 2014:29; for further critiques see Wray 2004 and Ingham 2004). The evidence that does exist is the long cuneiform record showing that the major initial monetary activity of most Mesopotamians was to pay fees and taxes, or buy products that palaces and temples made or imported, on credit provided or regulated by these large institutions.

As far as convenience is concerned, the simplest and least costly way to conduct exchange is to avoid direct payment in metal. Having to weigh money for retail or even larger exchanges would have maximized transaction costs. Yet when anti-government ideologues argue that commodity money and bank credit minimize these costs (Ober 2008:49-50, echoing the ideas of North 1992), they compare coinage only to barter, not to credit, *e.g.*, settling debts on the threshing floor at harvest time. The barter theory excludes the thought that palatial extending of credit and regulation of prices and debt payments served to minimize the use of money payments during the crop year (and hence, transaction costs), with fiscal stability maintained by administering the price schedule for payments to the palatial sector.

The barter theory's lack of evidence did not trouble Menger, because his logic was purely speculative: "even if money did not originate from barter, could it have?" Today's prehistorians and anthropologists would answer, "No, it couldn't have happened that way." Money always has been embedded in a public context, especially in its form as metal refined, certified and supplied by public authority. It hardly could have evolved without public catalysts and ongoing oversight to make it acceptable.

For starters, any practical payment system for credit and trade requires accurate weighing and measuring. That calls for public oversight as a check on counterfeiting and other fraudulent practice. Trust cannot be left to individuals engaging in barter or credit on their own. Crooked merchants historically have used light weights when selling goods or lending out money, so as to give their customers less, while using heavy weights when buying or collecting debts so as to gain an unduly large amount of silver or other commodities. (See Powell 1999 for discussion.)

Biblical denunciations of merchants using false weights and measures find their antecedents in Babylonia. Hammurabi's laws (gap §x [Roth 1997:98], sometimes referred to as §94 and §95) stipulate that merchants who lend grain or money by a small weight but demand payment using a larger measure should forfeit whatever they had lent. Alewomen found guilty of using crooked weights and measures in selling beer were to be cast into the water (§108 [Roth 1997:101]). Many other rulings deal with creditor abuses, which date back to the rule of Urukagina of Lagash ca. 2350 BC.

Such abuses are timeless. The 7th century BC prophet Amos (8:5-7) depicts the Lord as denouncing wealthy Israelites "who trample the needy and do away with the poor of the land" by scheming, "skimping the measure (making the ephah small), boosting the price (making the shekel great), and cheating with dishonest scales." Likewise, the prophet Micah (6:11) denounces merchants using "the short ephah, which is accursed? Shall I acquit a man with dishonest scales, with a bag of false weights?" (Kula 1986 reviews Biblical and Koranic examples.)

Leviticus (19:35-36) describes the Lord as directing Moses to instruct his followers not to use dishonest standards when measuring length, weight or quantity. Deuteronomy 25:1315 admonishes: "Thou shalt not have two differing weights in your bag – one heavy, one light. Thou shalt not have two differing measures in your house – one large, one small. You must have accurate and honest weights and measures … For the Lord your God detests … anyone who deals dishonestly."

Public regulation of weights and measures was a step beyond primitive barter among individuals. It needed official organization (just as exchange and credit needed supervision). As noted above, sexagesimal weights to denominate minas and shekels reflected the priority of transactions within Mesopotamian palaces and temples, deriving from their grain-based accounting system to schedule and distribute food and raw materials. Jewish temples likewise provided standardized measures (Exodus 30.13 and 38.2427, and Leviticus 27.25; for royal measures see 2 Samuel 14.26), as did the Athenian *agoranomoi* (public market regulators). Throughout antiquity markets were located in the open spaces in front of city gates or temples, providing easy access to official weights and measures to prevent fraud.

In addition to public oversight of weighing and measuring, quality standards were required for alloys of silver and gold. Sales and debt contracts from the second and first millennia BC typically specified payment in silver of 7/8 purity (.875 fine, the equivalent of 21 carats). To avoid adulteration, silver was minted in temples to guarantee specified degrees of purity. The word "money" derives from Rome's Temple of Juno Moneta, where silver and gold coinage was struck during the Punic Wars, mainly to arm soldiers, build a navy and pay mercenaries, not for barter exchange.

Formal coinage, however, was not required for metal to function as money. Weighed metal was sufficient, often stamped by temples to attest to its degree of purity. Long before coins were struck in the first millennium BC, raw silver (*hacksilver*) and weighed jewelry served the function that coinage did in classical times. Although coinage is not attested before the 7th century BC, Balmuth (1967 and 1971) may have found Near Eastern antecedents, citing an inscription by the Assyrian ruler Sennecherib (705-681 BC) saying that he "fashioned molds of clay and poured bronze therein, as in casting (fashioning) half-shekel pieces" (Balmuth 1971:2). The second-millennium Ugaritic epics of Aqht and Krt describe "flows of tears ... as resembling 1/4 shekels or pieces-of-four and 1/5 shekels or pieces-of-five." "Like markets, coinage was there before the Greeks," summarizes Powell (1999:22); "the only significant difference that coinage makes in money transactions is the guarantee of quality; in Babylonia, as elsewhere, silver coins were cut up just like other silver and put in the balance pan."

There were no public debts circulating as means of payment. Throughout antiquity temples were creditors, acting as society's ultimate sources of money in emergencies. Sacred statues were adorned with golden ornaments that could be melted down in times of need to pay mercenaries (or perhaps ransom or tribute; see Oppenheim 1949), much as were the Winged Victory statues of Athens during the Peloponnesian War. Indeed, silver owed its status to its role in making prestige handicrafts, largely to donate to the temples as well as to settle debt balances owed to the palace.

The monetary role of silver

Mesopotamia's and Egypt's economies were bifurcated. Entrepreneurial trade operated on a silver standard, atop a rural economy on a grain standard for paying agricultural fees and debts – on the threshing floor for grain, or in the shearing season for wool. Silver was used primarily by the palace and the entrepreneurs managing its trade and other enterprise. To import silver and supply it to the economy at large, Mesopotamia's palace mobilized crop surpluses to feed weaving and other workshops producing handicrafts to export.

Throughout the history of Sumer "the management of silver and gold, of textiles, and of other precious or 'luxury' goods is largely dominated by the royal palace," notes Garfinkle (2012:244-245 and 226). Even in Lagash ca. 2350 BC the temples "did not actively control the politically important treasuries," which were under control of the palace. In neighboring Umma numerous branches of the economy converted their primary goods annually "into tiny sums of silver, which were collected by the province and then delivered to the state in the form of donations to a religious festival. ... Luxury goods – textiles, silver and gold, meat, and special edible delicacies – are primarily found in one specific context, namely the palace."

Denominating prices in silver forced reliance on scales. To prevent the awkwardness of weighing relatively small pieces, silver was cast into jewelry, such as bracelets made with easily broken-off segments measured in shekels. Powell (1977) notes that the Middle Babylonian word for 1/8 shekel, *bitqu* (literally "cutting"), suggests silver rings and coils, and may originally have denoted "a piece of standard size cut off from such a silver coil." Such jewelry money gave way to officially stamped weights of precious metal as coinage in classical antiquity.

What is not well understood is how silver got into the hands of Mesopotamia's general population. Some would have been obtained by selling crops, textiles or other handicrafts to the palace (Sallaberger 2008, cited in Garfinkle 2012:245), or by entrepreneurs earning silver on their trade and management of public services. The palace also paid silver to mercenaries, and there are hints of rulers handing out silver tokens to soldiers after victory and perhaps at royal festivals. But most of the influx of silver from foreign trade was re-invested in more trade ventures or lent out in rural usury for current income and, ultimately, to acquire land. Silver lying around not lent out was called "hungry" for profit-making opportunities – for creditors who "ate" the interest.

Personal debts mounted up rapidly as a result of agrarian usury, and inability to pay them often resulted from crop failure, drought, or the debtor's illness or other misfortune. Royal proclamations cancelling these agrarian debts preserved economic viability on the land. Public oversight of money went hand in hand with management of debt, including the setting of interest rates and customary proclamation of royal amnesties for personal agrarian debts. Early Near Eastern rulers recognized that most of their population were in debt and hence needed to be protected from forfeiting their income and means of self-support to creditors. The aim was to maintain overall social balance, above all by saving the economy at large from being impoverished by keeping the magnitude of debt within the ability to be paid.

In contrast to the Near Eastern reality, the barter theory of money's origins treats money as a commodity, not as a public utility. It sees the original role of money as being to serve the interest of individual savers who preferred hard bullion to preserve the value of their savings, and of debts owed to them under "hard" debt collection rules. The theory has no regard for the economic disruption caused by the widespread inability of debtors to pay.

Archaic money and interest-bearing debt

The ancient words for interest – *máš* (goat) in Sumerian and Akkadian, and *tokos* and *fænus* (calf) in Greek and Latin – are used in the metaphoric sense of "that which is born or produced." What was "born" was not goats or calves, but interest, on the new moon each month. (Hudson 2000 discusses the semantics, elaborated in Hudson 2018 and Chapter 4 below).

Interest always has been an inherently monetary phenomenon and officially regulated. The practice first seems to have emerged as the means of financing Sumer's long-distance trade, and then of advancing land to its cultivators or managers. The most plausible explanation is that it was not created with a view to polarize economies between increasingly wealthy creditors and an increasingly impoverished debtor population, but to serve a more desirable social function. The standardized commercial "silver" interest rate suggests that palaces, temples and in time private suppliers consigned products for merchants to export, with the profits being shared by the entrepreneurial merchant-debtor paying the consigner double the original advance in five years.

The standard Mesopotamian interest rate for commercial loans denominated in silver dovetailed into palatial accounting practice at the "unit fraction:" one shekel (60th) per mina per month, 12 shekels a year (the equivalent of 20 percent annual interest in decimalized terms), doubling the principal in five years. Rates were set simply for reasons of mathematical simplicity in Mesopotamia's sexagesimal system of fractional weights and measures. This practice of setting interest rates in terms of the local "unit fraction" for ease of calculation was emulated throughout antiquity, *e.g.*, a troy ounce per pound in Rome. These rates remained traditional for centuries, not being related to productivity, profit levels or risk.

Ignoring the first three thousand years of interest rates, adherents of a purely individualistic "free market" idea of interest have put forth a pre-monetary productivity origin myth that steers entirely clear of any need for a public interface. According to this anti-state speculation, interest originally was paid by individual debtors "in kind," in crops or cattle that were produced from seeds or animals lent by creditors. (Böhm-Bawerk's *Capital and Interest* (1890 [1884]) surveyed and refuted what he called "naïve productivity" theories of interest.) This scenario depicts the origins of interest-bearing debt as being productive and hence economically justified – and occurring without monetary silver or other official money playing a role.

The classic attempt to depict such interest as existing already in the Neolithic (ca. 5000 BC) and reflecting the yield of crops or herds (and implicitly, profit rates) – and even taking into account the risk of non-payment – is Fritz Heichelheim's *Ancient Economic History, from the Palaeolithic Age to the Migrations of the Germanic, Slavic and Arabic Nations* (1958:54): "Dates, olives, figs, nuts, or seeds of grain were probably lent out ... to serfs, poorer farmers, and dependents, to be sown and planted, and naturally an increased portion of the harvest had to be returned in kind." In addition to fruits and seeds, "animals could be borrowed too for a fixed time limit, the loan being repaid according to a fixed percentage from the young animals born subsequently. ... So here we have the first forms of money, that man could use as a capital for investment, in the narrower sense."

Such "food-money" supposedly was lent out in the form of seeds and animals, at interest rates reflecting their reproduction rates. This scenario depicts "money" as originating not as the means of denominating and paying taxes, fees or other debts to palaces or temples, but as private personal capital in the form of seeds and animals, capable of producing an economic yield to be paid in kind as interest, at a rate reflecting physical productivity.

The problem with this myth is that the tribal communities known to anthropologists do not lend or borrow cattle, either for calf-interest or other payment (Sundstrom 1974:34 and 38, and Hoebel 1968:230). When seeds are advanced, it typically is by absentee landowners to sharecroppers. Debtors are obliged to pledge (and forfeit) their livestock (or their labor) to creditors, and pay usury out of their *own* resources, not from investing the creditor's livestock or seeds at a profit.

Like the barter theory of money, the productivity theory of interest takes interest out of its historical context, treating capital assets and money simply as commodities owned by individuals prior to any public oversight or regulation coming into being. If Heichelheim's scenario were valid, interest rates would have varied with the reproductive rates of cattle and seeds or mercantile profit rates. But interest rates remained standardized over many centuries, being set independently from productivity and profit rates.[1]

Barter-based "naïve productivity" theories of interest invert the historical line of development by envisioning transactions among individuals acting on their own account, with borrowers hoping to make a gain

---

[1] I discuss Heichelheim's speculations and productivity theories of interest further in Chapters 3 and 4 below.

out of which to pay their creditors. But in reality the paradigmatic interest-bearing debts were owed to Mesopotamia's palaces and temples. Interest charges did not reflect physical productivity or mercantile profit rates but were specifically monetary, paid in silver at the stipulated rate based simply on the unit-fraction for ease of calculation.

Most fatal to productivity theories of interest is that most Mesopotamian agrarian debts did not result from actual loans but accrued as arrears (Wunsch 2002). Agrarian interest often was charged only after the "due date" was missed. In such cases interest was paid for the *failure* of productivity to keep up with normal expectations.

Mesopotamia did not have banking in the modern sense of taking in deposits and lending them out at a profit. Even in Neo-Babylonian times "banking families" such as the Egibi were simply wealthy families. They paid depositors the same rate (equivalent to 20 percent) as they charged customers, so there was no intermediation markup as occurs in modern banking (Bogaert 1966).

Mercantile "silver loans" to commercial traders and managers were not subject to the royal amnesties wiping out the overgrowth of agrarian "barley debts" that tended to mount up in excess of the ability of cultivators to pay. This exemption from Clean Slate proclamations shows an implicit policy distinction between productive and unproductive credit – the contrast that medieval Church Fathers would draw between interest and usury.

Classical antiquity's changing context for money and credit

Interest-bearing debt is found spreading westward to the Mediterranean lands around the 8th century BC, mainly via Syrian and Phoenician traders establishing trading enclaves (Hudson 1994 and 2023). They brought with them weights and measures that were adopted by Greeks and Italians. A. E. Berriman's *Historical Metrology* (1953) points out that the carat originally was the weight of a carob grain, *ceratonia siliqua*, a tree native to the Mesopotamian meridian, weighing $1/60^{th}$ of a shekel. The Greek term is *keration* ("small grain").

Greek and Roman elites also adopted the Near Eastern practice of setting interest rates in accordance with the local unit-fraction, *e.g.*, Rome's duodecimal system dividing the pound into 12 troy ounces. One ounce per pound per year ($1/12^{th}$) was the equivalent of an $8⅓$ percent rate of interest. That was much lower than Mesopotamia's interest rate of one-fifth of the principal for commercial loans (and one-third for agrarian loans, based on the typical sharecropping rate), but debts in

Rome and Greece were inexorable and hence ultimately more burdensome as there were no more kings to proclaim Clean Slates.

Despite the different context for Greek economic practice, its experience confirms a number of generalities in keeping with earlier Near Eastern monetary development. Describing how the commercial Isthmus city of Corinth adopted coinage ca. 575-550 BC (a generation after the introduction of coinage in Aegina), Salmon (1984:170-172) supports the conclusion of the numismatist C. M. Kraay (1976:317-322) that "coinage cannot have been intended to facilitate trade, either at a local level or on a wider scale." Early money – including formal coinage in classical antiquity – was to finance credit transactions, not the exchange of goods: "From the earliest issues to the second half of the fourth century, at least in Corinth, the association between coins and trade was mainly that they offered a means of providing credit. If they had acted as an item of trade themselves we should have expected them to travel much further, and in far greater quantities, from Corinth than they in fact did. Their main function was to be lent at Corinth for purchase of items to be traded."

Money was mainly for paying taxes and fees, Salmon continues: Corinthian "coins were first issued in order to serve the purposes of the minting authorities. Cities would find it convenient if payments made to them – taxes, fines, etc. – were in the form of coins whose purity and weight were fixed; while payments made by the state from time to time for building schemes, mercenaries, and other purposes could be much simplified if trustworthy coins were available."

However, taxation developed only slowly in Greek cities. Greece and Rome obtained bullion not from tax revenue or public enterprise but from war booty, by levying tribute or, in Athens, from local silver mines. Spending was mainly to pay soldiers and hire mercenaries. In the Ionian cities of Asia Minor, money's primary role was to pay "allowances to the sailors manning the huge fleet being prepared by the rebels" (Figuera 1981:157). "Hectataeus of Miletus did not propose a large capital levy or other forms of taxation to build up the allied fleet, but a confiscation of the treasures at Branchidae (Hdt. 5.36.3-4). This may suggest that taxation was primitive in early 5th-century Ionia."

Military conquest remained the major source of monetary metal from Alexander the Great's looting of temples and palaces down through the end of antiquity in Rome. Armies brought minters along to melt down the booty and distribute it to their commanders and troops, with a tithe to the city-temple. When there were no more realms for imperial Rome to conquer and extract tribute, the inability to tax the oligarchic economy led to debasement of the coinage. Treating money simply as a commodity led, along with the unchecked dynamics of interest-bearing debt, to the concentration of wealth that impoverished the imperial Roman economy, ultimately forcing resort to barter.

The main difference between Greek and Roman economies and those of the Ancient Near East was the absence of debt relief, resulting in a long series of political crises extending from the 7th-century BC "tyrants" (populist reformers) in classical Sparta and Corinth down to Rome in the 1st century BC (see Hudson 2023). Mid-19th-century historians attributed these debt crises to the introduction of coinage around the 7th and 6th centuries BC, when Greek city-states issued coins imprinted with their city-images, such as the owls of Athens. But money-changers still weighed coins from the various cities, in keeping with the practice for weighed bullion that predated coinage by about two thousand years. The economic impact of coinage thus did not differ much from that of *hacksilver*. So it was not money, coinage or even interest-bearing debt by themselves that caused the polarization under classical antiquity's creditor oligarchies. The problem was the way in which society handled the proliferation of interest-bearing debt.

As credit was increasingly privatized, debt became a dynamic powerful enough to dissolve the checks and balances that had arisen in the social context in which money first developed. Mesopotamia had usury and debt bondage, but its rulers managed to avoid the irreversible disenfranchisement of smallholders and ultimate serfdom that plagued the Mediterranean lands. The Near Eastern aim was to preserve a land-tenured citizenry supplying the palace with corvée labor and military service. Despite the palace's role as the major creditor, it protected debtors by debt amnesties that undid the polarizing effect of agrarian usury. Most debts in early Mesopotamia were owed to the palace, so rulers basically were cancelling debts owed to themselves and their collectors when they proclaimed Clean Slates. These acts saved their economies from widespread debt bondage that would have diverted labor to work for creditors at the expense of the palace.

But in the Mediterranean lands of classical antiquity, debts came to be owed mainly to Greek and Roman oligarchies and no longer were cancelled, except in military or social emergencies to maintain the *demos*-army's loyalty. What came to be "sanctified" was the right of creditors to foreclose, not the cancellation of debts to restore economic balance. In contrast to what happened in Mesopotamia where money and interest-bearing debt originated, Greek and Roman oligarchies gained sufficient power to stop civic debt cancellations. Rural usury in Greece and

Rome expropriated indebted formerly self-supporting citizens from their land irreversibly, typically to find employment as mercenaries.

Today's mainstream ideology has maintained this shift to hard pro-creditor law, and depicts non-payment of debts as leading to chaos. Yet Clean Slates are what *saved* Near Eastern economies from the chaos of economic polarization and widespread bondage. Mesopotamia's economic takeoff could not have been sustained if rulers had adopted modern creditor-oriented rules.

Classical antiquity's takeoff was not sustained. By the closing centuries of the Roman Empire, wealthy elites had monopolized the land and stripped the economy of money, spending most of what they had on imports that drained monetary silver and gold to the East – leaving a barter economy in its wake as the "final" or "third" stage of monetization: impoverishment and polarization in which money was stripped away.

This oligarchic collapse into local self-sufficiency and barter was long after the origin of credit and fiscal practices in Mesopotamian palaces. That reverses the once-held idea that exchange evolved *from* barter via monetization to credit economies. Yet textbooks still repeat that sequence without recognizing the early role of credit, without mentioning the palaces and temples where monetization first evolved, and without citing the tendency of debts to be mathematically self-expanding when not overridden by debt writedowns and Clean Slates.

Also confused today is understanding of how the charging of interest originated. Instead of reflecting productivity, profitability or risk, interest rates were officially administered and remained remarkably stable in each region throughout antiquity, having been set by reference to the local unit fraction. Today's governments continue to regulate interest rates, yet mainstream economic theory continues to propose interest-rate models based not on Treasury fiscal and monetary policy but on profit rates, "risk" and consumer "choice."

Summary: The shifting historiography of money's origins

Money origin myths at odds with the historical record are the result of the conflict between vested interests and reformers over whether the monetary and credit system should be controlled by private commercial banks or by governments. Are credit and debt to be administered privately by creditor interests favoring themselves, or should they be regulated in the public interest, protecting resilience and prosperity for the indebted population at large? The way in which this question is answered turns out to be the key indicator of one's preference regarding the Barter or State Theory of the origins and character of money, credit and interest.

Assyriological and anthropological research confirms that money and interest were not created by individuals trucking and bartering crops and handicrafts or lending crops and animals to each other. Archaic economies operated on credit, using money as a means of settling debts to Mesopotamia's palaces and temples at harvest time or at the conclusion of trade ventures. Interest first seems to have emerged as the means of financing long-distance trade and then advancing land to its cultivators or entrepreneurial managers.

Recognition of these palatial origins of money and interest is at odds with the drive by commercial bankers to depict their own control of money and credit as being natural and primordial, and government money creation as a disruptive burden. Ever since Roman law became oligarchic and strongly favored creditors, the history of money, debt and banking has been written as a political lobbying exercise by bankers and other creditors to defend the view that the "sanctity" of debts having to be paid is natural and desirable, not to be questioned.

In contrast to Bronze Age Mesopotamia, today's monetary ideology recognizes no positive role for public money and credit creation except to benefit creditors. To oppose government monetization of deficit spending and policies that subordinate creditor demands to the goal of long-term economic growth, the innovative role of Bronze Age palaces and temples in creating money and interest charges is excluded from economic histories. The aim is to argue that interest on the economy's credit should be paid to banks and other private creditors, not to governments creating their own credit for the economy and self-financing their public budgets.

Also excluded from today's mainstream ideology is knowledge of the Bronze Age's checks and balances to protect economies from polarizing between creditors and debtors and being impoverished by debt. Recognition of such measures would endorse society treating money and credit as part of the overall economic system, not a matter of "individual choice," which turns out to be creditor choice in practice. To focus on contractual monetary and debt arrangements between individual lenders and borrowers without regard for how the overgrowth of debt may disrupt the economy is a travesty of economic history and a disaster for national economic policy. Failure to understand how the origins of money and interest-bearing debt went hand in hand with safeguards to protect economies from the predatory behavior of creditors blocking economic growth is a major factor responsible for today's resurgence of debt crises like those that plagued classical antiquity.

Bibliography

Balmuth, Miriam (1967), "Monetary Forerunners of Coinage in Phoenicia and Palestine in Antiquity," in A. Kindler, ed., *The Patterns of Monetary Development in Phoenicia and Palestine in Antiquity* (Jerusalem).

" (1971), "Remarks on the Appearance of the Earliest Coins," in David Gordon Mitten, John Griffiths Pedley and Jane Ayer Scott, eds., *Studies Presented to George M. A. Hanfmann* (Cambridge, Mass.):17.

Bell [Kelton], Stephanie A. and Edward J. Nell, eds. (2003), *The State, the Market and the Euro: Chartalism versus Metallism in the Theory of Money* (Cheltenham, Edward Elgar):1-25.

Bogaert, Raymond (1966), *Les Origines Antiques de la Banque de Depôt* (Leiden).

Böhm-Bawerk, Eugen von (1890 [1884]), *Capital and Interest: A Critical History of Economical Theory* (repr. New York, Kelley & Millman 1957).

Bongenaar, A. C. V. M., ed. (2000), *Interdependency of Institutions and Private Entrepreneurs* (= Proceedings of the Second MOS Symposium, Leiden 1998) (Nederlands Historisch-Archaeologisch Institute, Te Istanbul 2000).

Charpin, Dominique (1987), "Les Decréts Royaux a l'Epoque Paleo-babylonienne, à Propos d'un Ouvrage Recent," *Archiv für Orientforschung* 34:36-44.

" (1990b), "Les Edits de 'Restauration' des Rois Babyloniens et leur Application," in Claude Nicolet, ed., *Du Pouvoir dans L'Antiquite: Mots et Realities* (Geneva):13-24.

" (1998), "Les prêteurs et la palais: Les édits de *mîšharum* des rois de Babylone et leurs traces dans les archives privées," in Bongenaar 2000.

Cripps, Eric L. (2017), "The Structure of Prices in the neo-Sumerian Economy (I); Barley:Silver Price Ratios." http://cdli.ucla.edu/?q=cuneiform-digital-library-preprints.

Dalton, G. (1965), "Primitive Money," *American Anthropologist* 67:44-65.

Dercksen, J. G. (1999), ed., *Trade and Finance in Ancient Mesopotamia: Proceedings of the First MOS Symposium* (=MOS Studies 1) ([Leiden 1997], Istanbul 1999).

Dercksen, J. G., J. Eidem, K. van der Toor Nen and K. R. Veenhof, eds. (2016), *Silver, Money and Credit: A Tribute to Robartus J. van der Spek on the Occasion of his 65th Birthday on 18th September 2014* (Nederlands Instituut voor het Nabije Oosten, Leiden).

Englund, Robert (1988), "Administrative Timekeeping in Ancient Mesopotamia," *Journal of the Economic and Social History of the Orient* 31:121-185.
" (2004), "Proto-Cuneiform Account-Books and Journals," in Hudson and Wunsch 2004:23-46.
" (2012), "Equivalency Values and the Command Economy of the Ur III Period in Mesopotamia," in Gary Urton and John Papadopoulos, eds., *The Construction of Value in the Ancient World*, Ch. 21 (Los Angeles, Cotsen Institute of Archaeology Press):427-595.

Figueira, Thomas J. (1981), *Aegina: Society and Politics* (New York, Arno Press).

Finkelstein, Jack J. (1961), "Ammisaduqa's Edict and the Babylonian 'Law Codes,'" *Journal of Cuneiform Studies* 15:91-104.
" (1965), "Some New *misharum* Material and its Implications," in *Assyriological Studies* 16 (*Studies in Honor of Benno Landsberger on his Seventy-Fifth Birthday*):233-246.
" (1969), "The Edict of Ammisaduqa: A New Text," *Revue d'Assyriologie et d'archéologie orientale* 63:45-64.

Finley, Moses (1981), *Economy and Society in Ancient Greece* (London).

Garfinkle, Steven J. (2004), "Shepherds, Merchants, and Credit: Some Observations On Lending Practices in Ur III Mesopotamia," *Journal of the Economic and Social History of the Orient* 47:1-30.
" (2012), *Entrepreneurs and Enterprise in Early Mesopotamia: A Study of Three Archives from the Third Dynasty of Ur (2112-2004 BC)* (Bethesda, Md., CDL Press).

Gelb, Ignace J. (1965), "The Ancient Mesopotamian Ration System," *Journal of Near Eastern Studies* 24:230-243.

Goodhart, Charles (1998), "The two concepts of money: implications for the analysis of optimal currency areas," *European Journal of Political Economy* 14:407-432.

Graeber, David (2014), *Debt: The First 5000 Years* (Brooklyn, Melville Press).

Grierson, Philip (1977), *The Origins of Money* (London).

Hartman, L. F., and Leo Oppenheim, "On Beer and Brewing Techniques in Ancient Mesopotamia," Supplement to the *Journal of the American Oriental Society* 10 (1950).

Hawkins, J. D. (1988), "Royal Statements of ideal prices: Assyrian, Babylonian, and Hittite," in J. V. Canby et al., eds., *Ancient Anatolia: Aspects of Change and Cultural Development* (Essays in Honor of Machteld J. Mellink) (Madison):93-102.

Heichelheim, Fritz M. (1958), *An Ancient Economic History, from the Palaeolithic Age to the Migrations of the Germanic, Slavic and Arabic Nations*, Vol. I. (rev. ed., Leiden).

Hoebel, Edward Adamson (1968 [1964]), *The Law of Primitive Man: A Study in Comparative Legal Dynamics* (New York).

Hudson, Michael (1992), "Did the Phoenicians Introduce the Idea of Interest to Greece and Italy – And If So, When?" in Günter Kopcke and Isabelle Tokumaru, *Greece Between East and West: 10th-8th Centuries BC* (Mainz):128-143.
" (1996), "Privatization in History and Today: A Survey of the Unresolved Controversies," and "The Dynamics of Privatization, from the Bronze Age to the Present," in Michael Hudson and Baruch Levine, eds., *Privatization in the Ancient Near East and Classical Antiquity* (Cambridge, Mass., Peabody Museum, Bulletin #6).
" (2000), "How Interest Rates Were Set, 2500 BC-1000 AD: *Máš, tokos* and *fænus* as metaphors for interest accruals," *Journal of the Economic and Social History of the Orient* 43:132-161.
" (2002), "Reconstructing the Origins of Interest-Bearing Debt and the Logic of Clean Slates," in Hudson and Van De Mieroop 2002:7-58.

" (2003), "The Creditary/Monetarist Debate in Historical Perspective," in Bell and Nell 2003.
" (2004), "The Archaeology of Money in Light of Mesopotamian Records," in Wray 2004.
" (2004), "The Development of Money-of-Account in Sumer's Temples," in Hudson and Wunsch 2004:303-329.
" (2018), *"... and forgive them their debts": Lending, Foreclosure and Redemption from Bronze Age Finance to the Jubilee Year* (Dresden, ISLET).
" (2020), "Debt, Land and Money, From Polanyi to the New Economic Archaeology," in Radhika Desai and Kari Polanyi Levitt, eds., *Karl Polanyi and Twenty First Century Capitalism* (Geopolitical Economy Series, Manchester University Press).
" (2023), *The Collapse of Antiquity: Greece and Rome as Civilization's Oligarchic Turning Point* (Dresden, ISLET).

Hudson, Michael and Marc Van De Mieroop, eds. (2002), *Debt and Economic Renewal in the Ancient Near East* (Bethesda, Md., CDL Press).

Hudson, Michael and Cornelia Wunsch, eds. (2004), *Creating Economic Order: Record-Keeping, Standardization and the Development of Accounting in the Ancient Near East* (Bethesda, Md., CDL Press; repr. Dresden, ISLET 2023).

Humphrey, Caroline (1985), "Barter and Economic Disintegration," *Man, New Series* 20.

Ingham, Geoffrey (2004), *The Nature of Money* (Cambridge, Polity Press).

Innes, Alfred Mitchell (1913), "What is money?" *Banking Law Journal*, May:377-408, reprinted in Wray 2004.
" (1914), "The credit theory of money," *Banking Law Journal*, Dec./Jan.:151-168, reprinted in Wray 2004.

Jursa, Michael (2002), "Debts and Indebtedness in the Neo-Babylonian Period: Evidence from Institutional Archives," in Hudson and Van De Mieroop 2002:197-220.

Knapp, Georg Friedrich (1924 [1905]), *The State Theory of Money* (London, Macmillan).

Kraay, C. M (1976), *Archaic and Classical Greek Coins* (London).

Kraus, Fritz R. (1958), *Ein Edikt des Königs Ammi-saduqa von Babylon,* SD 5 (Leiden).

Kula, Witold (1986), *Measures and Men* (Princeton).

Lambert, Maurice (1960), "La naissance de la bureaucratie," *Revue Historique* 224:1-26.
" (1961), "Le premier triomphe de la bureaucratie," *Revue Historique* 225:21-46.
" (1963), "L'Usage de l'argentmetal a Lagash au temps de la IIIe Dynastie d'Ur," *Revue d'Assyriologie* 57:79-92.

Larsen, Mogens Trolle (1976), *The Old Assyrian City-State and its Colonies* (Copenhagen).
" (2015), *Ancient Kanesh: A Merchant Colony in Bronze Age Anatolia* (Cambridge University Press).

Laum, Bernard (1924), *Heiliges Geld: eine historische Untersuchung über den sakralen Ursprung des Geldes* (Tübingen).
" (1952), "Geschichte der öffentlichen Finanzwirtschaft im Altertum und Frühmittelalter," in Wilhelm Gerloff and Fritz Neumark, eds., *Handbuch der Finanzwissenschaft*, 2nd ed. (Tübingen):211-235.

Leemans, W. F. (1950), *The Old Babylonian Merchant: His Business and Social Position* (Leiden).

Manning, J. G. and Ian Morris (2005), *The Ancient Economy: Evidence and Models* (Stanford University Press).

Menger, Carl (1892 [1871]), "On the Origins of Money," *Economic Journal* 2:238-255.
" (1981), *Principles of Economics* (New York, New York University Press).

Michel, Cécile (2013), "Economic and Social Aspects of the Old Assyrian Loan Contract," *La Sapienza Orientale*, L'economia dell'antica Mesopotamia (III-I millennio a.C.) Per un dialogo interdisciplinare 9:41-56.

Ober, Josiah (2008), *Democracy and Knowledge. Innovation and Learning in Classical Athens* (Princeton, Princeton University Press).

Oppenheim, Leo (1949), "The Golden Garments of the Gods," *Journal of Near Eastern Studies* 8:172-193.

Polanyi, Karl (1944), *The Great Transformation* (Beacon Press).

Polanyi, Karl, Conrad M. Arensberg and Harry W. Pearson, eds. (1957), *Trade and Market in the Early Empires: Economies in History and Theory* (New York).

Postgate, J. N. (1992), *Early Mesopotamian Society and Economy at the Dawn of History* (London and New York).

Powell, Marvin A. (1999), "*Wir müssen alle unsere Nische nuzten*: Monies, Motives, and Methods in Babylonian Economics," in Dercksen 1999:5-23.
" (1977), "Sumerian Merchants and the Problem of Profit," *Iraq* 39:23-28.

Pritchard, J. B., ed. (1958 [1955]), *Ancient Near Eastern Texts* (Princeton).

Radner, Karen (1999), "Money in the Neo-Assyrian Empire," in Dercksen 1999:127-157.

Renger, Johannes (1979), "Interaction of Temple, Palace, and 'Private Enterprise' in the Old Babylonian Economy," in Eduard Lipinski, ed., *State and Temple Economy in the Ancient Near East* (Leuven) I:249-256.
" (1984), "Patterns of Non-Institutional Trade and Non-Commercial Exchange in Ancient Mesopotamia at the Beginning of the Second Millennium BC," in Alfonso Archi, ed., *Circulation of Goods in Non-Palatial Context in the Ancient Near East* (=Incunabula Graeca, LXXII, Rome):31-115.

Roth, Martha T. (1997), *Law Collections from Mesopotamia and Asia Minor*, 2nd ed. (Atlanta, Scholars Press).

Sallaberger, Walter (2013), "The Management of Royal Treasure: Palace Archives and Palatial Economy in the Ancient Near East," in Jane A. Hill, Philip Jones, and Antonio J. Morales, *Experiencing Power, Generating Authority: Cosmos, Politics and the Ideology of Kingship in Ancient Egypt and Mesopotamia* (University of Pennsylvania Museum of Archaeology and Anthropology, Philadelphia): 213-255.

Salmon, J. B. (1984), *Wealthy Corinth* (Oxford).

Samuelson, Paul (1973), *Economics*, 9th ed. (New York, McGraw Hill).

Steinkeller, Piotr (1981), "The Renting of Fields in Early Mesopotamia and the Development of the Concept of 'Interest' in Sumerian," *Journal of the Economic and Social History of the Orient* 24.
" (2002), "Money Lending Practices in Ur III Babylonia: The Issue of Economic Motivation," in Hudson and Van De Mieroop 2002:109-137.

Sundstrom, Lars (1974 [1965]), *The Exchange Economy of Pre-Colonial Africa* (New York).

Van De Mieroop, Marc (1995), "Old Babylonian Interest Rates: Were they Annual?" in *Immigration and Emigration within the Near East. Festschrift E. Lipinski* (Orientalia Lovaniensia Analecta 65; Louvain, Departement Oriëntalistick).
" (2002), "Credit as a Facilitator of Exchange in Old Babylonian Mesopotamia," in Hudson and Van De Mieroop 2002:163-174.
" (2002), "A History of Near Eastern Debt?" in Hudson and Van De Mieroop 2002:59-94.
" (2004), "Accounting in Early Mesopotamia: Some Remarks," in Hudson and Wunsch 2004:47-64.
" (2005), "The Invention of Interest," in William N. Goetzmann and K Geert Rouwenhorst, eds., *The Origins of Value: The Financial Innovations That Created Modern Capital Markets* (Oxford University Press):17-30.

van der Spek, Bert (2015), "Money, Prices and Market in the Ancient Near East," Yale University, New Haven, Economics Department, Economic History Seminar, March 30, 2015. https://economics.yale.edu/sites/default/files/yale_money-prices-markets.pdf.

Veenhof, Klass R. (1972), *Aspects of Old Assyrian Trade and its Terminology* (Leiden).
" (2010), "The Interpretation of Paragraphs t and u of the Code of Hammurabi," in Yayia Hazirlayan and Sevket Dönmez, eds., DUB.SAR E.DUB.BA.A: *Studies presented in honour of Veysel Donbaz* (Istanbul).

Ventris, Michael, and John Chadwick (1956), *Documents in Mycenaean Greek: Three Hundred Selected Tablets from Knossos, Pylos and Mycenae with Commentary and Vocabulary* (Cambridge, Cambridge University Press).

Wray, L. Randall, ed. (2004), *Credit and State Theories of Money: The Contributions of A. Mitchell Innes* (Cheltenham, Edward Elgar).

Wunsch, Cornelia (2002), "Debt, Interest, Pledge and Forfeiture in the Neo-Babylonian and Early Achaemenid Period: The Evidence from Private Archives," in Hudson and Van De Mieroop 2002:221-255.

2
Civic and Temple Origins of Ancient Coinage*

From its origins in the 7th century BC in Asia Minor, coinage was state money. As Aristotle emphasized, that made coins a creation of law (*nomos*). Their study (numismatics) shows how civic governments and their temples shaped monetary policy to promote their major fiscal objectives. In Greece these aims started with the need to provide a medium to pay taxes, fees and fines, for market trade at public games and festivals, and to finance armies and naval construction.

This Greek coinage experience had a similar motivation to Mesopotamia's palaces monetizing silver, grain and other commodities in order to standardize and co-measure fiscal collection and payments in a single set of integrated accounts, an innovation also requiring weights, measures and purity overseen and sanctified by temples.

In contrast to this Greek and earlier Near Eastern fiscal practice, Rome saw its coinage deteriorate into a crude commodity quasi-money, resulting in a "barter stage" of exchange. This was a consequence of the landed aristocracy breaking free from taxation. The state's weakening fiscal authority left coinage without its use in paying taxes and fees. As the post-Roman economy resorted to payment in kind with little fiscal function – that is, without a "market demand" for coinage to pay taxes, fees or debts to public institutions – there was little fiscal role for coinage beyond its commodity content.

Most 19th-century historians blamed classical antiquity's debt conflicts and related economic upheavals on the transition from payments-in-kind to cash payments. But ever since the third millennium BC in the Near East, weighed pieces of silver of standardized purity had served the credit functions later attributed to coinage. Metallic money therefore long predated coinage. No economic trauma was created by its introduction, because classical antiquity's mints did not change the basic character of money. Coinage did not even make market transactions more convenient, as weighing was still required. "Through most of the

---

* This chapter will also appear in Y. Nersysian and L. R. Wray, eds., *The Elgar Companion to Modern Money Theory* (Edward Elgar, Cheltenham, in press).

Middle Ages," notes one monetary historian, "many individual coins of the same issue differed substantially in weight and fineness. Indeed, prior to the 13th century, coinage methods hardly permitted less than a 5 to 10 percent variation in weight between individual coins struck from the same plate."[1] Such deviation was aggravated by wear, clipping and sweating of coins, requiring professional weighing to measure the actual bullion content of the proliferating diversity of coins.

Temples as Mints[2]

Commodity-money theorists have emphasized how silver compresses a high economic value into a relatively small space. It also is malleable, readily melted and shaped into coins, and does not spoil. But these qualities do not explain money's public fiscal origins. When economists "say that currency was devised to overcome the limitations and inconveniences of barter," the anthropologist Arthur Hocart has pointed out, "they are imputing to ancient man the motives which would sway a modern financier. They are victims of the dangerous fallacy that because a custom serves a certain purpose [in modern society] it was invented for that purpose. If we divest ourselves of our modern preconceptions and study the evidence, we are driven to the conclusion that currency had a religious origin."[3] And the practical fiscal reason for its innovation was to make payments to communal or civic authorities.

The most prestigious contributions to temples were silver and gold, associated with the lunar and solar deities respectively. Seeing metallic coinage as evolving out of religious tokens imbued with a sacred cosmology, Hocart suggested that India's square coins reflected the mandala's four directions, while the round shape of Western coins symbolized the sun's disc, as did the royal crown and the halo, with the coins impressed with the symbol or image of the local divinity under whose auspices they were issued.

As in Sumer and Babylonia, Greek temples played a central monetary role by refining silver and attesting to its purity. "Hence the religious character of all early coin-types," Barclay Head summarized. "Just as the word θEOI [THEOI] frequently stands at the head of treaties engraved on stone, so the emblems of the gods stand conspicuous on the face of

---

[1] Mélitz 1974:71, cited in Goodhart 2003.

[2] I discuss the public financial role of Greek temples and their mints in Chapter 6 of *The Collapse of Antiquity* (2023).

[3] Hocart 1952:99-101.

coins ... the gods being as it were called to witness to the good weight and purity of the coin."[4]

Money always has been a public institution, with its value administered in antiquity by civic authorities taking control of commerce and markets. Pheidon of Argos (in the southern Peloponnese, east of Sparta) is often said to have created the first silver coinage, the stater, on the neighboring island of Aegina. The mint probably was located in the sanctuary of Aphrodite, the island's "goddess of trade, and, as such, a promoter of international unity, identical with the Phoenician Astarte,"[5] goddess of the sea. Early Aegina coins bore Aphrodite's sacred symbol, the tortoise. In her capacity as Aphrodite Urania, the goddess "formed the kernel of every Sidonian factory, whence we find her worship on all the coasts of the Archipelago devoted to maritime intercourse. Every occupation, trade, or industry, such as fishing and mining pursued by the inhabitants, was under her protection. Through her means did the precious metals, with the Babylonian systems of value and weights, make their way into Greece. Her priests first introduced the metals as measures of value ... and marked with the symbol of the deity the ingots belonging to the temple-treasury, just as in the temple of Apollo the furniture belonging to the sacred inventory was marked with a lyre."[6]

Temples were relied on as minters and overseers of monetary silver and gold throughout all antiquity. "The Jews, in Roman times, struck sacred coins for offerings in the Temple, where money-changers set up their tables in the precincts to provide such coin in exchange for foreign money."[7] Our word *money* (as well as *mint*) derives from Rome's Temple of Juno Moneta, which issued Rome's first silver coinage in 269 BC.[8] The Latin word *monere* meant to warn or admonish – but not to warn against money-changers or usurers. According to legend, the honking of the geese at the site where the temple would later be built warned Rome of an imminent Gaulish attack in 390 BC.

---

[4] Head 1887:lvi-lvii.

[5] Head 1887:xxxv and xxxviii. Ernst Curtius 1870:99 noted that "in the temple of the goddess Hera at Argos he [Pheidon] hung up, in memory of the old order of things, specimens of the cumbrous bronze and iron bars, *obeliskoi*, which had served for money before his time."

[6] Curtius 1870:92-93.

[7] Gardner 1918:37.

[8] Thomson 1961 III:161 and 259-262, and I:33. The word *monera* meant "monster," in the sense of a warning omen.

Storerooms were located in the rear of Greek, Roman and Jewish temples to serve as treasuries for public savings (and often those of private individuals), as well as to store food and weapons: "Every temple of any degree of importance had a treasure, which consisted of the surplus of the proceeds from the lands dedicated to its use, the presents made, and of the income flowing from other sources of the god to whom the temple was consecrated. These treasures were under the care of the treasurers of the sacred moneys. In Athens important sacred treasure was that of Minerva in the citadel. Into this flowed – to say nothing of the public money therein deposited, beside the rich votive offerings, and large amounts of rent – many fines entire, of others the tenth part, and also the tenth of all booty, and of confiscated property."[9] Violating laws typically resulted in fines to expiate one's offense.[10] In cases where offenders were banished or proscribed, they might forfeit their estate to the temple. The Temple of Artemis in Ephesus was especially notable for being enriched by such sequestered properties.

Temples were creditors as well as depositories, lending at interest to the poor as well as to merchants, and to civic authorities in times of war or other crises, issuing early money to denominate payments to themselves and other public authorities. Temple treasurers, superintendents and sacrificers were responsible for handling the official savings of Athens, Thebes, Cnidus and Sicyon, the savings being kept in "sacred chests" or "public chests" at the Temple of Apollo in Delphi. But when Delphi was drawn under the influence of Corinth and Sparta of the Peloponnesian League, Athens extended its control over the temple of Delos, which in 478 became the first treasury and central meeting place of the Delian League, named after the temple.[11] Its strong-room contained row upon row of jars and other receptacles "on which was indicated the provenance of the contents or the purposes for which it is earmarked." One

---

[9] Boeckh 1857:217-219. See also pp. 568-571.

[10] The word for sin originally signified the debt owed as expiation or reparations, as in German *Schuld*. The parallelism exists in most Indo-European and Near Eastern languages (Hudson 2018, Chapter 4). It has caused much confusion for translators of the Lord's Prayer regarding "Forgive us our debts/sins."

[11] In 454 BC the League's treasury and headquarters were moved to Athens, turning what had been a defensive democratic alliance against Persia into an exploitative Athenian tribute system. One 60th of this tribute was dedicated annually to the goddess Athena.

series contained "over 48,000 drachmas which remained unopened from at least 188 to 169."[12]

In light of this monetary role of temples in antiquity, there is ample reason to call modern banks "temples of finance," with architecture often symbolically resembling that of ancient temples, and like them, typically towering over the skyline of their cities.

Democratic reforms and how Greek coinage democratized the character of money

Neither Greece nor Italy had specialized production on anything like the scale of Mesopotamian temples or palaces (or even those of the Mycenaean period) at the time Syrian and Phoenician traders brought Near Eastern commercial and debt practices westward around 750 BC. With no tradition of "divine kingship" to promote liberty from debt bondage, Greek and Italian chieftains adopted credit practices in the context of their own control of the land, trade and religion. Religious cults were under the control of a few aristocratic families who combined sacred, civic and economic power. Largely through the unchecked dynamics of interest-bearing debt, they concentrated commercial and financial wealth in their own hands, forcing families living on the edge of subsistence into clientage and bondage.

Coinage was struck in Greece and Asia Minor not by individuals bartering, but by "tyrants" and reformers who took control of trade and finance away from the autocratic families who had monopolized the land and held its cultivators in debt. Instead of this coinage causing debt crises, many of the "tyrants" who introduced coinage were known for cancelling debts and redistributing land as part of their sponsorship of standardized economic relations. These populist leaders (often emerging from the minor branches of the leading families) included Pheidon of Argos, Kypselos of Corinth and Solon of Athens.[13]

Ancient writers unsympathetic to democracy gave a negative autocratic connotation to the word "tyrant." The term is better translated as "demagogue," which retains the populist *demos* root of their policies. What subsequent oligarchies found so "tyrannical" was the assertion of public power over creditors by driving the dominant families into exile, redistributing their land and cancelling the debts that had deprived

---

[12] Larsen 1938:341. See also Finley 1973:174, and Boeckh 1857:219 and 565-566.

[13] I discuss the tyrant-reformers, Sparta and its iron money, Solon, and Athenian money creation in Chapters 2, 3, 4 and 5 respectively of *The Collapse of Antiquity*.

many clients of their liberty, much as Near Eastern rulers had cancelled debts and returned self-support land through Clean Slate proclamations.

The civic minting of coins emerged in the wake of this restructuring. An early step was taken by Sparta. One of the most prosperous city-states on the Greek mainland at the start of the 7th century, its "Lycurgan" anti-commercial revolution ca. 680 set it on a radically different path from others by rejecting the use of silver and even copper as money in favor of a fiat iron currency. That is the period's most obvious example of metallic value not being the key to monetary worth. Plutarch reports that this iron was treated with vinegar so as to make it too brittle to have a useful metallic value on its own as a store of monetary wealth.

Sparta also made the neighboring land that it conquered and assigned to its citizens inalienable so that it could not be forfeited. In Argos, Pheidon (ca. 710-670) overthrew the local aristocracy and, along with establishing standardized weights and measures and striking silver coinage, is said to have redistributed land to equalize its distribution. A generation later, Corinth became the richest Greek city-state under Kypselos (ruled 657-625) and his son Periander, who cancelled debts, redistributed the land and exiled the families who had monopolized it. They also reorganized exchange by striking coins. In addition to Pheidon, Kypselos and Periander, "the Phrygian king Midas's Kymaian wife; Hippias of Athens [the son of Peisistratos; and] Polykrates of Samos" were reformer-tyrants who struck coinage, notes Leslie Kurke. "The first mention of coinage in a Greek text (Alkaios fr. 69 V) links the 'staters of the Lydians' to the 'cunning-minded fox' who is presumably the tyrant Pittakos." Elected "tyrant" of Mytilene, the denunciation by aristocratic writers suggests that Pittakos emulated the policy of other reformers and drove out the old aristocracy, redistributed their lands and cancelled debts as well as issuing coinage. From Herodotus and other biographers, one can distil a "portrait of the tyrant as champion of egalitarian justice and opponent of aristocratic overreaching."[14]

Colin Kraay has described how – like silver money in Mesopotamia – Greek coinage was introduced to standardize payments made to and by the state for its fiscal transactions vis-à-vis the rest of the community.[15] By

---

[14] Kurke 1999:67-68. Kurke describes Lydia as issuing its early coinage in conjunction with sponsoring regional games as public festivals that provided an occasion for markets and payment to prostitutes (*porne*) as the democratic counterpart to the courtesans who served the wealthy in exchange for gifts rather than fixed monetary payments.

[15] Kraay 1964.

594 BC a debt and land crisis had developed in Athens. It was resolved by Solon's "shedding of burdens" that cancelled debts, banned debt bondage for Athenians and made land unalienable to outsiders to block aliens from foreclosing on the land of indebted Athenians. The first Athenian coins are dated a half-century later, minted by the Peisistratids.

Athens was unique in having its own silver mines at Laurion, owned by the city-state and leased to private operators. That helped lay the groundwork for Athenian democracy by enabling it to issue public coinage – the "owls" – standardizing the means for payments and denominating prices for trade in the *agora*, the marketplace in which merchants rented stalls from the city. Other elements of this civic program included public building and the staging of dramatic festivals to replace the religious cults controlled by the aristocratic families.

Much as was the case when Mesopotamia's palaces and temples monetized silver two thousand years earlier, classical antiquity's reformers who overthrew despotic aristocracies and introduced coinage acted as "straighteners," with tyrants being characterized "as *euthunter*, 'straightener,' the bringer of justice and law," the same metaphor used by Babylonian rulers who proclaimed *misharum* annulling rural debts, bringing "straight order" with connotations of distributive justice.[16] "Edouard Will argued some time ago that in the Greek polis *nomisma*, coinage, had strong associations with fair distribution; it described the relationship between citizens and the city," notes Sitta von Reden. "Not accidentally *nomisma* and *nomos*, law, had the same roots: both were the result of rightful distribution, a conventional standard, something used by custom or convention among a political community."[17] Kurke points out that the term that Aristotle used for coinage, *nomisma*, means "currency" – not necessarily money, for which the usual term was *chremata*. In addition to meaning "law" (*nomos*) or "rule," the root *nem-* meant "to allot, to distribute."[18]

Kurke describes the pre-tyrant aristocracies as refraining from creating public coinage or standardized prices and markets because they preferred to conduct exchange on a personal basis favoring their own powerful status according to circumstances. "Whether we etymologize it (with Will) as 'process or result of lawful distribution' or (with Laroche) as 'convention,' the term *nomisma* points to the political function of

---

[16] Kurke 1999:67-68, citing McGlew 1993:81-86.

[17] Von Reden 2002:53, citing Will 1954 and 1975.

[18] Kurke 1999:332 and 13-14.

coinage, either as a means of effecting redistributive justice or as an institution of consensus," as the reformers moved to replace the old elite's arbitrary demands and pricing.[19]

"As the polis used coins for its own payments and insisted on payment in coin," summarizes Randall Wray, "it inserted its sovereignty into retail trade in the agora ... wresting control away from the elite."[20] Kurke suggests that this democratic dimension is a major reason why civic coinage spread so slowly outside of the Greek sphere despite the flowering of trade in Egypt, Phoenicia and Carthage for many centuries. What catalyzed coinage was the conquest of Alexander the Great (356-323 BC) looting the region's temples, melting down their statues and ornaments into bullion and putting it into circulation as coinage.[21] Coinage henceforth was increasingly military in character.

Reviewing the American Numismatic Society's database MANTIS, Francois De Callataÿ finds that "the monetary mass of the Hellenistic world was overwhelmingly issued for military purposes (and it is likely that this statement – obviously true for the Roman world as well, whether Republican or Imperial – needs to be extended into the Classical and Archaic worlds)."[22] And reflecting the fact that Greek cities, kings and leagues produced their coinages more to pay soldiers than for market trade, coinage imagery was primarily chosen "to make coins accepted by the users" by being "related to power and military values such as helmet, thunderbolt, club, shield, and spear. Zeus appears increasingly after the conquests of Alexander," just as Rome's Severan emperors would favor the Mars type.[23] Alexander was the first to press

---

[19] Kurke 1999:41, citing von Reden 1995:173-174.

[20] Wray 2001.

[21] Kurke 1999:7 and 12.

[22] De Callataÿ 2016:129-130. He adds that the "mostly ephemeral, sometimes sporadic, very rarely continuous" character of Greek coin production was "much more suitable for military situations than for trade. Anyone who tries to argue that coins were produced to facilitate transactions has first to cope with this evidence. ... Military attributes such as helmet, shield, club and spear indeed come first in the list of inanimate objects. ... Soldiers are supposed to be more illiterate, rougher and rustic than the average population, more multi-ethnic too, thus favoring simple messages understandable by all."

[23] De Callataÿ 2016:116-117. As Head 1887:lxviii-lxix noted: "All through the history of free and independent Greece, and even until the death of Alexander the Great, the main object of the coin-type was to place before the people an ideal representation of the divinity most honored in the district in which the coin was intended to circulate."

coins with his own profile, providing the model for subsequent kings to depict their rule as divinely sanctioned.

Another public occasion for the use of coins, Head noted, were the festivals associated with the public games sponsored by the four great Greek temples: the Olympian games, the Pythian games at Delphi, the Isthmian and Nemean games. (Athens later sponsored the Delian games to offset the first four, all of which were held in Spartan-dominated Peloponnesia). These games were associated with markets and hence a need for coinage minted by the temples.[24]

The accepted position for the past half-century remains that of Kraay: "The issuer in all identifiable cases proves to be the supreme political power in each city or state; there is no evidence in the Greek world for the private issue of coins by bankers or merchants."[25] The monetary historian C. J. Howgego states bluntly: "There is no certain case in the whole of antiquity of coins being produced by individuals."[26]

Civic authority over the temples

Like Mesopotamia's monetary silver, Greek coinage was produced in the temples, which in turn were administered by civic authorities. Curtius summarizes the transition from temple to civic coinage and credit. In cases where donations were made jointly to the town and its deity,

> sacred money was under a mixed administration.
>
> This control exercised by the municipal authorities led, however, to an interference with priestly institutions. The state sequestered the priestly treasures, a sequestration which must have commenced at Athens during the time of the Tyrants, when the priesthood had an annuity conferred upon them, and when the great temple treasury was erected at the expense of the state, to serve at once as a treasury for the state and the temple.

---

[24] Head 1887:lvii notes: "Apparent exceptions to the almost universal rule as to the sacred character of the types of Greek coins are the so-called *agonistic* types commemorating victories in the games; but it should be borne in mind that all Greek games partook of a religious nature, and that the representation of a victorious chariot or other agonistic emblem would be in a certain sense symbolical of the god in whose honor the games were held."

[25] Kraay 1966:12.

[26] Howgego 1995:3. Greek temples organized smithing and metal-working into guilds. The mint in Athens was located in the Stephanophore temple devoted to Theseus.

> Now on the transfer of the temple treasures to municipal management, the money struck thence became state money, *i.e.*, the state took the issuing into its own hands, giving its own credit in the place of that of the priests. But as it was everywhere the endeavor to make the transfer as gently as possible (whence so few traditions of conflicts between states and the priesthoods) during the completion of the secularization, the form in which it was done was concealed, and the treasuries were built like temples, their officers being invested with a sacerdotal character, while the deity was left to all appearance in full possession of her property. Thus it was also with the temple currency; the religious character was left as if it still continued to be issued by the priests, but in token that the circulation of money struck under other than state authority was no longer permitted, and that the money was recognized as the state currency, the initials of the name of the town were placed as a profane mint-mark upon the reverse. ... It is the Government countermark to the priestly symbol which was left unchanged; its introduction marks the secularisation of the coinage, which it seems first took place in Kyzikos and Teos.[27]

"The treasurers of the goddess, therefore, were not merely treasurers of the temple in the narrower sense, but were at the same time keepers of the public treasure," noted August Boeckh in reference to Athens. After 419 BC, "these several treasurers of the temples, with the exception of the temple of Minerva, were all united in a single board called the 'Treasurers of the Gods, or of other Deities.'"[28]

The anti-government (essentially anti-socialist) "Austrian" barter theory of money's origins proposed by Carl Menger 1871 (translated into English to great popularity in 1892) sidestepped any acknowledgement of how money was civic and official from the outset. Despite publication of the research of Boeckh 1857, Curtius 1870, Jebb 1880, Middleton 1888 and Head 1887 regarding the primary and positive role played by public institutions in the genesis of money, the "individualist" school conjured up a censorial myth of how individuals acting by themselves might have developed money without any official oversight or purpose other than to truck and barter.

No anthropological or archaeological evidence has been found to support the fantasy of money having originally been developed for on-the-spot payment of goods and services. Most archaic economic relations were on credit, with payment typically being made at harvest time down

---

[27] Curtius 1870:108-109.

[28] Boeckh 1857:222.

to medieval Europe in the 12th and 13th centuries. The "Austrian" barter theory was developed by opponents of the rising state regulatory power in the late 19th century. Their ideological aim was to create an origin myth for money – and economic relations in general – that excluded any positive role for the state. That ruled out acknowledging the role played by civic authorities and their city-temples in the development of Greek and Roman coinage.

Temples were associated with coinage in two ways: First, as already described, their mints struck coins, typically stamped by civic authorities as a guarantee of purity, to pay mercenaries, taxes and for trade, especially at festivals and games. Second, temples lent their votive offerings to their local city-states to strike coins. Examples where temple treasure was lent for coinage include Athens, Syracuse and other Greek cities during the final decade of the Peloponnesian War (414-404 BC), and Rome toward the end of the Hannibalic Wars during 211-205 BC. Much civic coinage thus took the form of a public debt to the temples.[29]

For many centuries the fact that temples were sacred led them to be left intact by conquerors who did not hesitate to plunder private property. However, when the Phocian generals occupied Delphi during 356/346 BC, they seized its treasures to pay mercenary troops. They "melted down money from the votive offerings made of gold and silver, and minted coins and put them into circulation of the various states," mainly to hire more troops. Most of these coins were later deemed sacrilegious and re-melted, and some were cast into new images and offerings and returned to the Delphi temple.[30] But it soon became normal for Roman generals to bring minters with them to coin looted temple booty on the spot to pay their soldiers (and themselves). This was not an "economic" market exchange for commodity trade.

Temples and debt contracts

Antiquity's temples sanctified and its palaces created the social and legal context in which money and debt relationships evolved. Borrowers took

---

[29] During the Mithridatic Wars (87-83 BC) the Roman general Sulla looted the gold held by the Temple of Artemis, but later ordered the city of Ephesus to make restitution, in keeping with the traditional obligation of civic authorities to return all borrowings of gold after peace was restored.

[30] Plutarch, "The Oracles of Delphi," cited in Middleton 1888:283; see also p. 307. Subsequent Christian rulers from Roman times to medieval Europe broke traditional respect for religion by seizing alien temple wealth as being "pagan" (even that of Constantinople in 1204) and hence not sanctified by their own exclusive church.

sacred oaths, and creditors were obliged to swear that their claims were valid. To violate such oaths was a sacrilege rendering one an outcast, subject to Graeco-Roman infamy.[31] Land boundaries were protected by local gods such as those depicted on Athenian *horoi* stones. By the 4th century BC these markers came to be engraved with the mortgage terms on which their demarcated properties were pledged as collateral. To move or destroy them was a sacrilege for which offending parties could be fined, punished, outlawed, excommunicated or even reduced to bondage. And adopting the Neo-Babylonian practice of registering land sales in the Temple of Bel,[32] Greek and Asia Minor cities preserved records of mortgage loans and other debts in their major temples – which is why "the destruction of such archives and registries was a usual aim of social revolts."[33]

Temples lent to individuals for mortgages and to slaves to buy their liberty as well as to their city-states. The most detailed surviving archive is from Delos, which Athens took over during the Peloponnesian War as a counterpoise to Delphi, Olympia and other temples in territory controlled by Sparta's allies. Each year the outgoing *hieropoioi* (ministers of public worship) would go to the Delian Senate and hand over to their successors an inventory of "all the objects which they had received from their predecessors ... [and of those] acquired during their year in office" for the Temple of Apollo and other temples on Delos. These detailed lists included such items as a cow missing its left horn and a kettle that had lost its bottom and handles, as well as small amounts of gold dust.

---

[31] Middleton 1888:309 notes that at the Temple of Apollo in Delphi, "the form of excommunication for ασεβια (*asebeia*) with which the nonpayment of fines was punished, curiously resembles that used by the Medieval Church: 'Let the city (people or person) be devoted to the vengeance of Apollo, Artemis, Leto, and Athene Pronaia: let their land produce no fruit, their wives bear monsters, their cattle be barren. Let them be defeated in war and in tribunals of justice; let them and theirs perish, and let their sacrifice be unacceptable to Apollo, Artemis, Leto, and Athens Pronaia.'" The meaning is one of ungodliness. For Asia Minor's similar practice see Larsen 1938:357.

[32] Heichelheim 1958 III:71 cites San Nicolo's description that this registry enabled titles to mortgages to "be changed from the name of one creditor to that of another using simple book-keeping entries ... two creditors who each had mortgages on plots or houses belonging to the other could cancel or reduce, in the same way, these mortgages spontaneously without any money payments being necessary."

[33] Broughton 1938:226, describing official registries in the Roman Near East holding debt records, "especially in Jerusalem Sepphoris, Dura, Edessa and Antioch on the Orontes ... where both depositing and registering [debts] were possible."

> But the wealth of the Delian god did not consist merely in the contents of his temple. He was also a landowner and a moneylender. ... His revenues comprised rents of arable land, of pastures, and of houses. The house-property is multifarious – workshops, cellars, dwelling houses, lodging houses, an apothecary's shop, a bath. Apollo further levied taxes on the purple-fishery, on anchorage, and on the disembarkation of merchandise. ... The Delian temple, like other rich temples, put out the balance of its revenues at usury. The town of Delos, the island communities, and also private persons, appear as debtors in the temple register of loans. The capital sums were usually lent out for terms of five years, at an annual interest of ten per cent.[34]

A Delos temple document dating from 250 BC describes a mortgage loan extended "from the sacred money," giving the temple the right to foreclose on other property of the borrower and his guarantors in case of a loan default. A loan to a person named Autocles was extended "on the security of all the other property belonging to Autocles and his guarantors." If the mortgaged property's value did not suffice to cover the loan balance, "the authorities can seize other property belonging to the borrower and his guarantors." The temple's typical loan criteria and terms were similar to

> the rules governing the investment of the donation of Attalus at Delphi. The land mortgaged must have twice the value of the loan and be free of encumbrances. Guarantors acceptable to the administrators were required. If the loan was not repaid, the property pledged was to belong to the city and to be sold. If the sales price was less than the sum borrowed, the remainder could be collected from other property of the borrower and his bondsmen. If the interest was not paid when due, payment was to be enforced with a 50% penalty. Here too it is clear that the administrators of the funds could proceed directly to the enforcement of their claims without a preliminary lawsuit.[35]

However, Greek temples often gave debtors who fell into arrears extra time and opportunity to pay off the balance. No doubt this was especially the case with prominent local borrowers, but there was a general ethic of promoting viability.

---

[34] Jebb 1880:30. Larsen 1938:370-371 notes that the interest rate charged by Delos often was not specified. "When loans were repaid, the payment was simply entered as a payment of money which the city owed the god without any indication of how much was capital and how much was interest." See also Heichelheim 1958:74.

[35] Larsen 1938:375-377.

Secularization of credit in Greece and Rome

The role of Delos and other temples declined after the Peloponnesian War ended in 404. Civic governments came to dominate the temples, and most loans by temples in turn were to municipal city-state governments, which operated their own public banks and borrowed from the temple to lend at a markup.[36] In Asia Minor, "temples in or near the cities tended to come under civic control ... the development of private banking and the invention of the public bank tended to restrict the function of the temple to deposits and reserves. They had probably never engaged seriously in commercial loans, bottomry loans [on shipping] and other more hazardous kinds of credit, and so lost little as the private bankers took these functions over."[37] Temples were left to focus on mortgages and loans to the poor who otherwise would not qualify for credit.

Mortgage lending terms and interest charges for the economy at large were originally modeled on the formalities used by Greek temples and their Near Eastern predecessors. Lending practices, however, became secularized and privatized in the hands of the families that dominated civic government and administered the temples, in Italy as well as in Greece. But Western financial practices remained less sophisticated than those of the Near East. Although "money changing, pawn loans with interest, interest-free loans, interest loans on real estate, and deposit business of different patterns were early known as banking activities of temples and private persons," notes Fritz Heichelheim, there was no trade in bills of exchange nor were there prominent banking firms on the scale of Babylon's Egibi family from the 7th to 5th centuries BC or the Murashu firm in 4th-century BC Nippur.[38] Organizing tax collection and public finances on behalf of the imperial Persian regime, these two Neo-Babylonian firms were innovative in using their own trade credit

---

[36] Thucydides 1.96, 8.108 and 5.32 describes how Athens expropriated Delians from their own island, ultimately to be butchered by the Persian general Arsaces (who ruled from 247 to 217 BC). Strabo 10.5.4 states that after Rome destroyed Corinth, its merchants and bankers shifted their operations to Delos, by which time its role had become thoroughly commercialized, with private bankers playing a growing role.

[37] Broughton 1938:890, citing Ziebarth, "Hellenistische Banken," *Zeitschrift für Numismatik* 34 (1924):36-37.

[38] Heichelheim 1958 II:70-71. Cornelia Wunsch 2000 describes the Egibi family's activities, and Matthew Stolper 1985 those of the Murashu, who organized tax collection by creating a transportation and marketing network to turn sharecropping and other crop surpluses into cash payments. Their banking organization also organized irrigation networks to charge for water, and even sold beer.

and property management to monetize the economy's crop surpluses. And in Jerusalem, the major Jewish temple facilitated commercial shipping by enabling debts to be repaid "in regions far distant from those in which they had been incurred, especially in Rome; similarly debts incurred in Rome could be discharged in Syria."[39]

Rome's monetary deterioration under the Republic's oligarchy and the emperors

Money originated as an accounting technique used by Near Eastern palaces and temples to denominate and serve as the means of paying credit balances owed to these institutions at harvest time and at the conclusion of foreign trade ventures. And in the West from the outset of coinage in the 7th century BC, coinage's fiscal value derived from its acceptability for paying taxes and other public charges. That gave coinage its value, as shown most obviously by Sparta's iron-money. But as classical antiquity's creditor oligarchy gained power, it became increasingly able to avoid having to pay taxes as it appropriated the land of smallholders and also public land. Economies and their use of credit and money became increasingly privatized.

Rome's fiscal collapse ended the value of coinage for public purposes. After the Roman Republic gave way to the Empire in the 1st century BC, its tributary economy ran out of new conquests, and the imperial treasury was less able to collect taxes from the large landowners who had gained control of the land and resisted taxation while reducing cultivators to clients as sharecroppers, leading ultimately to serfdom, capping Rome's long process of economic polarization between creditors and debtors.[40] Unable to create a tax-paying need for its coinage, Rome's fiscally based monetary system broke down. Rome's emperors debased the metal content of coinage as their fiscal position fell into chronic deficit.

Metallists blame the resulting price inflation on the government issuing too much debased coinage, while adherents of the State Theory of money attribute Rome's need to resort to debasement to the state's inability to tax wealth that was becoming increasingly concentrated. Without civic fiscal value, the legal worth of coinage disappeared after the 4th century AD. When taxes could not be collected and as emperors

---

[39] Broughton 1938:224-226.

[40] I discuss Rome's polarization in *The Collapse of Antiquity* (2023), with Chapters 19 and 20 describing the Late Empire's fiscal squeeze, monetary depreciation, inflation, and collapse into feudalism.

used whatever metal the state had on hand to pay their soldiers, coinage was left only with its raw commodity value – the deteriorating silver content of the increasingly debased coinage. Money became more an item of barter for silver than a means of settling debts in what had begun as a credit economy. Rome's economy collapsed into payment-in-kind as economic life retreated to self-sufficient manors and Church estates on the land. The evolution of monetary systems thus went from credit to "money" and ended in barter, not from barter to bullion-money to a privatized credit superstructure as depicted in "Austrian" theory.[41]

Near Eastern rulers had avoided classical antiquity's fate by preventing a domestic creditor and landowning oligarchy from replacing the palace's taxing power with its own claims for debt and rent payments and labor services. By proclaiming Clean Slates cancelling debts, liberating bondservants from service to their creditors, and returning self-support land that had been alienated, Near Eastern rulers were able to maintain a broadly-based landholding and tax-paying class, periodically renewing fiscal balance and keeping the monetary system, prices, interest rates and land distribution stable for thousands of years.

The post-Roman aftermath

Like Near Eastern rulers, strong Byzantine emperors in the 9th and 10th centuries AD imposed fiscal checks on their financial elites. To prevent creditors from depriving the palace of the corvée and other fiscal obligations of smallholders and their service in the military, rulers reversed foreclosures and distress sales of self-support land.[42] But just as oligarchies had undermined the West Roman fiscal system, landholding elites weakened Byzantine power to the point where Constantinople was easily sacked by the Crusaders in 1204.

This looting provided a basis for revived banking and credit operations in Western Europe. The Venetian city-state, which had invested in the Fourth Crusade diverted to Constantinople in exchange for a share of the loot, along with the Knights Templar and Hospitaller, monetized much of the silver and gold looted by the Crusades. Commercial and mortgage lending revived, using legal formulae soon adopted by private bankers, supported by Church theologians re-legitimizing financial

---

[41] And only in medieval times did kings (*i.e.*, the government) begin to borrow from private bankers, mainly to finance their wars, as described below.

[42] I describe these reforms in the Eastern Roman Empire in Chapters 27 and 28 of *"... and forgive them their debts"* (2018).

charges for foreign exchange (*agio*) fees and commercial trade financing, which were deemed to be productive credit, in contrast to predatory usury. But "unproductive" loans were accepted by being extended to the top of the social pyramid, to enable kings to pay Peter's Pence tribute to Rome and wage wars on the papacy's behalf with loans from Italian bankers close to the Papacy.[43]

The monetary role of silver and gold was privatized, coming under the control of banking families who became creditors to increasingly indebted governments, mainly for war loans. This privatization of credit is a distinguishing feature of the post-Roman West, whose commercial recovery enabled bankers and other creditors to act independently of Church or secular public authority.

Money and credit creation and allocation has been institutionalized increasingly outside of public control as governments themselves have become subject to private-sector financial control. Instead of governments creating money (over and above what they raise as revenue from taxes, fees and public enterprise), governments have become debtors, financing their budget deficits by borrowing from the private sector while their central banks provide credit and reserves to serve as the basis for commercial banks to create their own credit. Instead of taxes backing public money creation, they give fiscal valuation to bank credit.

Banks and financial institutions thus have privatized the government's traditional role as money creator and administrator. This transformation has been rationalized by the claim (without historical support) that governments are irresponsible in creating their own money – as if public money creation to spend into the economy is more inflationary than commercial banks creating credit or bondholders providing their private savings for governments to spend. The privatization of money creation has also been supported by a self-promoting creditor ideology claiming that prosperity is best achieved by minimizing the legal and regulatory "transaction costs" of creditors transferring income and property into their own hands away from the economy at large.

Modern governments have indeed created their own paper money in wartime as well as on other occasions (as Modern Monetary Theory has explained). This option's success and effectiveness poses an existential

---

[43] By the early 14th century when France's Philip IV and other kings ran out of money, they "cried down" the coinage by simply redefining the face value of coins (much as Rome's emperors debased the metal content of coinage as their fiscal position fell into chronic deficit). That affected the payment of debts, making it easier for debtors but providing less real purchasing power to the Church, the nobility and banking families.

political threat to the money-creating privileges that private bankers have obtained over the past thousand years. It is largely to deter public money creation for government self-financing that bankers have sponsored an origin-myth that money had a metallist genesis independent of any public authority or issuer.

Bibliography

Balmuth, Miriam (1967), "Monetary Forerunners of Coinage in Phoenicia and Palestine in Antiquity," in A. Kindler, ed., *The Patterns of Monetary Development in Phoenicia and Palestine in Antiquity* (Jerusalem).
" (1971), "Remarks on the Appearance of the Earliest Coins," in David Gordon Mitten, John Griffiths Pedley, and Jane Ayer Scott, eds., *Studies Presented to George M. A. Hanfmann* (Cambridge, Mass.):17.

Bell [Kelton], Stephanie, and Edward Nell, eds. (2003), *The State, The Market and The Euro* (Cheltenham)

Boeckh, August (1857 [1842]), *The Public Economy of Athens* (Boston and London).

Broughton, T. R. S. (1938), "Roman Asia Minor. The First Mithridatic War, 89-84 BC," in Tenney Frank, *Economic Survey of Ancient Rome*, IV: *Roman Africa, Syria, Greece and Asia* (Baltimore):500-512.

Curtius, Ernst (1870), "On the religious character of Greek coins," *Numismatic Chronicle* 10:91-111 (translated by B. V. Head; original title "Ueber den religiosen Character der griechischen Münzen.")

De Callataÿ, Francois (2016), "Greek coin types in context: a short state of the art," *Pharos* 22 (1):115-141.

Dercksen, J. G., J. Eidem, K. van der Toor Nen and K. R. Veenhof, eds. (2016), *Silver, Money and Credit: A Tribute to Robartus J. van der Spek on the Occasion of his 65th Birthday on 18th September 2014* (Nederlands Instituut voor het Nabije Oosten, Leiden).

Finley, Moses (1973), *The Ancient Economy* (Berkeley and Los Angeles).

Gardner, Percy (1913), "Coinage of the Athenian Empire," *Journal of Hellenic Studies* 33.
" (1918), *A History of Ancient Coinage: 700-300 BC* (Oxford).

Head, Barclay V. (1887), *Historia Numorum: A Manual of Greek Numismatics* (Oxford).

Heichelheim, Fritz (1964), *An Ancient Economic History*, Vol. II (Leiden).

Hocart, A. M. (1952), *The Life-Giving Myth* (London):Chapter X: Money: 97-104.

Hudson, Michael (2000), "How Interest Rates Were Set, 2500 BC-1000 AD: *Máš, tokos* and *fænus* as metaphors for interest accruals," *Journal of the Economic and Social History of the Orient* 43 (Spring):132-161.
" (2003), "The Creditary/Monetarist Debate in Historical Perspective," in Bell and Nell 2003:39-76.
" (2004a), "The Development of Money-of-Account in Sumer's Temples," in Michael Hudson and Cornelia Wunsch, eds., *Creating Economic Order: Record-Keeping, Standardization and the Development of Accounting in the Ancient Near East* (Bethesda; repr. Dresden 2023):303-329.
" (2004b), "The Archaeology of Money in Light of Mesopotamian Records," in Wray 2004.
" (2018), "*... and forgive them their debts": Lending, Foreclosure and Redemption From Bronze Age Finance to the Jubilee Year* (Dresden).
" (2023), *The Collapse of Antiquity: Greece and Rome as Civilization's Oligarchic Turning Point* (Dresden).

Jebb, R. C. (1880), "Delos," *Journal of Hellenic Studies* 1.

Kurke, Leslie (1999), *Coins, Bodies, Games, and Gold* (Princeton).

Larsen, J. A. O. (1938), "Roman Greece," in Tenney Frank, *An Economic Survey of Ancient Rome*, Vol. IV (Baltimore).

Laum, Bernard (1924), *Heiliges Geld* (Tübingen).

Menger, Carl (1892 [1871]), "On the Origins of Money," *Economic Journal*, 2:238-255.

Middleton, J. Henry (1888), "The Temple of Apollo at Delphi," *Journal of Hellenic Studies* 9-10:282-322.

Powell, Marvin A. (1999), "*Wir müssen alle unsere Nische nuzten*: Monies, Motives, and Methods in Babylonian Economics," in J. G. Dercksen, ed., *Trade and Finance in Ancient Mesopotamia* (Istanbul):5-23.

Stolper, Matthew W. (1985), *Entrepreneurs and Empire: the Murašû Archive, the Murašû Firm, and Persian Rule in Babylonia* (Leiden).

Thomson, Rudi (1957-61), *Early Roman Coinage and its Evidence*, 3 vols. (Copenhagen).

von Reden, Sitta (1995), *Exchange in Ancient Greece* (London).
" (2002), "Demos' *Phialê* and the rhetoric of money in fourth-century Athens," in Paul Cartledge, Edward E. Cohen and Lin Foxhall, eds., *Money, Labour and Land: Approaches to the economies of ancient Greece* (London, Routledge).

Will, Edouard (1954), "De l'aspect éthique des origines grecques de la monnaie," *Revue historique* 212:209-231.
" (1975), "Fonctions de la monnaie dans les cités grecques de l'époque classique," in M. Dentzer, P. Gauthier and T. Hackens, eds., *Numismatique Antique: problèmes et méthods* (= 1975, Études d'archéologie classique) (Louvain):233-246.

Wray, L. Randall, Review of Kurke's "Coins, Bodies, Games, and Gold," *Journal of Economic Issues* (March 2001).
" ed. (2004), *Credit and State Theories of Money: The Contributions of A. Mitchell Innes* (Cheltenham).

Wunsch, Cornelia (2000), *Das Egibi Archiv* (Leiden).
" (2009), "The Egibi Family," in Gwendolyn Leick, ed., *The Babylonian World* (New York).

3

Social vs. "Individualistic" Theories of the Origins of Money and Interest*

The past century's research by anthropologists, philologists and Assyriologists has refuted the myth that money and interest-bearing debt emerged spontaneously by individuals bartering and lending amongst themselves. Every discipline except mainstream economics has found that general-purpose money was developed as part of public fiscal organization. This has not deterred "free market" economists from claiming that money is merely a veil for exchanging goods and services, so that no public agency is (or ever was) needed to oversee money and its associated creditor/debtor relationships. To defend this stance, they have composed hypothetical scenarios of how families living in an agrarian epoch might have developed metallic money and set interest rates for lending spontaneously on a merely interpersonal level.

History has not been the strong point of such speculation. "The great superiority of the historical method," the anthropologist Arthur Hocart has pointed out, "is that it assumes nothing which we do not know actually to occur."[1] The historical evidence shows Near Eastern palaces and temples developing money and debt rules to facilitate their forward planning and collection of rents and fees, with the paradigmatic monetized payments arising from transactions with these large institutions.

The claim that money and debt are not economically important

Opponents of public regulation of banking and finance feel so uncomfortable discussing money and credit that they claim that the topic does

---

* This chapter combines the basic analysis of two articles: "The Archaeology of Money in Light of Mesopotamian Records," in L. Randall Wray, ed., *Credit and State Theories of Money: The Contributions of A. Mitchell Innes* (Edward Elgar, Cheltenham, 2004):99-127, and "The Development of Money-of-Account in Sumer's Temples," in *Creating Economic Order: Record-Keeping, Standardization and the Development of Accounting in the Ancient Near East* (CDL Press, Bethesda, Md., 2004; now ISLET, Dresden, 2023):303-329.

[1] Arthur M. Hocart, *The Life-Giving Myth* (London, 1952):66 (from a 1922 essay, "The Origin of Monotheism").

not really matter, because economies basically function on barter. Money is viewed as just another commodity (*hacksilver* or *ponderata*), and markets simply as aggregations of individuals trading goods amongst themselves, without reference to money's role as a vehicle for taxes and other debt settlement. "If we were to reconstruct history along hypothetical, logical lines," posits Paul Samuelson in his *Economics* textbook, "we should naturally follow the age of barter by the age of commodity money. ... Even in the most advanced industrial economies, if we strip exchange down to its barest essentials and peel off the obscuring layer of money, we find that trade between individuals or nations largely boils down to barter."[2]

The reality is that archaic exchange was transacted on credit, not barter. All ancient societies ran up debts to bridge the gap between planting and harvesting, and between the consignment of goods to traders and their seasonal return from their sea voyage or caravan. But credit tends to become economically intrusive and destabilizing if not overseen by government. The claim by Samuelson (1967:52) that the origins of money are to be found in barter unrealistically ignores the linkage between money, credit and interest-bearing debt. Assuming that exchange is settled on the spot misses the all-important point that general-purpose money arose essentially as a means of paying debts. What Samuelson dismisses as "the obscuring layer of money" is credit – that is, debt on the liabilities side of the balance sheet. Instead of acknowledging the problem of debts mounting up in excess of the means to pay, mainstream economists depict creditors as acting in society's best long-term interest, not as concentrating ownership of land and monetary wealth in their own hands at the expense of the economy at large.

The polarizing dynamics of debt led to economic crises that deranged classical Greek and Roman antiquity's economic balance, just as debt polarizes today's domestic and foreign relations. In contrast to Bronze Age "debt management" in the form of royal Clean Slates designed to restore balance and equity to the monetary/debt system, the "barter" myth of money's origin denies any need for public authority to protect against monetary and debt dynamics distorting and polarizing economies.

An anthropological and philological perspective

Today's surviving tribal communities are rarely pristine. Most have had many hundreds of years to interact with more modern economies.

---

[2] Paul Samuelson, *Economics* (New York, 1967):52 and 54-55.

Describing the Kwakiutl of Northwest Canada a century ago, Marcel Mauss's *The Gift* (1925) focused on their gift exchange, headed by copper obtained by fur trade with the Hudson's Bay Company. The striking feature about the Kwakiutl was their competitive gift-giving, trying to bankrupt others by "topping" their gifts as a means of obtaining a status advantage. Mauss believed that such one-upmanship may have been the prototype for archaic interest charges. He viewed such charges as so universal that he took those of the Kwakiutl as proxies for early Western civilization. But it is hard to imagine civilization's takeoff occurred by dissipating wealth in such a way.

Mauss and other anthropologists were on the right track in recognizing that societies had debts long before they developed money. Some anthropologists have looked to classical Greece and Rome or medieval European common law for clues as to how exchange and money evolved in the West. Among the early social processes requiring means of settling debts not associated with market exchange of commodities were wergild-type fines to compensate victims of manslaughter and lesser injuries. These are found already in early Babylonia and seem to have been a universal archaic common law practice. It is from such reparation debts that the verb "to pay" derives, from the root idea "to pacify."[3]

Payments to the victims of injury or their families (and also bride-price and dowry payments) typically took the form of movable assets such as livestock, or servant-girls. These payments played no fiscal role, because they were to families, not to temples, palaces or the state. And fines for breaking noses and manslaughter hardly were "commodity transactions" or negotiated through the marketplace. The linguistic root of wergild is *wer* (Latin *vir*), "man," hardly an article of commerce (except in slavery). The victim was not a "creditor" in the modern sense of the term, but an injured party to whom a liability was owed. Such fines were part of reciprocity and gift exchange. Indeed, in classical Greece compensation for a wrong, *apoina*, was counted as a category of gift.[4]

The value of wergild debt was a "head price" determined by the victim's social status. The Greek word *timē*, used as a legal term, signified the penalty deemed appropriate in law – death, exile or monetary liability to compensate the victim. At first the word connoted "worth," "esteem" or "valuation," and subsequently "wealth" and hence in time

---

[3] My 2018 *"... and forgive them their debts"* provides an updated discussion of how the words for debt in nearly all languages are synonymous with "sin" or "guilt," reflecting an origin in reparations for personal injury.

[4] Moses Finley, *Politics in the Ancient World* (Cambridge, 1983):241.

"tax assessment." By the classical period *timē* came to denote "the nominal value of which an Athenian citizen's property was rated for the purposes of taxation, his rate of assessment, rateable property" (Liddell and Scott), and formed the root of the word *timocracy* – rule by property holders or other wealthy persons. The Athenian *timētes* was an official charged with appraising damages, penalties or taxes, similar in function to the Roman censor in charge of taking the census and rating the property of citizens. The line of evolution thus ran from common law based on reciprocity to a fiscal context based on land and wealth. Barter and trade were not involved.

However, wergild penalty debts brought into being the means of enforcing debt collection by impoundment of the debtor's property (the village pound). This institution took on a socially polarizing function when monetary indebtedness to wealthy creditors came into being.

Knapp's State Theory of Money and its offshoots

Theories of the public sector's dominant role in money's origins were developed most notably in Germany, which took the lead in public control of banking in the decades leading up to World War I with a three-way coordination between the government, banking and heavy industry (with emphasis on the military) to finance national growth, in contrast to British banking and stock brokerage extracting short-term financial returns, not financing long-term industrial capital investment.

Criticizing metallist theories for trying to deduce the genealogy of commodity money "without the idea of a State," Georg F. Knapp's *The State Theory of Money* in 1905 defined money as whatever governments "accepted at the public pay offices" for taxes, fees or the sale of public services.[5] The policy conclusion was that steering bank credit creation along productive industrial lines required state oversight to prevent private bankers from gaining undue influence.

---

[5] G. F. Knapp, *The State Theory of Money* (London, 1924):vii-viii, translated into English in 1924 at the urging of John Maynard Keynes. L. Randall Wray provides a review and bibliography of the State Theory of money in *Understanding Modern Money* (Cheltenham, 1998). I trace the ideological motivations behind metallist theories of money and the State Theory in "The Creditary/Monetarist Debate in Historical Perspective," in Edward Nell and Stephanie Bell, eds., *The State, The Market and The Euro: Chartalism versus Metallism in the Theory of Money* (Cheltenham, 2003):39-76. See also in that volume Charles Goodhart, "The two concepts of money: Implications for the analysis of optimal currency areas."

Knapp's logic found its antecedents in Aristotle, who described money as a creature of the state, and hence of law (Greek *nomos*, from which our word *numismatics* derives to signify the study of coinage). Around 325 BC, three centuries after the first electrum coins (an amalgam of gold and silver) were struck in Lydia, he observed that money had no "natural" value independent of its legal and political context. Providing the earliest documented statement of the rationale for minting coins, he explained (*Ethics* 1133) that money is called *nomisma* "because it exists not by nature, but by law (*nomos*), and it is in our power to change it and make it useless," as Sparta did when it issued iron slab-money treated with vinegar to make it brittle and hence useless except as money. The metallic content was incidental. Its value was set by public institutions. Likewise for Knapp, the value of early bullion and coinage was based on their acceptance by public institutions in payment of taxes and other fees.

Laum's proposed monetary origins

Knapp's approach inspired Bernard Laum to suggest that the Greek *oboloi* ("spit-money") and *drachmae* ("handfuls") derived from tax-like ceremonial food contributions to the temples that sponsored antiquity's communal festivals, and to their common-meal guilds and brotherhoods or other redistributive agencies. In subsequent writings he elaborated how fish money and other edibles fit into this category, whose value later was calculated in terms of the monetary metals. It would be a quantum leap to deem food contributions "money," but in time, Laum theorized, monetary tokens were used as exchange equivalents for the contribution or purchase of such food.[6]

Money was a logical extension of public oversight of weights and measures. Tax-like obligations would seem to be the bridge to money. The German word for money, *Geld*, derives from Gothic *gild*, "tax," but an early connection to paying fines is indicated by Old Icelandic *gjald*, "recompense, punishment, payment," and Old English *gield*, "substitute, indemnity, sacrifice."[7] This semantic metonymy combines the ethic of reciprocity with the idea of a standardized equality of contributions.

---

[6] Bernard Laum, *Heiliges Geld* (Tübingen, 1924) and "Geschichte der öffentlichen Finanzwirtschaft im Altertum und Frühmittelalter," in Wilhelm Gerloff and Fritz Neumark, eds., *Handbuch der Finanzwissenschaft*, 2nd ed. (Tübingen, 1952):211-235, esp. 216. An English-language summary of Laum's ideas appears in William H. Desmonde, *Magic, Myth and Money* (New York, 1962).

[7] Emile Benveniste, *Indo-European Language and Society* (Coral Gables, Fla., 1973):58.

A generation after Laum wrote, Karl Polanyi established a research group at Columbia University. Criticizing modernist economic approaches as being abstract and "disembedded," he analyzed the evolution of exchange as occurring in three stages: reciprocity (gift exchange), redistributive with administered price equivalencies, and modern markets with prices responding to shifts in supply and demand.[8] Mesopotamian and other Bronze Age economies dominated by their large institutions were "redistributive."

Leo Oppenheim, the major Assyriologist in Polanyi's group, described how sacred statues were adorned with golden ornaments that could be melted down in times of need to pay mercenaries (or ransom or tribute), as were the Winged Victory statues of Athens during the Peloponnesian War.[9] Throughout antiquity the public sector – including the temples – was in a surplus position, not the deficit position that it is in today, with debts owed to banks and other financial institutions.

Keynes wrote in his *Treatise on Money* (1930) that the principles underlying the State Theory of money could be traced back over four thousand years to Mesopotamia. Although having only a cursory familiarity with Sumerian records, he saw enough to deduce that money must have originated there as a unit of account: "Money itself, namely that by delivery of which debt-contracts and price-contracts are discharged, and in the shape of which a store of General Purchasing Power is held, derives its character from its relationship to the Money-of-Account, since the debts and prices must first have been expressed in terms of the latter." Such money, he explained, "comes into existence along with Debts, which are contracts for deferred payment, and Price-Lists, which

---

[8] See *Primitive, Archaic, and Modern Economies: Essays of Karl Polanyi*, George Dalton, ed. (New York, 1957) and Polanyi, *The Livelihood of Man* (New York, 1977):40-42. His approach is elaborated by Johannes Renger, "Patterns of Non-Institutional Trade and Non-Commercial Exchange in Ancient Mesopotamia at the Beginning of the Second Millennium B.C.," in Alfonso Archi, ed., *Circulation of Goods in Non-Palatial Context in the Ancient Near East* (= Incunabula Graeca 82, Rome, 1984):31-123.

Economists like to use their own jargon. John Hicks referred to the transition from "customary" to "command" pre-market societies (see Philip Grierson, *The Origins of Money* (London, 1977):19).

[9] A. Leo Oppenheim, "The Golden Garments of the Gods," *Journal of Near Eastern Studies* 8 (1949):172-193. His article "On an Operational Device in Mesopotamian Bureaucracy," *ibid.* 18 (1959):121-128, first suggested that early clay tokens were accounting devices and the inscriptions on their envelopes proto-cuneiform. See Denise Schmandt-Besserat, *Before Writing: From Counting to Cuneiform* (Austin, Texas, 1992):8-9.

are offers of contracts for sale or purchase."[10] Assigning price equivalencies to major commodities made them co-measurable. That enabled payments to be made in terms of any commodity listed on such a fiscal schedule, headed by barley and silver.

Measuring the value of goods and services was the essential function of Mesopotamia's money-of-account, and also of money in classical Greece. When Anacharsis, a Scythian 6th-century BC prince renowned for his admiration of Greek culture, was asked for what purposes the Greeks used money, he answered: "For reckoning."[11] As Aristotle concluded (*Ethics* 1133), "all things that are exchanged must be somewhat comparable. It is for this end that money has been introduced, and it becomes in a sense an intermediate; for it measures all things ... – how many shoes are equal to a house or to a given amount of food." In sum, he concluded, "Money acting as a measure, makes goods commensurate and equates them" by enabling them to be co-measured.

Aristotle's approach, along with what Knapp outlined in theorizing about modern finance and Keynes intuited for the origins of money, can now be filled in with much more historical detail from Mesopotamian payments of fees, rent and interest payments to the palatial economy's large institutions in the form of standardized measures of grain or weights of metal.

The individualistic anti-government approach

Economics students are indoctrinated with a fable about how money might have emerged out of the process of exchange among individuals, with no role played by public institutions. Markets are deemed necessary to enable individuals to buy each other's products. But what came first: marketplaces, or money in the form of metal pieces with which to enable people to make payments for specialized products? Who mined and refined metallic money?

The modern view that money emerged out of the barter process goes back to Aristotle, despite his description of money as being (or at least having become) the product of law. The reason why individuals invented money, he explained, was to make possible a division of labor so that everyone could specialize in what they were best at producing.

---

[10] John Maynard Keynes, *Treatise on Money* (London, 1930):3-7.

[11] Athenaeus, *Banquet of the Scholars* (I.iv.49). Marx quotes this in his chapter on money in *Capital* (London, 1887:73).

> When the inhabitants of one country became more dependent on those of another, and they imported what they needed, and exported what they had too much of, money necessarily came into use. For the various necessaries of life are not easily carried about, and hence men agreed to employ in their dealings with one another something which was intrinsically useful and easy to handle in general life, for example, iron, silver, and the like. Of this the value was at first measured simply by size and weight, but in the process of time they put a stamp upon it, to save the trouble of weighing and to mark the value.[12]

This explanation assumed that the specialization of labor already had occurred at the time money was introduced, and then money was created to facilitate easier exchange by providing a convenient set of proportions to co-measure diverse products and activities. "Barter" advocates assume a starting point of individuals exchanging commodities made by themselves rather than in a diversified institutional household with specialized tasks – what Sumerians called the "large house," é.gal, the palace that emerged out of temple precincts ca. 2750 BC. Such households supplied smiths, weavers and other institutional workers with food from their own landholdings rather than obliging employees to grow their own or sell their products in village markets in exchange for food, clothing and other necessities. There was smaller-scale local production, of course, but it occurred within the much larger context of the palatial economy.

In attributing the value of monetary metals to their raw bullion value, metallists neglect to observe that this value initially was set by the temples and palaces or subsequent civic institutions. Sumer's account-keeping system designated the value of a shekel of silver relative to that of barley and other commodities as administered bookkeeping prices to denominate the fiscal debts owed to these institutions. This system involved creating the weights and measures in which metals, crops and products were denominated. That was necessary to schedule, coordinate and forecast – in a word, to *plan* – the circulation of raw materials and rations within the large institutions and between them and the rest of society.

---

[12] *Politics* I.9 at 1257a, translated by B. Jowett (Oxford, 1921). Perhaps by the word "value" Aristotle meant "purity."

The historical origin of money-capital and interest was not livestock

Some confusion has arisen by conflating money's role of as a measure of value and means of paying debts with its use as capital ("a store of value") producing interest. Believing that the term "capital" derives from "cattle" (Latin *pecus*, as in "pecuniary"), many popularizers of the individualistic approach have assumed that cattle were a primordial form of money as pastoral capital. This suggests an animate origin of money used as capital to produce offspring in the form of young animals as proto-interest. The implication is that money's origins evolved from herding and farming economies to broader and more sophisticated uses in civilization's industrial and commercial stages.

In that reading, successful individuals lent productive assets to help debtors benefit and the economy grow, not to impoverish debtors and appropriate their land. This celebratory description of creditors was asserted most glaringly by Fritz Heichelheim's extravagantly entitled *Ancient Economic History, from the Paleolithic Age to the Migrations of the Germanic, Slavic and Arabic Nations,* first published in 1938 and greatly expanded in a 1958 English translation. He pointed out that livestock can reproduce themselves, "giving the lie to the doctrine of Aristotle that 'money is barren'" (*Politics* 1258a, Bk. I, ch. x).[13] If livestock were money, charging interest in the form of calves born to cattle lent out would have had a productive basis.

But anthropologists have shown that throughout the world, livestock used in debt transactions are pledged as collateral *to* creditors, not lent out *by* them. Creditors receive antichretic interest in the form of calves produced by the cattle that debtors pledge as collateral. This is unproductive to the debtor, who often ends up losing his means of livelihood and liberty. Interest-bearing debt in a rural context tends to absorb the economic surplus rather than finance its creation.

Heichelheim's idea that cattle were "money-capital" failed to realize that the use of archaic "birth" words for interest using livestock terminology was metaphoric, and did not come into general usage until about 2000 BC.[14] The philologist Emile Benveniste devoted a chapter on "Livestock and money: *pecu* and *pecunia*" to controvert this folk etymology,

---

[13] Heichelheim, *Ancient Economic History* (Leiden, 1958):111 and 184. See also the discussion of Heichelheim's speculations in Chapter 1 above.

[14] Piotr Steinkeller, "The Renting of Fields in Early Mesopotamia and the Development of the Concept of 'Interest' in Sumerian," *Journal of the Economic and Social History of the Orient* 24 (1981), and Chapter 4 below.

pointing out that the concrete devolved from the abstract: "All the indications point to the fact that the sense of 'livestock' is a restriction of the more ancient comprehensive term 'movable wealth,' applied as it was to the principal form of property in a pastoral society." He traced the derivation of the Indo-European terms for livestock back to an original meaning of "head," first used abstractly to mean "'person' and 'capital (financial)' and 'capital (of a province),' or head of a river, or chapter." He concluded that: "It was only by a special development of a pragmatic and secondary kind that *peku*, which meant 'movable wealth' became applied in particular to an item of the real world 'live-stock.'"[15] That occurred relatively late in German, as Gothic *faihu* (<*Vieh*) meant only "money" or "fortune," as does the English cognate "fee." In time, Benveniste concluded, "*peku* came to mean 'live-stock' (the first specialization), and specifically 'small live-stock' (the second specialization), and finally 'sheep' (the third and last specialization). But intrinsically *peku* does not designate either the flock or any animal species."[16]

No traces have been found of interest being paid in the form of the offspring of livestock lent as capital. If the capital:interest principle did not derive from that of livestock:calf, it is necessary to trace how monetary interest payments did evolve. One clue is that the earliest interest is attested to have been paid in silver. If money is to be defined as capital that earns interest, then silver rather than livestock (or Heichelheim's "seeds") represents the first such money. The linkage between money, payment of debts and charging interest was based on inanimate silver, not livestock. And that leads to an origin of interest in the sphere of foreign trade.

Silver, not cattle was the original basis for interest-bearing debt and money

The barter theory of money breaks down most conspicuously in its failure to explain how monetary silver was produced and put into circulation. On purely logical grounds it was by no means natural for prehistoric communities to have agreed to adopt silver as the preferred means of denominating loans, settling payments and holding savings. Why did individuals adopt a metal so little associated with the production process or with purely secular barter-like commodity trade?

---

[15] Benveniste, *Indo-European Language and Society* (1973):43 and *Problems in General Linguistics* (Coral Gables, Fla., 1971):254.

[16] Benveniste, *Indo-European Language and Society*:45 and 50-51.

If the explanation does not lie in any inherent technological use-value role, it must lie in the social role that imbued silver with its monetary desirability. The ancient monetary role played by silver seems to have evolved out of its ceremonial role. Its cosmological association with the moon – and hence with the lunar festival calendar – made it a major prestige material for donations to early temples,[17] and for personal amulets and jewelry, for gifts for burials to honor one's ancestors and on the occasion of marriage or other rites of passage. Silver thus was the most widespread prestige commodity. The silver objects that adorned temples, such as the ceremonial tripods dedicated in Greece, attested to the public-spirited character of their donors. Merchants presented silver offerings upon the successful completion of their voyages, and victorious generals set aside a *dekate* out of the booty they seized. Such philanthropy helped legitimize gain-seeking and public status. These status associations gave silver a character for relations with the community beyond that of just another commodity.

Like public institutions throughout antiquity, Near Eastern temples and palaces were creditors rather than debtors, and hence the largest early recipients of interest. Bronze Age Mesopotamian palaces obtained silver by consigning textiles and other handicrafts to merchants to export for metal and other raw materials. Most business debts owed to the palaces and temples, their officials and sub-contractors for public fees and the advance of land, boats or workshops were payable in silver or its equivalent measure of grain. That acceptability for public payments – what Knapp cited as the essential characteristic of money – led citizens to accept these monetized commodities as general means of settlement. Aristotle was simply describing long-established practice when he voiced the chartalist idea of money as being a legal institution, not merely a commodity. Governments determined its value.

Silver's monetary role emerged from its use as an administrative accounting measure to assign values to resource flows within the large institutions, and as a unit of account to measure the value of payment obligations owed by merchants to the temples and palaces, as well as to

---

[17] The fact that the word "money" derives from Rome's Temple of Juno Moneta, where coinage was struck during the Punic Wars, is indicative of the deep links between money, the refining of precious metals and religious sanctification. Many anthropologists have discussed the sacred associations of these metals, gold being identified with the sun and silver with the moon. Hocart, *Kingship* (London, 1927) and Mircea Eliade, *The Forge and the Crucible* (New York, 1962) deal with early money from this perspective.

denominate payments by the rest of the economy to these institutions. The palace was the ultimate guarantor of silver's value by accepting it in payment of obligations owed to it and to the temples. Its use as a means of settling debts outside the large institutions and as the preferred store of value followed from these transactions with the large institutions.

In addition to being the major recipient of silver, the palace was its major supplier. It was put into circulation by a number of ways, including palace purchases of surplus crops and wool. There are hints that the palace may have distributed silver to fighters after military victories, or perhaps on ceremonial occasions such as the New Year or a royal coronation as suggested by Hocart. Military conquest also played a role, with charioteers and mercenaries being paid out of tribute levied on defeated populations. Classical antiquity's generals brought minters on their campaigns to melt down booty and share it within the ranks of their victorious armies as well as with their home-city temple.

Gold also came to be associated with wealth acquisition. Around 1900 BC it was used for large-scale investment in Assyria's trade to the north. Investment contracts typically called for an advance of 2 minas of gold, with the merchant-debtor to return 4 minas in five years. But in subsequent Near Eastern documents it appears most often in the form of jewelry for dowries.

The fact that gold was much rarer and more expensive than silver deterred it from serving as general-purpose money. The ornate golden grave goods of Ur have been interpreted as *nouveau riche* prestige assets. Gold's dominant monetary role under Kassite rule (14th-12th century BC) seems to have reflected the preference of military warlords. In classical antiquity, the main occasion when Athens coined gold was when it melted down its statues of Winged Victory to pay mercenaries during its war with Sparta, much as Rome coined gold in the closing years of its war with Carthage.

It was mainly the well-to-do who obtained silver and gold, largely via their positions as merchants, collectors and officials in the palace bureaucracy. Entrepreneurial "big men" (lu.gal) operated workshops or other enterprises leased from the temples or palace. These workshops advanced textiles and other handicrafts to other merchants who traded them abroad and paid the consigner in silver or goods that had a silver equivalent. Petty usury became a lucrative source of wealth in the form of land and the labor of debtors.

Why temples were necessary issuers of metallic money

The "barter" depiction of silver being desired for its convenience overlooks the fact that it is not uniform in quality. It needs to be refined and alloyed. Babylonian sale and debt documents from the second and first millennia BC typically specify that monetary silver should be of 7/8 purity (.875 fine, the equivalent of 21 carats). Babylonian "wisdom literature" and the Old Testament are full of denunciations of merchants using false weights and measures or adulterating their products. Yet free-market ideology assumes that when traders and merchants exchanged products, they had little need for public oversight to protect themselves against counterfeiting or fraudulent dealing, or even to enforce standardized weights and measures to conduct exchange and payments in an honest manner. Down through classical Greece and Rome, this protection required temples to refine and supply monetary metals of attested purity as part of their role of overseeing weights and measures. Marketplaces were located in the vicinity of temples, whose authority helped sanctify weights, measures and other basic preconditions for organized commercial exchange.

Another presumed advantage of silver was that it compressed a large value into a small space. But this high value restricted its use to large transactions. A shekel "represented a month's pay" in the Old Babylonian period (2000-1600 BC), notes Marvin Powell. The usual "barter" explanation of metal's virtues as money also claims that metal was easily divisible, but ancient scales were not accurate for measuring small quantities of metal. Deviations could rise to about 3 percent for small weights.[18] Settling consumer transactions "on the spot" instead of on credit thus would have been awkward indeed.

At first silver fulfilled the money-of-account function with some interchangeability with grain, copper, tin, gold and other commodities, but gradually it emerged as the dominant monetary medium. Its dominance stemmed largely from the *lack* of its use value for making tools, weapons or other essential needs.

---

[18] Marvin Powell, "*Wir müssen alle unsere Nische nuzten*: Monies, Motives, and Methods in Babylonian Economics," in J. G. Dercksen, ed., *Trade and Finance in Ancient Mesopotamia: Proceedings of the First MOS Symposium* (=MOS Studies 1) ([Leiden, 1997], Istanbul, 1999):16.

Why public institutions developed money as a standard of value

Today's economic individualism assumes that individuals invented metallic money as a means of economizing on the transaction costs of their barter trade. That origin myth is controverted by the cuneiform record showing the paradigmatic monetary role of debt payments, specifically to Bronze Age temples and palaces. Sumerian accounting records show a complex administrative hierarchy by 3000 BC. During the third millennium, palaces and temples were endowed with their own land and herds to provide barley, dates and wool to the institutional labor force (largely war widows and orphans) employed in temple workshops to weave cloth and make other handicrafts. Temples consigned these products to merchants to trade for silver and other raw materials from across the Iranian plateau to the east, and from Cappadocia in central Anatolia to the west. "The fact that Enlil, the chief god of Nippur, bore the epithet 'trader of the wide world,' and that his spouse was called 'merchant of the world,' is an indication of the role of the Babylonian temples in the exchange of goods."[19]

A measurement system had to be developed to quantify and administer palace and temple resources on a monthly and annual basis, along with a schedule of key price ratios to strike an overall valuation. The resulting standardized price equivalencies – "book prices" – for crops, silver, wool and other key commodities enabled temples and palaces to coordinate their resource flows and dealings with the rest of the economy. Public fees and user costs for tools, draft animals, seeds or water, as well as fines, could be paid in barley or other products at administered prices.

The essence of Mesopotamia's money was its role as a set of common denominators established via price equivalencies to co-measure such payments. It emerged as a byproduct of the price schedule of commodities that could be used to pay the large institutions, and which enabled them to track their economic position with a unified set of accounts. The key monetary development was to make a shekel-weight of silver equal in value to the "bushel" (gur) of barley – the monthly institutional consumption unit. This enabled accounts to be kept interchangeably in silver and barley to co-ordinate production and land rents, trade and

---

[19] Henri Frankfort, *Kingship and the Gods* (Chicago, 1951):67. Guillermo Algaze, *The Uruk World System: The Dynamics of Expansion in Early Mesopotamian Civilization* (Chicago and London, 1993) describes Sumerian colonization efforts to find such raw materials in the Uruk expansion ca. 3500 BC.

services, debts and interest charges in a single balance sheet. It also enabled grain payments to settle debts at a stable silver-price equivalency, enabling cultivators to pay crops when they lacked silver.[20] Grain and silver thus were the first forms of money, and their role as the means of paying debts to Mesopotamia's temples and palaces established their economy-wide value.

Sumer's fiscal accounting system was civilization's essential monetary breakthrough. It was not affected by shifts in the supply of silver or barley or price variability that occurred outside of the palatial sector, as when crops failed late in the Ur III period ca. 2022 BC and the price of grain supplied by independent producers rose sharply.[21] Similarly, outside of the large institutions, petty usury rates for barley debts owed by distressed cultivators varied from rates on official transactions.[22]

The calendrical monetary denominations of measures, weights and interest rates

Administering prices for the transactions by which the palatial economy's departments interfaced with each other and with the rest of the economy required the design of measures and weights for commodities to assign them account-keeping value. These measures and weights were made calendrical so that food and materials could be distributed on a regular basis. The traditional lunar calendar would not do, because the lunar month ranged from 28 to 30 days, averaging 29½ days. To avoid this variability the temples created a 360-day administrative year

---

[20] Hammurabi's laws (ca. 1750) maintained this monetary convertibility to stabilize crop-rental relationships, ruling that silver debts and other fees could be paid in barley at the official rate. Other administered prices served to stabilize public/private leasing arrangements and the sale of commodities to the rest of the economy. The laws of Eshnunna ca. 2000 BC start by establishing such equivalencies. Assurbanipal's coronation prayer (668 BC) cites the prices of barley, oil and wool that one could buy for a shekel of silver.

[21] Thorkild Jacobsen, "The Reign of Ibbi-Suen," *Journal of Cuneiform Studies* 7(2) (1953):36-47.

[22] Benjamin R. Foster, "Social Reform in Ancient Mesopotamia," in K. D. Irani and Morris Silver, *Social Justice in the Ancient World* (Westport, Conn., 1995), points to examples of trade outside of these institutions at higher prices as demonstrating the "ineffectiveness" of public price ratios. But the aim of fiscal accounting prices was not to impose economy-wide price controls, but simply to stabilize transactions in and with the large institutions, leaving the rest of the economy free to respond to interpersonal and market pressures.

calendar, divided into artificial 30-day months. The 5¼-day excess of the actual year over the 360-day administrative year was made part of the extra-calendrical New Year festival (whose celebration spanned the 11-day gap between the normal 365-day solar year and the archaic 354-day lunar year).

The earliest quantitative measure appears to have been for a bushel (gur) of grain, being the quota of food for the 30-day administrative month. It was divided into units of 60, enabling two meals to be eaten each day. The earliest weight to quantify silver and other metals was the mina, which likewise was divided into 60 shekels to dovetail into the fractional system used to measure grain and other crops. This sexagesimal system enabled amounts expressed in terms of grain to be expressed equally in fractional silver counterparts.

With silver and grain being co-measurable on a 1:1 basis, the designated ratios for other key products were administered in conveniently round numbers to keep account-keeping as simple as possible. That integrated the commercial system involving foreign trade with the food-supply system. Commodities on the price schedule were readily convertible into labor time as measured by the rations that were disbursed. The commercial rate of interest was set at the unit fraction, a shekel per mina (that is, $1/60^{th}$) per month. This sexagesimal interest rate remained stable at customary levels century after century, regardless of the supply of silver. This is a further indication that the rate of interest was an administered price rather than reflecting profit or productivity rates (as Chapter 4 will discuss).

Modern economists deny that governments can control prices for long. Most explain price shifts by changes in the money supply. In analyzing ancient prices they start by tracking the supply of silver and/or grain. But this is too modernist an approach. No concept of the money supply would have been relevant, because payments scheduled to be paid in silver could be made in barley at the official price equivalence. Stabilizing the barley-silver conversion rate enabled exchange to occur without families needing silver to pay debts or buy products needed for their daily life.

Conducting transactions on credit enabled money *not* to be used as a means of payment for transactions on the spot. For small retail sales, such as occurred when ale women sold beer, the common practice was for consumers to "run up a tab," much as is done in bars today.[23] A large

---

[23] We know this because §§16-17 of the Edict of Ammisaduqa (1648 BC) annulled debts to ale women as part of the royal Clean Slate. The Edict is translated in Martha

proportion of Neo-Babylonian debt records from the 7th and 6th centuries BC did not reflect monetary loans, but were accruals of arrears for various agrarian charges, which normally were to be settled at harvest time.[24] Crops were brought to the threshing floor and measured out to pay debts owed to palace and temple collectors for rent, draught animals, tools or water. Then came debts to officials in the royal bureaucracy acting on their own account.

Financial instability arose not from monetary dynamics but from the accumulation of debt arrears. The problem was especially acute after bad harvests, floods or other natural disasters or military disruption. And to prevent debts from growing too large for the rural economy to pay even under normal circumstances, Mesopotamian rulers annulled agrarian "barley" debts at the outset of their first full year on the throne, and thereafter in times of crop failure or military conflict.

Cancelling crop debts when no crop money was available to pay kept the volume of such debt within the debtor's ability to remain viable and self-supporting on the land. The key principle was that instead of upholding the sanctity of debt claims, agrarian debts should be forgiven if paying them would have reduced families to bondage and loss of land to creditors. In an epoch when cultivators had only land rights and a few animals to support their families, the aim was to stabilize land tenure so as to maintain a self-supporting corvée labor and military force. Monetary and debt stability thus was the key to maintaining stable property relations and fiscal balance.

Mainstream ideology defends creditor claims over the indebted economy

Money came into being as a medium to pay debts, but today's monetary theory acts as if we are in a debt-free barter economy. When monetary problems arose, they were basically debt problems, which became more disruptive and polarizing as money and credit became more privatized over the course of antiquity, culminating in Rome's oligarchic economy.

The stages of monetary and financial development are the reverse of what the 19th century imagined to be a three-step sequence from barter

---

Roth, *Law Collections from Mesopotamia and Asia Minor*, 2nd ed. (Atlanta, 1997).

[24] Cornelia Wunsch, "Debt, Interest, Pledge and Forfeiture in the Neo-Babylonian and Early Achaemenid Period: The Evidence from Private Archives," in Hudson and Van De Mieroop, *Debt and Economic Renewal in the Ancient Near East* (Bethesda, Md., 2002):221-255.

to a monetized economy, culminating in modern credit economies. The primordial mode of exchange was credit, not barter or even the use of money for on-the-spot settlement. Debt arrangements were the norm for thousands of years before coinage emerged. Barter appears only as the final stage of debt-ridden economies, most notably in the monetary breakdown of the Roman Empire after the 4th century of our era capping a prolonged private-sector debt crisis.

Viewing monetary silver or gold simply as commodities – or convertible into "hard money" – strips away money's role as a social institution, and also its association with debt. That approach also fails to understand how Bronze Age palatial economies organized their monetary and debt management to maintain stability by preventing creditors from acting in the destructive ways that would later impoverish classical Roman antiquity – whose pro-creditor legal philosophy remains the basis for modern law governing debt and property relations.

The thought that money originated as a medium to settle debts rather than for bartering goods on the spot, and that the major monetary debts were owed to public institutions, creates great distress among free-market economists who still follow Adam Smith's description of money emerging from individuals "trucking and bartering," and who recognize no catalytic role for public institutions. Governments are supposed to have gotten into the act belatedly, causing instability by irresponsible money creation and making matters worse by imposing bureaucratic price controls in an attempt to contain the resulting inflation.

Economic orthodoxy is further disturbed by the fact that Bronze Age fiscal policy gave priority to preserving economic balance, not to enforcing creditor claims. Rulers proclaimed Clean Slates annulling debts owed to the palace, its collectors and other creditors.

These ideas – the origins of money as a means of paying obligations to public bodies, and cancelling debts to promote long-term stability and growth – seem unthinkable today. At the heart of the free-market resistance to the historical record of money's public origins, debt cancellations and the setting of early interest rates is the issue of whether governments or private creditors should be in charge of society's monetary and debt arrangements. For creditors, the great fear is that politicians will write down debts – the creditors' claims on the economy – to save their populations from austerity and dispossession. To protect the "security of contracts" for creditors, both domestic populations and entire nations are indebted and subjugated to bondholders and banks as debts grow in excess of the means to pay.

The political bias of pro-creditor ideology depicts public regulation and annulment of debts as increasing the "transaction costs" of credit contracts, supposedly slowing economic growth by "interfering" with creditor rights. The New Institutional Economics of Douglass North depicts money and credit as minimizing transaction costs if kept "free" of public regulation.[25] This exclusive focus on the "transaction costs" of financial contracts does not recognize the social costs of creditors foreclosing on the property and livelihood of defaulting debtors, nor the economic costs of wealth polarization and debt deflation.

Economic orthodoxy's failure to acknowledge the social polarization caused by the monetary and credit context for commodity trade finds its most extreme policy defense in Paul Samuelson's Factor-Price Equalization Theorem purporting to demonstrate, along his usual "hypothetical, logical lines," that free trade tends to equalize labor and capital proportions throughout the world, denying any need for governments to protect their economies from monetary dependency on creditors. Neither he nor the rest of the economic mainstream explain how the polarization of Western economies since 1980 results from financialization and the rising debt overhead. One is reminded of Thomas Mann's observation in *Magic Mountain*: "There are many different kinds of stupidity, and cleverness is one of the worst."

At the root of today's economic tunnel vision regarding the linkage between money and debt is the self-interest of bankers and their economic lobbyists, leading them to block public understanding and acknowledgement of the debt crises that creditors have caused throughout history. Depicting their loans as productive, modern high finance hopes to keep money and credit creation under its own control, seeks to block the public sector from creating its own money and credit, and insists that today's debt burden not be subject to a Clean Slate to prevent debts from leading to peonage and economic shrinkage. Promising that leaving credit and debt management to the banks and large financial institutions will lead to economic equilibrium and growth, this "free market" approach actually leads to debt deflation and concentration of wealth by extractive means that end up destroying monetary stability.

---

[25] Douglass North, "Transaction Costs, Institutions, and Economic History," *Journal of Institutional and Theoretical Economics*, no.140 (1984).

4

How Interest Rates Were Set, 2500 BC-1000 AD:
Máš, *tokos* and *fænus* as metaphors for interest accruals*

Charging interest was invented in Sumer in the third millennium BC. No contemporary evidence for interest-bearing debt has been found in the Indus civilization or the Hittite kingdom. The Hittite debt cancellation edict of Tudhaliya IV refers to wergild-type compensation owed for personal injury, not interest-bearing debt.[1] Egypt's *sed* festivals, unlike their Mesopotamian coronation or New Year-type counterparts, did not allude to debts. The fact that no archaic Egyptian debt records exist might theoretically be the result of destruction of the papyrus writing medium, but nearby regions that used clay tablets for public administration, such as Crete and Mycenaean Greece during 1600-1200 BC, likewise have left no hint of commercial credit, no pooling of money by partnerships, and – most telling of all – no agrarian debt cancellations. It is the nature of interest-bearing debt to be strictly calculated and documented. The absence of debt records outside of Mesopotamia prior to the first millennium BC is thus a strong argument for its absence.

Neither gift exchange, dowries or fines have stipulated interest rates. Gift exchange might involve customary repayments, and even the one-upmanship of an increased valuation – what Marshall Sahlins called "negative reciprocity." But that is not interest according to the formal economic definition of the term: a stipulated rate of return on a debt obligation (the principal) payable on a specific date. A failure to add something to the reciprocating gift does not lead to legal foreclosure, nor are sureties or contracts involved. Interest-bearing debts typically entail written contracts backed by witnesses and sureties, pledges of collateral,

---

* An early version of this paper appeared as "How Interest Rates Were Set, 2500 BC-1000 AD: *Máš*, *tokos* and *fænus* as metaphors for interest accruals," *Journal of the Economic and Social History of the Orient* 43 (Spring 2000):132-161. My discussion reviews the theories of interest that had been put forth prior to 2000. I have tightened up the article's language and organization.

[1] Westbrook and Woodard 1990, and Westbrook 1995:158-159.

and the rate of interest often is publicly regulated (although the degree of enforcement varies).[2] These formalities indicate arms-length transactions, usually among unequals, in contrast to the more free-floating gift-exchange obligations familiar to anthropologists. (Obligations among equals often are interest-free, *e.g.*, the *eranos* loans among classical Greek aristocrats.)

Modern economists have proposed numerous theories to explain why archaic society developed the practice of charging interest. These economic theories depict interest as being so natural that it is inherently universal, not a product of specific circumstances. And hardly by surprise, these theories assume that archaic Sumerians and others thought along lines quite similar today. But the modern way of thinking is as alien to that of Bronze Age communities as their world view is to ours. Yet economists pay almost no attention to the Mesopotamian world view – especially to its grounding in social cosmology in the context of the palatial economies that characterized the ancient Near East, the region where money, interest and other basic economic practices actually began.

What is known is that interest rates were set in three primary centers – Bronze Age Sumer, classical Greece and Rome – and remained remarkably stable in each society: the decimalized annual equivalent of 20 percent for Mesopotamia, 10 percent for Greece and 8⅓ percent for Rome, each rate being lower than that of its chronological predecessor. Many economists have tried to explain this downward trend in interest rates as reflecting profit and productivity levels, subject to risk. The 19th-century German economic historian Wilhelm Roscher attributed the decline in interest rates since antiquity to the "advance of civilization"[3] lowering the riskiness of investment, to improved social stability, market efficiency and the security of credit, and at the same time to the allegedly declining ability of business borrowers to pay interest as a result of shrinking profit margins.

Some economic historians speculated that the "kid" or "calf" words for interest (*máš* in Sumerian, *tokos* in Greek and *fænus* in Latin) reflected the growth of herds. But this begs the question of why such growth would have declined over time, from Sumer through Greece and Rome.

---

[2] Charging interest is different from imposing a penalty for late payment of an obligation. Archaic penalties often doubled the sum owed, but interest typically represented only a fraction of the debt obligation.

[3] Roscher 1878, Vol. II:111 and Vol. I:270.

Already a century ago, Eugen von Böhm-Bawerk rejected such "naive productivity explanations" of interest rates.[4]

The most obvious problem is that interest rates were not "economic" in the sense of being within the ability of most cultivators and other debtors to pay. The key polarizing financial dynamic of antiquity was debt arrears (including unpaid tax collections) mounting up *beyond* the ability of many borrowers to pay. That is what necessitated the royal amargi, *andurarum* and *misharum* "Clean Slate" proclamations cancelling Mesopotamian agrarian debts during the Bronze Age and early first millennium.

With regard to the early history of commercial credit, little has changed since Leemans acknowledged that he was unable to find an explanation for the origin of Mesopotamia's decimalized equivalent of 20 percent annual interest for silver loans.[5] As Steinkeller has pointed out: "Loan documents are in general quite rare before Ur III."[6] Why did some loans bear interest, and others not, Renger asks; and why did silver loans usually bear 20 percent interest, in contrast to the Old Babylonian period's 33⅓ percent for barley loans? He found that the answer "cannot presently be ascertained," and suggested that interest probably began in agriculture, simply by virtue of the fact that early economies were agricultural.[7]

The agrarian rate was not the most characteristic fixed rate of interest, however. That status belongs to the commercial rate of 1 shekel per mina ($1/60^{th}$) per month, hence $12/60^{ths}$ [=20 percent] per year. The commercial debts that bore this rate arose in the context of Mesopotamia's need to trade with other regions for the metal and stone not available in its alluvial soil. But to date [2000], nobody has suggested a firm explanation for the 20 percent rate's origins. No records of commercial profitability exist either for specific transactions or as earnings statements reported at regular intervals. A "normal" rate of mercantile profit rarely exists even in modern times. And when Sumerian and Babylonian commercial advances were repaid, the cuneiform tablets with the details were destroyed. My own view is to think of the silver-interest rate as a doubling time of five years, which probably was meant to result in a fair

---

[4] Böhm-Bawerk 1890.

[5] Leemans 1950.

[6] Steinkeller 1981:141. The Ur III period was 2111-2004 BC. The Old Babylonian period was 2000-1600 BC.

[7] Renger 1994:192.

profit-sharing split between the consigner advancing goods for export and the traveling merchant paying interest on the advance.

If a logical pattern is to be found, it should be based on official or customary rates of interest which, in each ancient society, remained remarkably stable over time, although variations in profit rates must have been frequent. The explanation for the decline in interest rates from Mesopotamia to Greece and Rome therefore must be institutional, as the decline cannot be explained in terms of documented profit or even reasonable productivity rates, much less by the pastoral economics of herding.

On the basis of Mesopotamian evidence, the present paper argues that the idea of birth of young animals was taken as a metaphor for interest being "born," with the rate set by numerical simplicity of calculation. I compare Greek, Roman and Byzantine evidence to show that subsequent societies adopted the Mesopotamian idea of setting interest rates purely arithmetically for simplicity of calculation in accordance with their local system of numerical fractions, counting and measuring. In each region, what was "born" as interest was the unit-fraction: $1/60^{th}$ per month (a shekel per mina) in Mesopotamia's sexagesimal system, $1/10^{th}$ (a *dekate*) in Greece's decimal system, and $1/12^{th}$ (a troy ounce per pound) in Rome's duodecimal system.

Ease of computation evidently played the key role. Instead of interest rates being set by economic factors such as productivity levels – with payment being made in kids or calves as suggested at first glance by the ancient words for interest – purely arithmetic considerations were at play. Although the words for interest in Sumerian, Greek and Latin all have an association with "birth" or "newborn," *what is meant seems to be the periodic accrual or birth of a local numeric system's unit fraction, not young calves or crops.*

A widespread common denominator – the local fractional system and its corollary weights and measures – appears to explain how ancient interest rates were set. This principle begins with Sumer's increments of a shekel per month, and continues down through the *dekate* in Greece and Rome's *uncia* (troy ounce) per pound. This suggests that the reason why interest rates declined over the course of classical antiquity was the change in the fractional arithmetic being used.

Table 1

Region	Smallest Fractional Unit	Normal Rate of Interest
Bronze Age Mesopotamia	1/60th (shekel)	1 shekel per month per mina owed. In the decimal system, 1⅔ percent = 20 percent per year.
Classical Greece	1/10th (*dekate*)	10 percent per year
Classical Rome	1/12th (*uncia*)	8⅓ percent (1/12th) per year
Byzantium - before Justinian	1/100th lb. (1 *nomismata*)	12 percent per year
" - Justinian	a *siliqua* per *solidus*	5 percent per year
" - after Constantine	1/72nd lb. (1 new *nomismata*)	8⅓ percent (1/12th) per year (=6/72^{nds})

As late as the Byzantine epoch the 12 percent rate worked out to a "penny per month." When the currency was devalued by reducing the number of *nomismata* from 100 to 72 per pound of gold after Constantine, "the fixed rate of interest tended to adjust itself to the new figure, to the lender's advantage: till by the Tenth Century 6 per cent. had changed to be 6 *nomismata* per 1 lb. of gold, that is to say 8.33 per cent.; and the maritime speculation would bring in 16.66 per cent."[8]

Archaic interest rates remained relatively stable over the centuries because they were administered – along with key prices and various fees (at least for paying fiscal duties) – by the temples, palace, or simply by tradition, not subject to variations in market supply and demand.

Why productivity explanations of ancient interest rates are anachronistic

Most economic historians have tried to explain interest rates as a usufruct reflecting the productivity of capital, and hence what borrowers can afford to pay their creditors. It is as if debtors calculate how much the loan is worth to them, based on what they can earn with what they

---

[8] Runciman 1956:138-139.

borrow. This approach assumes that interest rates reflect the debtor's productive use of creditor assets. Heichelheim's *Ancient Economic History*, for instance, speculated that such lending occurred as early as the Neolithic, with early "food-money" and credit becoming linked by about 5000 BC: "Dates, olives, figs, nuts, or seeds of grain were probably lent out ... to serfs, poorer farmers, and dependents, to be sown and planted, and naturally an increased portion of the harvest had to be returned in kind." In addition to fruits and seeds, "animals could be borrowed too for a fixed time limit, the loan being repaid according to a fixed percentage from the young animals born subsequently. ... So here we have the first forms of money, that man could use as a capital for investment, in the narrower sense."[9]

Seeing that profit expectations must be qualified for risk, Heichelheim imagined Neolithic peasants made an actuarial calculation: "Rich owners" who lent out their surplus stocks "had to demand a higher return in view of the possible losses from bad harvests or animal diseases." High rates of interest at the outset of civilization thus are assumed to have compensated creditors for risk-taking.

Such modernist reasoning has been carried to an extreme by Foster. Retrojecting modern principles of calculated risk-taking and supply and demand, he suggests that Sumerian and Babylonian debt cancellations increased the creditor's risk and led to high agrarian interest rates, and hence to low land prices.[10] This logic recalls Hillel's argument advocating the *prosbul* clause in the 1st century BC, by which Jewish borrowers waived their rights under the Jubilee Year. Hillel claimed that adhering to the Jubilee Year would deter lending (but he did not say that lenders would charge more interest).

Schneider, Leemans, Diakonoff and Steinkeller earlier had noted that the barley-loan interest rate in Mesopotamia was the same as the rental rate on the advance of sharecropping land.[11] Both rates were 33⅓ percent by the time documentation appears in Ur III. But Foster did not recognize this basic equivalency at the heart of the interest/rent relationship: The indebted sharecropper paid the creditor interest at the same rate that he paid rent to the field's owner: a third. (And this rate was a flat rate, not an annualized rate.) The creditor received as interest the same usufruct rate that could have been obtained by buying fields

---

[9] Heichelheim 1958:54-55.

[10] Foster 1995:167. See also Chapter 5 for further critique of this modernist reasoning.

[11] Schneider 1920, Leemans 1950:30, Diakonoff 1974:14, n12, and Steinkeller 1981:141.

outright and leasing them out on a sharecropping basis. The rent rate determined the agrarian interest rate.

There is no evidence that archaic creditors viewed interest rates as a rate of return net of risk, much less of their evaluating the likelihood of debt cancellation and setting their rates accordingly. Archaic interest rates showed no response to changes in risk levels, nor did changes in these rates affect land prices. Interest rates remained constant century after century. This was the Bronze Age, not modern Wall Street or the City of London.

Leemans observed that 33⅓ percent interest "seems outrageous to us," but if it were charged only on seed-grain – and assuming yields to have been 16 to 24 times the sowing-corn, or even more – then it would have amounted to just 1 percent of the crop.[12] Such agrarian interest was able to be paid out of the spectacular crop yields of Mesopotamia's rich alluvial soils. The problem was that most agrarian debts seem to have stemmed from payment arrears, not from entrepreneurial borrowing. It was more likely that the failure of a crop forced most cultivators into debt, not hopes for a prosperous bounty. Foster's reconstruction assumes that debts stemmed from advances of money by creditors (and hence, facing risks of non-payment). But most debts simply accrued as arrears on various types of fees and obligations owed to royal collectors. Instead of money being advanced there was an *absence* of harvest payments being made.

A pastoral origin of interest?

The word *capital* derives from Latin *caput*, a *head* of livestock, while *chattel* is a general term for property. The philologist Benveniste has pointed out that livestock seem to have been taken at some point as prototypical capital, in the sense that they produce calves. Taking as their starting point the usage of pastoral words such as "capital," as well as Greek *tokos* and Sumerian *máš* for lending and interest relations, some economists have jumped to the conclusion that credit must have started in herding economies. Heichelheim assumed that creditors lent cattle to debtors, producing calves that might have been paid as interest. Like his seed-grain theory of interest being paid out of the seeds' yield, this would mean that early agrarian loans were economically productive with mutual gain between creditors and debtors, not distress debts.

Yet little trace of cattle being lent out, either for calf-interest or for a stipulated money payment, has been found in any archaic or modern

---

[12] Leemans 1950:32.

tribal community. (There are scattered traditions of herd owners consigning cattle or other animals to shepherds who are compensated in the form of animals as their commission.) In any event, the attested interest rates do not lend themselves to easy divisibility of living animals. It would be hard to pay a twelfth, a tenth or a fifth of an animal – or its offspring – as interest.

Basically, Heichelheim and like-minded economists get matters backward. Studies of tribal economies throughout the world find insolvent debtors pledging their livestock as collateral, but not borrowing cattle. Anthropologists studying tribal economies have found that when cattle or land are part of the loan process, *it is as antichretic collateral* (that is, a pledge) that produces services or a usufruct *for the creditor*. Debtors do not receive cattle with which they generate a usufruct. The transfer of livestock invariably is to rich creditors *from* poor debtors who pledge their stock and other assets, in exchange for necessities, which are consumed or paid as taxes or fines rather than productively invested. It is the debtor's *own* productive asset that produces a usufruct, not borrowed animals. And in periods of crop failure or general need, it must have been hard for many debtors to redeem the assets they pledged or sold, even when no interest was charged.

The history of ancient agrarian usury shows that instead of the interest being paid out of growth in the debtor's income earned by investing the loan proceeds productively, interest charges devoured his already exhausted resources, making it hard to pay the debt. The proceeds of agrarian loans were not invested productively to generate an income out of which to pay interest to the creditor. The usufructs – and increasingly, the collateral too – were obtained by creditors. It thus is futile to try to explain interest rate levels by reference to productivity or profit rates. Roscher, Böhm-Bawerk and their contemporaries emphasized that archaic usury consisted of "distress debts in contradistinction to acquisition-debts."[13] Needy individuals borrowed out of abject necessity, not to earn a profit. Borrowing out of absolute need is what economists call price-inelastic: Borrowers were willing to pay virtually any interest rate.

So the reproduction rate of animals is not relevant for the lending terms, because such usury involving the pledge of livestock is a pure loss to debtors on the land. It is not paid out of income generated by the loan, nor out of profits earned on investing the loan's proceeds, but out

---

[13] Roscher 1878, Vol. II:128; see also Finley 1973.

of the debtor's own stock pledged as collateral. *The usufruct is not produced by the borrowed capital itself.*

The preferred forms of collateral through the ages have been the debtor's cattle, slaves, daughters, wives or sons to perform services in the creditor's household; and later, public privileges such as land rights, fishing privileges and mineral rights. But it is difficult to formally express the precise fraction of the debt principal that these antichretic yields represent. Cattle may give birth to calves and provide plowing services and milk, but no economist has come up with an explanation of how to translate the value of these activities into a precise rate of interest. Gelb (1967b) has translated a tablet on the growth of a herd of cattle, showing that the Sumerians knew that herds do not grow at $33\frac{1}{3}$ percent per year.[14] It hardly can be assumed that Sumerian livestock reproduced more rapidly than Greek livestock, or that the latter increased more quickly than those of Rome. Even at the Roman interest rate of $8\frac{1}{3}$ percent, animal herds and crop yields hardly could have increased regularly at these rates year after year.

The final problem with trying to explain interest rates by reference to pastoral and agricultural productivity rates or market conditions is the fact that interest rates have been administered by law throughout most of history. The Mesopotamian rate of $1/60^{th}$ per month – one shekel per mina – remained stable for over a thousand years, starting with the Third Dynasty of Ur shortly before 2000 BC and extending through the laws of Eshnunna and Hammurabi to Neo-Babylonian times.[15] Also stable for many centuries was Rome's legal rate of $1/12^{th}$, that is, an *uncia* (ounce) of copper per year on every *as* (pound). Greek bankers typically paid a decimalized $1/10^{th}$ (*dekate*) on deposits. Renger observes that "the unchanging rate of interest throughout the centuries constitutes a strong argument against the existence of a credit market," adding that "the same is true for rental dues which do not fluctuate, thus also indicating that they are not governed by the laws of supply and demand."[16] The fact that interest rates were legally administered and fixed over long periods strongly points against their reflecting supply and demand responding to agricultural or pastoral productivity, yields or even the ability of debtors to pay.

---

[14] Gelb 1967b. See more recently Nissen, Damerow and Englund 1993.

[15] Roth 1995:38, 61 and 97.

[16] Renger 1994:203.

The evolving meanings of máš: from kid to fee, (periodic) payment and interest

Philologists have found that the kid- or calf-words for interest, like their agrarian relative "usufruct," are relatively late pastoral analogies that postdate the first charging of money-interest by many centuries. Steinkeller has established this fact for the Sumerian language, and two decades earlier Benveniste found that the archaic Greek and Latin words for capital likewise came to mean "cattle" relatively late. The Indo-European root *peku (<Latin *pecus*) originally referred to "personal chattels, movables" in general, and only later narrowed to mean specifically livestock, and then their smaller offspring. "Similarly the English term cattle, French *chaptel*, goes back to Latin *capitale* 'principal property.'"[17]

The word *pecuniary*, meaning monetary or market-oriented, stems from Latin *pecus*, meaning cattle either singly or in herds. The word "fee" likewise derives from *pecus*, as does "feudal." It appears that a pecuniary standard was first introduced by the payment of fines (and perhaps of proto-taxes) in animals, silver or other capital items. To the extent that cattle were civilization's first pecuniary means of payment, it was not to buy market goods and services but to settle capital-type obligations. Fines for personal injury are the earliest documented "prices," at least for Indo-European speaking societies. (Bridewealth and brideprice were akin to capital transfers when families merged.)[18] But cattle hardly could have served as money as our epoch understands the term. Their value was too high for most exchanges of goods and services. They were for paying reparation fines (headed by manslaughter compensation), marriage obligations and proto-taxes such as contributions to communal sacrifices.

Sumerian economic records begin in readable detail in the Early Dynastic period, 2700-2435 BC. Around 2450, in the time of Urukagina's "reform" text, Sumerians had to pay the temples or palace a regular

---

[17] Benveniste 1973.

[18] Bernard Laum (1924) attributed the origins of money to the donation of cattle offerings to the temples and their feasts. Chapters 1 through 3 above have traced the origins of money to Sumer's palaces and temples, but not specifically to such donations. The Greek monetary spits (*oboloi*) and handfuls thereof (*drachmae*) suggest that cattle or some of the offspring were dedicated to the temple or other community institution annually as firstfruits, and that these proto-tax contributions became a kind of proto-money. But it is a speculative leap from such contributions to specific rates of interest for debt payments.

máš-fee.[19] It is not certain whether this was necessarily in the form of lambs or kids. Steinkeller reads the term *máš* literally in Ukg 4 iv.27: "the surveyors, the chief *bala*-priests, the chief stewards, the brewers, (and) the foreman had to pay silver" fees or offerings in the form of fleeces or young kids born to the herds pastured on public fallow lands. His reading is that "in the pre-Sargonic period *máš* was still used only in its literal sense." But it is not clear why surveyors, brewers and others should make payments relating to the use of grazing lands.[20]

Steinkeller suspects that the earliest references to *máš* payments designate a tax on the growth of flocks, probably paid in kind before being transformed into a silver obligation as Sumer's economy became more commercially oriented. He suggests a derivation from *wasabum*, "to increase," presumably referring to the growth of herds. But by the time the term *máš* can be documented in this new context, it seems to have taken on a broader meaning of birth or accrual.

The term *fee* seems especially appropriate for such public obligations, inasmuch as its linguistic root is *pecus*, a semantic counterpart to Sumerian *máš*. However, the payments seem to have been denominated mainly in silver, sometimes in crops. To be sure, Urukagina's text describes royal collectors seizing the assets of debtors, especially the cattle of cultivators in arrears on their public obligations, which seem to have been owed in silver or its barley equivalent, and to be in the character of irrigation fees or proto-taxes, not interest on money advances. These obligations were akin to debt payments mainly by being due periodically, but there is no direct confirmation of interest yet being charged on arrears for these fees.

Language frequently evolves by making semantic leaps that often are idiosyncratic and hard to reconstruct. Philological analysis is prone to the danger of taking words too literally and missing their often metaphoric dimension. Thus, in noting that a word for interest literally signified a kid or calf, we must beware of assuming that the earliest interest actually was paid in young animals or that the first interest-yielding usufruct-producing capital consisted of cattle. Words often assign a derivative meaning by analogy, and in the case of the ancient words for interest, taking this metonymy literally will miss the metaphoric usage of the terms.

---

[19] See *e.g.*, Cooper 1986:71-73.

[20] Steinkeller 1981:140.

Today's pro-creditor economic ideology is eager to accept the literal interpretation of archaic words for interest – *máš* in Sumerian, *tokos* in Greek and *fœnus* in Latin – and jump to the conclusion that kids or calves were the prototypical interest payments, which later became monetized. This implies a productive origin of interest-bearing debt; newborn animals appear to be a portion of the usufruct produced with the help of the creditor's loan.

But kids and calves are indivisible units. What happened to debtors who had only a few cattle to graze? By the time documentation can be picked up in the 2300s, even grazing fees were due in silver, not in calves. "The meaning 'interest' of *máš* is not attested before Ur III,"[21] Steinkeller concludes. Tracing how the word came to mean "interest," he points out that "the pre-Sargonic tenant farmer delivered a tax in silver for the yearly increase in the number of his goats and sheep." This tax "actually represented a fee for the right to utilize the rented field for grazing. The usage of *máš* in a transferred sense is first attested in the Sargonic period, when *máš* came to denote the tax itself. Once this change had been accomplished, only one step remained: since the tax for the yearly increase in a herd of animals offered an obvious analogy to the interest yielded during one year by a loan, in Ur III *máš* acquired the meaning 'interest.'"

The calendrical basis for Sumer's monthly $1/60^{th}$ rate of interest

Monetary transactions, especially payment of interest, require weights and measures. The first known examples were developed by Sumer's institutional households to distribute rations of food, oil and other periodic flows.[22] Calculating quantities of such distributions, prices and interest was kept relatively simple by setting the most important prices, fees and interest rates in round numbers.

The fractional divisions of counting, measures and weights were calendrical because disbursements needed to be coordinated on a regular basis. That need obliged Mesopotamian and Egyptian temples and palaces to replace the traditional lunar months, which varied in length from 28 to 30 days, with standardized administrative months comprising 30 days each. Adopting 30-day months and creating a sexagesimal (60-based) system of fractional measures and weights based on this calendar made it easy to distribute and divide monthly barley rations:

---

[21] Steinkeller 1981:131-132.

[22] Gelb 1965 and 1972, and Powell 1990.

the gur ("bushel") of barley was divided into units of 60, enabling 2 meals a day for an adult male. (Women and slaves received half this amount, and children still less, depending on their age.)[23]

Interest and rent obligations likewise were relatively easy to compute, thanks to the fact that the number 60 is divisible by eleven divisors: 30, 20, 15, 12, 10, 6, 5, 4, 3, 2 and 1. Economic relations were standardized in a way that integrated weights and measures, prices and ration levels into a single managerial system. Barley obligations were payable upon harvest, while commercial debts (including some rural obligations and fees) were denominated in silver. For temple and palace accounting purposes the value of barley was set at one gur-bushel per shekel of silver. That enabled accounts to be kept simultaneously in silver and barley, creating a bimonetary standard. In times of crop failure the market price of grain outside of the public institutions might rise substantially, but temple and palace accounts insulated themselves from market fluctuations by using standardized "book" prices.

This accounting practice explains early interest rates. Reflecting the sexagesimal measures for grain, the standard weight for silver, the mina, was divided into 60 shekels. Dovetailing into this system, the interest rate for commercial debts was set at one shekel per silver mina ($1/60^{th}$) per month – the simplest and most convenient fraction to compute for monthly accruals of interest.[24] This simplicity was emulated by the Greek *dekate* ($1/10^{th}$) and the Roman *uncia* per *as* – a troy ounce per pound ($1/12^{th}$). In Mesopotamian, Greek and Roman notational systems each rate represents the basic unit fraction.

Steinkeller points out that "the pre-Sargonic term for interest was *kudra usa*, from the verb *kud/kudr*, 'to cut off,' meaning 'portion' (cf. *nig. kud*, Akk. *miksum*)."[25] Powell suggests a concrete reference to silver rings and coils: The Middle Babylonian word for 1/8 shekel, *bitqu* (literally "cutting"), seems originally to have denoted "a piece of standard size cut off from such a silver coil."[26] Did this usage extend back to the third millennium?

The term "cutting" is semantically akin to the English shilling (from *skilja*, to cut) and the Russian rouble (from *rupit*, also meaning to cut).

---

[23] Lambert 1963:83-84 and Englund 1988.

[24] This fraction also was applied annually in cases where only a small public charge was deemed appropriate, *e.g.*, the storage of grain as stipulated in §121 of Hammurabi's laws.

[25] Steinkeller 1981:142.

[26] Powell 1978 and 1996.

Grierson points out that words for cutting are widespread for payment, as in the modern slang phrase, "What's his cut?" In 14th-century Russian, "when the word *rubl'* first occurs in the texts, the flans of Russian coins were cut from strips of wire hammered flat."[27] That seems to have been the meaning of Sumerian *kudr*, with interest being just one form of regular payment. The terminology suggests that interest was payable in silver (the commodity being cut), not barley or cattle. And that in turn suggests a commercial rather than agricultural context for the origins of charging interest, some time before pastoral terms for interest came into use. There is no indication of calf payments in this commercial sphere.

Birth metaphors for time, numbers and interest

The point of reference for commercial debts in Sumer was 60 months – five years, by which time a mina of capital (bearing interest at the commercial rate of one shekel per month) had reproduced itself by accruing 60 shekels. As an Egyptian saying put it: "If wealth is placed where it bears interest, it comes back to you redoubled."[28] It seems that at this five-year doubling point the Sumerians considered the principal to have become an "adult." Compounding did not begin until that point – as only adults are capable of reproduction.

Sumer's written notation reflects this "reproduction" idea. Prior to the Ur III period a somewhat confusing set of symbols was used for integers and their fractions. The distinction between the single unit ("1") and its unit fraction (1/60) originally was expressed by similar but different sized D-shaped symbols: The symbol D and the word *gesh* were used to signify 1, 60 or, alternatively, 1/60th.[29]

In the final century of the third millennium, this notational usage evolved into a place system that represented both the numbers 60 and 1 by Y (two perpendicular wedge indentations, crossing one another like a T), much as our 1 signifies 1, 10 or 100 depending on its placement. But inasmuch as cuneiform lacked the idea of zero, the same number symbol meant 1, 60 or 60^2 depending on its place value. Dilke observes that "The same symbols were also used for writing fractions. So 1 can

---

[27] Grierson 1978:14.

[28] Lichtheim 1976:135.

[29] This notational characteristic may help explain why the archaic term for interest was "kid." A number of ancient languages viewed the small unit fraction as a miniature model of the large unit. The Latin word *as* ("pound") is cognate to Greek *heis*, "one." Each of the 12 *unciae* (ounces) in an *as* was also a "one" (from *unus*, 'unity').

be 1/60 or 1/60², and so on. ... The result could be confusing even for the Babylonians. ... Everything depended on the order of the wedges, reading from left to right. So 𒌋𒌋 = 11. But it can also equal 601 (60 x 10 + 1) 𒌋𒌋 = 2, but ᵛᵛ = 61; the difference depends only on careful writing and reading."[30] Readers of cuneiform economic accounts therefore had to decide on the context to know whether a number referred to a fraction or a whole integer.

Diakonoff has defined an archaic language as one which, "on the lexical level, has no or only poorly developed means of expressing abstract ideas." Sumerian is a good example. The verb meaning "to kill," for instance, is composed of the roots "club, head, break." The language used metaphor and metonymy to convey abstract concepts. "There are no adequate means, either lexical or grammatical, to express such abstract ideas as 'time,' 'space,' 'subject,' 'object,' 'cause,' 'beauty,' 'liberty,' 'invention,' 'multiplication,' 'division' and many others, some of which appear to us elemental, as, *e.g.*, the distinction between 'darkness,' 'calamity,' 'illness,' and 'pain,' etc., or between 'good,' 'enjoyable,' 'kind,' 'happy,' 'useful,' 'lucky,' etc. ... In the absence of means to express general ideas, one resorts to generalization by tropes (metaphors and metonymies)."[31] It follows that words for abstract economic ideas such as interest likewise would be expressed metaphorically in terms of concrete images.

Bronze Age cosmologies depicted nature in terms of birth cycles,[32] a universal metaphor applied widely to the three basic measures of time: the month, the year and the day. Calendrical starting points had their respective points of conception at their darkest points: the narrow sliver of the crescent moon for a new month, the winter solstice heralding the new year, and midnight bringing a new day.[33]

The birth metaphor also was applied to numbers and their fractional "children." For if time had a gestation period, so did the numerical cycles used to demarcate it. Likewise, it was natural for the archaic ter-

---

[30] Dilke 1987:11.

[31] Diakonoff 1983:83.

[32] The gestation and birth process provides one of the most common metaphors of human culture. The word *metaphor* itself means literally pregnant with meaning – "to bear" (*pherein*) and "beyond" (*meta*).

[33] The winter solstice, December 21, by rights should be our January 1. But in 46 BC, Julius Caesar delayed January 1 in his calendrical reform to make the first day of his new year fall on the new moon.

minology for interest to be based on a birth metaphor, as interest after all is a payment for time.

In conformity with this birth metaphor, numbers were conceived in terms of gender. Seidenberg cites the Pythagorean dictum that "odd numbers are male, even numbers are female."[34] In some Australian, South American and South African societies, he points out, counting begins with two. The logic seems to be that a coupling must precede the generation of "children." A couple composed of a man, 1, and a woman, 2, gives birth to a child, making the number 3 ("many"). This trinity of numbers can generate the modular patterns that form the basic higher numbers, *e.g.*, 2 + 3 = 5 by addition and 2 x 3 = 6 by multiplication. These in turn may generate as "offspring" 5 x 6 = 30, and 30 x 12 = 360.

As early as the Old Babylonian period ca. 1800 BC (and probably earlier) each major deity was assigned a number that was a fraction of 60. As chief of the pantheon, Anu was symbolized by the sign for "1" ($60/60^{\text{ths}}$), with 22 "children," fractional numbers that divide roundly into 60: 30, 20, 15, 12, 10, 6, 5, 4, 3, 2 and 1, and their reciprocals (in our notation a half, a third, a quarter, a fifth, a sixth, a tenth, a twelfth, a fifteenth, a twentieth and a thirtieth). The Sumerians called these fractions "children of 60" or the "children of Anu."

Commenting in Roman times on the sexual anthropomorphism of numbers, Plutarch asserted that the ancient Egyptians knew the 3 x 4 x 5 "Pythagorean" right-angled triangle and the male and female deities associated with it. The upright perpendicular, measuring 3, represented Osiris.[35] The base, measuring 4 (an even number, as well as being horizontal, as a woman was supposed to be), signified Isis. Their offspring was Horus, the hypotenuse 5, a male odd number. The Pythagoreans called this "the marriage number," reportedly following Near Eastern tradition.

Plutarch called this triangle the Nuptial Figure. It probably had a long pedigree, for 3 x 4 x 5 = 60, the basis for the sexagesimal system, while 3 + 4 + 5 = 12, the number of months in the year. Stieglitz calls this line of reasoning *mathopoeic* to emphasize the numerical character of its abstractions: "the poet might say that the 'One' gave birth to a 'Female' (=2) and a 'Male' (=3), who in turn mated and thus begot successive generations of 'sons' and 'daughters' ($2^p 3^q 5^r$), formed in the 'image' of their pro-

---

[34] Seidenberg 1962b:2, citing Aristotle, *Metaphysics*, at 986a.

[35] Plutarch, *Isis and Osiris*, at 56.

totypes."[36] Sumer's sexagesimal system found cosmological significance in the fact that $2^2 \times 3 \times 5 = 60$, a number generated by multiplying twos and threes to generate offspring.

Once the gender of numbers was established, their ability to give birth to higher series of numbers (and fractions) followed naturally. So did the terminology for social processes using these fractions. The birth metaphor conceived of growth by incremental units, especially when this occurred on a periodic calendrical basis. The birthing of most animals occurs at a specific time of year, associating birth with calendrical regeneration, making a pastoral birth or calf metaphor especially appropriate for periodic calendrical social processes.[37] A baby unit emerges periodically from the full-sized parent.

The scheduling of paying debts and interest accruing was set at key calendrical points. For commercial debts this was the transition from one month to the next, with the monthly payment of a shekel – 1/60th of a mina – appearing as a newborn unit accruing each month, associated with the periodic renewal (rebirth) of the moon, the celestial patron deity of silver throughout antiquity. In 60 months the mina had produced a fully grown equal ("adult").

In an epoch when social organization and redistribution followed the periodicities of nature, the metonymy of the word *máš*, from offspring or birth to the interest yielded by the capital/debt relationship, established a neat formula: Interest was to capital as calves were to cattle. This explains how silver could be lent out to yield offspring. As payment for time, interest was expressed in the imagery of time being born anew, a silver calf on the new moon. The Chicago Assyriological Dictionary cites a proverb that making a loan is like making love; getting it repaid with interest is like having a baby.

This analogy between newborn and interest appears to have emerged during the Ur III period, by which time the means of payment were silver or barley, not livestock. The word *máš* signified the small units (silver shekels) being "born" of their financial parents (minas).

---

[36] Stieglitz 1982:257.

[37] The correlation of calendrical periodicities with animal reproduction cycles is found as early as Ice Age times. Marshack 1972 describes how Magdalenian cave paintings and inscribed batons reflect such calendrical events as the local area's mating and birthing of animals, the spawning of fish and the annual fructification of nature in general. Deer, fish and other important species to humankind at the hunting stage mate and give birth in specific seasons. (Humans are exceptional in giving birth throughout the year.)

Economists will recognize here the irony noted by Aristotle nearly two thousand years later: Silver is sterile. Metal does not give birth; only animate beings do. The metaphor of birth occurring on regular periodic dates, such as the new crescent moon (calend), is applied to a "baby" unit fraction, being "born" of the full unit, *e.g.*, the shekel from a mina. Silver minas invested at interest gave birth at the inception of each month. Similarly, Roman debts fell due and accounts were reckoned in the calendarium account book on the calend, the first day of the Roman month.[38]

Classical Greek and Roman calf/birth terminology for the payment of interest

I have argued elsewhere that the idea of charging interest was brought to Greece and Italy by Phoenician or Syrian merchants, probably in the 8th century BC, along with other commercial practices – and with them, the calf metaphor for interest.[39] The diffusion of social and economic practices rarely produces an exact copy, of course. The Mediterranean world ca. 750 BC conducted commercial enterprise mainly via family estates (the classical *oikos*), and credit was in private hands on a less centralized scale than that of the Bronze Age Near Eastern palaces. Workshops were self-financed, and agricultural credit took the form of usury, non-productive (*i.e.*, uneconomic) lending. We therefore must look to noneconomic explanations of Greek and Italian interest rates.

Already in their Linear B records the Mycenaean Greeks are found using a decimal system, probably reflecting Egyptian influence via Crete. As in Mesopotamia, Mediterranean interest rates were correlated with their fractional counting systems, and the Greeks seem to have adopted this practice from the Near East. The two major sources of public revenue in classical antiquity were votive offerings and the donation of war booty. A tithe (*dekate*) of military booty (including from piracy) typically was turned over to the temples.[40] As the Hellenic com-

---

[38] Etymonline.com (https://www.etymonline.com/word/calendar) explains that the words "calend" and "*calendarium*" derive "from *calare* 'to announce solemnly, call out,' as the priests did in proclaiming the new moon that marked the calends, from PIE root *kele- (2) 'to shout.' In Rome, new moons were not calculated mathematically but rather observed by the priests from the Capitol; when they saw it, they would 'declare' the number of days till the nones (five or seven, depending on the month)."

[39] Hudson 1992 and 2023.

[40] Pritchett 1971:93-95, with bibliography.

mercial flowering occurred, the *dekate* seems to have been adopted from this temple practice as the normal rate of interest.[41] The *dekate* (1/10th) was the smallest unit fraction in Greece's decimal system, just as the shekel was the basic unit fraction in Mesopotamia's sexagesimal arithmetic. And like Sumerian *máš*, the Greek term for interest/usury, *tokos*, signified a young animal and the idea of birth.

The linkage of Athenian debt practice to the periodicities of time was reflected in counting the days of the month backwards from midmonth or the third decade of the month (that is, the 20th). This indicated the number of days remaining before periodic obligations such as personal debts and rents fell due on the new moon (*i.e.*, at month-end, as with many debts in modern society). Merritt cites a scholion to Aristophanes' *Clouds* in which Strepsiades declaims:

> The fifth, the fourth, the third, and then the second,
> And then that day which more than all the rest
> I loathe and shrink from and abominate,
> Then comes at once that hateful Old-and-New day,

the day when his debts were due.[42]

Calendrical and numerical practices likewise seem to have influenced Roman interest rates via Rome's duodecimal arithmetic and its associated weights and measures. Just as the year was divided into twelve months, the copper *as* (pound) was divided into twelve *unciae* (the origin of the modern troy ounce system), and the XII Tables tradition set the legal rate of interest at 1/12th per year – a "baby" fractional unit being paid as interest on each large or "full" unit. The Latin term for loan interest was *fœnus*. Its prefix (*fe*) connoted the idea of fecundity, much as did the Greek word for interest, *tokos* (and earlier, Sumerian *máš*).[43]

This basic idea of setting interest rates on the basis of the local unit fraction continued into the Byzantine epoch. Justinian "found it necessary to give special protection to small holders in Thrace and Illyricum against lenders of money or of corn. He limited the annual rate of interest to one *siliqua* in the solidus (or slightly over 5 percent) on money loans, and one-eighth (or 12½ percent) on loans in kind, and enacted that if this were paid with the original debt, the lender must restore the land or

---

[41] Bogaert 1968.

[42] Merritt 1961:40, citing Aristophanes' *Clouds*, line 1131.

[43] Neither the Greeks nor Romans distinguished between the ideas of interest and usury. The choice of which modern term to use for *tokos* and *fœnus* thus reflects more the ideology of the translator than something inherent in the Greek or Latin language.

stock which he had seized. The lenders were, it appears, mainly officials, probably collectors of taxes or arrears, who made a practice of converting the obligation to the state into a private bond to themselves."[44]

Some consequences of "uneconomic" interest rates

Aristotle noted that unlike cows which reproduce themselves, metallic money lent out by usurers is sterile. This barrenness of metal is the central problem of usury: Interest is demanded on the basis of money-loans whose proceeds are not invested productively, much less at sufficient profit to pay the rates demanded by usurers. For good reason, Aristotle observed, the most hated form of money-making "is usury, which makes a gain out of money itself, and not from the natural use of it. For money was intended to be used in exchange, but not to increase at interest. And this term usury, which means the birth of money from money, is applied to the breeding of money, because the offspring resembles the parent."[45]

By classical times debt increasingly took the form of sterile agrarian and related usury. Creditors often broke up families by taking away their servant girls, daughters, sons or mother as debt pledges, while they themselves often refrained from marrying in order to keep their own family fortunes intact. The *naditu* heiresses of the Old Babylonian period lived in temple precincts in order to invest their families' money rather than marry and convey it out of their clan. Reflecting the sterility of usury, usurers through the ages have been portrayed as Shylocks, homosexuals or old men without families, typically outsiders. Ancient bankers frequently were money-changers, often aliens who had left their families behind – Near Easterners in Greece, Greeks and Phoenicians in Etruria, and just about everybody in 2nd century BC Delos. At the end of this line of development, Philip IV staged public show trials against Europe's major banking order, the Knights Templar in early 14th-century France, accusing them of sodomy as well as apostasy. Their persecution embodied what had become the traditional stereotype of the "sterile" usurer through Dante in his *Inferno*.

Given the sterility of usury, the explanation for antiquity's interest-rate trends is not "economic" in character. Commercial credit seems to have preceded agrarian interest-bearing debts. Mercantile interest rates were

---

[44] Jones 1992, Vol. II:775, citing Justinian's Novels xxii, xxxiii and xxxiv, and 535.

[45] Aristotle, *Politics*, Book I at 1258b (Jowett's translation).

lower and remained more uniform, but by classical antiquity came to be applied to commercial and agrarian debts alike. A seeming irony in the trajectory of interest rates in antiquity is that despite the increasing power of private-sector creditors in the face of declining royal authority, the standardized lending rate declined from Bronze Age Mesopotamia through classical Greece and Rome. Contrary to "economistic" views, the explanation is not to be found in rising security of credit or declining productivity, but simply reflects the different arithmetic fractions used for weights, measures and hence monetary denominations, moving westward over time.

Summary

1. Although ancient economies were predominantly agricultural, the practice of accruing interest seems to have been invented in the commercial sphere of Sumer, apparently with temples playing a catalytic role.

2. The terms *máš* in Sumerian and Akkadian, *tokos* in Greek and *fænus* in Latin signified a young animal, and hence the idea of birth. In time they came to mean interest. But in this sense, rather than deriving from the pastoral economics of herding and referring to the birth of animals literally, these terms referred to the periodic accrual or "birth" of the local unit fraction. The practice of using birth metaphors for interest started in third-millennium Sumer and diffused over about two thousand years to classical Greece and Italy.

3. Mesopotamia's commercial rate of $1/60^{th}$ per month made it easy to compute interest regularly. This practice found its counterpart in other regions – $1/10^{th}$ in Greece, and $1/12^{th}$ in Rome, reflecting their own respective systems of calculating fractions. It is thus a false trail to try to explain the long-term decline in interest rates on "economic" grounds. The apparent decline was an accidental byproduct of the numerical fraction system in each region, not reflecting economic rates of return or the debtor's shrinking ability to pay.

4. Interest rates in the commercial and agricultural spheres remained distinct throughout most of antiquity. Rates for agrarian debts tended to reflect land rents. In Sumer's case this was the sharecropping rate. Rents and agrarian interest rates both tended toward a norm of 1/3 by Ur III times, but there was more variation in agriculture than in the commercial sphere.

5. Although commercial lending in Mesopotamia did not seem to cause major society-wide problems, agrarian rates were above the "economic" rate that many cultivators were able to pay. The normal

resolution of debt problems was to lose one's family members and land-rights, until such time as the ruler might proclaim an agrarian debt cancellation. But such Clean Slates became less frequent after the Middle Bronze Age. Interest-bearing debt without royal cancellations led to economic polarization of the Babylonian, Greek, Roman and Byzantine economies.

6. There seems to have been a long tradition of considering the loan to be amortized when its interest payments had fully reproduced the principal. A hint of this idea is found in Hammurabi's law §117 liberating bondsmen after three years of service. His choice of three years may reflect the fact that agricultural interest rates typically were 1/3 per year. In three years the value of the crop payments or personal services provided by the debt-pledge would have repaid the original debt. Two thousand years later, Justinian's laws explicitly considered the debt was to have been paid off once the interest paid by cultivators had equaled the initial principal.[46] This ruling seems to reflect a long-standing Roman practice since the time of Julius Caesar.

---

[46] See Noonan 1957, pp. 39-41 and Grice-Hutchison 1978, p. 29, citing *Codex* 4:32:3; *Institutions* 3:14:2; *Digest* 12:1:2:1; 13:6, f.3, n.6 and f.4; 44:7:1:4; 50:16:121.

Bibliography

Azarpay, Guitty (1990), "A Canon of Proportions in the Art of the Ancient Near East," in Ann C. Gunter, ed., *Investigating Artistic Environments in the Ancient Near East* (Washington DC: Smithsonian Institution):93-103.

Benveniste, Emile (1973), *Indo-European Language and Society* (Coral Gables, Fla.: University of Miami Press).

Berriman, A. E. (1953), *Historical Metrology* (New York: Dutton [repr. Greenwood Press 1969]).

Bogaert, Raymond (1968), *Banques et Banquiers dans les Cities Grecques* (Leiden: E. J. Brill).

Böhm-Bawerk, Eugen von (1890), *Capital and Interest: A Critical History of Economical Theory* (repr. New York: Kelley & Millman 1957).

Charpin, Dominique (1986), *Le Clerge d'Ur au siecle d'Hammurapi* (Geneva-Paris: Librairie Droz).

Cooper, Jerrold S. (1986), *Sumerian and Akkadian Royal Inscriptions, I: Presargonic Inscriptions* (New Haven: American Oriental Society, Translation Series, Vol. I).

Crawford, H. E. W. (1973), "Mesopotamia's invisible exports in the third millennium BC," *World Archaeology* 5:232-241.

Diakonoff, Igor M. (1974), *Structure of Society and State in Early Dynastic Sumer* (Malibu: Monographs of the Ancient Near East 1[3]).
" (1982), "The Structure of Near Eastern Society before the Middle of the 2nd Millennium BC," *Oikumene* 3:7-100.
" (1983), "Some Reflections on Numerals in Sumerian: Towards a History of Mathematical Notation," *Journal of the American Oriental Society* 103:83-96.

Dilke, O. A. W. (1987), *Mathematics and Measurement* (London: University of California Press/British Museum).

Englund, R. K. (1988), "Administrative Timekeeping in Ancient Mesopotamia," *Journal of the Economic and Social History of the Orient* 31:121-185.

Finley, Moses I. (1973), *The Ancient Economy* (Berkeley and Los Angeles: University of California Press).

Foster, Benjamin (1995), "Social Reform in Ancient Mesopotamia," in Irani and Silver 1995:165-177.

Frankfort, Henry (1951), *Kingship and the Gods* (Chicago: University of Chicago Press).

Friberg, Joran (1982), *A Survey of Publications on Sumero-Akakadian Mathematics, Metrology and Related Matters: 1854-1982* (Goteborg: Chalmers University of Technology, Dept. of Mathematics).

Gelb, Ignace J. (1965), "The Ancient Mesopotamian Ration System," *Journal of Near Eastern Studies* 24:230-243.
" (1967a), "Approaches to the Study of Ancient Society," *Journal of the American Oriental Society* 87:18.
" (1967b), "Growth of a Herd of Cattle," *Journal of Cuneiform Studies* 21:64-69.
" (1972), "The Arua Institution," *Revue d'Assyriologie et d'Archaeologie Orientale* 6:8-12.

Grice-Hutchinson, Marjorie (1978), *Early Economic Thought in Spain: 1177-1740* (London: G. Allen & Unwin).

Grierson, Philip (1978), "The Origins of Money," in George Dalton, ed., *Research in Economic Anthropology: An Annual Compilation of Research*, Vol. I (Greenwich, Conn.: JAI Press):135.

Heichelheim, Fritz M. (1958), *An Ancient Economic History* (Leiden: E. J. Brill).

Hudson, Michael (1992), "Did the Phoenicians Introduce the Idea of Interest to Greece and Italy – And If So, When?" in Gunter Kopcke, ed.,

Greece Between East and West:10th-8th Centuries BC (Mainz: Philipp von Zabern):128-143.

" (1995), "Roscher's Victorian Views on Financial Development," *Journal of Economic Studies* 22:187-208.

" (2023), *The Collapse of Antiquity: Greece and Rome as Civilization's Oligarchic Turning Point* (Dresden: ISLET).

Irani, K. D. and Morris Silver, eds. (1995), *Social Justice in the Ancient World* (Westport, Conn.: Greenwood Press).

Jones, A. H. M. (1992), *The Later Roman Empire, 284-602: A Social, Economic, and Administrative Survey*, 2 vols. (Baltimore: Johns Hopkins University Press).

Kramer, Samuel Noah (1959), *The Sumerians: Their History, Culture, and Character* (Chicago: University of Chicago Press).

Kramer, Samuel Noah and John Maier (1989), *Myths of Enki, the Crafty God* (New York and Oxford: Oxford University Press).

Lambert, Maurice (1963), "L'Usage de l'argent metal a Lagash au temps de la IIIe Dynastie d'Ur," *Revue d'Assyriologie et d'Archaeologie Orientale* 57:79-92.

Larsen, Mogens Trolle (1976), *The Old Assyrian City-State and its Colonies* (Copenhagen: Akademisk Forlag).

Laum, Bernard (1924), *Heiliges Geld* (Tübingen: J. C. B. Mohr (Paul Siebeck)).

Leemans, Wilhelmus F. (1950), "The Rate of Interest in Old Babylonian Times," *Revue Internationale des Droits de l'Antiquite* 5:7-34.

Lewy, Hildegard (1949), "Origin and Development of the Sexagesimal System of Numeration," *Journal of the American Oriental Society* 69:111.

Lichtheim, Mary (1976), *Ancient Egyptian Literature: A Book of Readings*, 2 vols. (Berkeley and Los Angeles: University of California Press).

Marshack, Alexander (1972), *The Roots of Civilization* (New York: McGraw Hill).

Mauss, Marcel (1954 [1925]), *The Gift* (New York: Norton).

Menninger, Karl (1969), *Number Words and Number Symbols: A Cultural History of Numbers* (Cambridge, Mass.: MIT Press).

Merritt, Benjamin D. (1961), *The Athenian Year* (Berkeley and Los Angeles: University of California Press).

Nemet-Nejat, Karen Rhea (1993), *Cuneiform Mathematical Texts as a Reflection of Everyday Life in Mesopotamia* (New Haven: American Oriental Society, Monograph Series, Vol. 75).

Nissen, Hans J., Peter Damerow, and Robert K. Englund (1993), *Archaic Bookkeeping: Writing and Techniques of Economic Administration in the Ancient Near East* (Chicago: University of Chicago Press).

Pettinatto, Giovanni (1981), *The Archives of Ebla: An Empire Inscribed in Clay* (Garden City, N.Y.: Doubleday).

Postgate, J. N. (1992), *Early Mesopotamia: Society and Economy at the Dawn of History* (London and New York: Routledge).

Powell, Marvin (1977), "Sumerian Merchants and the Problem of Profit," *Iraq* 39:23-28.
" (1978), "A contribution to the history of money in Mesopotamia prior to the invention of coinage," in B. Hruska and G. Komoroczy, eds., *Festschrift Lubor Matous* (Budapest):211-243.
" (1990), "Masse und Gewichte," *Reallexikon der Assyriologie*, Vol. 7 (Berlin: Walter de Gruyter):457-530.
" (1996), "Money in Mesopotamia," *Journal of the Economic and Social History of the Orient* 39:224-242.

Pritchett, W. Kendrick (1971), *The Greek State at War*, Part I (Berkeley and Los Angeles: University of California Press).

Quiggin, Alison (Hingston) (1949), *A Survey of Primitive Money* (London: Methuen).

Renger, Johannes (1994), "On Economic Structures in Ancient Mesopotamia," *Orientalia* 18:157-208.

Roscher, Wilhelm (1878), *Principles of Political Economy* (New York: Henry Holt & Co.).

Rosengarten, Yvonne (1959), "La notion sumerienne du souverainete divine: Urukagina et son dieu Ningirsu," *Revue de l'Histoire des Religions* 156:129-160.

Runciman, Stephen (1956), *Byzantine Civilization* (New York: Longmans, Green & Co.).

Schneider, Anna (1920), *Die sumerische Tempelstadt* (Essen: G. D. Baedeker).

Seidenberg, A. (1962a), "The ritual origin of geometry," *Archive for History of Exact Sciences* 1:490-523.
" (1962b), "The ritual origin of counting," *Archive for History of Exact Sciences* 2:140.

Silver, Morris (1995), "Prophets and Markets Revisited," in Irani and Silver 1995:179-198.

Skaist, Aaron (1994), *The Old Babylonian Loan Contract: Its History and Geography* (Ramat-gan, Israel: Bar Ilan University Press).

Steible, Horst and Hermann Behrens (1982), *Die altsumerischen Bau- und Weiinschriften* (Wiesbaden: F. Steiner).

Steinkeller, Piotr (1981), "The Renting of Fields in Early Mesopotamia and the Development of the Concept of 'Interest' in Sumerian," *Journal of the Economic and Social History of the Orient* 24:113-145.

Stieglitz, Robert R. (1982), "Numerical structuralism and cosmogony in the ancient Near East," *Journal of Social and Biological Structures* 5:255-266.

Stone, Elizabeth (1987), *Nippur Neighborhoods* (Chicago: University of Chicago Press).

Thureau-Dangin, Francois (1936), "Textes Mathematiques Babyloniens," *Revue d'Assyriologie et d'Archaeologie Orientale* 33:65-84.

Walker, C. B. F. (1987), *Cuneiform* (London: University of California Press/British Museum).

Westbrook, Raymond (1995), "Social Justice in the Ancient Near East," in Irani and Silver 1995:149-163.

Westbrook, Raymond, and Roger Woodard (1990), "The Edict of Tudhaliya IV," *Journal of the American Oriental Society* 110:641-669.

5

How Clean Slates Restored Order: Circular vs. Linear Time*

When interest-bearing commercial and agrarian debt came to be incorporated into civilization's economic structure in the third millennium BC, it was accompanied by Clean Slates that liberated bondservants and restored to debtors the rights to the crops and land that creditors had taken. Their Sumerian prototypes are found in Lagash, proclaimed by the rulers Enmetena ca. 2400, Urukagina ca. 2350 and Gudea ca. 2150. By the second millennium in Babylonia these royal "restorations of order" became customary proclamations rescuing debtors whose family members had been reduced to bondage or who had lost their land to foreclosing creditors.

The Sumerians and Babylonians did not leave any treatise explaining the logic that underlay their policies. They no doubt thought that their response to the challenge of over-indebtedness was so obvious as to be self-evident. Anyone setting out to translate their inscriptions therefore is obliged to fill in many gaps – and where inference is called for, modern biases tend to raise their head regarding what seems natural. And nowhere are these biases stronger than in the conflict between creditor and debtor interests.

Anthropologists have looked at surviving tribal enclaves for ideas of how the Bronze Age takeoff may have been managed. But no tribal communities in today's world possess the outward-reaching dynamics of Mesopotamia during its commercial takeoff, which occurred in many ways that are alien to modern ways of thinking. The documentation describes an approach operating on different principles from those that most modern observers assume to have been primordial and universal.

---

* This chapter is based on "Reconstructing the Origins of Interest-Bearing Debt and the Logic of Clean Slates," in *Debt and Economic Renewal in the Ancient Near East* (CDL Press, Bethesda, Md., 2002), the colloquium to which references below to "this volume" refer. I have omitted background discussion that has appeared in other essays in this present collection and in my 2018 *"... and forgive them their debts"*.

The character of Bronze Age debt

The dynamics of interest-bearing debt are different from those of tribal gift exchange and related reciprocity obligations. Monetary credit arrangements bear a specific interest rate, and the date of payment is specified in advance rather than left open-ended. That requires debts to be recorded in writing and formally witnessed. Creditors may take foreclosure measures for non-payment, leading to the debtor's bondage or the loss of land rights.

Civilization's earliest written records, from Sumer in the third millennium, provide the best evidence for civilization's monetized debt relations "in the beginning." Two categories of debt existed, each associated with its own designated monetary commodity. Business obligations owed by traders and entrepreneurial managers, above all those associated with foreign trade, were denominated in silver. The agrarian economy operated on credit denominated in barley units, each assigned a value equal to the silver shekel in order to strike a common measure.

Rules for money loans described in scribal training exercises are found almost exclusively in the commercial sphere, especially in connection with long-distance trade. These loans were denominated in silver at the equivalent of a 20 percent annual rate of interest, doubling the principal in five years. Under normal conditions merchants were able to pay this rate to their creditors and keep a profit for themselves. Lenders shared in the mercantile risk, taking what in effect was an equity position. If caravans were robbed or ships and their cargoes lost at sea through no fault of the merchant, the debt was voided. There is no indication that payment of such mercantile debts led to problems requiring royal intervention.

Interest-bearing debt had initially arisen in the commercial sphere, taking the form of advances of assets by the large civic institutions to entrepreneurial recipients, enabling them to make an economic gain in commerce and land management. But throughout all antiquity the most problematic debts disrupting the economy's fiscal and social balance were in the agrarian sphere. The original objective of charging interest to sharecroppers and other cultivators, however, can hardly have been to reduce them to bondage or to expropriate them from their self-support land. Their labor was needed for the agrarian economy to function.

Origins of barley interest in land-rental agreements

It seems that rural usury and the consequent widespread forfeiture of lands were derivative of what began as advances of land, animals and tools to sharecroppers (or manager intermediaries) by temples and palaces. Sharecropping land and agricultural inputs were advanced for a rent of one-third of the (optimistically) estimated normal crop yield.[1] Interest was charged on arrears of this rent and other agrarian obligations not settled at harvest-time. The interest rate charged on these carry-over debts was the same as the sharecropping rental rate: one-third. Even arrears of unpaid debts for food or credit for other needs, such as priestly social services, were charged interest at the rate of one-third of the sum owed, simply mirroring the sharecropping rental return for creditors.

Arrears on agrarian obligations must have been frequent, given the ever-present risk of crop failure preventing anticipated crop payments from being paid. This volume's papers by Archi and Steinkeller show that agrarian interest rates denominated in barley are attested by the middle of the third millennium. Officials, collectors for the palaces and temples and merchants often acted in their own private capacity to make interest-bearing loans to cultivators for arrears of fees owed to the large institutions.

Rural usury thus emerged as well-to-do "big men" charged for arrears owed to the palace and temples, also lending food and other necessities to distressed cultivators. But agrarian interest-bearing debt, especially usury charged to borrowers in need, was always denounced as socially unfair. The question therefore arises as to just how such charges originated in the first place.

Few types of barley debt involved actual loans of money. What often are called "loan documents" should more literally be termed "debt records" or simply "notes of obligation." In this volume Marc Van De Mieroop points out that a debt record may reflect "any arrangement between two parties that entailed a delivery at a later date." Cornelia Wunsch's list of such obligations as they appear in the Neo-Babylonian Egibi archive shows that actual money loans represent only a minority of these debts. Even in the commercial sphere with its debts denominated in silver, textiles and other handicrafts that temple and palace workshops consigned to merchants for trade were recorded as debts. And when contractual work was to be performed, craftsmen gave customers tablets of obligation when they were given materials to make into a finished product.

---

[1] Although not clear from the records, it seems likely that agricultural inputs were advanced as part of a "package" with the land for a total rental of one-third of the crop.

The legal formulae used to draw up contracts treated all such advances as debts, reflecting the legal preference for building on precedent. The basic contractual formulae were well established by the end of the third millennium. Debt tablets state the sum owed, the due date and the names of witnesses, with the appropriate seals. Additional stipulations might include the pledges involved, guarantees by individuals who stood surety, and the interest rate to be charged (typically to accrue only if the debt were not paid on time). Some documents were given a title citing the reason why the debt was established.

Usually there is no such explanation, but agrarian debts mostly arose on rental agreements for land advanced by public institutions to intermediaries, who then subleased it to sharecroppers. Johannes Renger describes how land and workshops were administered directly by palace officials in Ur III (2111-2004 BC), but by the Old Babylonian period (2000-1600) the palace franchised the management of its fields and date orchards, herds of sheep, and workshops for brick-making and other handicrafts to "entrepreneurs" as *Palastgeschäfte*, "royal enterprises." These managers were entitled to keep whatever they could produce or collect above and beyond the amount stipulated by their contract with the palace, but if the sums they collected fell short, their arrears were recorded as a debt and they were obliged to pay the difference out of their own resources.

The rate of interest payable by cultivators on land rental debt arrears was, as described above, one-third, being the same as the rate charged for advances of sharecropping land. Cultivators were also charged this one-third rate of interest for unpaid arrears of charges for advances to buy food, beer or meet emergency needs on credit. If they lacked the means to pay out of whatever assets they had, they had to work off the debt charges in the form of their labor service or that of their family members (daughters, sons, wives or house-slaves), and ultimately they had to pledge their land rights.

How agrarian debt transformed land tenure

Barley debts had an annual character reflecting the crop cycle, falling due upon harvest, but Van De Mieroop finds that for short-term loans the full annual rate often was charged as a flat proportion, sometimes even more than one-third of the sum. The accrual of such debts did not reflect a parallel growth in the cultivator's ability to pay out of their harvest. Steinkeller's paper in this volume traces how creditors obtained work at harvest-time by extending loans whose interest was paid in the form of labor service, as labor-for-hire was not generally available in this epoch.

In addition to their labor, debtors were obliged to pledge their family members as bondservants, followed by their land rights. Self-support land had traditionally been conveyed from one generation to the next within families, not being freely disposable outside of the family or neighborhood. Land transfers did occur when families shrank in size and transferred their cultivation rights to distant relatives or neighbors. But starting with rights to its crop usufruct, subsistence land was pledged and relinquished to outsiders after 2000 BC.

Debtor families initially were left on the land after they lost their crop rights, but were forced off the land as the new appropriators turned to less labor-intensive cash crops such as dates. Debtors often ended up as members of rootless bands or mercenaries after the middle of the second millennium. Instead of crop and land rights being lost only temporarily – being returned to their original owners by royal edicts that restored the *status quo ante*[2] – such forfeitures became irreversible by the first millennium BC, especially in Greece and Italy to the west.

The logic of cancelling rural debts and reversing land forfeitures

An inability to meet obligations was inherent in the risks to which agrarian life was subject throughout antiquity: drought, flooding, infestation or an outbreak of disease, capped by military disruptions. The problem confronting rulers was how to prevent debts from mounting up to the point where they threatened to expropriate the community's corvée labor and fighting force, dooming debt-ridden realms to defeat by outsiders. If the indebted rural citizenry were to survive along customary lines, priority could not be given to creditors.

Mesopotamian rulers countered the rural debt problem not by banning interest outright, but by annulling barley debts. To restore the means of self-support, rulers issued edicts "proclaiming justice,"

---

[2] The classic studies of these edicts are F. R. Kraus, *Königliche Verfügungen in altbabylonischer Zeit* (Leiden, 1984), Jean Bottéro, "Désordre économique et annulation des dettes en Mesopotamie à l'époque paléo-babylonienne," *Journal of the Economic and Social History of the Orient* 4 (1961):113-164, J. J. Finkelstein, "Ammisaduqa's Edict and the Babylonian 'Law Codes,'" *Journal of Cuneiform Studies* 15 (1961):91-104, "Some New *misharum* Material and its Implications," in *Assyriological Studies* 16 (1965), *Studies in Honor of Benno Landsberger on his Seventy-Fifth Birthday*:233-246, "The Edict of Ammisaduqa: A New Text," *Revue d'Assyriologie et d'Archaéologie Orientale* 63 (1969):45-64, and the works of Igor Diakonoff and Dominique Charpin.

decreeing economic order and "righteousness." These proclamations date from almost as early as interest-bearing debt is attested, starting in Sumer with Lagash's rulers Enmetena ca. 2400 and Urukagina ca. 2350. Much as commercial debts were forgiven when the merchandise was lost through no fault of the merchant, Hammurabi's laws (§48) provided that cultivators would not be obliged to pay their crop debts if the storm-god Adad flooded their field and the crop was lost. The operative principle was that debtors should not lose their economic liberty by being held liable for "acts of God." And inasmuch as most barley debts were owed to the palace or royal officials, it was easy for rulers to cancel them. Letting officials and merchants keep the crops and labor of debtors would have deprived rulers of their ability to collect the customary royal fees and land rents for themselves and to obtain corvée labor and military service,

There was no modernist thought that the dynamics of interest-bearing debt might be self-stabilizing by letting "market forces" proceed unimpeded. There was no thought of Adam Smith's Deist god designing the world to run like clockwork, with checks and balances automatically maintaining equilibrium without any need for intervention by kings or priestly sanctions. Not even the wealthy voiced the ideology of modern free-market fundamentalism arguing that society's wealth and revenue would be maximized by letting it pass into the hands of the richest and most aggressively self-serving individuals reducing hitherto free families to bondage.

The modern historiography of Clean Slates

The Hebrew word used for the Jubilee Year in Leviticus 25 is *dêror*, but not until cuneiform texts could be read was it recognized as cognate to Akkadian *andurarum*. Before the early meaning was clarified the King James Version translated the relevant phrase as: "Proclaim *liberty* throughout all the land, and to all the inhabitants thereof." This passage was inscribed on America's Liberty Bell, when England's colonists in America were fighting for the freedom to legislate their own laws. But the root meaning of *andurarum* is to move freely as running water – or, for humans, as bondservants liberated to rejoin their families of origin.

The wide variety of modern interpretations of such key terms as Sumerian amargi, Akkadian *andurarum* and *misharum*, and Hurrian *shudutu* serve as an ideological Rorschach test reflecting the translator's own beliefs. The earliest reading was by Francois Thureau-Dangin (1905:86-87). He related the Sumerian term amargi to Akkadian *an-*

durarum and saw it as a debt cancellation. Ten years later Schorr (1915) related these acts to Solon's *seisachtheia*, the "shedding of burdens" that annulled the debts of rural Athens in 594 BC. In England, George Barton (1929) translated Urukagina's and Gudea's use of the term amargi as "release," although the Jesuit Anton Deimel (1930:9) rendered it rather obscurely as "security."

Maurice Lambert (1956) initially interpreted Urukagina's amargi act as an exemption from taxes, on the ground that most of the debts being annulled were owed to the palace. His subsequent 1972 discovery of Enmetena's kindred proclamation dating some fifty years earlier led him to see amargi as signifying a debt cancellation. F. R. Kraus had followed this view in 1954, and greatly elaborated his survey of Babylonian proclamations in his 1984 survey of rulers "raising the torch" to signal debt cancellations.

But in America, Samuel Kramer (1959) interpreted these acts as tax reductions. In a letter to *The New York Times* the day President Reagan took office in 1981, he even urged the president-elect to emulate Urukagina and cut taxes! The term amargi became popular with U.S. libertarians seeking an archaic precedent for their tax protests.

Kramer (1959:49) further belittled Urukagina's reforms as soon "gone with the wind," being "too little, too late," as if they were failures for not solving the debt problem permanently. In a similar vein Stephen Lieberman (1989) deemed Babylonian debt cancellations ineffective on the ground that they kept having to be repeated. "The need to repeat the enactment of identical provisions shows that the *misharum* provided relief, but did not eliminate the difficulties which made it necessary. ... What seems to have been needed was reform which would have eliminated all need for such adjustments." He did not suggest just what could have created an economy free of credit cycles.

Mesopotamian rulers were not seeking a debt-free utopia but coped pragmatically with the most adverse consequences of rural debt when it became top-heavy. Usury was not banned, as it would be in Judaism's Exodus Code, but its *effects* were reversed when the debt overhead exceeded the ability to pay on a widespread basis. These royal edicts retained the economy's underlying structure. The palace did not deter new debts from being run up, and kept leasing out land to sharecroppers, who owed the usual proportion of crops and were obliged to pay the usual interest penalties for non-delivery.

Dominique Charpin (1987:39) emphasizes that the word for "mother," *ama*, connotes "origin," so that amargi signifies a return to (or restoration of) the "mother situation" as its "point of origin." The aim was to restore the economic order that existed before the imbalances caused by debt. Babylon's *misharum* acts returned the debtor's wife, daughters or sons who had been pledged as bondservants, and also returned household slaves (typically women captured in war) to the debtors who previously owned them. So these acts freed bondservants, but not slaves.

Along similar lines Igor Diakonoff (1991:234) emphasized that "the word *andurarum* does not mean 'political liberation.' It is a translation of Sumerian amargi 'returning to mother,' that is, 'to the original situation.' It does not mean liberation from some supreme authority but the cancelling of debts, duties, and the like. Also, 'cleaning' is a *terminus technicus* for 'release from payments.'" This was something more specific than freedom in the abstract. It connoted liberty from the bondage that had been brought about by the overgrowth of debt, and from being displaced from one's self-support land.

The Assyrian term "washing the tablets" (*hubullam masa'um*; see Grayson 1972:7) may refer to dissolving them in water, akin to breaking or pulverizing them. Likening it to the Babylonian term meaning "to kill the tablet," Kemal Balkan (1974:33) explained that the idea was to cancel grain debts by physically destroying their records. Along more abstract lines, Raymond Westbrook (1995) likens the idea of "washing" to a ritual cleansing of the population from inequities that would displease Sumerian and Babylonian patron deities. Urukagina's edict thus was held to have cleansed Lagash from the moral blemish of inequity.

Some Assyriologists have interpreted Assyria's *andurarum* proclamations as free-trade acts waiving palace charges. Julius Lewy (1958a:99) believed that when the ruler Ilushuma decreed that the copper of Akkadians should be "washed," this signified a free movement of copper and other goods by exempting them from tariffs or other duties. Mogens Larsen (1976:74-76) likewise believes that *addurarum* was a free-trade policy "to attract traders from the south to the market in Assur by giving them certain privileges," such as enabling raw copper to be refined. But Postgate (1992:196) warns against limiting such acts to trade only. Ilushuma was doing just what Babylonian rulers did when they proclaimed *andurarum*: revoking enslavement for debt and annulling personal debts.

The archaeological context for Assyria's *andurarum* inscriptions shows its rulers embedding them in the walls of their city-temple. One of Ilushuma's *andurarum* acts was proclaimed after building a temple for Assur's patron goddess Ishtar, and another describes the façade and new wall for a temple the ruler built (Grayson 1972:7 and 1987:15; see also *Chicago Assyriological Dictionary* E321a.). This hardly seems an appropriate setting for something so worldly as a free-trade edict. Tellingly, a text of one of his successors, Erishum, concludes with the words, "May (justice) be established in my city," using the word *misharum*, familiar from Babylonian royal edicts. Analyzing the Akkadian terms *kittum* and *misharum*, Ephraim Speiser (1953:874) and Bottéro (1992:182) have pointed out that the idea of "straight" with which the terms are associated connotes the idea of *rectitude*, an egalitarian idea of "straight order" and social equity.

Some anachronistic creditor-oriented views of Clean Slates

Instead of enforcing debt contracts at the cost of social and military instability, Sumer and Babylonia preserved economic viability via Clean Slates. Today's creditor-oriented ideology denies the success of Clean Slates overriding free-market relations. It depicts the archaic past as much like our own world, as if civilization was developed by individuals thinking in terms of modern orthodoxy, letting interest rates be determined simply by market supply and demand, duly adjusted for risk of non-payment.

Modern economic theory assumes that debts normally can be paid, with the interest rate reflecting the borrower's profit. The implication is that the fall in interest rates from Mesopotamia to Greece and Rome resulted from falling profit rates and/or the greater security of investment. In this view, debt cancellations would only have aggravated debt problems, by increasing the creditor's risk and hence the interest rate.

Some Assyriologists have followed this market-based explanation of interest rates. Benjamin Foster (1995:167) attributed Mesopotamia's historically high rates for agricultural borrowers – a third to half the debt principal, compared to the 20 percent annualized rate normal for commercial loans – to the moneylenders' risk that royal debt cancellations might annul their claims. "We need not be advanced economic theoreticians," he wrote, "to suppose that there might be a relation between such high rates of interest and the possibility of an edict abolishing debt, although we may ask which was first, the risk or the rate." It is as if the agrarian interest rate included a calculation of risk, not simply, as I believe, an application of the same rate that the palace charged for advances of sharecropping land: one-third. Suggesting that Clean Slates were self-defeating, he wondered "if the edicts did not in fact favor moneylenders in the long term, even if unintentionally – and, thus, we may wonder whose benefit the edicts ultimately served."

Foster did not consider that the interest – and the debts being annulled – were owed to the palace or its collectors. Most seriously, he treated agrarian debts as stemming from prior money loans, not from crop failures leading to shortfalls in crop payments. That assumption followed the views of his Yale predecessor Jacob Finkelstein (1965:246), who wrote that the anticipation of *misharum* acts should have deterred creditors from making loans whose claims for payment soon were likely to be annulled. (That is what Rabbi Hillel argued with regard to the Jewish Jubilee Year.) "If our hypothesis proves valid, the years immediately preceding a *misharum* should show a low rate of frequency in transactions in general, higher interest rates, lower sales prices for real estate, etc. (the risk to the potential buyer and creditor being then much greater)."

But Charpin (2000:203) finds that not to have been the case in Babylonia. "The majority of loans were contracted in the months preceding the *misharum*. ... Obviously, whatever risk was incurred did not discourage the creditors from extending interest-bearing loans." The increased indebtedness, especially in times of crop failure or warfare, would explain why *misharum* proclamations were needed as a response.

Modernist assumptions distract attention from what actually happened. No writer in antiquity is known to have related interest rates to profit rates or risk, or to the use of seeds or breeding cattle to produce offspring. We may well ask whether it was fortunate for the survival of Babylonian society that its rulers were not "advanced economic theoreticians" of the modern sort. If they had not proclaimed Clean Slates, creditors would have reduced debtors to bondage and taken their lands irreversibly. But in cancelling crop debts, rulers acknowledged that the palace had taken all that it could without destroying the economy's foundations. If they had demanded that debt arrears be made up by cultivators forfeiting their family members and land rights to royal collectors (who sought to keep debt charges on the crop yield for themselves), the palace would have lost the services of these debtors for corvée labor and in the armed forces to resist foreign attack.

Markets indeed became less stable as economies polarized in classical antiquity. Yet it was only at the end of antiquity that Diodorus of Sicily (I.79) explained the most practical rationale for Clean Slates. Describing how Egypt's pharaoh Bocchoris (720-715 BC) abolished debt bondage and cancelled undocumented debts, Diodorus wrote that the pharaoh's guiding logic was that:

> the bodies of citizens should belong to the state, to the end that it might avail itself of the services which its citizens owed it, in times of both war and peace. For he felt that it would be absurd for a soldier, perhaps at

the moment when he was setting forth to fight for his fatherland, to be haled to prison by his creditor for an unpaid loan, and that the greed of private citizens should in this way endanger the safety of all.

That would seem to be how early Mesopotamian rulers must have reasoned. Letting soldiers pledge their land to creditors and then lose this basic means of self-support through foreclosure would have expropriated the community's fighting force – or led to their flight or defection. By the 4th century BC the Greek military writer known as Tacticus recommended that a general attacking a town might promise to cancel the debts owed by its inhabitants if they defected to his side. Likewise, defenders of towns could strengthen the resistance of their citizens by agreeing to annul their debts.

This emergency military tactic in classical antiquity no longer reflected a royal duty to restore economic self-reliance as a guiding principle of overall order. What disappeared was the relief of debtors from their obligations and reversal of their land sales or forfeitures when natural disasters blocked their ability to pay or after a new ruler took the throne. The oligarchic epoch had arrived, abolishing any public power able to cancel the society-wide debt overgrowth.

The cosmological dimension of Clean Slates

What saved Mesopotamia from classical antiquity's fate was its "divine kingship." The prefatory passages of Babylonian edicts cited the ruler's commitment to serve his city-god by promoting equity in the land. Myth and ritual were integrated with economic relations and were viewed as forming the natural order that rulers were charged with overseeing, including by cancelling debts to fulfill their sacred obligation to their city-gods. Commemorated by their year-names and often by foundation deposits in temples, these amnesties appear to have been proclaimed at a major festival, replete with rituals such as Babylon's ruler raising a sacred torch to signal the renewal of the social cosmos in good order – what Mircea Eliade has called "the eternal return," the idea of circular time that formed the context in which rulers restored an idealized *status quo ante*. By integrating debt annulments with social cosmology, the image of rulers restoring economic order was central to the archaic idea of justice and equity.

The occasion for such proclamations resembled a New Year festival or coronation ceremony in the sense that they "periodically" restored order out of the chaos into which the social cosmos tended to fall. Such proclamations may have been part of the enthronement ceremony at the outset of the ruler's first full year on the throne. Gudea appears to have cancelled debts at a New Year celebration ca. 2100 (Jacobsen 1987 and Edzard 1997). There was no fixed periodicity in the sense of a mathematically regular cycle such as is called for in the Jubilee Year. After their initial coronation proclamation rulers repeated these edicts as conditions warranted, such as military hostilities or crop failures, or a major public achievement such as rebuilding a city-temple. But when rulers are described as "periodically" clearing the slate, the chronological meaning is loose. Proclaiming Clean Slates at the outset of the ruler's first full year on the throne (technically his second year) was thought of as starting a new cycle – which was simply a new beginning, much as inaugurating a new European ruler down through feudal times was viewed as starting a new cycle, with years numbered from the start of their rule and which often included an amnesty for criminals, the last vestige of archaic Clean Slates.[3]

For many years these royal edicts clearing away the most adverse consequences of rural indebtedness were dismissed as being merely symbolic ritual formalities. At some point they indeed became a vestigial *topos*, but they certainly were enforced in Sumer and Babylonia to reverse the imbalances that had been mounting up since the last royal proclamation. This is confirmed by the extent to which their "small print" was elaborated over the centuries to close the loopholes by which creditors sought to keep the land, bondservants and other assets they had taken from debtors, culminating in Ammisaduqa's 1646 edict that countered the most prevalent creditor stratagems.

The first-millennium aftermath

A century ago it was widely assumed that production, trade and credit evolved from a small private scale to a larger, ultimately public context. But the course of economic enterprise developed in just the reverse direction. The scale and complexity of Sumer's temples and palaces far exceeded that of private *oikos* estates in classical Greece and Rome. That scale was necessary to call into being the accounting, credit and

---

[3] There is a hint that Babylonian rulers may have annulled agrarian debts on the occasion of celebrating "a month of years" of their rule (thirty years), as in the case of Hammurabi's *misharum* proclamation of 1762. With regard to just how precisely the Babylonian idea of regularity may have been reflected in the timing of *misharum* acts, see the not very persuasive article by G. Komoroczy (1982).

monetary arrangements necessary to organize and articulate basic commercial and pricing relations.

Just as important as scale was the philosophy that guided credit relations and land tenure. Economic and social practices changed radically in the process of being transplanted from complex Near Eastern palatial economies to those of the Aegean and Italy – from large to small scale units, from economies with checks and balances to less regulated ones. The decontextualization of interest-bearing debt was much like the effect of new plants or animal species growing unchecked when transplanted to a new environment.

The result was an out-of-context adoption of the Near Eastern debt system and related commercial practices as trade and industry were concentrated in the households of Greek and Italian chiefdoms. The Clean Slates that had checked over-indebtedness and land concentration in Mesopotamia did not accompany the spread of interest-bearing debt to regions that lacked the large civic institutions and "divine kingship."

The most severe problem was agrarian usury. Lack of local traditions of annulling agrarian debt buildup left no means to reverse debt bondage and the forfeiture of land rights stemming from the tendency of debts to grow in excess of the ability to pay. Economic polarization became irreversible in the Mediterranean lands, and hence much more devastating in Greece and Italy than had been the case in the earlier Near East.

Baruch Levine's oral presentation to this colloquium (not included in this volume) developed his 1989 study tracing the Hebrew word *derôr* used for the Jubilee Year back to Akkadian *andurarum* used for Clean Slates from the Old Babylonian through Neo-Assyrian epochs. The biblical compilers would have become familiar with the tradition during the Babylonian captivity (586-538 BC). Like its Babylonian prototype, Leviticus 25 annulled rural debts, liberated bondservants and returned the land to families that had lost it under economic duress. The Biblical narrative describes kings as becoming oppressive by the first millennium, leading Judaism to elevate the Jubilee Year to a central position in the Mosaic covenant, out of the hands of kings and given a regular cyclicality at the center of the religion as part of Judaism's covenant with the Lord.

Details of first-millennium debt-remissions are better documented in Judah's great enemy Assyria a century or so earlier. Finding that Assyrian rulers "might initiate an 'amnesty' ... that ... would lead to the cancellation of enslavement for debt," Nicholas Postgate (1973:231 and 1974:417, text #132) concludes that Sargon II (late 8th century BC) and his successors had adopted the practice. The hints suggested by Michael

Jursa in this volume remain the firmest evidence of Neo-Babylonian debt annulments, and new Neo-Assyrian examples have come to light. Kindred policies are reflected in Egyptian inscriptions as late as the Ptolemaic-era Rosetta Stone (196 BC).

A major reason why debt cancellations did not spread to the Mediterranean lands was that the new economies were run by chieftains and warlords in the Greek and Italian city-states that emerged from the turmoil of the 1200-750 Dark Age, creating oligarchic political systems. In Athens, Solon's *seisachtheia* debt cancellation in 594 BC was a one-time response to emergency conditions. After the Gracchan attempts at reform in Rome in 133 BC, a century of civil warfare settled the debt problem in favor of the creditor-landholder oligarchy that presided over an economy shrinking under the weight of its debt overhead. The only imperial debt annulments one hears of were tax abatements, mainly to free the wealthiest landowners of their fiscal burden, which was shifted onto the less affluent as Rome's economy polarized.

Clean Slates based on the distinction between productive and unproductive credit

Over and above the Bronze Age distinction between productive and unproductive credit (silver loans vs. barley loans) was an awareness that debt pressures, if left to accumulate unchecked, would distort normal fiscal and landholding patterns to the detriment of the community. In this respect the ancients were in advance of modern economic equilibrium theorizing. They perceived that debts grow autonomously under their own dynamic by the exponential curves of compound interest rather than adjusting themselves to reflect the ability of debtors to pay. This idea never has been accepted by modern economic doctrine, which assumes that disturbances are cured by automatically self-correcting market mechanisms. That assumption blocks discussion of what governments can do to prevent the debt overhead from destabilizing economies.

Like the subsequent Biblical prophets, Mesopotamians denounced usury yet voiced no complaint about commercial trade financing. The distinction between productive and unproductive credit was never made explicit, but rulers only cancelled rental arrears, distress loans and other "barley" debts, not "silver" business debts. That reflects their epoch's implicit distinction between productive lending and socially corrosive usury.

Productive loans provide resources enabling borrowers to repay the loan with the stipulated interest charge. Although antiquity knew of almost no loans to create means of production, advances of money or merchandise enabled merchants to earn enough to pay their creditors and still keep a profit under normal conditions, thereby providing a mutual gain between debtor and creditor. The Sumerians and Babylonians left such mercantile loans and investments intact when they annulled crop debts.

Hebrew *tarbit* and *neshek* reflect the distinction between the ideas of growth and diminution, *i.e.*, interest on productive commercial debts representing a share of the mercantile gain vs. a "bite" in the sense of the food crop bitten off by the creditor (whom Akkadian usage described as "eating" the interest), using usury as a lever to pry land away from smallholders.

Christianity originally deemed all lending at interest to be usurious. But medieval Church doctrine changed this teaching to legitimize bank credit while retaining the condemnation of extortionate lending to the poor. The Churchmen provided room for the revival of loan charges in the sphere of foreign trade, initially in the form of an *agio* to remunerate bankers for transferring commercial payments from one currency to another, and they distinguished the charging of "interest" from "usury." The medieval term "interest" had a connotation of lenders sharing in the fortunes of their commercial borrowers, literally having an *interest* in the success of their ventures.

The essence of the modern idea of progress is not only a "free market" (one free of public regulation of credit, debt and other forms of economic rent), but also irreversibility of economic polarization – linear time, not a need for fresh economic renewal. This linearity has come to signify not only the secular progress of knowledge and technology, but also the buildup of debt and with it the widespread transfer of property to creditors. The concept of circular time had made it easy for Mesopotamian rulers to restore the traditional social order by annulling the economic imbalances that had built up.

At the deepest level is the need for economic renewal to restore balance. Amnesties for past offenses and their fines may have provided Mesopotamia's rulers with a precedent for the forgiveness of personal monetary debts as these proliferated. By limiting the buildup and consequences of rural debt to only temporary duration, Mesopotamia's restorations of economic order avoided classical antiquity's emergence of creditor oligarchies fighting against popular demands to cancel debts and redistribute land as the economy polarized. Never since have debt strains been dealt with in so comprehensive a way as at the outset of civilization's debt dynamic.

Some safety net is provided by today's bankruptcy laws wiping out debts on a case-by-case basis. But debt and land ownership are not regulated by taking into account the broad economic context. Since late antiquity, economic freedom for individuals has been based on the demand that governments should stand by passively while indebted individuals lose their land and economic liberty.

That predatory economic ideology is what weakened the Roman economy from within. The major creditors no longer were public institutions, but private individuals eager to expand their landholdings at the expense of debtors. By the 7th century BC debt crises wracked Sparta, Corinth and Athens, and by the end of antiquity Livy, Plutarch and Diodorus described usury as the main culprit in their epoch's collapse. Men dispossessed from the land had little means of support except to become hired mercenary fighters.

Most historical writers have explained Rome's resulting decline by focusing on the military attack from without. But the raiders were always there. What enabled them to sack Rome was the loss of internal balance that early civic policy and, indeed, religious values had sought to preserve. As far as the evolution of civilization is concerned, the Roman oligarchy turned out to be the barbarians *within* the gates.

Classical antiquity ended economic renewal by making the loss of economic balance and mutual aid irreversible. The ideal of linear progress has seen Western civilization fall prey to the financial polarization that the Bronze Age Near East managed to avoid. Roman contract law making the loss of land and personal liberty irreversible replaced the ideology of social equity and balance that had characterized Mesopotamian Clean Slates. Today's world is still carrying the legacy of Rome's pro-creditor law to a degree that is polarizing economies along lines similar to those that polarized the late Roman Republic.

Bibliography

Balkan, Kemal (1974), "Cancellation of Debts in Cappadocian Tablets from Kultepe," *Anatolian Studies Presented to Hans C. Guterbock* (Istanbul):29-36.

Barton, George (1929), *The Royal Inscriptions of Sumer and Akkad* (New Haven).

Bottéro, Jean (1961), "Desordre economique et annulation des dettes en Mésopotamie à lá epoque paleo-babylonienne," *Journal of the Economic and Social History of the Orient* 4:113-164.
" (1992), *Mesopotamia: Writing, Reasoning, and the Gods* (Chicago [Paris 1987]).

Charpin, Dominique (1987), "Les Decréts Royaux à l'Époque Paléo-babylonienne, à Propos d'un Ouvrage Recent," *Archiv für Orientforschung* 34:36-44.
" (1990), "L'*andurârum* à Mari," MARI 6 (1990):253-270.
" (2000), "Les prêteurs et la palais: Les édits de *mîsharum* des rois de Babylone et leurs traces dans les archives privées," in Bongenaar, A. C. V. M., ed., *Interdependency of Institutions and Private Entrepreneurs* (= Proceedings of the Second MOS Symposium, Leiden 1998)(Nederlands Historisch-Archaeologisch Institute, Te Istanbul):185-211.

Deimel, Anton (1930), *Sumerische Tempelwirtschaft der Zeit Urukaginas und seiner Vorgänger* (Rome).

Diakonoff, Igor M. (1991), "The City-States of Sumer" and "Early Despotisms in Mesopotamia," in *Early Antiquity* (Chicago):67-97.

Edzard, Dietz O. (1957), *Die zweite Zwischenzeit Babyloniens* (Wiesbaden).

Finkelstein, J. J. (1961), "Ammisaduqa's Edict and the Babylonian 'Law Codes,'" *Journal of Cuneiform Studies* 15:91-104.
" (1965), "Some New *misharum* Material and its Implications," in *Assyriological Studies* 16 (*Studies in Honor of Benno Landsberger on his Seventy-Fifth Birthday*):233-246.

" (1969), "The Edict of Ammisaduqa: A New Text," *Revue d'Assyriologie et d'Archaéologie Orientale* 63:45-64.

Foster, Benjamin (1995), "Social Reform in Ancient Mesopotamia," in K. D. Irani and Morris Silver, eds., *Social Justice in the Ancient World* (Westport, Conn.):165-177.

Frankfort, Henri (1951), *Kingship and the Gods* (Chicago).
" (1952), "State Festivals in Egypt and Mesopotamia," Journal of the Warburg and Courtauld Institute.

Gelb, Ignace (1967), "Approaches to the Study of Ancient Society," *Journal of the American Oriental Society* 87:1-8.

Grayson, A. K. (1972), *Assyrian Royal Inscriptions* (Wiesbaden).

Heichelheim, Fritz (1958), *Ancient Economic History, from the Paleolithic Age to the Migrations of the Germanic, Slavic and Arabic Nations* (Toronto).

Hudson, Michael (1992), "Did the Phoenicians Introduce the Idea of Interest to Greece and Italy – And if So, When?" in Gunter Kopcke, ed., *Greece Between East and West: 10th-8th Centuries BC* (Berlin):128-143.
" (2000a), "How Interest Rates Were Set, 2500 BC-1000 AD: *Máš, tokos* and *fænus* as metaphors for interest accruals," *Journal of the Economic and Social History of the Orient* 43:132-161.
" (2000b), "The Mathematical Economics of Compound Interest: A Four-Thousand Year Overview," *Journal of Economic Studies* 27 (2000):344-363.
" (2018), "*... and forgive them their debts:" Lending, Foreclosure and Redemption From Bronze Age Finance to the Jubilee Year* (Dresden).

Hudson, Michael, and Baruch Levine, eds. (1996), *Privatization in the Ancient Near East and Classical Antiquity* (Cambridge, Mass: Peabody Museum, Bulletin #6).
" (1999), *Urbanization and Land Ownership in the Ancient Near East* (Cambridge, Mass: Peabody Museum, Bulletin #8).

Innes, A. Mitchell (1913), "What is Money?" *Banking Law Journal.*
" (1914), "The Credit Theory of Money," *ibid.*:151-168.

Jacobsen, Thorkild (1987), *The Harps that Once ...: Sumerian Poetry in Translation* (New Haven).

Komoroczy, G. (1982), "Zur Frage der Periodizität der altbabylonischen *misharum*-Erlasse," *Society and Languages*:196-205.

Kramer, Samuel (1959), *History Begins at Sumer* (New York).

Kraus, Fritz (1958), *Ein Edikt des Königs Ammisaduqa von Babylon*, SD 5 (Leiden).
" (1984), *Königliche Verfügungen in altbabylonischer Zeit*, SD 11 (Leiden).

Lambert, Maurice (1956), "Les 'Reformes' d'Urukagina," *Revue d'Assyriologie* 60:169-184.
" (1971), "Une Inscription nouvelle d'Enteména prince de Lagash," *Revue du Louvre* 21:231-236.

Larsen, Mogens T. (1976), *The Old Assyrian City-State and its Colonies* (Copenhagen).

Lewy, Julius (1958a), "Some Aspects of Commercial Life in Assyria and Asia Minor in the Nineteenth Pre-Christian Century," *Journal of the American Oriental Society* 78.
" (1958b), "The Biblical Institution of *Deror* in the Light of Akkadian Documents," *Eretz-Israel* 5.

Levine, Baruch (1989), ed., *Leviticus: The Traditional Hebrew Text, with the new Jewish Publication Society Translation* (Philadelphia).
" (1996), "The Hebrew Bible as a Repository of References to Economic Developments in the Ancient Near East," in Hudson and Levine 1996.

Lieberman, Stephen J. (1989), "Royal 'Reforms' of the Amurrite Dynasty," *Bibliotheca Orientalis* 46:241-259.

Maidman, Maynard (1996), "'Privatization' and Private Property at Nuzi: The Limits of Evidence," in Hudson and Levine 1996.

Mauss, Marcel (1954 [1925]), *The Gift* (New York).

Nelson, Benjamin (1960 [1949]), *The Idea of Usury: From Tribal Brotherhood to Universal Otherhood*, 2nd ed. (Princeton).

Postgate, J. N. (1969), *Neo-Assyrian Royal Grants and Decrees* (Rome).
" (1973), *The Governor's Palace Archive* (= British School of Archaeology in Iraq, Cuneiform Texts from Nimrud II).
" (1974), "Royal Exercise of Justice under the Assyrian Empire," in Paul Garelli, ed., *Le Palais et la Royaute* (Paris).
" (1992), *Early Mesopotamia: Society and Economy at the Dawn of History* (London and New York).

Renger, Johannes (1994), "On Economic Structures in Ancient Mesopotamia," *Orientalia* 18:157-208.

Schorr, M. (1915), "Eine babylonische Seisachthie aus dem Anfang der Kassiten-Zeit" (SHAW, Phil.-hist. Kl.).

Speiser, Ephraim (1953), "Early Law and Civilization," *Canadian Bar Review* 31:863-877.

Thureau-Dangin, Francois (1905), *Les Inscriptions Royales de Sumer et d'Akkad* (Paris).

Veenhof, K. R. (1997), "'Modern Features' in Old Assyrian Trade," *Journal of the Economic and Social History of the Orient* 40:336-366.
" (1999), "Silver and Credit in Old Assyrian Trade," in J. G. Dercksen, ed., *Trade and Finance in Ancient Mesopotamia: Proceedings of the First MOS Symposium* (=MOS Studies 1) ([Leiden], Istanbul):55-83.

Versnel, H. S. (1970), *Triumphus: An Inquiry Into the Origin, Development and Meaning of the Roman Triumph* (Leiden).

Westbrook, Raymond (1995), "Social Justice in the Ancient Near East," in K. D. Irani and Morris Silver, eds., *Social Justice in the Ancient World* (Westport, Conn.):149-163.

Westbrook, Raymond, and Roger Woodard (1990), "The Edict of Tudhaliya IV," *Journal of the American Oriental Society* 110:641-659.

II

Land Tenure: From its Fiscal Origins to Financialization

6

How the Organization of Labor Shaped Civilization's Takeoff*

> In the primitive economic situation ... there is, of course, no 'solitary hunter,' living either in a cave or otherwise, and there is no man who 'makes by his own labor all the goods that he uses,' etc. ... There is no reasonable doubt but that, at least since mankind reached the human plane, the economic unit has been not a 'solitary hunter,' but a community of some kind.
>
> – Thorstein Veblen

It is now more than a century since Veblen poked fun at armchair philosophers postulating a primitive idyll of individuals making products to "truck and barter" with each other, as Adam Smith put it. Such simple schemes of economic life "throw into the foreground, in a highly unreal perspective, those features which lend themselves to interpretation in terms of the normalized competitive system."[1]

This individualistic approach does not recognize a productive role for communal or public institutions. Palaces appear as a blind alley leading to Oriental Despotism, typically in the image of Egyptian overseers whipping slaves to build pyramids. There is no thought of communities allocating land as a way to mobilize labor to perform collective tasks, or of a large institutional bureaucracy innovating entrepreneurial monetary and commercial practices. Government is seen as a burdensome overhead, necessary only to wage war and protect property and financial claims.

---

* The first version of this paper appeared as "How the Organization of Labor Shaped Civilization's Takeoff," in *Labor in the Ancient World* (ed. with Piotr Steinkeller, ISLET, Dresden, 2015):649-664, the work to which references below to "this volume" refer. Many of the authors cited are contributors to that "Labor" volume, whose findings I summarize in the present paper. I have reorganized and edited sections for continuity with other chapters in the present collection.

[1] Thorstein Veblen, "Professor Clark's Economics," *Quarterly Journal of Economics* 23 (February 1908), reprinted in *The Place of Science in Modern Civilisation, and other Essays* (New York, 1919):180-230.

By the Bronze Age, society's survival required the organization of communal labor to provide corvée services and conscription in the military. Members of the community, citizens and "sons of the city" worked on publicly organized projects such as building temples and city walls and digging local irrigation ditches. Sumer, Babylonia, Egypt and Mycenaean Greece developed account-keeping largely to organize labor, land tenure, credit and commercial enterprise to provision corvée groupings and temple and palace workshops.

By the time written records appear in the third millennium BC, labor had long been mobilized for large building projects that must have involved entire communities. From the early Neolithic, this mobilization was organized on different principles from those of the modern world. Corvée labor obligations were linked to fiscal systems based on land tenure. Most members of the community were self-supporting on the land, with land-tenure rights associated with obligations to perform public labor services. This must have been organized on a voluntary basis, given the ever-present option of flight.

The archaic employment of labor could not have been based on barter or market sales of crops or handicrafts, because (apart from working to produce its own subsistence) labor initially was organized to construct public ceremonial sites and buildings, irrigation works, and to serve in the military. No exchange value was initially involved. We see the vestiges of this system in classical antiquity. Greece imposed public *leiturgoi* expenses on large landholders, and the Roman concept of class was defined by the landed wealth needed to outfit and support oneself at a given military rank.

From ceremonial community-based labor to the corvée

Carl Lamberg-Karlovsky describes the monumental ritual center of Göbekli Tepe, ca. 10,000-9000 BC in southeastern Anatolia, built by hunter-gatherers drawn from what must have been a broad territory to spend decade after decade carving its remarkable pre-pottery statuary. Such sites hosted gatherings for the rituals that integrated archaic communities by customary gift exchange and intermarriage.

Four or five thousand years after Göbekli, populations came together at Avebury, Stonehenge and other ceremonial sites.[2] This still was long

---

[2] No doubt their gatherings and feasts were coordinated by calendrical turning points based on the lunar and solar cycles so that widely scattered groups would know when to converge. The cosmology extends back to the Ice Age caves described by Alexan-

before profit-seeking trade or state coercion developed. Excavations show that a large volume of gazelle, auroch cattle and other animals fed Göbekli's builders, but who supplied them is not recorded. No doubt a similar organizational practice guided the mobilization of labor that built Sumerian, Babylonian and Egyptian monuments and infrastructure.

The labor requisitioned for such projects did not produce goods for sale. But someone had to organize it. A byproduct of Neolithic monument building was thus a managerial class, headed by chieftains who acted as calendar keepers and organizers and centralized some specialized or dependent labor in their own households. By the Pre-Pottery Neolithic-B period these men "held religious authority that legitimized their right to rule," Lamberg-Karlovsky explains. "Supernatural sanction, confirmed and certified by specialist practitioners, offered not only the legitimacy of rule, but the structure of order within the earliest villages." Social status reflected the authority of individuals responsible for allocating resources, organizing rituals and mobilizing labor for building monuments, temples and other public works, presiding "over ritual centers, the nascent forms of the later temples that became the focus of centralized political and economic power."

What was "produced" already in preliterate times at Tal-i-Bakun ca. 6000 BC and Tell Abyad ca. 5500 BC, Stonehenge and sites in Central Asia thus were not only public works and ceremonial centers but also nascent control mechanisms and administrative hierarchies. By the Mesopotamian Bronze Age this managerial class controlled wealth via the temples and palaces to produce textiles, metal working and prestige goods for long-distance trade.

The Neolithic thus bequeathed to the Bronze Age a complex of socio-economic relationships: (1) food provisioning and the hosting of feasts, requiring (2) empowerment of a managerial class, with (3) customary crop rights and land tenure as a byproduct of (4) fiscal policy to allocate responsibility for mobilizing labor, food and other resources.

Corvée labor as the primordial proto-tax defining land rights

A common theme of the papers in this volume is that supplying corvée labor and military service was the prototypical "tax" obligation, leading

---

der Marshack in "Space and Time in Pre-agricultural Europe and the Near East: The Evidence for Early Structural Complexity," in Michael Hudson and Baruch A. Levine, eds., *Urbanization and Land Ownership in the Ancient Near East* (1999):53. See also Chapter 9 in this collection.

land tenure to be defined in fiscal terms. "The man responsible for the tax was the 'owner' [of the land] as far as the state was concerned."[3] Property "belonged" to its holders in exchange for their meeting public obligations. Land rights were allocated in proportion to the holder's obligation to supply corvée labor for public work and military service.[4]

Ogden Goelet defines corvée labor as "unpaid, unskilled manual labor exacted in lieu of taxation in the form of money or goods. ... it generally entailed involuntary service and normally involved a great mass of people from a given locality." In Egypt, "the impressment was temporary and may have been based on a quota that local officials had to meet." Through the fiscal labor obligations attaching to land, a crop and manpower surplus was extracted from landholders, much as a surplus was extracted from merchants and entrepreneurs for their leasing or control of property, trade and palace enterprises.

Land was plentiful in Mesopotamia but required irrigation, which was provided by local communities (or over a larger territory in the case of major canals), evidently availing themselves of the corvée labor obligations. But property holders always have had a tendency to avoid their fiscal and social obligations, and indeed to use their privileges to gain control of the state administration in predatory and extractive ways. The development of civilization has seen a constant struggle by fiscal authority to link ("burden") property rights to public obligations to serve society's growth, equity and ultimately its survival.

Corvée labor and feasts

Piotr Steinkeller emphasizes the major problem for organizing labor prior to classical antiquity: a chronic labor shortage.[5] The problem was how to get self-sufficient cultivators to work at manual labor consisting

---

[3] Christopher J. Eyre, "How Relevant was Personal Status to the Functioning of the Rural Economy in Pharaonic Egypt?" in Bernadette Menu, ed., *La dépendence rurale dans l'Antiquité égyptienne et proche-orientale* (BdÉ 140, Cairo, 2004):174. Goelet adds: "Historically, the delegation of fiscal responsibility to the richest local residents has been normal in Egypt. ... as holders of liturgies in the Ptolemaic period, or as village headmen (*shaykh/umda*) in later periods. They were personally responsible for the flow of revenues to the 'lords of the land.'"

[4] This is the reverse of Locke's attempt to justify land ownership by the labor that landlords put into the land by clearing and improving it.

[5] Goelet cites the corollary observation from Eyre about land-holding in Egypt: there always seems to have been enough land available for cultivation, but "[l]and was valueless without people." "Village Economy in Pharaonic Egypt," in A. K. Bowman and

largely of carrying baskets of earth and transporting building materials during the non-planting season.

Seth Richardson cites Babylonian efforts to promote "public joy" for participants in corvée activities by "invest[ing] such occasions with an atmosphere of feasting and plenty." That made these tasks "something closer to a prebend, an opportunity, a festival" with the benefit of group membership and identity. Indeed, he asks:

> Would it even be *possible* to create a corps of 'forced,' 'unfree' or 'semi-free' laborers to toil under adverse conditions – for no more than one week a year? Would workers who had toiled for 150 days of the year in the dirt and mud to grow barley for state and bare survival choose to resent a few days of collective labor, in the company of neighbors and with the prospect of feasting and song? Should we really imagine teams of tens of thousands groaning under the weight of massive building blocks under the stern eyes of whip-wielding overseers, when the average work-account text deals with teams of workers numbering fewer than two hundred?

Most corvée labor was seasonal so as not to interfere with the crop cycle. Richardson estimates that institutional building work in Babylonia "only comes to something like 4% of the farming work" needed for families to produce their own sustenance – "not more than a week of work compared to six months of farming." In Egypt, the workers' town housing the specialized labor force that "worked hard on the pyramids (such as moving megaliths)" was, in Mark Lehner's description, "a rather elite place of high-status royal service and possibly higher-quality recompense than recruits might have known in their home districts."

In contrast to what Richardson characterizes as "our very modern assumption that labor is a social and economic disutility," what was being built was not just monuments and palaces but communal identity, a ceremonial expression of creativity akin to Veblen's Instinct of Workmanship, along with great feasts and drinking parties when projects were completed (and probably in between). Lehner describes an Egyptian causeway scene showing "the completion of the king's pyramid by the dragging and setting of the capstone (*pyramidion*) with a celebration of feasting, singing, and dancing" by the work crews, "perhaps a special feast out of the many regular feasts that we know so well from tomb and temple texts ... We see racks of hanging meat, to be shared and consumed for the occasion." Such feasts must have been a major source

---

E. Rogan, eds., *Agriculture in Egypt from Pharaonic to Modern Times* (Proceedings of the British Academy 96; Oxford, 1999):46.

of meat for many Bronze Age corvée attendees, not to mention the vast amounts of beer provided.

Public feasts continued in classical antiquity. In Homer's *Odyssey*, "Alcinous has the Phaeacians build a ship for Odysseus and promises a public feast and rations for the sailors, offering to reimburse the other lords for gifts to him through a levy on the demos. ... the treasurers (*tamiai*) of the temple of Athena, who managed sacred revenue, and the so-called 'ham-collectors' (*kolakretai*), [referring] to their original function apportioning shares at public feasts, who perhaps by the time of Solon also collected city revenue and paid out money, for example, to travelling envoys."[6]

Ambitious Sumerian empire builders retained the loyalty of leading towns by granting exemption from the *bala* in-kind tax, and the well-to-do hired stand-ins to perform their corvée duties. But Steinkeller sees a political byproduct of bringing labor from distant provinces by the Ur III period (ca. 2112-2004 BC): "National building projects were an extremely important tool of political and cultural integration," a "nation-building" effort instilling an idea of proto-national solidarity as workers came to think of themselves as "fellow members of a united Babylonia."

Local abuses of labor

Palaces remained dependent on local officials or contractors to supply labor, resulting in a political tug of war as local authorities sought to divert labor for their own purposes. Assyriologists have found a reliance of Ur III and Babylonian rulers on local clan heads or *lu-gal* "big-men" acting as contractors to supply labor and military support, especially in Mesopotamia's Intermediate Periods. Sometimes in history a central authority deters such power grabbing, as in England's Star Chamber in the 16th and 17th centuries that dealt with complaints against aggressive local nobility. But the Bronze Age Intermediate Periods saw central power wane vis-à-vis that of local clan heads, chieftains and "big-men."

Describing Egypt's First Intermediate Period, Goelet finds that "the power of the local elites apparently outweighed that of the monarch. The end result was that the status of mrt-[corvée] laborers and other lower class individuals generally had declined from being serfs bound to the land to becoming purchasable chattel." The Horemheb and Nauri

---

[6] Andrew Monson, review of Hans van Wees, *Ships and Silver Taxes and Tribute: A Fiscal History of Archaic Athens* (2013), *Bryn Mawr Classical Review*, August 2014 #42.

decrees show that: "Those who were 'corvéable' ... might be subject to the arbitrary control of some powerful local official acting on his own interests without state sanction. This was by no means a minor problem since the unauthorized removal of personnel appears as a central concern for the institutions to which they were attached ..."[7]

Enmetena, Urukagina, Ur-Nammu, Shulgi, the rulers of Hammurabi's Babylonian dynasty, Hurrian and Amorite rulers proclaimed debt moratoriums to assert palace claims on labor over local creditors seeking to hold labor in bondage. Such bondage threatened to prevent labor serving in the army or being called up for corvée labor. Rulers restored fiscal priority by annulling agrarian "barley" debts, liberating bondservants to return to their families, and returning land and crop rights to debtors who had pledged them to creditors. Such royal proclamations provided the model for the Biblical Jubilee Year of Leviticus 25, as our 2002 volume on *Debt and Economic Renewal in the Ancient Near East* has documented. The effect was to re-start a ruler's reign with the economy in financial balance. (Commercial "silver" debts were exempt from such proclamations.)

No interest-bearing debt is found in the Linear B records, but a similar tension existed between the palace and local authorities. Tom Palaima distinguishes Mycenaean palace administrators from "collectors" or "mobilizers" acting as entrepreneurial contractors. He suggests that mobilization of labor in the outlying areas relied on pre-existing systems headed by "local big men ($g^w asilēwes$) or sib groups, clans and elders (*gerontes* and *geronsiai*)."

After Mycenaean palace control ended ca. 1200 BC, administrative power reverted to local heads. As our 1996 volume on *Privatization in the Ancient Near East and Classical Antiquity* has described, *basilai* managers disappear from palace records with the ending of Linear B documentation in 1200, and reappear around the 8th century BC as "kings" independent of central authority. In this sense one can view classical antiquity as a long "intermediate period" of lapsed central control until Roman times.

---

[7] Goelet elaborates: "In the Horemheb Decree, those people most directly affected by the abuses appear to have been the independent individuals typical of rural life such as fishermen, herdsmen, or the agricultural workers called nḥmw, who might be comparable to our notion of freemen. ... All such edicts aimed to shelter people who were deemed to be working on the king's behalf, especially if they were on institutional lands. ... it seems that the peasantry was often vulnerable to compulsion or even long-term subjugation by powerful individuals. This is hardly surprising, yet these edicts show that occasionally this vulnerability extended even to the wealthier stratum, including the administrative class, in the countryside."

From the corvée to commodity-producing enterprise

The third millennium saw large-scale commodity production employ dependent manual labor, and also specialized skilled labor. The driving force was southern Mesopotamia's need to trade to obtain metals and stone not found in local soils. This challenge was met by organizing workshops to produce exports, mainly by dependent and proto-wage labor overseen by a temple or palace managerial class of scribe accountants, foremen and chief administrators. Egyptian sources suggest that scribes were not from elite families. Their profession was independent from property owning. But their planning, writing and accounting functions helped support authority and economic control. Organizing labor in temple and palace workshops was innovated by officials and merchants whose fortunes emerged in a symbiotic relationship with these institutions. A merchant class was required to organize and conduct this Mesopotamian trade. Also required were credit formalities to reimburse the large institutions for their consignment of goods.

Textiles were Mesopotamia's major export,[8] and the employment of non-slave labor is best typified by the widows and war orphans assigned to weaving and making other handicrafts in the temple and palace workshops. In contrast to the public infrastructure created by corvée labor, commodity production for trade aimed at gaining a monetary surplus by what today's economists call profit centers.

Half a century ago Maurice Lambert described how the Sumerian bureaucracy squeezed out an economic surplus from the widows and orphans taken out of the family-based context on the land to weave textiles in temple workshops, remunerated at a set rate, making products for sale to import silver, tin and gold.[9] During Lagash's war with Umma under Lugalanda, the city-state's nubanda administrator Eniggal re-

---

[8] These were woven mainly by poorly paid female labor – full-time dependents ("widows and orphans") and also part-time labor employed by the large institutions. No doubt the latter normally were dependent on their husbands. One finds even today low-wage female labor producing exports in Korea, where their husbands earn enough working in the domestic economy to subsidize such export production. For a discussion of Ur III textile production see H. Waetzoldt, "Compensation of Craft Workers and Officials in the Ur III Period," in M. A. Powell, *Labor in the Ancient Near East* (New Haven, 1987):117-142, and Rita Wright, *Gender and Archaeology* (University of Pennsylvania, 1996). Women also were employed in corvée construction work.

[9] Maurice Lambert, "La naissance de la bureaucratie," *Revue Historique* 224 (1960):1-26, and "Le premier triomphe de la bureaucratie," *Revue Historique* 225 (1961):21-46.

structured the accounting system to minimize rations.[10] The dependent work force (which included enslaved mountain girls) had little alternative but to submit, being dependent on the administration to provide food and shelter.[11]

Corvée labor was treated much better. Steinkeller points out that Ur III "building narratives emphasize the fact that among the workers employed on such projects 'no one received a higher or a lower wage,' an indication of the remarkable – and quite unusual – degree of equality that existed among the participants of these undertakings." Wages for major building projects "were very generous, since, apart from a monthly salary of between 30 and 60 liters of barley, they included a daily food allowance, consisting of 2 liters of bread, 2 liters of beer, and 2 shekels of fat," and often dates, cheese and sesame bran. By the Neo-Babylonian period (7th-6th centuries BC), Michael Jursa reports: "While there were differences in the size of rations owing to age, there were few and far less pronounced distinctions on the basis of profession and rank." Apprentices received 60 liters of barley a month, unskilled labor 90 liters and trained workers 180. Remuneration for skilled labor was negotiable.

The standard adult male wage of 2 sila per day seems to have remained remarkably stable over the millennia.[12] This stability reflects the fact that there was no labor "market" fluctuating in response to shifts in supply and demand, and no natural tendency for wages to reflect rising productivity or profit rates.

---

[10] Lambert, "Recherches sur la vie ouvriers," *Archiv Orientlni* 29 (1961):427-438.

[11] Lambert, "La Guerre entre Urukagina et Lugalzaggesi," *Rivista degli Studi Orientali* 41 (1966):34-36.

[12] This was the equivalent of 1.6 to 2 liters of barley rations. Summarizing the points he outlined in "Zur Rolle von Preisen und Löhnen im Wirtschaftssystem des alten Mesopotamien an der Wende vom 3. zum 2. Jahrtausend v. Chr. - Grundsätzliche Fragen und Überlegungen," *Altorientalische Forschungen* 16 (1989):234-252, Johannes Renger's paper at the colloquium (not included in this volume) notes: "Over centuries the amount of the barley rations did not change. According to the Persepolis documents (4th cent. B.C.) the daily ration was still ca. 2 sila. Even in the Mediterranean in the 16. cent. A.D. the annual provision for an able bodied worker was the same as in Mesopotamia in the 3rd and 2nd millennium." See also W. Scheidel, "Real Wages in Early Economies: Evidence for Living Standards from 1800 BCE to 1300 CE," *Journal of The Economic and Social History of The Orient* 53 (2010):425-462. The exception to normalcy occurred in emergencies, such as when Lagash was attacked by Umma.

Skilled and specialized craft labor was centered in temple and palace workshops, but individuals also worked "off the books,"[13] evidently on a piecework basis for whomever could pay for their services. It seems that wives and daughters from the free community earned money working by weaving or making other handicrafts in addition to their household work on the land. Jursa's paper shows that private for-hire contracts became widespread by the Neo-Babylonian period.

Managerial innovation in organizing and provisioning labor

More complex and productive technology required managerial innovation, starting with account-keeping. Babylonian training exercises called for calculating the labor time and hence food needs (easily converted into silver-value) for corvée labor to make bricks and build walls, move earth and dig canals. From prehistoric Uruk to Ur III Babylonia we find a labor-time/dietary basis for economic planning by accountants calculating monthly food needs per worker, categorized by male, female, older and younger children. Weights and measures, money and salaries had to be standardized, along with prices, to schedule the flow of food and raw materials. Only large complex institutions could have created these measures needed for market exchange to develop.

All this required cost accounting to regularize the distribution of food and raw materials. An administrative managerial calendar with equal 30-day months enabled grain disbursements to be convertible into bread equivalents, and into silver at standard ratios for accounting purposes, valued in terms of common monetary denominators. These calculations were a prototype of modern input-output tables.

So in addition to (1) writing, the resulting account-keeping system involved (2) standardization of measures and weights to supply labor with food and raw materials, (3) cylinder seals to establish administrative responsibility for receipt of goods and their storage, and (4) a schedule of administered prices to monetize payments to the palace and

---

[13] But not altogether out of the cuneiform record. In his paper to the colloquium (not included in this volume), Johannes Renger points out that *naditu* are documented as hiring workers to tend their fields, citing M. Weitemeyer, *Some Aspects of the Hiring of Workers in the Sippar Region at the Time of Hammurabi* (1962) and other studies. Regarding such informal labor, Goelet observes: "Once a member of the crew, that state (or royal) affiliation does not seem to have prevented the village's craftsmen from occasional work on their own behalf, even leading to an 'informal workshop' for which they could produce funerary goods for other private individuals, separately from their regular activities on behalf of the state."

its collectors. Silver acted as the main monetary measure, against which barley, copper and other basic commodities were valued in a grid with fixed price ratios for payments to and within Mesopotamian temples and palaces.

As Chapters 3 and 4 have described, these flows of food and materials required (5) a standardized administrative calendar of equal 30-day months to replace the lunar months of variable length. The sexagesimal (60-based) system of fractions provided the basis for denominating (6) calendrical weights and measures, and an easily calculated rate of interest ($1/60^{th}$, a shekel per mina per month) on advances to merchants and entrepreneurs.

Unfree labor that lost its liberty and self-support land

Goelet states a principle for Egypt that applies from Mesopotamia to Rome: "One way or another, from the pharaoh or from the inter-related nobility that controlled Egypt's land, the entire working class of Egyptian society – effectively 95% of the population – was effectively unfree and bound to the orders of some superior from childhood right through old age." But some labor was more unfree than others.

Slavery was not an important source of public labor in Egypt in the New Kingdom, except for war prisoners consigned to near-death work in the mines. Male slavery was relatively secondary, and often took the form of debt bondage that likely was subject to pharaonic amnesties, as in Mesopotamia. Most bondservants and slaves in both regions were female house servants – the daughters and slave girls pledged to work as year-round household servants for creditors, with sexual overtones.

Earlier volumes have pointed to debt bondage as a path of least resistance to obtain labor services. But at least Near Eastern bondservants were liberated by royal Clean Slates enabling them to return to their families of origin. These amnesties ended by classical antiquity. And the condition of slaves worsened as their role shifted from that of family members (the Latin word *familia* means "slave," a normal member of households) to being put to work in large-scale agricultural and handicraft production. In Athens slaves were foreign, and public labor was drudgery performed mainly by non-citizen metics. Dispossessed Roman citizens became mercenaries, fighting to extend the empire that had expropriated them for debt.

Handicraft production in classical antiquity was manned increasingly by servile labor. "The very wages the laborer receives are a badge of slavery," wrote Cicero.[14] By imperial Roman times a quarter of the population was reduced to debt bondage or slavery, ending up being housed in barracks on landed estates as economic life de-urbanized.

Unlike the takeoff of modern capitalism, labor was not forced off the land to seek a livelihood as landless wage earners. But flight from the community occurred in times of economic hardship or oppression, natural disasters, crop failure, drought or flooding. Fugitives from the land after 1600 BC in Babylonia joined bands as migrant workers or outlaws.[15] The word *hapiru* has been used to refer to such outcasts. Rome described its own origin as a place of refuge for such runaways and migrants – as was North America in more modern times.

Summary

To trace how the changing organization of labor shaped economies, fiscal policy and property rights over time, this summary colloquium in our five-part series has focused on eight major themes:

Theme #1: Steinkeller emphasizes that instead of a "reserve army of the unemployed" driven off the land, labor was in short supply throughout the Bronze Age. One consequence was that corvée labor service had to be organized with widespread assent. Organizing work to build basic infrastructure could not have been too coercive, because its participants might have run away. Lehner's report of large volumes of remains of slaughtered animals indicating great feasts for Egypt's pyramid builders seems to reflect long-standing practice throughout the ancient Near East to make such work acceptable.

Theme #2: Being organized communally for public construction projects in the first instance, the "output" of corvée labor was not marketable and had no exchange value. The work produced social value, creating ceremonial buildings, city walls, irrigation systems and roads as "social capital." Hence, modern supply and demand curves for labor and remuneration rates based on the market value of its output are not relevant.

Third-millennium temple and palace records show manual labor paid at standardized rates, ranked by sex and age (and in time by occupation). The basis for most salaries was what adult men, women and

---

[14] Cicero, *De Officiis* I:150f-151. "To work for a private employer was regarded as 'slavery,'" writes Sarah C. Humphreys, *Anthropology and the Greeks* (London, 1978):147.

[15] See Johannes Renger, "Flucht als soziales Problem," in D. O. Edzard, ed., *Gesellschaftsklassen im Alten Zweistromland und in den angrenzenden Gebieten* – XVIII. Rencontre assyriologique internationale, München, 29. Juni bis 3. Juli 1970 (1972):167-182.

children needed for basic sustenance. Schoolbook exercises calculated the food needed per worker, denominated in grain or bread equivalents directly convertible into standard weight units of silver money. By Neo-Babylonian times such wages were paid in silver.

Theme #3: Skilled craft labor was employed mainly by the large institutions. Craftsmen were only a small part of the labor force, but required a broad range of supporting activities to supply raw materials, schedule their delivery and provide tools. Being of large scale, this required management, oversight, account-keeping and credit, and therefore was centered in the temples and palaces (and on large estates whose owners usually were associated with the temples or the royal family).

Theme #4: Mesopotamian institutions and households obtained wealth largely by foreign trade, producing handicrafts and consigning them to merchants in a symbiotic relationship with the temple or royal bureaucracies. These merchants played a catalytic role in entrepreneurial trade. As temple and palace activities were increasingly privatized in the hands of merchants and lessors of land or public enterprises, the resulting mixed economies had what today would be called a conflict between public and private interests.

Theme #5: Labor-for-hire started as a marginal phenomenon. Well-to-do citizens could hire surrogates to perform their corvée duty – typically younger brothers or other relatives. Unlike manual labor for construction, handicraft work outside the large institutions typically was remunerated on a piecework basis. Weavers worked at home, much like those in England before power looms were introduced.[16] Piecework labor by skilled craftsmen became more frequent by Neo-Babylonian times, as did seasonal harvesting labor.

Theme #6: Agrarian and personal usury became a major means to obtain labor services through debt bondage, and in time to pry away land rights. Local "big men," *tamkarum* merchants and palace collectors sought control of labor at the expense of the palace's fiscal authority that sought to maintain land tenure rights/obligations as a means of assigning responsibility for providing corvée labor and service in the army.

Theme #7: Mesopotamia's large institutions were creditors not debtors. Most personal and agrarian debts took the form of obligations to these

---

[16] Renger, "Zur Rolle ...": 234-235 cites the Law-book of Daduša from Ešnunna §14 stipulating wages paid based on the weight of a garment to be finished by bleaching or washing.

institutions for advances of agricultural inputs or consumer goods. Collectors in the royal bureaucracy charged usury on arrears for these advances. Such debts increased sharply in times of drought, flooding and military hostilities. Falling into debt became the major dynamic leading to economic inequality as citizens lost their personal liberty and land tenure rights. Enforcing debt claims led to creditor foreclosure on the liberty of debtors, and ultimately their land rights.

Theme #8: The way in which debt problems were resolved became the major factor determining the status of labor.

Rulers restored fiscal stability, corvée labor and military service – as well as the personal liberty of debtors – by proclaiming royal Clean Slates that rescued debtors from bondage by clearing away the personal debts, bond servitude and land forfeitures that had occurred since the last such edict.

But by the 8th century BC, Near Eastern commercial practices were brought westward to Mediterranean lands that lacked the traditions of entrepreneurial temples and royal Clean Slate edicts. The replacement of kingship and Clean Slates by oligarchies distinguishes classical Greek and Roman economies from those of the earlier Near East. Populations became more debt-ridden, and debt bondage became a major means of obtaining dependent labor and ultimately monopolizing the land, driving the citizenry into clientage and bondage by the time of the Roman Empire.

Landholders and creditors at the top of the Late Roman Empire's economic pyramid managed to avoid tax obligations, creating a fiscal and monetary breakdown. Demographic and commercial shrinkage ensued as the domestic market was impoverished. The modern world has likewise dissociated landholding rights and wealth from their former social responsibilities. Land has been "freed" from the fiscal obligations originally attached to it. Land has ceased to be a public utility and has become an investment vehicle, increasing labor's cost of shelter and the mortgage debt typically attached to it.

Housing and land tenure ("a home of one's own") no longer is a right or indeed criterion for citizenship. Its financialization and increasing concentration of ownership has shifted the fiscal burden increasingly onto labor, obliging wage-earners to pay payroll tax withholding and regressive income and sales taxes, along with other wage set-asides for health care and retirement, while facing rising indebtedness to cover the cost of their basic needs. As occurred in late antiquity, this is polarizing society economically and financially by forcing labor into deepening dependency, with no periodic restoration of financial and economic balance and equity.

7

Land Tenure:
From Fiscal Origins to Financialization*

Summary

The earliest attested land tenure evolved in Mesopotamia and Egypt as part of the palatial levy of corvée labor and military service. Self-support land was allotted to citizens in exchange for these duties. However, the long historical trend has seen the net yield or rental value of land shift away from the community or palatial economy to creditors. Nominal landholders typically have served as intermediaries to pay the rental value initially to the tax collector and increasingly to mortgage lenders.

Early economies needed credit to bridge the gap between planting and harvesting. Debts incurred during the agricultural season were paid on the threshing floor at harvest time. Fiscal problems arose as this credit passed into the hands of individuals acting on their own account. Debtors were obliged to pay interest in the form of crops or their personal labor (debt bondage) to their creditors at the expense of palatial claims on their public service. By the second millennium BC, Babylonian debtors began to pledge their land to creditors.

For many centuries royal edicts kept such labor obligations and land transfers to creditors from disrupting traditional fiscal arrangements more than temporarily. New rulers restored the *status quo ante* when taking the throne, and when circumstances called for such Clean Slates. These acts prevented an independent oligarchy from emerging in the early Near East. But an inherent tension existed between the palace rulers and private creditors seeking to become large landowners. In classical Greece and Rome, which lacked the Near Eastern tradition of

---

* This chapter and Chapter 8 have their origins in "Land Monopolization, Fiscal Crises and Clean Slate 'Jubilee' Proclamations in Antiquity," in Robert C. Hunt and Antonio Gilman, eds., *Property in Economic Context*, University Press of America, Monographs in Economic Anthropology 14 (1998):139-169. I have restored the Byzantine discussion, which the publisher asked to be cut in order to meet the volume's page limit. In the process, I have taken the liberty to edit and improve the language.

strong palatial authority, debt bondage became much harsher than was the case in the Near East, and an independent creditor oligarchy quickly emerged. Land transfers to large estate holders and the subjugation of labor became irreversible in this Aegean and Mediterranean periphery. The result was an increasing polarization between large absentee landholders and smallholders.

The financialization of land tenure has intensified down to today's world, hand in hand with its democratization since the late 19th century. Nearly two-thirds of the U.S. population own their homes, as do 85 percent of Scandinavians. But taking on mortgage debt is a precondition for most homebuyers, and commercial real estate is even more highly debt-leveraged. The inflation of real estate prices on credit has enabled the financial sector to pry most of the land's economic rent away from the tax collector and also from private owners.

Since classical antiquity the "security of property ownership" has been subordinate to creditors holding mortgage claims. The nominal landholder's legal rights are less secure than those of creditors. This shift reflects a long-standing political maneuvering between creditors and public authorities over who will end up with the land's rental value. The fight peaked in the 19th century when classical economists sought to recapture land rent for the nation by taxing it or outright nationalization of the land and other rent-yielding resources.

The two broad approaches to the origins of land tenure

Like the historiography of money's origins, there are two approaches to the origins of land tenure. Just as the individualistic approach imagines money to be a product of individuals bartering, it depicts property rights as being created primordially by individuals acting by themselves to clear land with their own labor. Such theorizing is a product of writers whose ideology opposes active government regulation and ownership. By contrast, the historically grounded approach by archaeologists, Assyriologists and Egyptologists finds the origin of money in the palatial economy, and land tenure to have taken form in the Late Neolithic or Early Bronze Age by communities assigning self-support land rights to families in proportion to their ability to provide corvée labor and serve in the military, as Chapter 6 has described. (For a general review see Hudson 2019 and 2004, Hudson and Levine 1996 and 1999, and Steinkeller and Hudson 2015.)

The individualistic approach appears in Rome, and is associated with personal greed ending a utopian Eden. As Seneca (4 BC-AD 65) wrote

(*Epistula* 90.34, cited in Lovejoy and Boas 1935:272-273): "There was once a fortune-favored period when the boundaries of nature lay open to all, for men's indiscriminate use, before avarice and luxury had broken the bonds that held mortals together." Virgil (70-19 BC) expressed this typical view in his *Georgics* (I.125-128):

> No ploughman tilled the soil, nor was it right,
> To portion off the boundaries of property.
> Men shared their gain, and earth more freely gave
> Her riches to her sons who sought them not.

But Rome's landlord class was predatory, and its landlordship was blamed on greed. As Pliny (AD 23-79) complained: "The latifundia have ruined Italy."

John Locke viewed land tenure as personally carved out, but found this perfectly justified. His guiding axiom was that all men have a natural right to the fruits of their labor and he viewed land as a product of this labor, not as a site provided by nature. No labor duties were acknowledged by Locke as being owed to the community or state, and in fact he makes no reference to the land's rental value, only a right to its yield.

> Though the earth and all inferior creatures be common to all men, yet every man has a property in his own person ... The labour of his body and the work of his hands, we may say, are properly his. Whatsoever then he removes out of the state that nature hath provided and left it in, he hath mixed his labour with, and joined to it something that is his own, and thereby makes it his property. ... For this labour being the unquestionable property of the laborer, no man but he can have a right to what that is once joined to, at least where there is enough and as good left in common for others. (Locke [1689] 1947:134)

Locke wrote as if most rent derived from the landlords' own labor, not that of their tenants or the economy at large – and as if the landholder did not owe any labor to the community's governing body as a condition of his land rights. Absentee landownership does not appear in Locke's view, although an implicit corollary is that landlords have a right only to what they themselves produce, not to exploit and appropriate the labor of their tenants (or for that matter, what the community provides in support services). Locke did not acknowledge the reality of how military conquerors imposed rents on the indigenous landholders, nor how illicit land grabbers, foreclosing creditors and their heirs down through the generations imposed groundrent to free themselves from having to provide productive labor.

Since the 19th century the rising price of land sites has occurred independently of effort by landlords. The rent they charge reflects the economy's prosperity and the value of public infrastructure investment increasing the rent-of-location, along with the land's economic rent being paid out as interest, capped by debt-driven asset-price inflation. These matters play no role in the Roman or Lockean view of the origins of land tenure.

Fiscal origins of land tenure

Early Mesopotamian languages had no word for "property." As part of a person's basic needs, land was viewed as an extension of its holder. "Although the term LUGAL (in Sumerian) and *bēlum* (in Akkadian) are habitually translated as proprietor, one does not find in the Sumerian and Akkadian vocabulary a term which designates 'property' in the abstract sense of law of property" (Szlechter 1958:121; see also Cardascia 1959).

All landholders – and the population in general – were subordinate to a higher authority, headed by the palace ruler or pharaoh and their temples. These authorities allocated land tenure as part of an overall archaic fiscal system requiring citizens to provide the labor for large public projects and service in the military. To support the citizens subject to these duties, Mesopotamian and Egyptian land was divided into standardized lots and distributed to these citizens. (The word "lot" derives from chance, as in drawing lots for sites calculated to produce a standardized crop yield under normal conditions.)

In contrast to Locke's view of labor creating land as an asset, land rights created labor obligations to the community, leading land tenure to be defined in fiscal terms. Land rights were linked to the holder's obligation to supply corvée labor to the palatial authority and serve in the army. "The man responsible for the tax was the 'owner' as far as the state was concerned" (Eyre 2004:174, discussed in Hudson 2015:651-653).

Land tenure and its fiscal labor obligations, debt and monetary means of payment developed together in a symbiosis. Commercial "silver" loans financed foreign trade ventures. The agricultural cycle required credit for advances of seed and other agricultural inputs, as well as personal credit such as running up tabs at Babylonian ale houses ca. 1800-1600 BC. These agrarian debts were typically denominated in barley and were due at harvest time.

Money emerged as a means of paying these agrarian and commercial debts, above all to the palaces and temples. Silver and grain formed a bimonetary standard, with a gur "quart" of grain equivalent to a shekel of silver for denominating such debt payments.

Interest charges became the easiest way for creditors to obtain labor before a labor-for-hire market developed. Creditors extended loans in exchange for work (antichretic payment of interest), and ultimately obtained the debtor's land rights. That enabled creditors and large landholders to grow powerful enough to avoid their fiscal obligations by the second millennium BC, especially in Mesopotamia's and Egypt's Intermediate Periods when central power waned relative to that of local chieftains and "big men."

Exemption from agrarian obligations in cases of drought or flooding

The ability to repay agricultural credit was subject to the disruptions of weather, military fighting and disease. A flood or drought prevented the expected crop yield and hence personal debts from being met. Rulers were pragmatic enough to recognize that debts (even to their palace) could not be paid without driving debtors to borrow from private creditors and hence owing their labor to them instead of to the palace. The laws of Hammurabi (§48, ca. 1750 BC) specified that agrarian debts would not have to be paid in times of flood or drought – an archaic example of "acts of god" (in this case the storm god Adad) freeing rural debtors from liability. And rulers regularly proclaimed Cleans Slates upon taking the throne, and when faced with military conflict. Near Eastern monarchies in the first millennium BC still recognized that it would be self-defeating to permit much of the population to fall into bondage to enrich an independent oligarchy.

Self-support land tenure

The self-support land of smallholders was protected from permanent alienation so as to preserve an agrarian population owing military service and corvée labor to the palace. Land tenure preserved the continuity of families on the land of their forefathers by giving hereditary preference to clan members as part of common law. Creditors sought to use this patriarchal practice to circumvent restrictions on the sale or forfeiture of land to outsiders by the ploy of having debtors adopt them as sons. (Stone 1987 and Stone and Owen 1991 provide many examples.) The creditor-"son" would take the land into the creditor's own family and might well be older than the debtor-"father."

Land tenure for large institutions (temples and palaces) and the military

From the earliest records down through the modern world, land owned by temples and other public institutions was set aside in the form of perpetual holdings subject to their own rules of taxation. Temple land provided food, wool and other materials to supply dependents who could not work in agriculture because of being widowed or orphaned, or because of illness, blindness, birth defects or other infirmities. Many were employed in workshops to produce textiles and other handicrafts (or beer) to be sold.

Endowing temples with land, herds of animals and other assets enabled them to be self-supporting. That was the archaic alternative to taxation. Most of this land was let out on a sharecropping basis, usually via palace managers as middlemen, the rental rate settling at a third of the crop by the end of the third millennium. Whereas private land transfers were limited in duration, sales to the large institutions were permanent, and temple land and that of the palace could not be alienated. That made the temples and palace holders of such land the first documented irreversible absentee landholders collecting a regular rent-usufruct.

Rulers purchased lands from the communal groupings (as documented for instance on the Stele of Manishtushu in the Akkadian period ca. 2250 BC). Hammurabi turned hitherto clan-tenured land into inalienable royal property and leased it to soldiers, commissaries and feudatories subject to *biltum* and *ilkum* "taxes" for labor and military service or crop rents (Charpin 2003:117 and Roth 1997:85-86). This land could not be sold or alienated for debt, as Hammurabi's laws (§37) invalidated any sale of rural fields, orchards or houses belonging to soldiers, and §38 prevented them from being pledged as collateral (see also §48 and §§43-44.). (Similar prohibitions on the alienability of cropland held by the military and smallholders were imposed as late as the Byzantine period in the 9th and 10th centuries AD, discussed below.)

In sum, Bronze Age tenure for cropland had too many public obligations attached to it to be deemed "private" in the modern sense of being able to be freely sold or otherwise alienated without future recovery rights. What is called the "free market" for land tenure is essentially the "right" (actually, the liability) of its owners to pledge and permanently forfeit land to creditors or sell it under duress to whomever they choose. Near Eastern rulers made such alienation reversible by royal proclamation in order to maintain a self-supporting citizen-army owing corvée labor. Modern "free alienability" of subsistence land would have to await Roman and subsequent law.

Freely alienable real estate

Merchants and other well-to-do citizens were able to freely buy or sell townhouses, including individual floors or rooms. These properties were not part of the subsistence sector, so there was no pressing need for rulers to redistribute them when they "proclaimed order." Ownership of such property was left intact, as were commercial silver-debts for mercantile activities.

The guiding logic was evidently that while merchants and other well-to-do might be obliged to sell or forfeit their townhouses, they still would have self-support land to provide for their basic needs as citizens. Only subsistence lands were protected from permanent alienation, so as to preserve a self-supporting rural population.

Clean Slates restore the status quo ante of land tenure

For thousands of years Near Eastern realms from Babylonia to the Levant (as in Judaism's Jubilee Year) recognized that for society to survive, it needed to help its indebted citizens recover their financial solvency. Without mutual aid, low-surplus economies suffered a flight of the population or civil warfare. To prevent this, rulers forgave personal debts.

There is no record of archaic ideological claims that economic growth would be maximized by letting individuals use their wealth to obtain the labor of debtors and monopolize the land for their own gain. There was general recognition that early economies could not afford to lose the corvée labor and military service of their citizens to creditors who used loans to obtain this labor. However, a proto-oligarchic class began to emerge, whose self-interest was to abolish the power of rulers to protect debtors from losing their liberty and finally their land as personal and agrarian debts mounted up faster than the ability to be paid. Defaults and foreclosures led to the concentration of land and wealth ownership in the hands of an oligarchy making itself into a hereditary aristocracy. That became the economic dynamic of classical antiquity.

Near Eastern rulers avoided this dynamic by asserting their authority and annulling agrarian "barley" debts, liberating bondservants to return to their families, and returning the land's crop rights to debtors who had pledged them as collateral. Self-support land could be alienated only until the next *misharum* proclamation. Hammurabi's laws insisted on the proper dating of contracts so that they could be rendered void in years when a *misharum* permitted debtors to reclaim their land.

Only thousands of years after the Near Eastern economic and commercial takeoff did Greek and Italian oligarchies break "free" of the

Clean Slates that cancelled debts and preserved land tenure for smallholders. For debtors in classical antiquity, a free market in land meant loss of their own self-support and liberty.

Classical Greek revolutions organize formal land tenure

There are no economic records from the Greek Dark Age (1200-750 BC). That is what makes this period "dark" to modern eyes. It seems to have been a period of warlord chieftains monopolizing the land and reducing much of the population to clientage. Throughout Greece these autocracies were overthrown by "tyrants" and other social reformers in the 7th and 6th centuries BC, from the Corinthian Isthmus region down to Sparta with its radical "Lycurgan" reforms, capped by Solon's reforms in Athens.

All these city-states reinvented their own land tenure arrangements on an *ad hoc* basis. The new, less anarchic systems allotted land to soldiers (the demos). This was easiest to achieve on land that was conquered or where new colonies could be established. But in due course the oligarchies that emerged grabbed the conquered public land and that of smallholders increasingly for themselves, especially in Italy.

According to legend, these 7th and 6th-century revolts featured a combination of land redistribution and cancellation of the debts that obliged subjects to work the land of their creditors. Sparta's 7th-century reforms were the most radical. The local oligarchy retained its land monopoly in Sparta itself, but assigned the lands it conquered and their populations to serve as helots producing food for the rest of the citizenry (*homoioi*, "equals"), equal in their holdings of these conquered territories only.

In Corinth, the Cypselid family reorganized the city to make it a commercial center and put in place a self-supporting population by land redistribution and apparently debt cancellation. Athens experienced a series of crises that peaked in 594 when Solon was appointed archon ("dictator") to cope with the same problems of land monopolization and debt slavery that had brought tyrant-reformers to power in other cities.

Solon cancelled personal debts and banned outright debt slavery. He was widely expected to redistribute the land as reformers had done in other cities, but he only removed the *horoi* stones demarcating absentee land ownership. (Debtors still owed labor services, but remained free citizens, not slaves.) He also banned landownership by foreigners, thereby preventing foreign creditors from foreclosing on Athenian land.

However, creditors in Greece and Rome were strong enough to prevent debt cancellations and land redistribution after the 6th century

BC. The size of one's landholding determined one's ranking for public office and the military, but the wealthiest families avoided fiscal obligations and defeated attempts by popular leaders to cancel debts and redistribute the land. Sparta's kings Agis IV and Cleomenes III sought to do this in the late 3rd century BC, but were defeated by neighboring oligarchies, which called on Rome to defeat Sparta. Within half a century, Rome would conquer, devastate and loot all of Greece, finishing off the devastation in the Mithridatic Wars (88-63 BC).

A distinguishing feature of classical antiquity was its increasingly oligarchic character, blocking central authority to limit land appropriation and creditor claims by the most powerful families. This "individualistic" (in practice, oligarchic) breakaway is, in my view, the essence of Western civilization.

The Roman oligarchy's fight to avoid tax liability and restrictions on land size

Roman land tenure was based increasingly on the appropriation of conquered territory, which was declared public land, the *ager publicus populi*. The normal practice was to settle war veterans on it, but the wealthiest and most aggressive families grabbed such land for themselves in violation of early law.

The die was cast in 486 BC. After Rome defeated the neighboring Hernici, a Latin tribe, and took two-thirds of their land, the consul Spurius Cassius proposed Rome's first agrarian law. It called for giving half the conquered territory back to the Latins and half to needy Romans, who were also to receive public land that patricians had occupied (Dionysius of Halicarnassus, *Roman Antiquities* 8.77.2). But the patricians accused Cassius of "building up a power dangerous to liberty" by seeking popular support and "endangering the security" of their land appropriation. After his annual term was over he was charged with treason and killed. His house was burned to the ground to eradicate memory of his land proposal (Livy, *History of Rome* 2.41).

The fight over whether patricians or the needy poor would be the main recipients of public land dragged on for twelve years. In 474 the commoners' tribune, Gnaeus Genucius, sought to bring the previous year's consuls to trial for delaying the redistribution proposed by Cassius (Livy 2.54 and Dionysius 9.37-38). He was blocked by that year's two consuls, Lucius Furius and Gaius Manlius, who said that decrees of the Senate were not permanent law, "but measures designed to meet temporary needs and having validity for one year only." The Senate could renege on any decree that had been passed.

A century later, in 384, M. Manlius Capitolinus, a former consul (in 392) was murdered for defending debtors by trying to use tribute from the Gauls and to sell public land to redeem their debts, and for accusing senators of embezzlement and urging them to use their takings to redeem debtors. It took a generation of turmoil and poverty for Rome to resolve matters. In 367 the Licinio-Sextian law limited personal landholdings to 500 iugera (125 hectares, under half a square mile; see Livy 6.35-36). Indebted landholders were permitted to deduct interest payments from the principal and pay off the balance over three years instead of all at once.

Most wealth throughout history has been obtained from the public domain, and that is how Rome's latifundia were created. The most fateful early land grab occurred after Carthage was defeated in 204. Two years earlier, when Rome's life and death struggle with Hannibal had depleted its treasury, the Senate had asked families to voluntarily contribute their jewelry or other precious belongings to help the war effort. Their gold and silver was melted down in the Temple of Juno Moneta to strike the coins used to hire mercenaries.

Upon the return to peace the aristocrats depicted these contributions as having been loans, and convinced the Senate to pay their claims in three installments. The first was paid in 204, and a second in 202. As the third and final installment was coming due in 200, the former contributors pointed out that Rome needed to keep its money to continue fighting abroad, but had much public land available. In lieu of cash payment they asked the Senate to offer them land located within fifty miles of Rome, and to tax it at only a nominal rate. A precedent for such privatization had been set in 205 when Rome sold valuable land in the Campania to provide Scipio with money to invade Africa.

The recipients were promised that "when the people should become able to pay, if anyone chose to have his money rather than the land, he might restore the land to the state." Nobody did, of course. "The private creditors accepted the terms with joy; and that land was called *Trientabulum* because it was given in lieu of the third part of their money" (Livy 28.46).

Arnold Toynbee (1965 II:250-251; see also 341-373) describes this giveaway of Rome's *ager publicus* as the turning point polarizing its economy by deciding, "at one stroke, the economic and social future of the Central Italian lowlands." Most of this land ended up as latifundia cultivated by slaves captured in the wars against Carthage and Macedonia and imported *en masse* after 198. This turned the region into "predominantly a country of underpopulated slave-plantations" as the formerly free population was driven off the land into overpopulated industrial towns. In 194 and again in 177 the Senate organized a program of colonization that sent about 100,000 peasants, women and children from central Italy to more than twenty colonies, mainly in the far south and north of Italy. Some settlers lost their Roman citizenship, and they must have remained quite poor as the average land allotment was small.

In 133, Tiberius Gracchus advocated distributing *ager publicus* to the poor, pointing out that this would "increase the number of property holders liable to serve in the army." He was killed by angry senators who wanted the public land for themselves. Nonetheless, a land commission was established in Italy in 128, "and apparently succeeded in distributing land to several thousand citizens" in a few colonies, but not any land taken from Rome's own wealthy elite. The commission was abolished around 119 after Tiberius's brother Gaius Gracchus was killed (Hopkins 1978:61-63).

Appian (*Civil Wars* 1.1.7) describes the ensuing century of civil war as being fought over the land and debt crisis.

> For the rich, getting possession of the greater part of the undistributed lands, and being emboldened by the lapse of time to believe that they would never be dispossessed, absorbing any adjacent strips and their poor neighbors' allotments, partly by purchase under persuasion and partly by force, came to cultivate vast tracts instead of single estates, using slaves as laborers and herdsmen, lest free laborers should be drawn from agriculture into the army. At the same time the ownership of slaves brought them great gain from the multitude of their progeny, who increased because they were exempt from military service. Thus certain powerful men became extremely rich and the race of slaves multiplied throughout the country, while the Italian people dwindled in number and strength, being oppressed by penury, taxes and military service.

Dispossession of free labor from the land transformed the character of Rome's army. Starting with Marius, landless soldiers became *soldati*, living on their pay and seeking the highest booty, loyal to the generals in charge of paying them. Command of an army brought economic and political power. When Sulla brought his troops back to Italy from Asia Minor in 82 and proclaimed himself Dictator, he tore down the walls of towns that had opposed him, and kept them in check by resettling 23 legions (some 80,000 to 100,000 men) in colonies on land confiscated from local populations in Italy.

Sulla drew up proscription lists of enemies who could be killed with impunity, with their estates seized as booty. Their names were publicly posted throughout Italy in June 81, headed by the consuls for the years 83 and 82, and about 1,600 *equites* (wealthy publican investors). Thousands of names followed. Anyone on these lists could be killed at will, with the executioner receiving a portion of the dead man's estate. The remainder was sold at public auctions, the proceeds being used to rebuild the depleted treasury. Most land was sold cheaply, giving opportunists a motive to kill not only those named by Sulla, but also their personal enemies, to acquire their estates. A major buyer of confiscated real estate was Crassus, who became one of the richest Romans through Sulla's proscriptions.

By giving his war veterans homesteads and funds from the proscriptions, Sulla won their support as a virtual army in reserve, along with their backing for his new oligarchic constitution. But they were not farmers, and ran into debt, in danger of losing their land. For his more aristocratic supporters, Sulla distributed the estates of his opponents from the Italian upper classes, especially in Campania, Etruria and Umbria.

Caesar likewise promised to settle his veterans on land of their own. They followed him to Rome and enabled him to become Dictator in 49. After he was killed in 44, Brutus and Cassius vied with Octavian (later Augustus), each promising their armies land and booty. As Appian (*Civil Wars* 5.2.12-13) summarized: "The chiefs depended on the soldiers for the continuance of their government, while, for the possession of what they had received, the soldiers depend on the permanence of the government of those who had given it. Believing that they could not keep a firm hold unless the givers had a strong government, they fought for them, from necessity, with good-will." After defeating the armies of Brutus, Cassius and Mark Antony, Octavian gave his indigent soldiers "land, the cities, the money, and the houses, and as the object of denunciation on the part of the despoiled, and as one who bore this contumely for the army's sake."

The concentration of land ownership intensified under the Empire. Brown (2012:330, 366 and 327) notes that by the time Christianity became the Roman state religion, North Africa had become the main source of Roman wealth, based on "the massive landholdings of the emperor and of the nobility of Rome." Its overseers kept the region's inhabitants "underdeveloped by Roman standards. Their villages were denied any form of corporate existence and were frequently named after the estates on which the villagers worked, held to the land by various forms of bonded labor."

A Christian from Gaul named Salvian (*De gubernatione Dei* ["The Government of God"] 5.9.45, paraphrased and discussed in Brown 2012:433-450) described the poverty and insecurity confronting most of the population ca. 440:

> Faced by the weight of taxes, poor farmers found that they did not have the means to emigrate to the barbarians. Instead, they did what little they could do: they handed themselves over to the rich as clients in return for protection. The rich took over title to their lands under the pretext of saving the farmers from the land tax. The patron registered the farmer's land on the tax rolls under his (the patron's) own name. Within a few years, the poor farmers found themselves without land, although they were still hounded for personal taxes. Such patronage by the great, so Salvian claimed, turned free men into slaves as surely as the magic of Circe had turned humans into pigs.

Church estates became islands in this sea of poverty. As deathbed confessions and donations of property to the Church became increasingly popular among wealthy Christians, the Church came to accept existing creditor and debtor relationships, land ownership, hereditary wealth and the political status quo. What mattered to the Church was how the ruling elites used their wealth, regardless of how they obtained it as long as it was destined for the Church, whose priests were the paradigmatic "poor" deserving of aid and charity.

The Church sought to absorb local oligarchies into its leadership, along with their wealth. Testamentary disposition undercut local fiscal balance. Land given to the Church was tax-exempt, obliging communities to raise taxes on their secular property in order to maintain their flow of public revenue. (Many heirs found themselves disinherited by such bequests, leading to a flourishing legal practice of contesting deathbed wills.) The Church became the major corporate body, a sector alongside the state. Turning from early Christianity's concerns for the poor, the Church's critique of personal wealth focused on personal egotism and self-indulgence, not anything like the socialist idea of public ownership of land, monopolies and banking. In fact, the Crusades led the Church to sponsor Christendom's major secular bankers to finance its wars against the Holy Roman Emperors, Moslems and Byzantine Sicily.

The fight by Byzantine emperors to reverse land transfers to the dynatoi

The archaic Near Eastern tension between palace rulers and creditors who sought control of the labor and land of tax-paying smallholders was still being played out in the Byzantine Empire, coming to a head in the 9th and 10th centuries. Basil I (ruled 867-886) took the lead in limiting the alienability of tax-paying land. His successor Leo VI (886-891) supported demands by the aristocracy for a free market in land, letting it be sold to any purchaser (McGeer 2000:35-36). But Romanos Lekapenos (920-944) saved the peasantry from being turned into landless clients by reviving the Law of Pre-emption that gave kinsmen and village neighbors the right of first refusal for land being alienated. *Dynatoi* (the powerful) who were not relatives were prevented from acquiring village land by adoption, gift, testamentary disposition or foreclosure. (The law is translated in McGeer 2000:46 and discussed by Ostrogorsky 1969:275-276.)

The historically cold winter of 927/8, when the ground was frozen and crops failed, made this law urgent. Romanos wrote a prologue explaining that his ruling was "beneficial to the common good, acceptable to God, profitable to the treasury, and useful to the state." He nullified sales of land for less than its true value, expelling the purchasers without a refund.

Toynbee (1973:175-176) describes the basic dynamic at work: "In protecting the small freeholders, civilian and military, against the designs of the large-scale landowners, the East Roman Government was not contending for the rights or for the independence of the small fry. The truth is that it was defending its own rights – its rights to the peasants' payments and services, which the feudal lords were trying to capture from the Government. ... The small landowners were merely the object of that contest; their payments and services were the prize that was at stake." That judgment may be extended back through the entire course of recorded history. The fight was by the oligarchy of creditors and large landowners to limit public power over themselves.

Constantine VII (945-959) moved to restore imperial control over military land and to recover the tax yield and services of its soldiers by preventing sales "below the fair price," defined at the remarkably high level of four pounds of gold for military land and two pounds for sailors' land (McGeer 2000:105 and 18-19). His successor Romanos II (959-963) ruled that any land sold since Constantine had taken the throne in 945 was to be "restored without obligation to reimburse the buyers" (McGeer 2000:81).

After a cold winter in 989 forced many peasants to sell out, Basil II (976-1025) moved against the leading oligarchic families, headed by the military aristocracy of Cappadocia and Anatolia that had gained dominance in the Byzantine court and church. But he was the last strong Byzantine emperor. The Byzantine *dynatoi* fought back by creating their own armies and using political stratagems to oppose royal control of land and natural resources. The Comneni Dynasty (1081-1184) disbanded military land tenure, shifting the army to professionals and foreign mercenaries paid out of tax revenues.

As was the case from Babylonia through Rome, most Byzantine landed estates were assembled by creditors foreclosing on subsistence lands pledged as collateral by debtors. Once these transfers no longer were reversed by royal fiat, the oligarchy took the surplus in the form of land rent for themselves and avoided paying taxes. The Byzantine Empire's fiscal ability to defend itself weakened to the point where it was easily conquered and sacked by Christian Crusaders in 1204.

Church banking orders break down local constraints on land alienation

Medieval European sanctions against lands being sold, forfeited or bequeathed to outsiders were eroded mainly by the Church bankers. Eager to gain endowments, especially from landlord-knights embarking on the Crusades, the Knights Templar and Hospitaller pressed for the land to be bequeathed freely – that is, to themselves – instead of keeping its tenure in local communities. The Church catalyzed tolerance of such alienations. Once land could be forfeited to the Church's banking orders, thanks mainly to the Church's dominant social status and the high status of its debtors, the legal path was opened for land to be transferred in due course to other outsiders by outright sale or to foreclosing creditors.

The Christian banning of usury had two major effects on the relationship between banking and land tenure. The first related to the loophole that permitted bankers to charge money-changing fees – *agio* – for foreign exchange or payments among countries. This effectively revived the distinction that ancient Near Eastern practice had drawn between commercial silver loans and agrarian barley debts. The Church thus re-invented the distinction between productive and unproductive credit. As a result, until the late 19th century, banks made most of their profits on international trade, not domestic mortgage lending.

Meanwhile, the ban on domestic-currency debt led to borrowing from the Jews. Secular rulers welcomed this, especially in England, whose kings heavily taxed the Jews as "the king's serfs." They were blocked from owning land outside of the ghettos in which they were forced to live. That prevented a symbiosis between money-lending and real estate such as that which developed from the late 19th century onward as land and home ownership were democratized.

Classical rent theory as a rationale for land nationalization or full taxation

The 19th century saw classical political economy create a revolutionary logic for freeing society from the power of landlords. Unlike earlier times, the aim was not to protect smallholders or increase tax revenue. This time the beneficiaries of the land tax proposed by the French Physiocrats, Adam Smith, John Stuart Mill and the "Radical Ricardians" were to be the industrial capitalists. Minimizing land rent by taxing landlords instead of labor, commerce or industry would minimize the price of food, the cost of living and hence the wages that industrial employers had to pay. That would free economies from the landlord class's extraction of rent.

A land tax also would increase industrial exports and foreign trade by making the economy more competitive internationally. This would benefit bankers, whose major market was trade financing and foreign exchange (with its *agio* charges). Bankers no longer were acting in alliance with landlords as in antiquity. Their leading spokesman in England's Parliament was David Ricardo, whose 1817 *Principles of Political Economy and Taxation* refined the definition of land rent in terms of value and price theory. He defined rent as the excess of market price over real cost value. It therefore was unearned, not having any labor cost of production, because (contra Locke) land was provided by nature, not the landlord's efforts. In Ricardo's logic the rental overhead extracted by landlords was the major block to Britain's export trade in manufactures.

In addition to deciding who would end up with the land's rent (the landlord, the tax collector or the mortgage lender) was the issue of the tax rate. That rate determines what the price of rent-yielding land will be. The higher the tax rate, the lower the capitalized value of the after-tax rent. The question for 19th-century reformers was whether to tax the full land rent as the basis of public revenue (instead of income or excise taxes on labor and capital), or to nationalize the land outright and set the rent rate for public purposes.

Seeing that parliaments throughout Europe were dominated by the upper house (such as Britain's House of Lords) controlled by the hereditary landlord class, the classical economists realized that land could not be taxed without far-reaching political reform. Land tenure, tax policy and constitutional reform thus went together, as had been the case with reform attempts in classical Greece and Rome. In Britain a parliamentary crisis arose in 1909/10 when the House of Commons passed a land tax but the Lords vetoed it. The situation was much like the fight between Rome's Senate and the plebeian assembly. But in Britain the crisis was resolved by legislating that the House of Lords never again could block a revenue act passed by the Commons. The Lords were deprived of the political monopoly that had enabled them to block progressive taxation and other democratic policies that threatened their *rentier* interests.

The logic for taxing the full land rent on economic productivity grounds was set back, ironically, by the most popular journalistic advocate of rent taxation, Henry George. He eloquently denounced American robber barons and England's absentee landlords in Ireland, but his muddled economic logic rejected classical value, price and rent theory in an attempt to show how original he was. In the 1880s he sought to create his own sectarian party, attacking socialists as rivals. His platform excluded all industrial labor reforms, consumer protection and financial reforms as distractions from his Single Tax attack on landlords. To make matters worse, his libertarian opposition to strong government prompted socialists and other reformers to leave land tax advocacy to his followers, turning their focus to industrial labor problems and monopolies.

Today's FIRE sector backs the financialization of land tenure

Landlords and their allied *rentier* interests rejected the classical concept of land rent as unearned income. John Bates Clark's "value-free" economics, like subsequent free market doctrine down to the present day, denied that any form of income and wealth was unearned. The academic mainstream reverted to a Lockean assumption that the land's cost of production and rental income reflected the landlord's enterprise.

The banking and financial sector shifted its position to oppose rather than support land taxation. A middle class was emerging, home ownership was becoming democratized and bankers found real estate becoming their largest loan market. Today, some 80 percent of commercial bank lending in the United States, Britain and other industrial economies is mortgage credit. As savings grow exponentially at the top of the economic pyramid, they are recycled into the residential and commercial real estate market. Along with endogenous credit creation by banks, the effect is to bid up prices for housing on credit, with a rising share of property values owed as debt. As of 2018, less than half the value of U.S. housing was homeowners' equity; most of the property value was owed to lenders.

Bankers understand that whatever rental income the tax collector relinquishes is available for new buyers to pay as debt service. As financial wealth and credit increase faster than the economy has grown, bankers have increased their lending terms from 80 percent of the purchase price to 100 percent (thereby requiring no down payments), while making interest-only mortgages instead of the once-normal 30-year self-amortizing mortgages.

The Finance, Insurance and Real Estate (FIRE) sectors have joined together in the United States and other countries to try and persuade voters to blame the high cost of housing on property taxes, hoping to lower this tax further so as to increase the proportion of rent that can be paid out as interest.

The high housing-debt overhead, along with high costs for privatized essential services, is causing the rest of the economy to shrink. Rising defaults concentrate property in the hands of the financial class, which is becoming an absentee owner class – resulting in a rental economy that reverses the democratization of land ownership and the 19th-century's classical economic aim of freeing society from land rent (along with monopoly rent, including financial charges).

Oligarchic vs. democratic reform of land tenure and its public obligations

Only a strong government can override the combination of the *rentier* landed and financial interests that today, as in antiquity, seek to weaken public regulation and taxation. Today's world once again is seeing a fight between democracy and oligarchy. Opposing the oligarchy from Greece to Rome, reformers called for land redistribution and cancellation of the debts that threatened loss of land and liberty. That would have required a strong government. Oligarchies want weak governments, unless they are controlled by the oligarchy itself, as was Rome's patrician Senate.

When it comes to land tenure, finance and other economic structures, politics rules all. Oligarchies want no protection for mortgage debtors or renters. Called neoliberalism today, this idea of a "free market" and weak democratic policy means unfreedom for the population falling into dependency on wealthy *rentiers* for housing, credit and other basic needs.

Bibliography

Asheri, D. (1963), "Laws of inheritance, distribution of land and political constitutions in ancient Greece," *Historia* 12:1-21.

Brown, Peter (2012), *Through the Eye of a Needle: Wealth, the Fall of Rome, and the Making of Christianity in the West, 350-550 AD* (Princeton).

Cardascia, George (1959), "La concept babylonien de la propriete," *Revue Internationale des Droits de l'Antiquite* 6:19-32.

Charpin, Dominique (2003), *Hammurabi of Babylon* (London and New York).

Eyre, Christopher (1999), "Village Economy in Pharaonic Egypt," in A. K. Bowman and E. Rogan, eds., *Agriculture in Egypt from Pharaonic to Modern Times*, Proceedings of the British Academy 96 (Oxford):33-60.
" (2004), "How Relevant was Personal Status to the Functioning of the Rural Economy in Pharaonic Egypt," in Bernadette Menu, ed., *La dependence rurale dans l'Antiquité égypienne et proche-orientale* (BdE 140, Cairo):157-186.

Hopkins, Keith (1978), *Conquerors and Slaves* (Cambridge).

Hudson, Michael (1998), "Land Monopolization, Fiscal Crises and Clean Slate 'Jubilee' Proclamations in Antiquity," in Robert C. Hunt and Antonio Gilman, eds., *Property in Economic Context*, University Press of America, Monographs in Economic Anthropology 14:139-169.
" (1999), "From Sacred Enclave to Temple to City," in Michael Hudson and Baruch Levine, eds., *Urbanization and Land Ownership in the Ancient Near East* (Cambridge, Mass., Peabody Museum):117-191.
" (2004), "The Archaeology of Money in Light of Mesopotamian Records," in L. Randall Wray, ed., *Credit and State Theories of Money: The Contributions of A. Mitchell Innes* (Cheltenham, Edward Elgar).
" (2012), *The Bubble and Beyond: Fictitious Capital, Debt Deflation and Global Crisis* (Dresden, ISLET).
" (2015), "How the Organization of Labor Shaped Civilization's Takeoff," in Steinkeller and Hudson 2015:649-664.

" (2018), *"... and forgive them their debts": Lending, Foreclosure and Redemption from Bronze Age Finance to the Jubilee Year* (Dresden, ISLET).

" (2020), "Origins of Money and Interest: Palatial Credit, not Barter," in S. Battilossi, Y. Cassis, and K. Yago, eds., *Handbook of the History of Money and Currency* (Singapore, Springer):45-65

Hudson, Michael, and Baruch Levine, eds. (1996), *Privatization in the Ancient Near East and Classical Antiquity* (Cambridge, Mass., Peabody Museum, Bulletin #6).

Hudson, Michael and Marc Van De Mieroop, eds. (2002), *Debt and Economic Renewal in the Ancient Near East* (Bethesda, Md., CDL Press).

Locke, John (1947 [1689]), "Of Property," *The Second Treatise of Civil Government* (New York).

Lovejoy, Arthur O., and George Boas (1935), *Documentary History of Primitivism and Related Ideas in Antiquity* (Baltimore, Johns Hopkins).

McGeer, Eric (2000), *The Land Legislation of the Macedonian Emperors* (Toronto, Pontifical Institute of Mediaeval Studies).

Ostrogorsky, George (1969), *History of the Byzantine State*, rev. ed. (New Brunswick, NJ, Rutgers University Press).

Roth, Martha T. (1997), *Law Collections from Mesopotamia and Asia Minor*, 2nd ed. (Atlanta, Scholars Press).

Steinkeller, Piotr, and Michael Hudson, eds. (2015), *Labor in the Ancient World* (Dresden, ISLET).

Stone, Elizabeth (1987), *Nippur Neighborhoods* (Chicago).

Stone, Elizabeth, and David I. Owen (1991), *Adoption in Old Babylonian Nippur and the Archive of Mannum-meshu-lissur* (Winona Lake, Ind.).

Szlechter, Emile (1958), "De quelques considérations sur l'origine de la propriété foncière privée dans l'Ancien Droit Mesopotamien," *Revue Internationale des Droits de l'Antiquite*, 3rd ser. 5:121-136.

Toynbee, Arnold (1965), *Hannibal's Legacy: The Hannibalic War's Effects on Roman Life*, 2 vols. (Oxford).
" (1973), *Constantine Porphyrogenitus and his World* (London).

Yoffee, Norman (1977), *The Economic Role of the Crown in the Old Babylonian Period* (Malibu).

8

Land Monopolization and Taxation from Antiquity to Post-Roman Europe*

Public obligations of landholders to perform corvée labor and military service are documented from the earliest written records in the Near East. By the second millennium BC we find private landlordship built up mainly through debt foreclosure, and wealthy families avoiding such obligations, often by shifting them onto the land's former holders. Such transfers of communally allocated subsistence land – and labor to cultivate it – impaired the fiscal and military position of governments. Rulers countered this proto-oligarchic drive by proclaiming Clean Slates cancelling agrarian debts, liberating citizens from debt bondage and restoring their land rights so as to guarantee them the right to the means of self-support. That was the traditional idea of social fairness and equity.

Classical Greece and Rome had no central authority to prevent the wealthiest landowning families from expropriating smallholders and shifting taxes onto the classes below them. The same tax shift is found in the East Roman (Byzantine) Empire from the 9th through 11th centuries AD, and it still characterizes today's world. And as most land rent is now paid out as interest to mortgage bankers, debt liability to the financial sector is the main factor in the allocation of land ownership.

Social functions of archaic land tenure

Self-support was the key to the survival of archaic communities – mutual aid, overseen by the palace in the Bronze Age. Land tenure was allocated to citizens whose status was defined by their rights to land in return for the labor obligations attached to it for seasonal corvée work on public infrastructure projects and military service in the draft.

---

* Like Chapter 7, this chapter has its origins in "Land Monopolization, Fiscal Crises and Clean Slate 'Jubilee' Proclamations in Antiquity," in Robert C. Hunt and Antonio Gilman, eds., *Property in Economic Context*, University Press of America, Monographs in Economic Anthropology 14 (1998):139-169. I have restored the Byzantine discussion, which the publisher asked to be cut in order to meet the volume's page limit. In the process, I have taken the liberty to substantially edit and improve the language.

The aim was largely military, in an epoch when armies were composed of all able adult male citizens. In addition to their military service, their labor typically was requisitioned for public construction projects and related communal tasks. The circular flow of credit and debt settlement was disrupted when men were called away from their land to fight. Some families fell into arrears and forfeited their children, wives, slave girls and cattle to local notables or members of Babylonia's royal bureaucracy in settlement of unpaid obligations. In time they pledged their land, starting with its crop usufruct as debtors were left on the land to plant and harvest its crops, or worked off their debts by cultivating the estates of their creditors instead of being available to perform their communal duties.

Archaic interest rates were high, so property once mortgaged often was lost. That is why Mesopotamian communities, where such interest-bearing debt is first attested, blocked the land from being forfeited to absentee owners for more than merely temporary duration. To preserve land in the hands of local kinship groupings rather than letting it be alienated, lots could be alienated temporarily as pledges for loans or other obligations, or even sold for emergency money, but were expected to be redeemed by the debtor, or at least relatives or neighbors were to be given the right of first refusal. And royal Clean Slates restored self-support land to debtors who had lost it.

The idea of property in conjunction with the palace and temple institutions

Southern Mesopotamian land tenure involved numerous types of property. (Diakonoff 1982 provides the classic review.) Agricultural land allocated to citizens as their means of self-support appears to have been redistributed periodically, normally to the heirs of its customary holders. Transfers thus were subject to redemption by the debtor, his relatives or neighbors as soon as economic conditions permitted.

Failing such redemption, transferred land was restored to its customary owners when rulers proclaimed "economic order" (amargi in Sumerian [Lambert 1972, Lemche 1979:16, Charpin 1987:39 and Postgate 1982:95], *andurarum* in Akkadian and Babylonian [Edzard 1957, Diakonoff 1991:234, Balkan 1974, and Postgate 1969 and 1973], the related word *misharum* in Babylonian [Kraus 1984, Bottero 1961, and Finkelstein 1961, 1965 and 1969], *shudutu* in Hurrian [Lacheman 1962]), a measure reflected in the *deror* legislation of Leviticus 25 (the Jubilee Year; see Weinfeld 1982, and Levine 1996).

These proclamations prevented creditors from interfering with the "originally" envisioned balanced order. Royal *misharum* acts restored the idealized and symmetrical "straight order" by returning to customary holders the land that they had forfeited for debt or, what almost was the same thing, sold under economic duress. A new debt-free fiscal start restored the ability of local communities to perform the citizenship duties on which the palace depended.

Sumerian communities also set aside land in the form of perpetual holdings for their temples and the palace to provide sustenance for their administrators and for the indigent (widows, orphans and the blind), and captured slave-women employed in their workshops. Having this land, as well as herds of animals and other assets, enabled these large institutions to be self-supporting.

These endowments also made their institutional holders the first documented landlords, in the sense of absentee landlords collecting a net usufruct from the land. Most land held by them was rented out on a sharecropping basis, usually via palace managers, typically for a third of the crop by the end of the third millennium. Temple and palace lands thus represent history's first documented "permanent" property devoted to producing a regular rent-usufruct, and they could not be alienated. But rulers purchased land from the communal groupings, and made these transfers irreversible (as documented on the Stele of Manishtushu in the Akkadian period ca. 2250 BC; see Gelb, Steinkeller and Whiting 1991).

Merchants and other well-to-do citizens acquired townhouses, which they could buy or sell freely without being subject to any repurchase options or other redistributive measures. Inasmuch as these properties were not part of the subsistence sector, there was no need to redistribute them when rulers "proclaimed order." Their ownership was left intact, as were commercial silver-debts as opposed to agrarian and personal barley-debts. Only subsistence lands were protected from permanent alienation, so as to preserve a self-supporting rural population alongside a commercial urban economy.

What concerned rulers was that, in addition to debtors losing their status as citizens if they lost their land, foreclosures caused a fiscal problem. Creditors wanted the land's usufruct, at the expense of the palace. Debtors bound to their creditors as servants were not available for the army or to provide corvée labor services and pay fees. That is why rulers cancelled the debts stemming from payment arrears and obligations to temple officials and merchants, and reversed the loss of personal liberty and forfeitures of land to palace collectors and other creditors. These "restorations of order" were proclaimed at least once each generation, when new rulers took the throne and when economic and military conditions warranted.

Restoring traditional land tenure helped guarantee the supply of labor services to the palace sector as part of the reciprocal responsibilities between community members, the palace and its administrative bureaucracy. Absentee land acquisition on the part of members of the palace bureaucracy and *tamkaru* merchants interrupted this reciprocity. Many such Babylonian officials obtained land and animals by acting on their own account in the process of collecting fees and other obligations owed to the palace and temples. They established creditor claims on community members by paying on their behalf the barley or other crop values due – arrears that mounted up at interest. And when debtors couldn't pay, these creditor-officials appropriated their property and labor for themselves.

Communal capital investment took priority over privatized land appropriation

Ancient Mesopotamian experience controverts the idea of the "tragedy of the commons" (Hardin 1968), according to which communal resource users are deemed unable to devise rules to restrain overgrazing and other selfish exploitation of communal resources. A corollary is that communal ownership is not conducive to capital investment. These ideas have been used to defend private property's alleged natural superiority by claiming that improvements on the land will occur only if private ownership replaces communal use rights – as if no workable means exist to productively allocate the use of land and natural resources communally. But economic history suggests the reverse tendency: *privatized property finds its interest to be asset-stripping and acting in economically and socially corrosive ways.* A narrow layer of families monopolizes land and wealth, shirking fiscal responsibility for society's basic survival needs.

Hardin himself recanted in 1991, but advocates of privatization ignore the obvious reason why large-scale capital investment and resource management in early antiquity was public: Individual families lacked the means to build transport and irrigation canals, city walls and gates, temples and other gathering places. Sumer's endowment of city-temples with the means to organize land use and commercial craft production occurred as part of a mixed economy, in which opportunities for gain typically followed from one's interface with the temple and palace institutions.

Assyriologists have traced how the inception of writing was developed in response to the need for account-keeping as a check on the behavior of public administrators. Auditing annual balance sheets was part of an institutional complex that included annual meetings, the invention of weights and measures, and the regularization of economic activity in general to standardize exchange between buyers and sellers. The temples and palaces established uniform rent and interest rates, and stipulated incomes and professional fees for public servants, formalized in written entrepreneurial contracts.

Privatizing the debt system and its monetary claims led to the conversion of communally allocated land into private property as needy commoners pledged and forfeited their customary communal allocations – their right to self-support on the land – as collateral for debts. This practice caused disorder, which increased as land transfers became less easily reversible late in the Old Babylonian period (2000-1600 BC). Making such transfers irreversible replaced (and indeed, inverted) the traditional idea of order based on economic balance and self-support by smallholders with the idea that we have today: security of contracts for appropriators, with no thought of restoring viability to losers, taking no account of the social consequences.

The idea of freedom and liberty

"Free-market" land ownership, in the sense of cultivators being able to alienate their lands free of communal restrictions, was slow to come into being. Mesopotamia's idea of freedom was not that of modern-day free markets, but protected the rural community from the adverse effects of economic polarization. The idea of order was not one of freedom for creditors to foreclose irreversibly on the lands and bondage-pledges of the economically weak – what Douglass North euphemizes as "security of contracts." Rulers annulled personal debts and reversed debtor forfeitures of family members and land, restoring liberty in the form of returning the means of self-support to citizens.

In practice this concept of social order and liberty meant that the land – and hence the economic freedom to be self-sufficient – was inalienable, much as America's Bill of Rights describes life, liberty and the pursuit of happiness. This trinity was expressed by John Locke in 1689 as "life, liberty, and estate," that is, property. Mesopotamian families could not sell their lands under duress without recourse, nor could they forfeit them permanently to creditors. That made the earliest private absentee landlordship only temporary, except for that of the large institutions and, in due course, heads of state beginning with members of Sargon's family.

Increasing private character of land and enterprise

The Middle Bronze Age – the half-millennium from 2100 to 1600 BC – is one of the most important transition periods in the history of civilization, precisely because it was one of decentralization and breakdown. What gave this half-millennium its quality of "middleness" was the dissolving of centralized institutional ownership, creating a power vacuum that enabled land and enterprise to become increasingly private in character. Rights to crop revenues on earmarked lands were inherited and subdivided, bought and sold. A growing market developed for townhouses, and even for cropland, and civilization's first "stock market" developed for shares in the prebend revenue generated by temple properties.

Bureaucratic decentralization left authority – and in time, property – in the hands of local administrators, chieftains and notables, especially as temple offices and their revenue were privatized (as discussed in the next section). Regarding the Inanna temple at Nippur, Zettler (1984:441 and 461) makes the point that "the family archive of the chief administrator is mixed in with records of the temple operations." Stone (1987:17-18) finds that business was conducted increasingly in the private apartments of temple administrators, and adds that "a few offices had associated prebend fields," but the best estimate of their value "is that they entitled the owner to a share of the sacrifice." By the Isin-Larsa period (2000-1800 BC) these revenue flows "had become a kind of private property which could have been passed on to the heirs of the owner."

Yet there are no Bronze Age words for property as such. Emile Szlechter (1958:121) finds that although there are terms and regulations for deposit, pledge, pawn and so forth, "One will look in vain in the Babylonian sources for a general orderly definition of the notion of property. ... although the expressions LUGAL (in Sumerian) and *bēlum* (in Akkadian) are habitually translated as *proprietor*, one does not find in the Sumerian and Akkadian vocabulary a term which designates 'property' in the abstract sense of *law of property*." The closest the Middle Bronze Age came to using a term for property was "domain of the lord," indicating temples as the first permanent absentee landowners.

Although claims on crops and labor were increasingly privatized, formal land tenure had not yet evolved into fully autonomous ownership as the modern world knows it. Bronze Age land had too many public-service obligations attached to it to be deemed "private" in the modern sense of the term. It also lacked one of the most important hallmarks of private property: the ability to be freely sold or otherwise transferred outside of its local kinship grouping (as will be discussed further below).

Acquisition of land and temple property by palace rulers and warlords

Temple officials had been losing ground to the palace and its nominees at least since the 25th century BC. Circa 2360, the ruler Lugalanda is found in control of the major Lagash temples, as was his successor Urukagina. A generation later, the conqueror Sargon of Akkad placed members of his family (female as well as male) in key priesthood positions throughout southern Mesopotamia. His successors obtained title to large tracts of hitherto group-held land (Gelb, Steinkeller and Whiting 1991:16-17 and 26).

To win the adherence of local chieftains to his ambitious plan of conquest, Hammurabi co-opted them into the palatial economy by privatizing hitherto public offices. He assigned control of temple land to local chieftains and headmen in place of the earlier temple and palace bureaucracies. In contrast to the centralization of southern Mesopotamia's economic surplus in palace hands, as in the third millennium, he sponsored its decentralization.

This feudalization of royal authority blurred the distinction between public and private. Concerned mainly with securing an overall income and supply of soldiers, the palace levied obligations on local communities to supply soldiers and related support from their headmen. Well-placed individuals served in effect as public proxies absorbed into the royal bureaucracy, leasing out public land as part of the *quid pro quo* for getting chieftains and headmen to acquiesce in the palace's empire-building, and allowing local headmen broad leeway as long as they provided the palace with soldiers and proto-taxes and contributions. The result was a kind of feudal arrangement. "Many of these new bureaucrats," finds Yoffee (1979:13), "appear to have come from mid- to upper-level elites of the community who had certain connections to resources embedded in local organizations that the crown wished to mobilize."

Temple offices and their revenues were organized along the lines that modern economists call profit centers. Each produced an earmarked usufruct. As this revenue was bequeathed to family members of the new bureaucrats, it came to be subdivided into smaller and smaller units. The earliest contracts relating to temple offices "record the control of whole or half offices," notes Stone (1987:21), "suggesting that these offices had either only been in the family for a short period of time or that they were neither heritable nor divisible before the time of the first contracts." Her hypothesis is that "the offices became heritable and divisible at the time they were given to these families," whose possession of substantial agricultural land suggests a rural foundation.

As background for how this state of affairs may have come about, Stone (1987:72-74 and 124) observes that the *Lamentation over the Destruction of Nippur* describes how, during the reign of Ishme-Dagan (1953-1935), "active warfare penetrated the city itself." The city was attacked, most likely by Amorite tribesmen who had entered from the northwestern Arabian-Syrian desert. Their first incursions into Mesopotamia are cited during the reign of Shu-Sin (2037-2029 BC), who built a long-fortified wall (the Martu or Western wall) to keep them out, but which the Amorites breached in 2022.

What may have stopped the fighting, Stone suggests, was the decision by palace rulers to buy off "the leaders of these rural, tribal groups. ... To stem future rebellion, the king moved them into the city, provided them with a large area of urban real estate, and co-opted the leaders with gifts of real estate and temple offices." Probably Iddin-Dagan (1974-1954) and his Isin successors, beginning with Ishme-Dagan, "initiated a program designed to pacify the countryside. Like the British during the mandate period, they brought the tribal leaders into the cities where they could be controlled." The chieftains were given temple positions, or at least the prebend revenues traditionally attached to these positions to support temple officials.

One result was to separate temple revenue flows from the actual performance of administrative functions. It would have been a travesty if each individual receiving temple income actually had tried to carry out the associated position for just a few days. Whereas there was only a single *ugula-e* (head administrator) receiving income from the Inanna temple in the Ur III period (ca. 2112-2004), "by Old Babylonian times, when up to one hundred may have shared a single office, the ownership of an office can have had little to do with the bureaucratic activities implied by the title," because these titles remained indivisible. There was only one responsible functionary in any given period. Ownership was divorced from management – precisely what Adolph Berle and Gardner Means described in the 1930s as representing the "new capitalism" of our modern epoch!

Based on a study of the clergy of Ur in Hammurabi's dynasty, Charpin (1986:260-262) concludes that the subdivision of temple prebend incomes must have begun late in the Ur III period. He finds that after 180 to 200 years so many successive bequests and partitions of these prebends had occurred that some holders received only a few days' income per year. Typical subdivisions are 15 days ($1/24^{th}$ of the 360-day administrative Mesopotamian year), 7½ days ($1/48^{th}$), 5 days ($1/72^{nd}$), 3⅔ days, and just 1⅔ days per year. "The result, after a century and a half of successive divisions, is an extreme parcellisation of prebends: When we see an individual owning five days of service a year in the Nanna temple, we may conclude that this theoretically signifies that the income is divided among 71 other persons for that year." (The number depends on how many heirs were left by successive generations of each branch of the original family.) The result was an economic organization of temples "as a kind of joint-stock company whose shares have passed into the hands of the town notables." By the first millennium BC this became standard practice throughout the Near East.

Ownership rights to temple usufruct flows came to be sold with increasing liquidity. Stone (1987:18 and 25) finds that after about 1800 BC, temple offices "carried none of the alienation restrictions which applied to the more traditional kinds of property, *i.e.*, fields and houses," for unlike the case with rural fields and properties, the sale of temple offices was not restricted to one's kinsmen. A new economic class thus came into being: a *rentier* class of temple prebend holders, history's earliest attested sinecures and permanently private absentee owners.

Turning land from a natural right into rentier *property*

Alienation of subsistence landholdings through debt foreclosure occurred especially in times of flood or drought, pestilence, and when men were called away to fight. Most cultivators initially had little to pledge as collateral except for their family members – their wives, daughters, sons or servants. As an alternative, cultivators looked for something else that could be pledged. The most desirable asset was land. But as already noted, land was long treated as a public utility, provided to citizens as a basic right, subject to the liabilities attached to it.

What creditors wanted was its crop usufruct, which they took as payment of interest. Debtors continued to work land that had been foreclosed, for without their labor, land rights would not have been very valuable to creditors in the early centuries of land mortgaging. There was not yet a body of "free" (that is, disenfranchised) seasonal labor for hire.

As land began to pass out of the hands of the community into those of wealthy appropriators, one of the first objectives of absentee owners was to avoid paying taxes and related obligations. Despite losing their land rights, debtors in principle remained liable for the public duties tied to their lost land for military obligations and corvée labor, but in practice they were liable to their creditors. The new landholders were not subject to local military service, so their foreclosures on the debtor's labor threatened the palace with a loss of military service. The fiscal shortfall caused by absentee ownership gave rulers good reason to block such land transfers, especially when the new owners were local officials or chieftains assembling power bases of their own.

As credit also became more privatized and commodified, merchants, palace collectors and others sought immunity from royal proclamations restoring economic order. Wealthy landowning creditor families emerged in most major Babylonian towns in the first half of the second millennium BC, but disappeared from the cuneiform record after a few generations. Still, the seeds for an oligarchy were being sown as palace control weakened and its overrides to land appropriation were undercut.

Creditor stratagems to circumvent Clean Slate proclamations

Most Babylonian debts were due in the barley-harvesting month, Simann, the third month of the year, corresponding to our own late May and early June. Just prior to the harvest, cultivators found their resources to be at their lowest ebb. Matters were especially serious if a drought or other natural disaster gave creditors reason to believe that debts were about to be cancelled, leading them to try to anticipate matters by extorting what they could. To prevent creditors from prematurely trying to collect their debts by coercing debtors to pay and then refusing to refund their money when *misharum* was proclaimed, the Edict of Ammisaduqa (§5, ca. 1646 BC) prescribed that if a creditor "prematurely collected by means of pressure, he must refund all that he received through such collection or be put to death."

A century earlier, §37 of Hammurabi's laws ca. 1754 BC annulled any sale of rural fields, orchards or houses that belonged to soldiers, commissaries or feudatories. §38 prohibited such soldiers, commissaries and feudatory tenants from pledging their fief-fields, orchards and houses as collateral for any obligation, or deeding them to their wives or daughters. However, §39 permitted property that already had been bought for cash to be resold, pledged for debt or deeded, evidently on the ground that such market property had passed out of the traditional communal or public sphere.

These restrictions against alienating the land were part of long-standing Mesopotamian tradition. Szlechter (1958:133) points out that although pre-Sargonic records attest to land sales, "when the lease-fields become 'private property' they refer only to houses, orchards or fields, whose area is relatively small." The sellers were professional bodies, and the buyer invariably was the palace (Diakonoff 1982:8-19, 36-48 and 67-69). This is not the same thing as property being transferred among individuals acting on their own account to obtain land and its rents at prices set by market forces.

Royal proclamations deterred absentee landlords from becoming a vested oligarchy by ruling that the sale or forfeiture of self-support land was only temporary, until the next *misharum* act restored the *status quo ante*. When rulers enacted *misharum*, all debt tablets were supposed to be handed over to the authorities to be broken, along with all land-property contracts. "Astounding as it must appear to our normally skeptical eyes," concludes Finkelstein (1965:244-246), instead of the *misharum* institution being "a pious but futile gesture," the fact is that "at the promulgation of the *misharum* formal commissions were established to review real-estate sales."

Finkelstein (1969:58) comments on Ammisaduqa's edict and its predecessors that "the provisions of these acts anticipated a certain amount of skullduggery and fraud aimed at circumventing the effect of the edict." When one creditor tried to collect the amount nominally due on a debt tablet predating one of Hammurabi's four *misharum* acts, the debtor sued and won on the ground that *misharum* had been declared since the document was drawn up. The judges symbolically broke a clod of earth in lieu of the tablet so that the latter should be considered null and void if the creditor ever again tried to collect.

One way in which creditors sought to evade such proclamations was to get debtors to waive their rights following a Clean Slate. A Mari text dated to the sixth year of one of Hammurabi's contemporaries, Zimri-Lim, stipulates that "if an *uddurarum* is instituted, this silver will not be subject to that measure" (ARM VIII 33, discussed by Lemche 1979:17, Durand MARI 1 1982:107 and Charpin 1987:39). By writing this clause the creditor got his debtor to formally renounce any benefit of the debt remission.

Julius Lewy (1958:24-25) cites similar contractual clauses from another upstream town, Hana, during the reign of Kashtiliashu in the late 1700s. One clause contains "a brief reference to an oath pledging the contracting parties not to contest the validity of their agreement by raising claims against each other." If the complaining party seeks to recover his land, his head is to be "smeared with hot asphalt." Inasmuch as Kashtiliashu's date formulae indicates that he "established (social) justice" at least twice, Lewy infers that it was considered necessary to insert this clause into the contract because "without such a statement, the landed property ... might have been liable to reversion to its former owner." Ammisaduqa's edict of 1646 banned such clauses, but their spirit is echoed in Rabbi Hillel's *prosbul* clause formulated nearly two thousand years later to circumvent the biblical Jubilee Year debt cancellations called for in Leviticus 25.

Anticipating that some creditors might try to perpetrate a deception by having their claims "drawn up as a sale or a bailment and then persist in taking interest," §6 of Ammisaduqa's edict voided such documents, thereby annulling the transfers. Creditors who attempted to "sue against the house of an Akkadian or an Amorite for whatever he had loaned him" were threatened with the death penalty, by §5. (This was the opposite of subsequent Roman law, which threatened only complaining debtors with death.) §7 laid down a similar punishment against creditors who claimed they had not given barley or silver as an interest-bearing loan, but rather as an advance for purchases or equity investment for mutual profit, or some similar form of credit exempted from debt cancellation by §8.

Restoring liberty to bondservants included restoring the land to its traditional role in preserving household structures. But here, too, creditors found a loophole around the protective clauses of these royal acts.

The "fictive adoption" stratagem

Just as land tenure was undercut by the rural usury process, so were the customary family lineage structures. Prior to being able to mortgage their land rights, all that cultivators had to pledge were their family members, who became bondservants to their creditors. Inasmuch as interest typically mounted up at an annualized rate of $33\frac{1}{3}$ percent by 2100 BC, rural debtors often were unable to redeem these pledges. So disruptive was their loss that the laws of Hammurabi ruled that bondservants should be freed after three years, probably on the logic that creditors had got back their capital in this period.

Middle Bronze Age creditors could not purchase land directly or get it pledged as collateral for loans on more than a temporary basis. To avoid the traditional Mesopotamian land-tenure arrangements preventing land from being sold or pledged as collateral for debts – by limiting its transfer only to the heirs of its customary holders – a strategic ploy was devised: The creditor would arrange to inherit the land upon the death of its seller/debtor by being "adopted" as his legal son and heir. Such "fictive adoptions" are found in Babylonia by the 18th century BC, spreading upstream along the Euphrates to Nuzi by the 16th century.

This ploy opened the gates for major inroads to be made into the conservative force of communal traditions based on the principle of self-sufficiency for landed kin-groupings. Debtors driven to the wall by economic need adopted their creditors as sons. When the debtor-landholder died, his adopted creditor-son inherited the land, to the exclusion of the debtor's own biological sons. It probably was from such arrangements that the Babylonian proverb arose: "A creditor has many relatives."

In her study of *Adoption in Old Babylonian Nippur* (1991:2-3), Stone elaborates how the debtor might receive an adoption payment as the *de facto* loan, stipulating "the monthly and annual rations which are to be delivered by the adoptee [the creditor] to support his new father [the debtor] until his death." These payments served as compensation for the right to inherit the land. The witnesses to such contracts are listed, and "the penalties for breaking the contract are spelled out."

One such contract finds a debt-ridden cultivator, Ur-Lumma, unable to support himself, yet "prevented by contemporary alienation restrictions from converting his property into cash through sale." The only way to alienate his property to obtain cash and security in his old age was through the back door of adoption. He solved the problem by adopting the well-to-do Lu-Bau, son of a prominent temple official, "as his heir in exchange for support. The text includes an oath in which Ur-Lumma and his heirs foreswear all claims to Lu-Bau's new inheritance." That was the only way for Lu-Bau to obtain good land. As matters turned out, Lu-Bau died without issue. The natural sons of Ur-Lumma pressed their traditional claims to inherit the property and, "thanks to the accident of Lu-Bau's childlessness, they regained control" (Stone 1991:9-10).

The effect of the fictive adoption stratagem was to concentrate land in the hands of an emerging oligarchy, at the expense of poorer lineages. Such arrangements broke up the customary family-lineage system as creditor/debtor relations become the new basis for kinship arrangements. But the basic economic tension in Babylonia stemmed from the fact that, despite it being the case that most creditors were *tamkaru* serving in the royal bureaucracy, they put their own interests above that of the palace, taking the land's usufruct formerly available to pay the palace.

Turning this crop over to creditors prevented it from being paid as royal sharecropping rent or sold to the palace. That was what Hammurabi's laws sought to address, forbidding *tamkaru* from taking land from the families of smallholders. *Misharum* acts, the palace's response to rural subsistence landholders pledging and forfeiting their land-tenure rights to creditors after falling into debt arrears, restored the *status quo ante* by returning self-support land, freeing bondservants and annulling all claims denominated in barley, that is, personal debts. These claims for payment included those of "ale-women" and other public or quasi-public officials, whose debts to the palace simultaneously were annulled.

Bronze Age rulers never spelled out the logic underlying their Clean Slates, but the Roman historian Diodorus (I.79), writing ca. 40-30 BC, got to the heart of matters when he explained why Egypt's pharaoh Bocchoris abolished debt-servitude and cancelled undocumented debts, by ruling "that the repayment of loans could be exacted only from a man's estate, and under no condition did he allow the debtor's person to be subject to seizure." The social context for this act was the growing military threat from Ethiopia. According to Diodorus, Bocchoris's rationale was that "the bodies of citizens should belong to the state, to the end that it might avail itself of the services which its citizens owed it, in times of both war and peace. For he felt that it would be absurd for a soldier, perhaps at the moment when he was setting forth to fight for his fatherland, to be haled to prison by his creditor for an unpaid loan, and that the greed of private citizens should in this way endanger the safety of all."

That is much how Bronze Age rulers must have reasoned when they blocked creditors from taking for themselves the usufruct and labor of tenants on royal and communal land that owed manpower and military service to the palace. Rulers had not yet become heads of their realm's aristocracies, as subsequent kings have been from the Roman emperors down to modern times.

Classical antiquity's oligarchies end royal power to proclaim Clean Slates

Clean Slates did not survive outside of the Near East and Egypt. No palace or temple authority existed in the classical Aegean and Italy to make such proclamations.[1] The Mycenaean palaces were a hybrid form, and in any case did not survive after 1200 BC. Where local chieftain-kings emerged from the Dark Age convulsions of 1200-750 BC in Greece and southern Italy, they ended up being unseated by landed aristocracies, much as England's aristocracy curtailed royal power from the 13th century AD onward. Thus, no central authority survived in Greece or Italy to institute the checks and balances that in the Near East had preserved self-sufficiency and order once it was disturbed by the dynamics of debt and growing oligarchic power in the conflict between creditors and debtors, and between wealthy landowners and the dispossessed.

---

[1] My 2023 book *The Collapse of Antiquity* emphasizes this change as being a defining feature of subsequent Western civilization.

The Biblical examples of creditor and landowner greed denounced by Isaiah 5:8-9 became most pronounced in Rome, which never created the checks and balances that preserved self-sufficiency in Mesopotamia and the Levant. Cicero (*De Officiis* 2.78-80) reflected the spirit of his times in condemning land redistribution and debt cancellation. Matters were especially serious for soldiers called away from their land to engage in the almost constant fighting that enabled Rome to conquer central Italy. In effect, smallholders were fighting for their own expropriation, forced into debt and absorbed (along with their land) into the estates of their creditors. The wealthiest families managed to gain immunity from the public obligations that landholders traditionally had owed their communities. Taxes became regressive and the economy polarized between rich and poor, ultimately stifling the Roman Empire's fiscal position in the western half.

The Byzantine survival[2]

The Empire's capital was shifted to Constantinople in 396 AD, and the eastern Byzantine half regained its economic momentum by the 7th century. Just as Babylonia's army and those of early classical antiquity had been recruited from the ranks of peasant freeholders, so was the Byzantine army. The best Byzantine emperors also came from this class. To preserve rural stability, imperial rulings (called Novels) prohibited mortgaging the land and its monopolization by large landowners, on much the same military and fiscal rationale that had motivated Bronze Age rulers: maintenance of a self-supporting class of smallholders available to pay taxes and fight in the army.

Basil I (867-886) founded a dynasty that replenished the army's ranks by ordering that the debt vouchers of insolvent debtors be burned. His lawbook, the *Epanagoge*, prohibited creditors from taking fields as collateral. To prevent a recurrence of rural instability, he banned agrarian lending at interest, except for permitting the estates of orphans and other minors to be lent out to provide an income for their support. Basil's laws restricted the sale of land by giving family members, owners of adjoining lands and neighbors the right of first refusal (Toynbee 1973:147).

---

[2] I emphasize the Byzantine echo of Near Eastern debt cancellations by emperors seeking to deter an independent creditor-landowning oligarchy (the *dynatoi*) in Chapters 27 and 28 of *"... and forgive them their debts"* (2018).

However, Basil's successor Leo VI (886-912) permitted rural interest of 5½ percent to be charged, claiming that banning rural mortgages would burden the economy. His Novel 114 removed Basil's Novel that had limited the right of first refusal to local community members. These rulings opened the way for the large *dynatoi* to re-appropriate the land. After a six-year turmoil following Leo's death, the imperial crown passed to Romanos Lekapenos (920-944), the son of a soldier who had held a military allotment.

Land tenure and credit problems came to a head after a cold winter in 927/8 caused a famine across the countryside. Many peasants mortgaged their lands to wealthy creditors, who absorbed the properties into their own holdings and enserfed the former freeholders. With the memory of the polarization of land ownership under Leo VI still fresh, Romanos sought to protect the lands of soldiers and other cultivators who were the basis for Byzantine taxation and its army. He issued a Novel (probably in 929) limiting the ability of large estates or absentee buyers to displace smallholders. His preamble explained that with Byzantium's recent victory over rebels on its eastern frontier, "We have left nothing undone to liberate districts and villages and cities from the enemy. ... Now that we have achieved these magnificent successes in putting an end to the aggression of the foreign enemy, what about the domestic enemy in our own household? How can we refrain from dealing severely with him?" (Toynbee 1973:153).

A new Novel in 934 lay down the guiding principle of Romanos's rulings: "Small property is particularly useful for the payment of taxes and the performance of military service. Everything would be imperiled if it disappeared" (Bréhier 1977:111). The Novel reversed all land transfers, gifts and legacies made since 922, and ruled that any property that had been acquired for less than half the reasonable price should be handed back without indemnity.

Romanos's Novels intensified the conflict with the large landowners, who had become powerful enough to weaken the fiscal position by not paying taxes, as had occurred in the Late Roman Empire. The ensuing fiscal squeeze impaired Constantinople's ability to field an army. Large landowners fielded their own military resistance in their role as commanders, threatening to turn their troops against Constantinople to block the emperor's ability to collect taxes and deter their concentration of land ownership.

Matters were stabilized by the nearly 50-year rule of Basil II (976-1025), the longest in Byzantine history. During his early twenties two warlords, Bardas Sclerus and Bardas Phocas, vied to seize control of the

Empire. Basil defeated them and mounted a fight against the landlords to prevent future challenges by reversing the forfeiture of lands that had taken place and rescuing the peasantry from being reduced to clientship and serfdom. On New Year's Day, 996, he ruled "that all lands which had been acquired since the first law of Romanus Lecapenus in 922 must be restored to their original owners without any indemnity, even those taken over by the Church" (Bréhier 1977:150).

Basil's rule resembled that of Hammurabi not only in its exceptional length but by establishing the security of land held by soldiers and freeholders, reversing its transfer to absentee buyers. His "chief weapon against the maintenance of large properties was a reform of the so-called *allelengyon* ... [the] system whereby local communities were jointly responsible for an annual sum payable to the imperial fisc." This was changed to exempt the poor from taxes, which were shifted onto the owners of large estates (Bréhier 1977:150).

The problem of tax exemption for Church property

In contrast to early Judeo-Christian denunciation of large landowners, the Middle Ages saw the most powerful bishops and officials of both the Roman and Eastern Churches headed by supporters of the landowning aristocracy. And just as the Knights Templar and Hospitaller would become large landholders and help break down Western European restrictions against alienating land out of the local communities (by gifts or sale of land to the banking orders during the Crusades), so the Byzantine Church sought to aggrandize its landholdings.

Religious institutions have enjoyed fiscal exemption in nearly all known societies. Their pedigree can be traced back to the Middle Babylonian *kudurru* exempting local towns and temple precincts from royal taxation to secure their loyalty to the palace. Similarly, when the Byzantine army conquered Bulgaria in 1018, Basil II quelled the revolt of local potentates by issuing *exkousseia*, "excusances" rewarding "those who remained faithful to the emperor in order to secure their support" by making clerical properties tax-exempt (Oikonomides 1988:321-322).

In Byzantium itself, Nicephoros Phokas (963-969) and Basil II abolished the ecclesiastical exemption from taxes, corvées and *leiturgoi*, but bishops were allowed to distribute a specified number of exemptions to individuals within their sees. "Consequently, the new approach created automatically a client relationship between the prelates and their subordinates." This loosened "the tight structure of the monarchic state in favor of the centrifugal forces of the privileged aristocrats, among whom the church formed a part," with the priestly hierarchy filled with scions of Byzantium's leading landed families (Oikonomides 1988:323-325).

In earlier centuries Late Roman tax exemptions had been granted to the clergy and other bodies by virtue of their public roles. But "the medieval privileges, on the contrary, emanating from a personal and exceptional favor ... could easily be considered as hereditary, especially when granted to members of large and powerful families. They were easily granted and in large numbers in moments of political instability, when local magnates – or church representatives, like those who obtained Basil's exemptions – could influence or even bring pressure to bear on the central authority." And by renting from the church, tenants (*paroikoi*) gained exemption from the royal land tax (*klerikotopion*). The exemption of these tenants "from certain fiscal burdens profited mainly the bishop, who received at least part of the exemption and who was thus in a better position to attract to his lands the manpower necessary for their cultivation, by offering prospective lessees more advantageous conditions than those of non-exempt landowners."

Land monopolization leads to military defeat

Byzantium was weakened fiscally by the 11th century, impairing its ability to defend itself. The last stand against landlords was made by Alexius I (1081-1118), the founder of the Comnenos dynasty. In the year of his accession he consolidated support by making land "grants or *charisticia* to the profit of individuals from the possessions of monasteries in exchange for the military services of their tenants (*paroikoi*)." But after Alexius the Comnenos dynasty, supported by the nobility, "abandoned the time-honored offensive of the central government against the great landowners and, to consolidate their dynasty's power, they favored the formation of large apanages and the unlimited increase of monastic properties, thus weakening the authority of the state" (Bréhier 1977:207 and 202).

The new Byzantine emperors were unable to hold power and secure Church support without strengthening the nobility, which opposed royal overrides to its land monopolization and special fiscal privileges. Unable to raise taxes to pay the army, and fearful of leaving troops in the hands of commanders drawn from the ranks of rivals in the upper aristocracy, the emperors had few resources to counter the pressures from the Turks gaining control in the eastern Arab states, Normans pressing in from Italy and finally the Crusaders joined by the navies of Venice and Genoa. In 1204 Byzantium fell before the army of Crusaders who looted Constantinople.

The relevance of Bronze Age and classical history for today's economic crisis

This essay has traced how the dynamics of debt, absentee land ownership, monopolization and economic polarization have overpowered societies repeatedly throughout history. The landed aristocracy undercut economic viability by overthrowing public oversight of land tenure and credit systems and "freeing" land of its historic fiscal and social obligations, destroying the basic fiscal principle of Near Eastern civilization. The liability attached to land tenure in the modern world is not part of a socially viable plan of economic growth, but obliges most land rent to be paid to mortgage bankers, not to the tax collector.

Today's debt overhead once again is transferring land and natural resources (oil and other minerals, and forest products) and infrastructure monopolies into the hands of a *rentier* class of bankers, bondholders and other creditors and their clientele of landlords, natural resource owners and monopolists. The U.S. oil industry's depletion allowance, fictitious transfer pricing and related tax breaks for mining and real estate, and tax-deductibility for interest payments represent notorious tax exemptions for rent-extractors. Matters are especially pronounced in the Global South countries, whose governments have been directed by U.S. diplomacy to provide special concessions to foreign investors. Under distress conditions, sell-offs of rent-yielding assets are used to pay foreign debts that have accumulated to a point where they create a chronic fiscal and foreign exchange crisis – a debt dynamic much like that which confronted antiquity's indebted smallholders.

Governments were not debtors in antiquity. They typically were creditors, and in the Bronze Age developed general-purpose money as a means of collecting payments on credit that they extended during the crop year and the foreign-trade cycle. Today's budget deficits and privatizations are the price of refraining from taxing land, natural resources and monopoly rents. Most wealth takes the form of rent-yielding assets, whose holders have broken free of taxation. This drive is crowned by minimizing and often abolishing the capital-gains tax, inasmuch as most "capital gains" (that is, asset-price gains) in today's world are from rising prices for debt-financed transfers of land, natural resources and infrastructure monopolies.

Fiscal obligations owed by landholders, above all for military service and corvée labor, have a pedigree going back at least to Sumerian times. Almost as old a phenomenon is the striving by wealthy families to avoid such obligations on the holdings that they are able to appropriate. This appropriation was done mainly by debt leverage prior to the development of a land market. The transfer of land to large property owners helped consolidate oligarchies to the point where their power was able to undercut that of centralized authority. The ensuing privatization of property rights and economic power squeezed governments fiscally and led to their economic and military collapse.

The conflict of interest between government and oligarchic power is age-old. Antiquity's rulers were confronted by aristocratic leaders and the wealthiest families opposed to royal protection of smallholders. Mesopotamian rulers countered this dynamic of rising oligarchic power by proclaiming Clean Slates cancelling debts and limiting the time period for debt bondage and the loss of property to foreclosing creditors or wealthy patrons. But this practice did not survive into Greek and Roman antiquity. Irreversible debt servitude and dependency replaced proclamations restoring economic order.

Rome became antiquity's most extreme oligarchy. Its legal principles favoring creditors over debtors have survived to endorse the transfer of land and financial wealth to the increasingly powerful oligarchy that has characterized the Western world ever since. Today's principles of linear economic progress and "security of contracts" that support the ideology of privatization and financialization have replaced the Bronze Age principle of "circular time" with its periodic restorations of social order to prevent economic polarization and impoverishment of the citizenry at large by a *rentier* class.

The train of consequences stemming from agrarian debt and usury

1. Interest and penalties are levied for late payment of debts. Arrears accumulate as these charges tend to exceed the borrower's normal ability to pay, especially in times of crop failure or military disruption.

2. Debtors who cannot pay these charges lose their labor and personal liberty (and that of their wives, children and house-slaves pledged for their debts).

3. Debt bondage initially is limited in duration, but tends to become permanent, degrading the status of debtors to that of disenfranchised clients, runaways or outlaws.

4. As an alternative to personal bondage, borrowers pledge the rights to their land, starting with its crop usufruct. Where formal land rights could be transferred only within the family clan, debtors are adopted

by creditors as their heirs so that the land can be bequeathed to them instead of passed on to the debtor-seller's own children.

5. In time this charade is abbreviated by a market sale, enabling creditors to take direct possession of the land. At first society holds the land-rights of indebted smallholders to be inalienable for more than a relatively short period. The land reverts periodically to its customary holders, along with their personal liberty, through the proclamation of Clean Slates. But gradually the alienation of land and personal clientage or bondage to creditors becomes permanent.

6. At first the creditors-become-landlords leave debtors on their land to work it and perform the labor obligations attached to it. Over time, debtors become attached to the soil in a serflike relationship. This may result in sharecropping arrangements such as the Athenian "sixth-parters" (*hektemoroi*).

7. To maximize their income, large landlords shift land-use away from traditional food production to latifundia-type plantations and export crops such as wine and olive oil in classical antiquity.

8. Creditor-landholders gain sufficient power to become an aristocracy, able to overthrow palace rulers and destroy any central power capable of overriding their acquisitiveness. The leading families create a modern type of ruler supporting the oligarchy instead of regulating it.

9. The resulting polarization of wealth weakens the economy by creating a class of landless peasant-tenants and smallholders living on the brink of subsistence. The wealthiest landholders succeed in throwing the fiscal burden onto the community's weaker and poorer families, most notoriously onto the Late Roman *curialis* class.

10. Foreclosures on debtors lead to depopulation, undercutting membership in the traditional rural-based army of cultivator-infantrymen. Mercenaries are hired, with the resulting additional tax burden falling on the less wealthy classes.

11. A policy debate develops around the debt problem, bringing religion and secular philosophy to bear. Early traditions criticizing money-addiction and limiting creditor abuses, the duration of debt-bondage and the loss of hereditary subsistence lands as violations of divine law, are replaced by a new religion and moral philosophy reflecting creditor-oriented values and celebrating selfishness as the progressive mainspring of economic growth and prosperity.

12. Societies wage war to seize from foreigners the surplus that no longer can be produced at home. In classical antiquity, prisoners were captured and enslaved to work on latifundia and in the mines. The slowing of Roman warfare and slave markets led to feudal serfdom, which was created to address depopulation.

13. Modern wars and financial conquests aim at seizing rent-yielding land, natural resources and basic infrastructure monopolies, which are privatized from the public domain and duly financialized in a symbiotic relationship between the banking and financial system and the rent-extracting sectors.

Bibliography

Balkan, Kemal (1974), "Cancellation of Debts in Cappadocian Tablets from Kultepe," *Anatolian Studies presented to Hans C. Guterbock* (Istanbul):29-36.

Bottero, Jean (1961), "Desordre economique et annulation des dettes en Mesopotamie a l'epoque paleo-babylonienne," *Journal of the Economic and Social History of the Orient* 4:113-164.

Bréhier, Louis (1977), *The Life and Death of Byzantium* (Amsterdam).

Charpin, Dominique (1986), *Le Clerge d'Ur au siecle d'Hammurabi* (Geneva-Paris).
" (1987), "Les Decrets Royaux a l'Epoque Paleo-babylonienne, a Propos d'un Ouvrage Recent," *Archiv für Orientforschung* 34:36-44.

Dandamaev, Muhammed (1984), *Slavery in Babylonia, from Napopolassar to Alexander the Great (626-331 BC)* (De Kalb, Ill.)

Diakonoff, Igor (1969), *Ancient Mesopotamia: Socio-Economic History* (Moscow).
" (1982), "The Structure of Near Eastern Society before the Middle of the 2nd Millennium BC," *Oikumene* 3:7-100.

Edzard, Dietz Otto (1957), *Die zweite Zwischenzeit Babyloniens* (Wiesbaden).

Finkelstein, Jack J. (1961), "Ammisaduqa's Edict and the Babylonian 'Law Codes,'" *Journal of Cuneiform Studies* 15:91-104.
" (1965), "Some New *misharum* Material and its Implications," in *Assyriological Studies* 16 (*Studies in Honor of Benno Landsberger on his Seventy-Fifth Birthday*):233-246.
" (1969), "The Edict of Ammisaduqa: A New Text," *Revue d'Assyriologie et d'archéologie orientale* 63:45-64.

Gelb, Ignace, Piotr Steinkeller, and Robert M. Whiting Jr. (1989, 1991), *Earliest Land Tenure Systems in the Near East: Ancient Kudurrus* (Chicago, Oriental Institute Publications 104).

Guerdan, René (1956), *Byzantium: Its Triumphs and Tragedy* (London [French ed., 1954]).

Hardin, Garrett (1991), "The Tragedy of the *Unmanaged* Commons," in Robert V. Andelson, ed., *Commons Without Tragedy* (London).

Hudson, Michael (1992), "Did the Phoenicians Introduce the Idea of Interest to Greece and Italy – And If So, When?" in Günter Kopcke and Isabelle Tokumaru, *Greece Between East and West: 10th-8th Centuries BC* (Mainz):128-143.
" (1995), "The Privatization of Land: How it all Began," *Land and Liberty* 102 (January-April):7-12.

Hudson, Michael and Baruch Levine, eds. (1996), *Privatization in the Ancient Near East and Classical Antiquity* (Cambridge, Mass.).

Kraus, Fritz R. (1984), *Königliche Verfügungen in altbabylonischer Zeit*, SD 11 (Leiden).

Lacheman, Ernest. R. (1962), "The word šudutu in the Nuzi tablets," *25th International Congress of Orientalists (1960)* (Moscow) I:233-238.

Lambert, Maurice (1972), "L'Expansion de Lagash au temps d'Entemena," *Rivista Degli Studi Orientali* 47:1-22.

Lemche, Niels Peter (1979), "*andurarum* and *misharum*: Comments on the Problems of Social Edicts and their Application in the Ancient Near East," *Journal of Near Eastern Studies* 38:11-18.

Levine, Baruch (1996), "Farewell to the Ancient Near East: Evaluating Biblical References to Ownership of Land in Comparative Perspective," in Hudson and Levine 1996.

Lewy, Julius (1958), "The Biblical Institution of *Deror* in the Light of Akkadian Documents," *Eretz-Israel* 5.

Oikonomides, N. (1988), "Tax Exemptions for the Secular Clergy under Basil II," in J. Chrysostomides, ed., *Kathegetria: Essays Presented to Joan Hussey for her 80th Birthday* (Camberley, Porphyrogenitus):317-326.

Oliva, Pavel (1971), *Sparta and her Social Problems* (Amsterdam and Prague).

Postgate, J. N. (1973), *The Governor's Palace Archive* (=British School of Archaeology in Iraq, Cuneiform Texts from Nimrud II).
" (1974), "Royal Exercise of Justice under the Assyrian Empire," in Paul Garelli, ed., *Le Palais et la Royaute* (Paris):417-426.
" (1976), *Fifty Neo-Assyrian Legal Documents* (Warminster).
" (1992), *Early Mesopotamian Society and Economy at the Dawn of History* (London and New York).

Rostoftzeff, Mikhail (1926), *The Social and Economic History of the Roman Empire* (Oxford).

Steinkeller, Piotr (1981), "The Renting of Fields in Early Mesopotamia and the Development of the Concept of 'Interest' in Sumerian," *Journal of the Economic and Social History of the Orient* 24.

Stone, Elizabeth (1987), *Nippur Neighborhoods* (Chicago).

Stone, Elizabeth and David I. Owen (1991), *Adoption in Old Babylonian Nippur and the Archive of Mannum-meshu-lissur* (Winona Lake, Ind.).

Szlechter, Emile (1958), "De quelques considérations sur l'origine de la propriété foncière privée dans l'Ancien Droit Mesopotamien," *Revue internationale des droits de l'antiquite*, 3rd ser. 5:121-136.

Toynbee, Arnold (1965), *Hannibal's Legacy: The Hannibalic War's Effects on Roman Life*, 2 vols. (London).
" (1973), *Constantine Porphyrogenitus and his World* (London).

Weinfeld, Moise (1982), "'Justice and Righteousness' in ancient Israel against the background of 'Social Reforms' in the Ancient Near East," in Hans-Jorg Nissen and Johannes Renger, eds., *Mesopotamien und Seine Nachbarn* (Berlin):490-519.

Yoffee, Norman (1977), *The Economic Role of the Crown in the Old Babylonian Period* (Malibu).

" (1979), "The Decline and Rise of Mesopotamian Civilization: An Ethno-archaeological Perspective on the Evolution of Social Complexity," *American Antiquity* 44:5-35.

Zettler, Richard (1992), *The Ur III Temple of Inanna at Nippur* (Berlin).

III

Urban Origins, Social Cosmology and Privatization

9

After the Ice Age:
Calendar-Keeping and the Archaic Urban Cosmos*

I first met Alex Marshack in 1982 at a public evening lecture he gave in New York City, where we both lived. That evening he described the Paleolithic "time-factored" notational systems and monuments that traced the rhythms of the moon and sun, and how Neolithic calendars governed the rhythms of planting and harvesting, as well as the rites of passage and social integration via festivals that were occasions for gift exchange and intermarriage. After the talk I introduced myself to him, and more than twenty years of friendship followed.

I was just beginning to trace the genesis of interest-bearing debt and how early societies dealt with the problems it caused. This led me to note the calendrical timing of early debt payments, along with the standardization of money and interest rates as a byproduct of weights and measures calendrically based for periodic distribution of food and other resources by Mesopotamia's temples and palaces. Alex saw immediately the convergence between my research, working backward from classical antiquity to the Early Bronze Age, with his own studies going forward from the Paleolithic. He introduced me to the Peabody Museum's director, Carl Lamberg-Karlovsky, who helped me organize a group of Assyriologists and archaeologists to publish what are now five colloquia volumes on the genesis of money and account-keeping, debt, urbanization and land tenure, privatization and labor.

At our second colloquium, held at New York University in 1996 on urban development in the ancient Near East, Alex summarized his views on how the time-keeping practices that began in the Paleolithic laid the foundations for civilization in the Near East and Europe. Using many of the same slides from the lecture I had heard him give fourteen

---

* First published as "After the Ice Age: How Calendar-Keeping Shaped Early Social Structuring," in Paul G. Bahn, ed., *An Enquiring Mind: Studies in Honor of Alexander Marshack* (American School of Prehistoric Research Monograph Series, Oxford and Oakville, Oxbow Books, 2009):149-153.

years earlier, he described the calendrical orientation of early ceremonial sites, reflecting their role as seasonal gathering places. The literal meaning of orientation, after all, refers to the east, facing the rising sun, whose annual return to this precise orientation made these meeting grounds part of a dependable regularity, linking such sites – and in time, temples and entire city plans – to the rhythms of the cosmos, "on earth, as it is in heaven." The videotape operator became so fascinated as soon as Alex took the podium that she forgot to press the "on" button on her machine.

The fact that Neolithic agriculture was dependent on the seasons, Alex explained, made the calendar the key to post-Paleolithic social organization, shaping "the way in which archaic communities structured their modes of cultural complexity" inasmuch as agriculture "increasingly requires 'time-factored' divisions of labor and skill, allotted times and places for specialized activities, and calendrically precise times for ritual, aggregation, and exchange."[1] The same may be said of trade and warfare. Sea commerce depended on the annual winds, and even war-making traditionally was waged after the harvest was in.

Calendrical rhythms determined the times when sparse populations came together in the seasonal gatherings that were the occasions for exchange – of family intermarriage as well as gifts. The ritual sites for these gatherings typically were on rivers, often near distinguishing natural features such as caves. The most famous sites were orientated to the rising or setting of the sun at the four major points of the year, the solstices and equinoxes. The calendrical setting of these gatherings was further reflected in their art, whose seasonal references Alex showed to reflect the rhythms of fish mating, deer molting and vegetation sprouting.

Based on the spread of artifacts reflecting a diversity of notational systems – signs that had been viewed simply as decorative markings prior to his 1972 article on the Blanchard bone's lunar notations ca. 28,000 BC – he postulated a worldview extending from the Atlantic to the Russian plain. "Long-distance movements and a dispersal of cultural influences were clearly present during this [Magdalenian] period." "On the Russian plain ... there were summer and winter sites along [the network of rivers that flow toward the Black Sea], including riverside

---

[1] Alexander Marshack, "Space and Time in Pre-agricultural Europe and the Near East: The Evidence for Early Structural Complexity," in Michael Hudson and Baruch A. Levine, eds., *Urbanization and Land Ownership in the Ancient Near East* (Peabody Museum of Archaeology and Ethnology, Harvard University, 1999:19-63):19 and 53.

sites that were specialized for seasonal resource exploitation and for seasonal symbolic performance and production."[2]

Alex concluded that rather than trying to explain "the rise of agriculture in the essentially material and materialistic terms of regional resources, changes in climate and demography, technology, and modes of harvesting and storage, or in terms of the self-domestication of plants and cereals through periodic harvesting," archaeologists and prehistorians "may now also have to consider the long and incremental cognitive and conceptual preparation that made these other processes viable."[3] He traced this cognitive development largely to the development of calendrical observation and its associated social structuring. "The well-known urban tapestries of temples, records, astronomies, and regional calendars, day-and-night hours, scheduled debts, and debt amnesties, and the increasing specialization of skills and the times and places for their use, all required a developing, increasingly precise, and carefully monitored calendar."[4]

That paper was the closest he came to publishing his *long durée* synthesis. Alex often spoke of writing a sequel to *The Roots of Civilization* describing how classical social structuring, myth and ritual preserved traces of Paleolithic cosmology. And what makes the Ice Age so relevant, after all, is how its time-structuring led to subsequent social practice – the civilization dimension of his book. The idea of organizing worldly life on calendrical regularities led to practices that survived even into the Bronze Age and classical antiquity. But Alex concentrated so much effort on defending his interpretation of Ice Age notational systems that he never got around to further elaborating his view of the Paleolithic as the matrix out of which subsequent thought evolved.

What he did elaborate was how time-factored notation evolved into arithmetic. Alex emphasized that tracing lunar patterns did not have to involve mathematical calculation. Paleolithic calendar keeping was pre-mathematical, predating actual arithmetic in the sense of counting in the abstract. It represented sequence (as do the alphabet and the musical scale) but not *numbering* as such. But it was the matrix out of which counting systems developed, inasmuch as the first phenomena to be counted seem to have been the rhythms of the moon and sun, not one's fingers. The key number 28, for instance, evidently was derived

---

[2] *Ibid.*:40 and 32.

[3] *Ibid.*:57.

[4] *Ibid.*:53.

from the days of visibility in the lunar month, to which Alex attributed the prominent role of the number 7 as its divisor.[5] This suggested that the first phenomena being counted were calendrical, and special significance came to be given to numbers in an increasingly abstract sense.

It was in the Neolithic, he believed, when some individuals began to count everything and developed more abstract mathematics, searching for a clue to the order of nature, as expressed first in its calendrical rhythms and then in natural musical and more abstract cosmological proportions. This search for order was the inspiration for science, as well as for myth and ritual.

Some people seem to have found remarkable parallels between calendrical fractions and those of tuning the musical scale. The 12 months of the year found their counterpart in the 12 tones of the musical scale, and the "Pythagorean comma" found its analogue in the gap between the solar and lunar years. These parallels fascinated Alex, and he arranged for us to meet with music historians. But he realized how speculative it was to infer how far archaic individuals had gone along these lines. How could we know whether we were being anachronistic? *We* had found these parallels, but the dangerously speculative waters of reconstructing archaic awareness dissuaded us from publishing until we could make a more thorough case.

One nonetheless can deem the pattern-seeking individuals who embedded these proportions in ancient mythology to have been proto-scientific, given their power of abstraction and ability to find connections. Myth and ritual, religion and social structuring sought ordering in nature, and also social equity. In a sense Alex himself was like a shaman in seeking to re-create the cosmological template that had led chieftains to organize social rhythms to coincide with calendrical cycles.

The problem in trying to re-create the archaic mental template, of course, is that surviving tools, inscribed bones, art and burials, monuments and buildings are only a shadow. There are suggestive inferential phenomena, but the only conclusive facts that could prove Alex's reconstructions would be written narratives. But only in classical antiquity did writers begin to explain the logic behind their policies. All that one finds earlier are records of what was done, not why, so there is no way in which the grand schema that Alex postulated can be more than inferential.

---

[5] Some New Guinea and Indonesian counting systems started from the fingers and went up across the arm and neck and down the opposing arm, up to 28 points. See Aletta Biersack, *The Logic of Misplaced Concreteness: Paiela Body Counting and the Nature of the Primitive Mind* (American Anthropological Association, January 1982).

Recognizing that artifacts have little conclusive to say about the social structures that produced them, he scoured the anthropological literature for studies about what chieftains and shamans did, viewing the latter as kindred spirits. To suggest the ways of thought that may have inspired Paleolithic calendar-keepers and civilization's cognitive takeoff, he compiled a library ranging from archaeoastronomy to classical myth and ritual, seeking clues in the practices of chieftains among the Native Americans and other surviving tribal enclaves.

The line of analysis that Alex initiated did not fit into any academic box in the sense of a discipline and departmental definition. That was his strong point. But it also made it hard to fit his discoveries into the curriculum, even that of anthropology and archaeology, quite apart from the fact that his background as a science writer did not include the PhD that has become the union card for modern professorships.

As a coda to my reminiscences of our discussions, I will briefly sketch the train of effects on which we agreed about how the calendar shaped the development of urban centers, weights and measures, and political divisions into calendrical tribes (thirds, fourths and twelfths). Of particular importance was the shift from lunar to solar calendars, and how early societies handled the disparity between the 356-day lunar year and the 365¼-day solar year, with a New Year interregnum of chaos, after which order was restored to start the new year in balance.

Early weights and measures in the Near East were divided into calendrical fractions for distribution of food and other resources on a monthly basis. This required the standardization of months, and hence the creation of a solar year with artificially standardized 30-day months. The mina's fractional division into 60 shekels in turn determined the rate of interest – $1/60^{th}$ per month, doubling the principal in five years.[6] Based it seems on the division of the year into 12 months, Rome adopted a 12-fold numerical division, and its rate of interest was $1/12^{th}$.

---

[6] I have traced the calendrical basis for the payment of debts, weights and measures in "How Interest Rates Were Set, 2500 BC-1000 AD: *Máš, tokos* and *fœnus* as metaphors for interest accruals," *Journal of the Economic and Social History of the Orient* 43 (Spring 2000):132-161; "Reconstructing the Origins of Interest-Bearing Debt and the Logic of Clean Slates," in Michael Hudson and Marc Van De Mieroop, eds., *Debt and Economic Renewal in the Ancient Near East* (CDL Press, Bethesda, 2002):7-58; and "The Development of Money-of-Account in Sumer's Temples," in Michael Hudson and Cornelia Wunsch, ed., *Creating Economic Order: Record-Keeping, Standardization and the Development of Accounting in the Ancient Near East* (CDL Press, Bethesda, 2004; now ISLET, Dresden, 2023):303-329. See also Chapters 3 and 4 of the present collection.

Serving as a cosmological model for social organization, the calendar found its spatial analogue as the template for early walled cities, which typically had four gates (sometimes as many as twelve) reflecting the cardinal points of the year (or months). Major streets often were aligned to the rising or setting sun, except where adjusted for wind factors.[7]

Greek city-states divided society into calendrical tribal fractions (halves, thirds, fourths or twelfths) as a means of rotating administration of their ceremonial and increasingly political center. It seems that each city-state sought to do so in its own way as a sign of distinction, but shared a common denominator in changing the calendar and tribal divisions together as new tribes were added. Each tribe was assigned its proportional period of rotating control of the center on a seasonal basis (for "four-square" tribal divisions) or monthly basis for twelve-tribe nations. When the calendar was changed, so were the tribal divisions.[8]

Alex and I often spoke of how such social structures imitated astronomical rhythms to create what must have been perceived as early social cosmology, aiming to establish regularities in earthly structures to reflect those of the heavens in a kind of "sympathetic logic." This ran the danger of becoming magical, as in astrology and much medical philosophy and other logic associated with early societies. But the attempt to create an ancient "general field theory" of society and nature also provided the intellectual impetus for what has become civilization.

---

[7] I elaborated this idea in my own contribution to *Urbanization and Land Use in the Ancient Near East*, "From Sacred Enclave to Temple to City." See Chapter 10 of the present collection. John Chapman has followed the idea of seasonal cosmological sites as "cities" in "Houses, households, villages, and proto-cities in Southeastern Europe," in David W. Anthony, ed., *The Lost World of Old Europe: The Danube Valley 5000-3500 BC* (Princeton, 2010):74-89.

[8] When the Athenian Cleisthenes changed the number of tribes from 12 to 10 late in the 6th century BC, for example, he adjusted the public prytany calendar accordingly, from a 12-month to a 10-month basis.

10
From Sacred Enclave to Temple to City*

The social sciences have long viewed the earliest cities as playing much the same role as they do in modern times: to serve as centers of government and to undertake commerce and industry, reflecting the economies of scale resulting from their population growth.

Such speculation assumes an almost automatic and inevitable urbanization stemming from material causes, a combination of increasing population density and new technologies (the agricultural revolution). To the extent that political and military dynamics are recognized, their character is regarded as being like that of classical antiquity, not as having cosmological roots in Neolithic Asia Minor and Early Bronze Age Mesopotamia where civilization's earliest urban centers began – as gathering places before becoming year-round occupation sites with specialized economic functions.

To be sure, not all pre-modern cities developed in the same way. Each region had its own particular characteristics. But from the vantage point of our modern civilization, the first great catalytic urbanization occurred in Mesopotamia. What gave its cities their distinctive character was their commercial and industrial role – by which I mean the specialized handicraft industries organized primarily by the temples and palaces. The unique way in which these urban functions developed was influenced strongly by southern Mesopotamia's ecological imperative to trade.

The word "town" derives from the German *Zaun* (fence), typically referring to the walled military camps planted across Europe by the Roman emperors in standardized designs. But the first urban areas were not that kind of town. From Ice Age caves to sites such as Çatal Hüyük in the sixth millennium BC, they seem to have had a cosmopolitan

---

* This chapter is based on "From Sacred Enclave to Temple to City," in *Urbanization and Land Ownership in the Ancient Near East* (ed. with Baruch Levine, Peabody Museum (Harvard), Cambridge, Mass, 1999):117-146. One change that I have made throughout this new edited version from the original presentation is to avoid the term "public" to describe Bronze Age palaces and temples. Subsequent assyriological studies have shown that the word "public" has too many modern connotations for these institutions, which came to be organized corporately distinct from their community's family-based sector on the land. The term "large institutions" is now the preferred term to describe them.

neutrality from local tribal or other tribal centers, apparently sanctified from raids and typically unwalled. (Although Jericho appears to have been a walled center by about 9000 BC, its walls may well have been flood walls.) Walled fortifications to defend inhabitants gathering in towns do not appear in southern Mesopotamia until relatively late, circa 2800 BC (Adams 1981).

Centered on their city-temples, archaic urban sites served as neutral zones for diverse groups to come together to transact arms-length commerce under an umbrella of common agreed-upon rules. I therefore suggest that if we are to take our clue from classical times, the model to be examined should be amphictyonic sites such as Delphi and Delos, where diverse groups seem to have come together freely without fear of attack – until they became the treasuries for rival Greek city-states.

To perform this neutral role, such sites tended not to develop at the center of their communities, but at boundaries or natural crossroads *between* diverse communities, or on islands. Assur, for instance, sat astride the Tigris intersecting central Mesopotamia's major east/west trade route, and many other entrepots likewise were situated near the sea or on major transport rivers. The landlocked town of Çatal Hüyük seems to have been the center of its own regionwide trading network (see Gelb 1986:165 for some qualifications). Being host to a diversity of groups, such towns hardly would have been centers of political control over the land. This paper therefore focuses on the public ceremonial character of the earliest cities as gathering places and ritual centers, and on the role played by their temple precincts.

The earliest urban sites were sanctified, commercial and peaceful

The physical orientation and cosmological symbolism of archaic cities, their streets, gates, and the architectural character of their civic buildings and monuments reflect their role as sanctified commercial and ritual meeting places and temple areas existing long before centralized war-making, political control and taxation developed. As commercial entrepots they functioned as havens both in the sense of ports (German *Hafen*, as in what Karl Polanyi called ports of trade) and as asylums, literally *havens* from the surrounding land.[1]

---

[1] Sarah Humphreys (1978:53), reviewing the ideas of Karl Polanyi, writes: "The port of trade is Polanyi's name for a settlement which acts as a control point in trade between two cultures with differently patterned economic institutions – typically, between a market and a non-market economy, or rather between a non-market society and

Specialized meeting areas for ritual, exchange and socializing may be found as early as the Ice Age in seasonal gathering spots. These sites initially were occasional rather than year-round settlements. It therefore is appropriate to view them as social constructs independent of their scale, performing urban functions long before they came to grow in size and attract year-round settled populations.

Temples and their precincts comprised the earliest city centers. Set corporately apart from the community at large to serve as self-supporting households of the city-god and/or ruler, they were larger, more specialized and more internally hierarchic than personal households. They also included many dependents whose families on the land were unable to care for them, *e.g.*, the blind and infirm, war widows and orphans, and others who could not function in normal family contexts. Placed in the institutional households that served as the ultimate sanctuaries, these individuals were put to work in handicraft workshops or other professions distinct from the agrarian family-based economy (*e.g.*, the blind musicians) in an early form of welfare/workfare.

It appears that archaic populations felt that the best way to keep handicraft production and exchange in line with traditional social values was to organize such activity under the aegis of temples, or at least to establish a strong temple interface as a kind of Chamber of Commerce. Public ritual and welfare functions already existed as the germ out of which this economic role would flower. As gathering places, temples became natural administrative vehicles for sponsoring trade. In retrospect it seems quite logical that the temple's ritual functions broadened in time to include the role of sponsoring markets. Populations attending sacred ceremonies engaged in trade and exchange, much as they did at the fairs of medieval Europe. Out of this commerce developed temple sponsorship and enforcement of trade obligations.

Much like the ancient cities of refuge (such as that to which Cain withdrew in Genesis 4, and which Numbers 35 and Joshua 20 describe as being established throughout Israel), temples served as sanctuaries for

---

professional traders, who may belong to the market pattern even if the society from which they come, as a whole, does not." Polanyi "saw that the port of trade controlled by a non-market power was a device which shielded the controlling state from influences which would otherwise have disrupted its economy and society. 'Trade was here treaty-based, administered, as a rule, by special organs of the native authorities, competition was excluded, prices were arranged over long terms.'" She adds (p. 54) that "The essential features of the port of trade are that it stands as a 'buffer,' both politically and economically, between the trader and the hinterland whose products he wishes to buy."

fugitives from the retaliatory fury of local feud justice. They also served as sanctuaries to store the savings of their communities – gold and silver, seeds, tools and other sanctified assets deemed free from attack by neighboring communities that shared a common religious belief that such seizure would be sacrilegious.

If the earliest urban zones are to be viewed as *regimes*, the archaic concept of regime was not our modern idea. The word is semantically related to *regulate*, and also reflects the idea of *regularity*, connoting the spirit of equity and even-handedness which is called for in arms-length dealings and the adjudication of disputes. The underlying spirit is one of standardization. Weights and measures are regularized, as are contractual commercial dealings. Parties are treated equally and symmetrically rather than dominated, and relations are formalized to minimize dispute.

To implement their regulatory functions, temples (and later the palaces) developed specialized bodies of law, beginning with rulings and prices governing their own sphere of activities. The resulting regime was essentially urban, but was not necessarily one of political control or "the state." At first the temples regulated the services that they performed directly – marriage and burial ceremonies, handicraft production via distinct guilds, and the prices and interest rates that merchants, palace collectors and other professionals could charge, especially in serving as intermediaries between the large institutions and local and foreign communities.

Bronze Age temples were administrative nodes

In viewing cities as evolving out of ritual and related sanctified functions, I have no intention of reviving ideas from the 1920s and 1930s about the so-called temple-state. Temples did not even have the power to tax (although they charged user fees, sharecropping rent and interest). In any event there was little private surplus to tax, a fact that obliged the Bronze Age large institutions to be self-supporting, and indeed to act as entrepreneurs.

Temples housed the workshops where most export textiles were woven (in contrast to the homespun cloth for subsistence use). They were endowed with resources to support their community's dependent labor to weave these textiles and undertake other export production. Toward this end, much of the community's land was set aside for use by the temples to support their nonagricultural labor force and official staff. Additional land was held by the temples (and in time the palace) for grazing their herds, above all the sheep whose wool was woven into the textiles exported for the raw materials not found in the Mesopotamian alluvium.

It was from this commercial production and export trade that southern Mesopotamia's pioneering economic innovations evolved. It was the temples that organized trade and established embassies in founding foreign trade colonies, sponsoring these embassies as temple cults for merchants operating abroad. The temples thus provided an umbrella for commercial arrangements among disparate peoples, in large part precisely because their sacred status enabled them to serve as forums to settle debts and disputes between local residents and foreign merchants. In sum, temples were administrative nodes governing external contacts.

While social organization on the land remained kinship-based, that of the cities became part of a higher and more cosmopolitan social ordering. Neolithic urban sites, for instance, seem to have begun as publicly demarcated spaces cut out from the surrounding land, where different groups gathered for ritual, exchange and intermarriage. Bronze Age Mesopotamian cities had corporately distinct palaces and temples alongside the communal sector with its own common law. Classical antiquity was different. Mediterranean trade and handicraft production typically was concentrated in the personal households of chieftains, military headmen and other well-placed families based on the land. The cities that arose from these private households became centers of government by the leading families, creating oligarchies free of palace rulers. And following classical antiquity, the modern Western state developed out of the private/communal sector's families governing all society, not out of a corporately distinct civic sector.

Eight characteristics of archaic Near Eastern urbanization

This paper makes eight points with regard to archaic urbanization.

(1) Cities were not an automatic byproduct of population pressures expanding over the land, but were a planned response to the need to conduct external relations, above all trade. Southern Mesopotamia's city-temples organized commerce in ways intended to minimize conflicts by resolving them in mutually agreed-on ways. Urban development thus consisted of heterogeneous groups coming together to engage in commerce and communal rituals.

(2) Early southern Mesopotamian cities took their character from their temples, which played a major role in this trade. Prior to the Bronze Age these temples served as ritual centers and gathering places, and their commercial functions initially evolved out of this role. The largest example in the fourth millennium was Uruk and its sacred Eanna district.

(3) Although textile weaving, pottery work, metalworking and other crafts began early, they were first systematically organized on a large scale in the temples and the palace. As the first corporate entrepreneurs, these large institutions organized craft workshops that employed the community's dependent population consisting largely of "unfortunates" (Babylonian *mushkenu*) – individuals who could not make a go of things in their traditional family context on the land. The blind and infirm, war widows and orphans were put to work at whatever tasks they might be able to perform, supplemented by outsiders such as slaves and war captives. (See Gelb 1965 and 1972, and also Kramer and Meier 1984 for the Sumerian epic in which the god Enki specifies tasks for each type of misfit.)

(4) The evolving structure and organization of Near Eastern cities reflects shifts in the character of their temples, from organizing sacred rituals to a growing commercial and handicraft role, followed by more worldly military concerns as the palace became increasingly important after circa 2800 BC.

(5) The privatization of real estate immune from royal Clean Slates redistributing land started with townhouses for the merchants and collectors who interfaced between the private/communal sector and the large institutions. These houses occupied the city area that originally was the public space. Classical antiquity's cities were privatized as towns became economic areas whose commerce was concentrated in the hands of individual households (the classical Greek *oikos*) rather than being centralized in the temples, palaces or other corporately distinct institutions.

(6) Only as cities became domiciles for the population at large (rather than public areas) did the state develop as modern writers define it. Whereas temples had been organized as autonomous corporate entities, military organization of the citizenry involved all society. Palace or aristocratic rule became predominantly military, creating for the first time truly general society-wide laws instead of separate rules for the large institutions. The land's oral common law came to be recorded in writing, adopting the practice of royal laws and proclamations inscribed on stone and wood and publicly displayed.

(7) Archaeologists find that secularization, an increasingly military focus of social organization and the privatization of economic life went hand in hand with a trend toward smaller economic units. The scale of industry became smaller, as did that of cities.

(8) The militarization of classical antiquity led to empire building. Whereas no Sumerian city was able to hold the "kingship of Sumer" in the third millennium, imperial Athens and Sparta, followed by Rome, extended the scale of the political and urban unit beyond merely local scope. As recipients of tribute they built up grandiose public structures as well as imperial bureaucracies.

Looking at the broad sweep of antiquity from the Early Bronze Age through the imperial Roman climax, one sees the function of cities shifting from amphictyonic or ritual centers to political capitals. At the end of this process Rome was simultaneously a military, governing and industrial center. This combination did not occur under the sponsorship of temples, whose social functions became much more limited than had been the case in Bronze Age Mesopotamia.

Nonetheless, capitals still sought to retain the cosmological idea of cities as centers of order such as had inspired the earliest temple-centered sites. However, the idea of order was made more difficult by wealthy families asserting their economic interests at the expense of society at large. They made public order impossible after the 4th century AD. Roman society polarized economically, cannibalizing its internal market and becoming deurbanized. Economic life reverted to self-sufficient agriculture, with complex organization surviving mainly on the monastic estates in the countryside.

Temple forerunners of cities – their ritual permanence

The origin of urban forms reflects above all that of the temples which served as the focal point of the earliest gathering sites. The seeds are found already in the Ice Age. It therefore is appropriate to begin the discussion with the extent to which Ice Age, Neolithic and Early Bronze Age ritual sites share the characteristics that urban historians subsequently have associated with cities.

It may seem unusual to begin the history of urbanization in the Ice Age, but that is a logical corollary of viewing cities as originating in sacred cosmological functions – ordering their communities, supporting astronomical observers who helped administer the festival calendar, and sponsoring festivals of social cohesion – while simultaneously organizing external relations (trade and war) with the objective of preventing external trade and warfare from deranging the ordered proportions that governed domestic social life.

Organizational structures are more important than physical scale in tracing these proto-urban dynamics. I therefore begin by reviewing the Marxist anthropologist V. Gordon Childe's 1950 discussion of ten common features of urbanization, to show how these characteristics are found in ritual sites before the Bronze Age emergence of formal cities. Childe's criteria of urban development apply equally well to pre-urban sacred sites and their temples because trade and exchange long remained ritual or "public" functions during the Neolithic and Bronze Age Near East. It was out of these functions, above all the economic role of temples in this region, that the first cities emerged.

Anthropologists recognize seven primary urban sites. Following the three great Bronze Age civilizations in the third millennium BC – Mesopotamia, Egypt and the Indus valley – are the North China plain, the Maya and Central Mexican cities, the pre-Incan Andes, and Nigeria's coastal Yoruba territory. Tracing the urban forms for each of these seven regions back to their beginnings, Dennis Wheatley (1971:9 and 225) observes that "we arrive not at a settlement that is dominated by commercial relations, a primordial market, or at one that is focused on a citadel, an archetypal fortress, but rather at a ceremonial complex. ... The predominantly religious focus to the schedule of social activities associated with them leaves no room to doubt that we are dealing primarily with centers of ritual and ceremonial activity. ... Beginning as little more than tribal shrines ... these centers were elaborated into complexes of public ceremonial structures ... including assemblages of such architectural items as pyramids, platform mounds, temples, palaces, terraces, staircases, courts, and stelae. Operationally they were instruments for the creation of political, social, economic, and sacred space, at the same time as they were symbols of cosmic, social and moral order." The first urban sites were thus predominantly public areas. They consisted above all of temples.

Functionally speaking, specialized ritual exchange centers are found already in the European Ice Age, between 30,000 and 10,000 BC, thousands of years before hunting and gathering bands settled down to cultivate the land on a year-round basis. By the Early Bronze Age for all practical purposes the temples (and in time the palace) *were* the city.

Mesopotamian merchants and "big men" built, bought and sold townhouses to interface with the palace and temples to trade their workshop wares abroad, collect barley-rents and interact in related ways as intermediaries with these large institutions. To the extent that urban areas were islands in predominantly agrarian societies, they were closely linked with the large institutions. Many pre-urban traditions remained to shape their urban cosmologies. It was these traditions that helped provide a forum for diverse groups to come together at these sites for interactions between the large institutions, their officials and merchants.

In setting the materialistic tone for most modern discussions in his above-mentioned 1950 article, Childe described the urban revolution as having occurred circa 3500-3000 BC, contemporaneously with the origins of writing. Not concerning himself with the cosmological aspects of archaic cities, he focused on their overt physical characteristics and material economic conditions. Using this approach, he found towns to be more or less automatic results of the agricultural revolution that began around 9000 BC. The cultivation of crops and domestication of animals enabled enough food, oil and wool to be produced to support a permanent superstructure of handicraft, mercantile and administrative occupations.

This labor was concentrated in urban complexes, especially in the temples and palaces that served as households of their local city-deities. Childe did not elaborate on the paramount role of temples in structuring the social ordering that formed the context for civilization's first urbanization. But upon examination, the ten characteristics he listed as constituting the urban revolution all describe temples so well that their role should have been readily apparent.

Childe found the most obvious characteristic of cities to be their size: "relatively large numbers of people in a restricted area." Their scale had to be large enough to support the second key urban feature: a specialized division of labor. This was associated with a third characteristic: social stratification, replete with hierarchies of authority, going hand in hand with the fourth characteristic: centralization of the economic surplus. This often was achieved by imposing taxes, and by a fifth urban feature: foreign trade, mainly in luxuries for the emerging stratum of wealthy landholders, merchants, officials and warriors.

A sixth urban feature was the shift of political representation away from kinship ties to local territorial districts. Voting in the assemblies was done by neighborhood or ward (*e.g.*, the Athenian *deme*) rather than by the clan membership that defined earlier communities.

A seventh urban characteristic was monumental ceremonial and/or administrative architecture. Writing (an eighth feature) was needed to coordinate record-keeping, production and contracts, and promoted a ninth feature: development of the exact sciences, starting with astronomy and mathematics, and flowering into physics and engineering. Childe held the tenth urban characteristic to be naturalistic art, especially portraiture to reflect the vanity of the emerging bourgeoisie.

Being a materialist (and indeed a technological determinist) and seeking universals, Childe viewed cities as developing automatically as a byproduct of growing population density, specialization of labor and the social stratification that came with a managerial class. From his perspective cosmological considerations and the role of temples seemed merely an incidental superstructure to this basic foundation. His approach led him not to remark on the degree to which his ten urban characteristics all are found in preurban ritual contexts.

Childe presented these urban characteristics as relatively late phenomena, more descriptive of the first millennium BC than the fourth or third millennia. His materialistic approach focuses upon what the Romans called *urbs* (the root of English *urban*), connoting cities primarily in their physically extensive dimension. His list says nothing explicitly about archaic cities being centered around temples, nor did he emphasize their multiethnic, often multilingual character. It therefore is relevant to review the temple antecedents which were the germs out of which increasingly secularized private-sector urban structures flowered. Tracing these urban characteristics requires looking further back in time, and to think of them as traditions of social intercourse, of *civitas* focusing on social structures. Even before the development of towns (and indeed, before agriculture), public traditions must have provided a foundation for group behavior by establishing – and indeed, sanctifying – its rules. It therefore is appropriate to review how Childe's ten urban criteria reflect this cosmology and its ritual functions.

Preurban and Urban Traditions of Social Intercourse

Cities as Formal Urban Sites (after Childe)	Temples in Third-Millennium Mesopotamia and Earlier
1. Concentrate people in a compact site.	Ritual ceremonies sanctify public space and incorporate its diverse occupants into an ordered community.
2. Specialization of labor.	The first formal professions were workers organized into temple guilds and specialized cult-families.
3. Social stratification.	Social stratification began in the public temples and palaces. The word "hierarchy" has sacred connotations.
4. Centralized economic surplus.	Temples were civilization's first public storehouses and "containers," sanctifying their food, seed, tools and precious metals from outside seizure or domestic misappropriation.

5. Foreign Trade.	Temples housed civilization's first handicraft workshops, producing goods for export to exchange for foreign metal, stone and other raw materials. In Mesopotamia they had the largest herds of sheep to provide wool for their textile-making labor.
6. Territorial organization takes precedence over family lineages.	Sacred space was set aside from ownership or control by any specific families. (Rulers did not speak of their parentage but described themselves as being nurtured or chosen by the gods, or "reborn" as members of sacred cults.)
7. Monumental public architecture.	The first stone architecture was civic and ceremonial.
8. Writing and account-keeping.	These originally were palace and temple functions to schedule the allocation of resources to feed and supply their dependent labor force.
9. Development of the exact predictive sciences.	Prediction began with calendar-making, for scheduling omen-taking and prognostication.
10. Naturalistic art, especially portraiture.	Subordination of realism to standardized traditions, often of a cosmological character in the depiction of rulers.

1. **Concentrations of people first occurred at ritual sites.** Only if we assume that the earliest gatherings of people were year-round does it follow that urban forms could not have developed prior to the agricultural revolution. But seasonal gathering sites existed already in Paleolithic times. The idea of sanctifying their ground must have survived to play a germinal role in patterning more permanent cities. The focal points of the rhythms of antiquity's economic and social life remained calendrical, for rituals associated with the harvest (and its debt settlements), markets and general coming together of groups that were more diffuse most of the time.

Contrary to Childe's emphasis on scale, there is no indication that archaic rulers or the augurs who functioned as early city planners thought of urban entities primarily in terms of size. Bronze Age cities appeared to their contemporaries primarily as temple and palace enclaves serving specialized functions. The Sumerian language used the word uru (Akkadian *alu*) to express the idea of village, town and city without regard to size. For instance, in the time of Gilgamesh, ca. 2600 BC, Uruk had fifty thousand inhabitants and spread over 400 hectares, extending a further 15 kilometers beyond the city walls. This made it the largest city prior to Republican Rome (Adams 1969 and 1981:85). Yet

Oppenheim (1977:115) points out that what seems to have been the key to it and other Mesopotamian cities was neither their size nor their walls, but the fact that they were situated on a water course. That was essential for the trade in which every Mesopotamian city needed to engage.

Rulers were called *en* or *lugal* regardless of whether they ruled large cities or were chieftains of small tribal bands (Hallo 1991). Throughout the Bronze Age we find rulers of small towns communicating with more important rulers on the basis of equality, exchanging gifts seemingly without regard for the relative weight of their realms. Function rather than scale was thus the essential feature. For instance, all of the Indus civilization's excavated settlements, from small villages to towns, exhibit a similar physical profile regardless of size (Miller 1985 and Morris 1979:14).

2. **Specialization of labor is documented most extensively in Mesopotamia's temple and palace workshops.** Families living on the land always have had to be relatively self-sufficient. Rural families throughout most of history have grown their own food, made their own clothes and built their own homes and furnishings. Craft specialization has been carried to the furthest degree in cities.

When this specialization was first being formalized at the outset of the Bronze Age, the temples took the lead in organizing handicraft workshops. Gelb (1965 and 1972) has shown how widespread has been the idea of setting aside a dependent specialized nonagricultural population in the large institutions, especially to weave textiles. Ancient Mesopotamia (like India and Incan Peru) established weaving workshops staffed with dependent labor, largely that of women and children. The laws of Hammurabi (§274) ca. 1750 BC list seal cutters, jewelers and metalsmiths, carpenters and house builders, leather workers, reed workers, washer/fullers, felt makers and doctors as institutional professions. Throughout the Bronze Age most specialized professions seem to have been organized as guilds.

Largely in response to the centralized production of most handicrafts for export to exchange for foreign raw materials, Mesopotamia's temples and palaces developed on a larger scale than did the households of chieftains and headmen in the less centralized periphery, including the Mediterranean lands where such workshops were located mainly on private estates (as they were in medieval Europe). Early urban industry thus was characteristically an institutional phenomenon.

3. **Social stratification began in the temples and palaces.** The word *hierarchy* derives from Greek *hiero* (sacred). Babylonian social stratifica-

tion and wealth stemmed largely from economic status gained by interfacing with the temples and palaces as official or quasi-official *tamkarum* merchants, royal collectors or other temple and palace administrators (Yoffee 1988 and 1981). Profit-seeking activities spread from the large institutions to the rest of society as ritual and administrative functions provided the major opportunities for wealth-seeking in socially acceptable ways.

4. **Concentration of the economic surplus in the temple sector.** Temple workshops were set corporately apart from their communities and endowed with their own land, dependent labor, herds of animals and stores of precious metal to support their handicraft activities and generate commercial surpluses. Many temple and palace lands were farmed by community members on a sharecropping basis, typically for a rent of a third of the crop or some other fixed proportion. Indeed, as history's first documented landlords, the temples received the first known land-rent. Administrators were assigned such usufructs to provide food for their support, and may have exchanged some of this barley-revenue for luxuries (Ellis 1976 and Archi 1984). The resulting "redistributive" system of production and consumption preceded market trade and pricing by thousands of years. Also, as business corporations (in contrast to family partnerships), temples appear to have earned interest.

Temples also served as repositories for the surplus grain and in time savings of the community, protected from theft and even from foreign military attack by sanctifying their precincts. Out of this role they became centers for attesting to the purity of silver that was used as money, and also oversight of the weights and measures for the money being used to settle obligations within the institutional economy and for trade.

In short, **profit-accumulating enterprise and the accumulation of surpluses (mainly grain and silver) was institutional before being privatized.** That explains why economic accounting and the organization of large-scale handicraft industry appear first in temple and palatial contexts. Temples systematized profit-seeking in ways that only gradually became acceptable for private individuals acting on their own. (Wealthy individuals were expected to use their resources openhandedly or consume them in conspicuous displays such as burials or marriage feasts.) Indeed, the temples' entrepreneurial functions emerged out of their sacred status "above" the community's families at large. The first organized surplus-yielding property thus was institutional rather than private (Hudson and Levine 1996).

Unlike the case with communal lands held by the population at large, temple and palace properties were not periodically redivided among community members. They were marked by boundary stones inscribed with cosmological symbolism of their permanent and irreversible alienation from their former communal-sector owners, *e.g.,* as on the stele of Manishtushu ca. 2200 BC. (Gelb, Steinkeller and Whiting 1989-91 provide a survey.) No such markers have survived for individually allotted lands from this period, suggesting that any such markers were merely temporary.

5. **Temple production played a central role in foreign trade.** In setting up trading posts or colonies to obtain foreign metal, stone and even hardwood, merchants acted in association with their home-city temples to establish local branches as a kind of trade association (for example, the Assyrian trade colony of Kanesh in Asia Minor. See Leemans 1950 and 1960, Oppenheim 1964, Larsen 1976 and Archi 1984, as well as Hudson 1992). Mesopotamia's temple workshops consigned their luxury textiles and other goods to merchants, and many temple professions dealt with imported materials.

The Uruk expansion ca. 3500 BC appears to have been organized by the temples, planting colonies and trade missions westward across Syria to Asia Minor, southwest to Egypt, and eastward across the Iranian plateau (Algaze 1989). Likewise in archaic Greece, the Delphi temple played a major role in planning and allocating trade outposts and colonies. Organization of foreign trade via temple outposts lasted throughout classical antiquity even in free-enterprise zones such as Delos.

6. **The urban shift away from family-oriented to territorial space began with temple-centered cults.** Individuals were initiated into corporate groupings that replaced their biological families for the purposes of political representation. Paternal authority and family structures were transposed onto the temple and palace households, cults and professional guilds with their own hierarchies of authority.

Over a century ago the American anthropologist Lewis Henry Morgan's *Ancient Society* (1878) placed civilization's urban watershed in the 6th century BC. He focused on the reforms of Cleisthenes in Athens (508) and Servius in Rome (537) as replacing the clannish family contexts, based on rural landholding, with neighborhood political units. Toynbee (1913) followed with a similar analysis for Sparta's changes in the 7th century BC. Subsequent archaeologists, however, have established that cities were organized on a district or ward basis thousands of years earlier. Already in Bronze Age Mesopotamia and Egypt each local area took responsibility for maintaining its irrigation dikes and canals.

Assyriologists have noted that early Mesopotamian rulers downplayed their family identity by representing their lineage as deriving from the city-temple deities. Sargon of Akkad, often taken as a prototype for the myth of the birth of royal heroes (including Moses and Romulus), emphasized his "public family." Archaic clan groupings seem to have been relatively open to newcomers. There is little Bronze Age evidence for the closed aristocracies found in classical antiquity. Mesopotamia seems to have remained open and ethnically mixed for thousands of years, and the Sumerians probably incorporated strangers as freely as did medieval Irish *feins* and many modern tribal communities. After all, labor was the factor of production in shortest supply.

Clan lineages seem to have consolidated themselves (along with their property ownership) more readily in the Western periphery. Mycenaean chieftains built up economic power by adopting the organizational and accounting techniques of the large Near Eastern institutions. And after 1200 BC warlord aristocracies parceled out Greek lands among their own ranks. When urbanization developed anew in the classical epoch, cities once again administered themselves on the district basis described by Morgan.

7. **Monumental architecture likewise originated in the temples.** The temple was the archaic skyscraper as well as the social and economic center of Bronze Age cities. Long before Near Eastern families adopted stone construction for their own homes, the temple symbolized the permanency of the palatial economy's institutions. The earliest stone architecture seems to have been used for official administrative buildings, legal stelae and boundary stones in Mesopotamia, as well as for tombs in Egypt and other regions (Raglan 1964:175-180). In Egypt and elsewhere, monumental stone architecture was used for funerary structures, which had an official, often ceremonial character. The significance given to their astronomical alignment and mathematical symbolism reflects the attempt to imbue administrative and ceremonial buildings with "natural order" (and the spirits of the dead with "eternity" as reflected in the chronological motion of the heavens).

In sum, civic buildings of stone reflected the eternal cosmos in an epoch when private residences were made of less permanent mud bricks and reeds. And as noted above, the use of stone boundary markers rather than wooden or clay ones indicated that alienations of land to the large institutions (usually to the palace) were irreversible, in contrast to communal land tenure.

With regard to the urban characteristics of monumental architecture, and also what Childe describes as naturalistic art, it may be relevant to note that sculptural aesthetics, civic art and urban cosmology dovetailed neatly with each other in a line that can be traced back to a common origin in temple architecture. Snodgrass (1980:179-181) points out that the carving of statues presupposed a marble industry, which derived first and foremost from architectural demand, above all for building sanctuaries and temples. During the flowering of Greek city-states in 650-575 BC, "statues were still often produced by men whose professional training had been as masons or quarrymen." The Attic marble statues whose production flourished after 600 BC found their epitome in dedications to sanctuaries and grave monuments (*ibid.*:145-146).[2]

8. **Writing originated as a palatial and temple function.** Record-keeping served as a centralized control and scheduling device long before writing became a vehicle for personal self-expression, literature or abstract philosophy. The earliest notations and cylinder seals were developed to hold temple administrators accountable for their receipt and disbursement of rations and other resources. By the middle of the third millennium, written accounts were being used to schedule product flows. The other great inspiration for symbolic notation and counting was calendar-keeping, traditionally a priestly task.

9. **Arithmetic and predictive sciences also were developed and formalized in a palatial administrative context, often to aid in rituals.** Archaic counting apparently derived from calendar-making, as did astronomy and other predictive sciences, along with astrology and the taking of auguries. Such forecasting was used for palatial institutional functions long before diffusing to the population at large.

---

[2] Snodgrass (1980:179) adds that although the Athenian statues of standing male figures (*kouroi*) seem at first glance to be a naturalistic rendering, their typical pose actually "is an unnatural one, both feet being flat on the ground even though the position of the legs is for walking." He explains this pose as probably being designed "to require the minimum modification of a tall, prism-shaped block of about 6 feet by 1 foot by 1½ feet ... equivalent to two small building blocks superimposed on end." The front, profile and back views could be drawn on the appropriate faces of the block, and carving would then follow the outline. Indeed, "'pre-carved' *kouros* statues either *in situ* at a quarry, or nearby," have been found (*ibid.*:143). This standardization of design was made all the easier by virtue of the fact that "accepted ratios existed for the various measurements."

Of a more practical calendrical nature were Mesopotamia's sexagesimal fractions and higher mathematics, developed in the third millennium. The 360-day administrative year helped provision the institutional labor force on a regular monthly basis. Large-number computation was used to schedule the food and beer rations and manpower needed to dig canals and for similar engineering projects. The 360-day calendar also provided a modular format for the circular geometry to divide the ecliptic and zodiac, and hence to predict celestial cycles. In sum, Bronze Age mathematical, astronomical and related knowledge was ritualistic as well as used for institutional enterprise long before classical antiquity applied it to more secular tasks.

10. **The first representational art is found in ritual contexts.** One cannot say that the phenomenon of "naturalistic" art is specifically urban. Long before settled agriculture supported year-round urbanization, the remarkably naturalistic imagery of the European Ice Age had depicted the seasonal behavior and appearance of animals and fish, including the moulting of pelage, the growth and shedding of antlers and the appearance of spring vegetation. Reviewing over twenty thousand years of Ice Age art and iconography, Marshack (1972 and 1975) gives persuasive reasons for regarding much of that imagery as being referential in its seasonal contexts, probably because it was produced for seasonal ritual and mythic purposes. (For instance, animals are shown in their seasonal molting or mating seasons, so one typically can see what time of the year the imagery refers to.)

What Childe seems to term naturalistic art is simply that which *lacks* the traditional dimension of symbolic cognitive meaning. But classical portraiture and statuary only gradually dispensed with the iconographic formalities traditionally used in the Bronze Age to indicate status. Although much statuary and portraiture appears naturalistic at first glance, the proportions of the head to the body and other ratios reflect a sexagesimal arithmetic in Mesopotamia and decimalized proportions in Egypt and Greece (Azarpay 1990). Even rulers such as Gudea, whom one would expect to be pioneers of individualistic rendering, were regressed into a set of standardized features (Winter 1989). Such symbolic and mathematized idealizations are the opposite of naturalism.

To sum up, all ten of Childe's urban characteristics turn out to be grounded in preurban ritual activities that long retained an institutional character, above all those activities associated with Bronze Age temples, their communal storage facilities, handicraft workshops and sponsorship of the festivals that were the focal point of the archaic calendar. As a Marxist, Childe might have emphasized how cities, like every social organism, evolved in the womb of their predecessor. Instead, he focused on cities simply as material consequences of a technological revolution, without tracing their genesis as sacred ritual sites.

No doubt if we could travel back in time to ask a Bronze Age Mesopotamian, Egyptian or Canaanite about how to go about founding a town, or even to ask a classical Greek or Roman augur who knew the appropriate rites, we would hear little about Childe's materialist criteria for cities. There was no archaic or classical discussion of population pressure and democratic density, or of how the division of labor led to social stratification or to lower costs (and hence higher economic competitiveness), but only to higher-*quality* output as a result of specialization (Lowry 1987:68-70 and Finley 1974). Nor did ancient writers discuss the urban character of writing and institutional architecture, science, engineering and the secularization of art. As for the idea that cities tended automatically to grow larger and more complex over time, it took many centuries for classical Greece and Rome to achieve anywhere near the degree of specialization found in Bronze Age Mesopotamia, and their industry was never as large-scale.

Even as cities became more secular in classical times, their administrative focus remained shaped to a large extent by sacred rituals. Town planners were augurs, more concerned with reading omens than with the more pragmatic aspects of city planning. In an epoch when medicine was ritualistic and doctors often were like shamans, the idea of promoting health was to perform proper rituals at the city's foundation rather than to place cities on slopes for good drainage. (It was considered auspicious to build Rome around the mosquito-ridden Forum.) Material considerations were incorporated to the extent that they could be reconciled with the guiding social cosmology.

Entrepot cities as enclaves from the laws of their lands and secular power

The heterogeneous and multiethnic character of Near Eastern cities reflected their function as enclaves *from* the law of the land, *e.g.*, as free trade areas. In this respect the earliest archaic urban sites were specialized islands – ritual centers, trading entrepots, and occasionally (but relatively late) imperial capitals and military outposts such as those of Sargon and his Akkadians. What is not found among early Near Eastern cities is the general-purpose *polis* of classical antiquity, whose citizen-landholders made laws covering their community at large and carried on industry through their own households rather than via corporately distinct institutions. Many millennia were required before a common body of law came to govern the city and the land, temples and palaces in a single code. *Polis*-type cities and their law codes combining hitherto separate institutional and private, sacred and secular functions were relatively late.

Having summarized the various characteristics of the earliest urban sites, we are now in a position to turn to one of the most economically important types of archaic city: the trade entrepot. Beginning with Çatal Hüyük in Asia Minor ca. 5500 BC, the earliest cities were multiethnic entrepots. They might range in size from a trading post (French *pôt*) to a full-fledged port city. Such commercial centers would have had to provide equal treatment for all parties, reinforced by the usual array of rituals. These towns were different in principle from centers of political government or military power representing one territory's interests as distinct from those of other such groupings.

Near Eastern cities were centered around temples which gave them a sacred status. The temples served as commercial administrators as an extension of their employment of dependent labor as described above. Not being controlled by any one tribe, family or locality (at least "in the beginning"), these temples were endowed by diverse parties as autonomous institutions to serve broad community-wide interests. This institutional status explains why the earliest towns were militarily stable despite their lack of fortifications. Their cosmopolitan, often multiethnic character made their urban identity broader than local hierarchies and chiefdoms.

An important characteristic of entrepot cities was that they were founded at the external margin rather than in the center of their communities. The fact that they often were on water-courses or similar natural points of confluence reflects the fact that one of their major purposes was to deal with outsiders, above all through trade. Similar entrepot areas were built up on conveniently situated offshore islands. Such islands had the political advantage of keeping foreign mercantile contact out of local communities. That made them a path of least resistance as neutral commercial entrepots facilitating politically autonomous contacts.

Egypt, for instance, restricted foreign contacts to the Delta region where the Nile emptied into the Mediterranean. The Etruscans confined their foreign commerce with the Phoenicians and Greeks in the 8th and 7th centuries BC to the island of Ischia/Pithekoussai, which became a base for Corinthian and other merchants to deal with the Italian mainland. Cornwall's tin was exported via the Scilly Isles. The north Germans may have conducted the Baltic amber trade by way of the offshore island of Helgoland. Athens traded via its Piraeus port area.

Muhly (1973:227) notes the significance of island entrepots: "The early Greek commercial settlements in the west were made not on the mainland but on small offshore islands, such as Ischia, in the Bay of Naples, and Ortygia, just off Syracuse. The early Phoenician settlements in the west followed the same pattern, as shown by the settlements at Motya, off the western tip of Sicily, and at Gadir, in Cadiz Bay." Rhys Carpenter (1966:206-207) has attributed this to the fear felt by seaborne traders of "mainland native treachery." Other such islands include the Scilly Isles off the coast of Cornwall as noted above, and the Bahrain islands, as well as Ru'ush eg-Gibal in the Gulf of Oman. Muhly adds (1973:99) that Fagerlie (1967) discusses the offshore islands of Øland and Gotland in northern Europe's amber trade. Homer's Odyssey has the Phaecians trade from an offshore island. (Note Hong Kong's role in today's world.) This long historical tradition stands behind today's offshore enclaves.

These commercial entrepots were stateless in the sense of lying outside the jurisdiction and control of any single territorial government. They often were islands figuratively if not literally, and many were situated at key transport junctions. The basic idea was to separate foreign mercantile activities from mainland social and economic relations. (We find this same idea in the *karum* areas where trade was conducted, even in inland colonies such as karum Kanesh to handle the Assyrian trade in Asia Minor. Larsen 1976 provides details.)

Such "cosmopolitan" exchange occurred on quite different principles from exchange within domestic economies. These transactions with outsiders were highly formalized and standardized, in contrast to relationships within domestic economies with their own hierarchies and status. Commercial debts were not cancelled by royal decrees that annulled domestic agricultural personal debts. Taxes were imposed on foreign trade in contrast to domestic commerce.

A characteristic of commercial entrepots was their exemption from control by any single regional or kinship-based grouping. Their inhabitants were treated equally (at least in principle), regardless of their private status. In the third and second millennia we find such cities marked by *kudurru* stones attesting to their exemption from tribute and quasi-taxes, something like Germany's medieval free cities.

The multiethnic character of southern Mesopotamian cities (and others as well) led them to formalize rituals of social integration to create a synthetic affinity. Urban cults were structured to resemble the family – an institutional family or corporate body with its own foundation story such as that of Abraham of Ur for the Jews, or heroic myths for Greek cities. Over these families stood the temples, "households of the gods," whose patron deities were manifestations of a common prototype and given local genealogies with a common archaic pattern.

Commercial contacts led to cultural interchange and new cultural forms. Residents of gateway centers staged pageants to celebrate and cement their association. Olympia, Delphi, Nemea and the Corinthian Isthmus staged pan-Hellenic games as friendly competitions to help integrate the Greeks (Raschke 1988). Such festivities have provided occasions for trade throughout much of history. Their ceremonial character enabled them to provide an umbrella of peace over a market for commercial wares.

Cities of refuge

The first city that appears in the Bible (Genesis 4) is not a commercial port, administrative capital or military outpost, but the city of refuge located "east of Eden ... in the land of Nod," to which Adam's son Cain withdrew after he killed his brother Abel. This city evidently was already established and populated, but we are not told by whom.

Such cities of refuge are found not only in the Old Testament but also in Native American communities at the time of their first contact with white men, suggesting a nearly universal response to the problem of what to do with public offenders. Throughout history, exile has been a widespread punishment for manslaughter and other capital crimes, including treason. The exile is obliged to leave his native community on pain of death, liable to retaliation by the victim's family taking revenge. Sanctuaries for such fugitives must have been well peopled, for an early myth says that Romulus helped populate Rome by founding an asylum for them.

The Israelites are said to have created twelve cities of refuge, one for each tribal region. Genesis 9 stipulates: "Whoever sheds the blood of man, by man shall his blood be shed." Exodus 21 qualifies this by adding that as long as there was no deliberate murder with premeditated guile, "if he does not do it intentionally, but God lets it happen, he is to flee to a place I will designate." Numbers 35 reports that the Lord commanded Moses to "Speak to the Israelites and say to them: 'When you cross the Jordan into Canaan, select some towns to be your cities of refuge, to which a person who has killed someone accidentally may flee.

They will be places of refuge from the avenger, so that a person accused of murder may not die before he stands trial before the assembly.'" Six towns were so appointed, to be overseen by Levite priests. More details are provided by Joshua 20, a veritable manual for how to inaugurate a city or new society:

> The Lord said to Joshua: "Tell the Israelites to designate the cities of refuge, as I instructed you through Moses, so that anyone who kills a person accidentally and unintentionally may flee there and find protection from the blood-avenger.
>
> When he flees to one of these cities, he is to stand in the entrance of the city gate and state his case before the elders of that city. Then they are to admit him into their city and give him a place to live with them. If the blood-avenger pursues him, they must not surrender the one accused, because he killed his neighbor unintentionally and without malice aforethought. He is to stay in that city until he has stood trial before the assembly and until the death of the high priest who is serving at that time. Then he may go back to his own home in the town from which he fled."

Such cities are often assumed to have been placed on hills, mountains or other prominent spots plainly marked, as described in Deuteronomy 19, but Levine finds them to be temples in the city itself. In any event, each year public workers are reported to have been sent to repair the roads leading to them, and to maintain signposts guiding manslayers. Such cities were to be of ready access, situated "in the midst of the land" rather than in remote corners, so that they could be reached by a single day's journey. Presumably they were emptied in the general amnesties which find their roots at least as early as the Babylonian *misharum* Clean Slates and Egyptian *sed* festivals early in the second millennium.

Archaic cities as gateways

Entrepots throughout history have been multiethnic, attracting merchants and travelers from all over. The logic of their social relations has dictated that when disputes arise, they should be settled by administrative bodies or juries composed of all parties. To establish a standard of behavior (and of pricing, responsibility and liability) these areas developed their own rules, which seem to have been the first to be written down. The most characteristic applications of early royal laws pertained to exchange and contact among alien-equals, and between the institutional professions and the communal/private sector. As noted above, such laws were distinct from the common law of the land, which took the form of oral traditions.

A variety of languages often were spoken in ancient entrepots, just as they are in modern Hong Kong with its Chinese and English, Panama with its Spanish and English, and Lebanon with its Arabic and French. As historians of writing and the alphabet have described, phonetic symbols enabled scribes to transcribe the sounds of alien names and towns to render them from one language to another. The urban tradition of writing thus may be attributed to the multiethnic commercial character of archaic cities, and their need for record-keeping to seal contracts and treaties, and to keep accounts.

Some parallels between archaic entrepots and modern offshore banking centers

A discussion of the origins of urbanization may provide some insight into the character of modern social problems by highlighting the long historical dynamic at work. It may not be out of place here to point out that anti-states are well known in the modern world, above all in what the U.S. Federal Reserve Board classifies as eleven offshore banking centers. Five such enclaves are in the Caribbean: Panama, the Netherlands Antilles (Curacao), Bermuda, the Bahamas and the British West Indies (Cayman Islands). Three enclaves – Hong Kong, Macao and Singapore – were founded to conduct the China trade. The remaining three are Liberia, Lebanon, and Bahrain at the mouth of the Persian Gulf – the island which Bronze Age Sumerians called Dilmun when they used it to trade with the Indus valley and the Iranian shore.

Nothing would seem more modern than these offshore banking and tax-avoidance centers. They are the brainchildren of lawyers and accountants in the 1960s seeking to weave loopholes into the social fabric – to provide curtains of secrecy ("privacy") to avoid or evade taxes, and to serve as havens for ill-gotten earnings as well as to facilitate legitimate commerce.

Whereas modern nation-states enact laws and impose taxes, these enclaves help individuals evade such regulations. And whereas nation-states have armies, these centers are the furthest thing from being military powers. They are antibodies to nationhood, yet more may be learned about Ice Age, Neolithic and even Bronze Age gathering and meeting sites by looking at these modern enclaves than by examining classical city-states such as Athens and Rome.

A clue to the common character of today's commercial enclaves and their Bronze Age forerunners is **their lack of political autonomy.** Instead of being politically independent, the modern offshore banking centers and free trade zones are small former colonies, *e.g.*, the Caribbean islands as well as the Chinese entrepots. The Grand Cayman Island was a Jamaican dependency until 1959, when it chose to revert to its former status as a British crown colony so as to benefit from what remained of imperial commercial preferences. Liberia and Panama are U.S. dependencies lacking even their own currency system. (Both use the U.S. dollar.) Hong Kong did not gain title to its own land until Britain's leases expired in 1997. Panama did not gain control of its canal until 1999.

In sum, whereas political theorists define the first characteristic of modern states (and implicitly their capital cities) as being their ability to enact and enforce laws, offshore banking centers are of no political significance. In the sense of being sanctuaries from national taxes and law authorities, such enclaves are in some ways akin to the biblical cities of refuge. If they are not sanctuaries for lawbreakers personally, they at least provide havens for their bank accounts and corporate shells.

Like most archaic entrepot-cities, modern offshore banking centers are **situated at convenient points of commercial interface between regions,** typically on islands or key transport navels such as the Panamanian isthmus. They are separated as free ports politically, if not physically, from their surrounding political entities. They often are centers of travel and tourism ("business meetings"), and for gambling. In antiquity they typically were centers for sacred festivals or games such as were held at Delphi, Nemea, the Corinthian Isthmus or Olympia (whence our modern Olympic games originated in a sacred context).

Although Delphi and Olympus were landlocked (as was Çatal Hüyük), they were centrally located for their local regions. They served as religious and cultural centers, whose festivals and games could be conveniently attended by the Hellenic population at large. Even visitors who were citizens of mutually belligerent city-states enjoyed **sacred protection against attack**. Of course, today's enclaves no longer claim sacred status, except for the Vatican and its Institute for Religious Works promoting money-laundering functions (Yallop 1984:92-94). Their commercial focus has become divorced from the religious setting associated with international commerce down through medieval Europe with its great fairs. And indeed, their attraction is especially to wealthy individuals avoiding the tax laws and criminal codes of their own homeland.

Today's enclaves **rarely have armies of their own,** yet they are militarily safe. Thanks to their unique apolitical status, and indeed to their ultimate dependence on larger powers, their neighbors have little motive to attack them and every reason to use them as business channels and even for government transactions such as arms dealing, money laundering and related activities not deemed proper behavior at home. The resulting commerce thrives free of regulations and taxes, conducted in militarily safe environments without the cost of having to support standing armies, and hence less need to levy taxes for this purpose, or to monetize national war debts.

To create such enclaves has been an objective of mercantile capital through the ages. It patronizes the world's politically weakest areas as long as they do not do what real governments do: regulate their economies. The search for "neutral territory" expressed itself already in the chalcolithic epoch, many millennia before private enterprise developed as we know it. The result of this impetus is that neolithic towns such as Çatal Hüyük, Mesopotamian temple cities such as Nippur, island entrepots such as Dilmun, the Egyptian Delta area, Ischia/Pithekoussai, and the biblical cities of refuge share the following important common denominator with today's offshore banking centers: **Instead of being centers of local governing, legal and military power, they were politically neutral sites established outside the jurisdictions of local governments.**

Whether the status of these urban sites was that of sanctified commercial entrepots or amphictyonic centers, they provided a forum for rituals of social cohesion to bolster their commerce. These rituals included the exchange of goods and women (intermarriage) – commerce and intercourse in their archaic sexual meaning as well as in the more modern sense of commodity exchange.

I have cited above the archaic practice of conducting trade via island entrepots. The sacred island of Dilmun/Bahrain in the Persian Gulf represents history's longest lasting example of such an enclave. It served as an entrepot linking Sumer and Babylonia (whose records refer prominently to the "merchants of Dilmun") to the Indus civilization and the intervening Iranian shore.[3] Its status as a sacred as well as commercial center may have been promoted by the fact that its waters were a source of pearls, prized as sacred symbols of the moon (being round, pale and associated with deep water). It also seems to have served as a high-status burial ground for prosperous individuals, or at least for parts of their bodies. Lamberg-Karlovsky 1982 reports that there are more fingers and other limbs than full skeletons, as the Sumerians partook piecemeal in

---

[3] Dilmun's weights and measures were those of the Indus basin (Zaccagnini 1986).

the island's sanctity (although some commentators believe that this may be simply the result of grave robberies through the centuries; see Moorey 1984). In any event, these social and commercial virtues helped make Dilmun one of the most expensive pieces of Bronze Age real estate, not unlike modern Bahrain.

The sacred status of such entrepots facilitated commercial development in ways that did not abuse Bronze Age sensibilities, **much like the sacred status of temples did when they became the major economic and textile production centers.** While creating the economic conditions and organization of large-scale enterprise within traditional social values and order, Bronze Age institutions provided leeway so as not to stifle commercial development with overcentralized control. This may be part of the reason why trade was conducted *outside* the city gates. The philosophy was to create "mixed economies" in which institutional and private sectors each had their proper role.

Delos: A classical prototype of modern Panama

This paper began by describing civilization's earliest cities as gateways and neutral zones. They were places where corporately distinct institutions – first the temples and later the palace – were endowed with resources to generate economic surpluses in profit-seeking ways not yet deemed proper for individual families. By the Hellenistic period in the 2nd century BC, Delos exhibits the mirror image: a trading enclave enabling private individuals to escape from social rules, turning its temples into commercial embassies of the crassest sort.

During the millennium extending from about 700 BC to AD 300 the unchecked dynamics of commerce and usury, warfare and slavery polarized Greece, Italy and the Mediterranean region as a whole. From Persia to Italy, palace workshops and temple households gave way to smaller-scale and less formal family-based estates (*oikoi*) of warrior aristocracies. Most commercial wealth passed into private hands freed from the checks and balances of central authority. That was particularly true after Alexander the Great's empire was parceled out among his leading generals following his death in 323 BC. The ensuing Hellenistic regimes provided a free-for-all for wealthy families to do virtually as they wished.

Like most other Aegean islands, Delos was dominated by Athens until one of Alexander's generals, Ptolemy, gained control in 315 BC. Although poor in land and other natural resources, and despite the fact that its port and harbor were not very good, Delos flourished as a commercial entrepot. Its Temple of Apollo had long established the island as a deposit-banking enclave. Sacred oversight of deposits by Apollo's attendants was of critical importance in an epoch when no such thing as national deposit insurance existed.

Matters were catalyzed when Rome threw its support behind oligarchies throughout the Aegean and Greece, achieving suzerainty over the Mediterranean in 168 BC with the battle of Pydna. Until this time Delos had been overshadowed by the neighboring island of Rhodes. The latter was an ally of Rome, but its business standards were too high to facilitate the quick killings sought by Italian speculators, and in any case Rhodians had kept non-Greeks out of local banking and commerce. In 168 the Roman Senate undercut the island's power by making Delos a duty-free port.

This diverted much business away from Rhodes, and gained for Italian merchants and bankers a major foothold in the Aegean. The Delian temple and general economic administration were turned over to Rome's ally Athens, which expelled many Delians and replaced them with Athenians, supplemented by an influx of Italian and Levantine adventurers. These newcomers used Delos as a locus for the Aegean grain trade and the maritime lending and insurance that grew out of it.

The island's commercial role was spurred in 146 BC when Rome destroyed Corinth and Carthage, and by the general breakdown of authority in the Aegean resulting from the fact that in destroying Rhodian naval power, Rome removed the single major check on piracy. Delos did not take Rhodes' place in keeping Aegean commerce free from pirates. Indeed, it became their major market!

Matters were greatly aggravated after 142 BC when an ambitious military officer, Diodotus Tryphon, led a revolt to break Cilicia (in what is now southern Türkiye) and neighboring Syria away from their Seleucid rulers. He organized the Cilicians into pirate fleets, and his freebooters managed to take over such government as there was in the region. The pirates quickly monopolized the most lucrative trade of the period – that in slaves. As Strabo (XIV.5) described matters: "Prisoners were an easy catch, and the island of Delos provided a large and wealthy market not far away, which was capable of receiving and exporting ten thousand slaves a day. Hence the proverb: 'Merchant, sail in, unload, everything is sold.' ... The pirates seeing the easy gains to be made, blossomed forth in large numbers, acting simultaneously as pirates and slave traders." They sold spoils and captives from Asia Minor, Syria and Egypt to the burgeoning southern Italian market to work as slaves on the large plantations, in handicraft workshops, or simply as household servants.

The Temple of Apollo, sun-god of justice, supporting rather than curtailing the activities of the pirates, merchants and usurers flocking to Delos, provided a protective screen for the basest commercial speculations. The historian Mikhail Rostovtzeff (1941:542-544 and 292) has described how "the free port of Delos [was] left completely in the hands of bankers, merchants and traders ... While in the early days of Delos the city was an annex to the temple, now the temple became a kind of appendix to the community, bankers with the corresponding amount of labor, mostly servile." Each of the island's ethnic and professional groupings formed its own cult association to represent its mercantile, shipping and banking interests. From southern Italy, for instance, came the cults of Mercury and Maia, Apollo and Poseidon. A Phoenician cult was centered in a temple replete with porticoes to display its members' merchandise (Tarn 1952:261, citing Hatzfeld, *Les Trafiquants Italiens dans l'Orient hellenique*).

Yves Garlan (1988:183) refers to pirate-controlled Cilicia and its emporium on Delos as "counterstates," and Rostovtzeff calls them "a new phenomenon among the city-states of Greece." Tarn (1952:264-266) describes Delos's relationship with the Cilician pirates as an "unholy alliance ... Delos became the greatest slave-market yet known, and as the eastern governments began to grow weaker their subjects were drained away; Bithynia is said to have been half depopulated." He concurs that Delos represented "a unique kind of form ... the foreign business associations became 'settlers,' and in their totality constituted 'Delos,' seemingly without any city forms at all, but under an Athenian governor; that is, political precedents were subordinated to the requirements of trade." Thus, just as in today's world Panama and other offshore banking entrepots operate as the antitheses to nationhood, so in Rostovtzeff's description "the motley population of Delos had not the slightest inclination to become a city. They were perfectly happy to live the peculiar life of a free merchant community with no civic duties to fulfill and no liturgies [taxes] to bear."

The last thing the Delian merchant class wanted was a public authority to regulate its entrepot trade in captured cargoes, slaves or, for that matter, honest goods. "It is evident that the residents of Delos were not very much interested either in the temple or in the city," concludes Rostovtzeff.

> Delos was for them not their home but their business residence. What they cared for most was not the city or the temple but the harbors, the famous sacred harbor, and especially the three adjoining so-called basins with their large and spacious storehouses. It is striking that while these

storehouses are open to the sea there is almost no access to them from the city. This shows that very few goods stored in them ever went as far as even the marketplaces of the city. Many of them came to the harbor, spent time in the storehouses, and moved on, leaving considerable sums in the hands of the Delian brokers. In fact in the Athenian period the city of Delos was but an appendix to the harbor. So soon as the activity of the harbor stopped, the city became a heap of ruins and it was again the temple which towered over these in splendid isolation.

This characteristic of Delos's warehouses being only open outwards, not inland, finds a parallel in modern Panama's Canal Zone, whose warehouses likewise are bonded and set aside from the local economy (save for the National Guard's pilfering and shakedowns). Panama's imports from Asia are destined for other Western Hemisphere countries rather than for local consumption. Drug and arms shipments provide another analogue to Delian contraband. Finally, Panama's sizeable Asian and European population working as brokers and bankers recalls the adventurers who made their way to Delos. Both that island and Panama became what are now called "dual economies": The Delian export trade involved the native population only minimally, much as is the case in Panama and other modern enclaves.

The anti-Roman leader Mithradates of Pontus received support from the Cilician pirates, and in turn gave his support to Delos. An uprising against Rome resulted in the massacre of Italian merchants and creditors throughout Asia Minor and Greece in 88 BC. Some 20,000 Romans and their retinues reportedly were killed on Delos and the neighboring islands. The pirates later looted Delos. Rome retaliated, and the accession of Augustus a half-century later finally cleared the Mediterranean of piracy and restored peace. That dried up the sources of the Delian trade in slaves and pirate contraband.

As free-enterprise havens for their respective criminal undergrounds, both the Delian and Panamanian enclaves attracted the usual riffraff. What would be needed to complete the parallel between Panama and Delos would be a massacre of Americans in the Canal Zone comparable to that of Roman tax farmers and creditors in the 1st century BC. Even without so grizzly a climax, an obvious parallel remains: Just as Rome finally closed down Delos, so the 1988-89 American invasion to topple Noriega lay waste to Panama's economy. (However, whereas Rome proceeded to clean up Mediterranean piracy as a whole, the United States has not sought to close down criminal-enterprise zones in the Caribbean except for the Canal Zone.)

Summary: Near Eastern temples and their urbanizing functions

Bronze Age trade entrepots and temples were not governing centers to establish general laws and policies for their local landed communities. Even less were they in the character of military centers. Entrepots did not have taxing authority beyond their local enclave limits. (That would have smacked of imperial tribute.) Tribute was imposed by conquerors on defeated populations, but the major Mesopotamian cities were freed from such tribute in the Middle and Late Bronze Age. This freedom was marked by *kudurru* stones (Oppenheim 1977). Nippur, for instance, was "tax-free." Mesopotamian rulers exempted it from tribute. In this status as a "free city" we find the characteristic of modern commercial havens. No doubt this status was related to the fact that many of antiquity's trade enclaves were established literally as **islands of free enterprise**.

Such cosmopolitan islands were anything but "states" as usually described by political theorists. Indeed, today's ideas of state power are not much help in analyzing Bronze Age institutions. Hammurabi's laws applied specifically to relations between the palace sector and the community at large, reflecting the fact that palaces and temples were set corporately apart. The community had its own common law to deal with personal injury and other relations not involving the palatial sector. Conversely, by not viewing states as having a directly commercial role, modern political theorists miss the key characteristics of archaic urbanization and the large Bronze Age institutions. Mesopotamian temples and palaces were economic producers in an epoch when production had not yet passed into private hands.

While the temples had important worldly social functions, governing was not one of them. They evolved out of seasonal ceremonial gathering centers to solve the most pressing economic problem of their time – to undertake the commercial enterprise aimed at securing foreign raw materials. Rather than being subject to the laws of any single territory, they had their own special laws, originally limited only to their own territory and governing their specialized functions. They made economic policy in that they established prices for food and other products, rented out sharecropping lands as history's first absentee landlords, extended credit at the first regularly attested interest rates, produced exports in their workshops, oversaw weights, measures and economic accounting, and stored seed, savings, money and economic records. Yet in performing these functions most Bronze Age cities and their temples fell short of the criteria of modern states as described by today's political theorists:

the ability to make generally binding laws, declare war and tax. The city-temples may best be thought of as public utilities. It was as such that they were accountable, whereas private partnerships were not. (Throughout antiquity the only business corporations that could be formed were for the purpose of undertaking public functions such as construction and tax farming.)

Inevitably, as towns developed into regional trade systems, their prosperity inspired local military rivalries while attracting the attention of alien raiders. Military and other secular forces played a growing role by the third millennium, and sought to legitimize themselves by adapting the traditional repertory of cosmological symbolism, sacred and civic architecture and at least the outward forms of archaic ritual functions to their evolving circumstances.

Bibliography

Adams, Robert Mc.C. (1969), "The Study of Ancient Mesopotamian Settlement Patterns and the Problem of Urban Origins," *Sumer* 25:111-123.
" (1981), *Heartland of Cities* (Chicago).

Algaze, Guiellermo (1989), "The Uruk Expansion: Cross-Cultural Exchange in Early Mesopotamian Civilization," *Current Anthropology* 30:571-608.

Burkert, Walter (1984), *Die Orientalisierende Epoch in der griechischen Religion und Literature* (Heidelberg).

Carpenter, Rhys (1966), *Beyond the Pillars of Hercules* (Delacorte Press).

Childe, V. Gordon (1950), "The Urban Revolution," *Town Planning Review* 21:3-17.

Crawford, H. E. W. (1973), "Mesopotamia's invisible exports in the third millennium BC," *World Archaeology* 5:232-241.

Diakonoff, Igor M. (1982), "The Structure of Near Eastern Society before the Middle of the 2nd Millennium BC," *Oikumene* 3:7-100.

Ellis, Richard S. (1968), *Foundation Deposits in Ancient Mesopotamia* (New Haven).

Fagerlie, J. M. (1967), *Late Roman and Byzantine Solidi Found in Sweden and Denmark* (New York).

Finkelstein, J. J. (1981), "The Ox that Gored," *Transactions of the American Philosophical Society* 71:Part 2.

Finley, Moses I. (1974), *The Ancient Economy* (Berkeley and Los Angeles).

Garlan, Yves (1988), *Slavery in Ancient Greece* (Ithaca).

Gelb, Ignace J. (1965), "The Ancient Mesopotamian Ration System," *Journal of Near Eastern Studies* 24:230-243.

" (1967), "Approaches to the Study of Ancient Society," *Journal of the American Oriental Society* 87:1-8.

" (1971), "On the Alleged Temple and State Economies in Ancient Mesopotamia," in *Studi in Onore di Edoardo Volterra* VI:137-154 (Milan).

" (1972), "The Arua Institution," *Revue d'Assyriologie* 66:1-21.

" (1986), "Ebla and Lagash: Environmental Contrast," in Harvey Weiss, ed., *The Origins of Cities in Dry-farming Syria and Mesopotamia in the Third Millennium B.C.* (Guilford, Conn.):157-167.

Gelb, I. J., Piotr Steinkeller, and R. M. Whiting Jr. (1989, 1991), *Earliest Land Tenure Systems in the Near East: Ancient kidurrus* (Chicago).

Gernet, Louis (1981), *The Anthropology of Ancient Greece* (Baltimore).

Hatzfield, Jean (1919), *Les trafficantes Italiens dans l»orient hellenique* (Paris).

Haywood, Richard Mansfield (1967), *Ancient Rome* (New York).

Herzog, Ze'ev (1986), *Das Stadttor im Israel und in den Nachbarlaendern* (Mainz).

Hocart, Arthur M. (1950), *Caste* (London).
" (1927), *Kingship* (London).

Holland, Louise Adams (1961), *Janus and the Bridge* (Rome).

Humphries, Sarah (1978), *Anthropology and the Greeks* (London).

Jacobsen, Thorkild (1978), *The Treasures of Darkness* (New Haven).

Kraeling Carl H., and Robert M. Adams, eds. (1960), *City Invincible: A Symposium on Urbanization and Cultural Development in the Ancient Near East, Dec. 4-7, 1958* (Chicago).

Lamberg-Karlovsky, Carl C. (1982), "Dilmun: Gateway to Immortality," *Journal of Near Eastern Studies* 41:45-50.

Lambert, Maurice (1960), "La naissance de la bureaucratie," *Revue Historique* 224:1-26.

Larsen, Mogens Trolle (1976), *The Old Assyrian City-State and its Colonies* (Copenhagen).

Leemans, W. F. (1950), *The Old-Babylonian Merchant: His Business and his Social Position* (Leiden).
" (1960), *Foreign Trade in the Old Babylonian Period* (Leiden).

Lethaby, W. R. (1974 [1892]), *Architecture, Mysticism and Myth* (London).

L'Orange, H. P. (1953), *Studies in the Iconography of Cosmic Kingship* (Oslo).

Lowry, S. Todd (1987), *The Archaeology of Economic Ideas* (Durham).

Marshack, Alexander (1972), *The Roots of Civilization* (New York).
" (1975), "Exploring the Mind of Ice Age Man," *National Geographic* 147(1):62-89.

Mellaart, James (1975), *The Neolithic of the Near East* (New York).
" (1987), "Common Sense vs. Oldfashioned Theory in the Interpretation of the Cultural Development of the Ancient Near East," in Linda Manzanilla, ed., *Studies in the Neolithic and Urban Revolutions. The V. Gordon Childe Colloquium, Mexico, 1986* (BAR International Series #349, Oxford):261-269.

Miller, Daniel (1985), "Ideology and the Harappan Civilization," *Journal of Anthropological Archaeology* 4:34-71.

Moorey, P. R. S. (1984), "Where did they bury the Kings of the IIIrd Dynasty of Ur," *Iraq* 46:1-18.

Morgan, Lewis Henry (1978), *Ancient Society* (New York).

Morris, A. E. J. (1979), *History of Urban Form: Before the Industrial Revolutions*, 2nd ed. (London).

Muhly, J. D. (1973), "Copper and tin: the distribution of mineral resources and the nature of the metal trade in the Bronze Age," *Transactions of the Connecticut Academy of Arts and Sciences*, TR 43[4] (New Haven):155-535.

Muller, Werner (1961), *Die heilige Stadt. Roma quadrata, himmlisches Jerusalem und die Mythe vom Weltnabel* (Stuttgart).

Murakawa, Kentaro (1957), "Demiurgos," *Historia* 6:385-415.

Murray, Oswyn, and Simon Price (1990), *The Greek City From Homer to Alexander* (Oxford).

Oppenheim, A. Leo (1977 [1964]), *Ancient Mesopotamia* (Chicago).

Pfeiffer, John E. (1982), *The Creative Explosion: An Inquiry into the Origins of Art and Religion* (New York).

Raglan, Lord (1964), *The Temple and the House* (London).

Rostovtzeff, Mikhail (1941), *Social and Economic History of the Hellenistic World* (Oxford).

Rykwert, Joseph (1988), *The Idea of a Town: The Anthropology of Urban Form in Rome, Italy and the Ancient World* (Cambridge, Mass.).

Snodgrass, Anthony (1980), *Archaic Greece: The Age of Experiment* (London).

Soffer, Olga (1985), *The Upper Paleolithic of the Central Russian Plain* (New York).

Stone, Elizabeth (1988), *Nippur Neighborhoods* (Chicago).

Struve, V. V. (1969 [1933]), "The Problem of the Genesis, Development and Disintegration of the Slave Societies in the Ancient Orient," translated in I. M. Diakonoff, ed., *Ancient Mesopotamia* (Moscow):17-69.

Tarn, W. W. (1952), *Hellenistic Civilization* (New York).

Toynbee, Arnold (1913), "The Growth of Sparta," *Journal of Hellenic Studies* 33:254-275.

Unwin, George (1918), *Finance and Trade under Edward III* (London).
" (1958 [1927]), *Studies in Economic History: The Collected Papers of George Unwin* (London).

van Buren, Elizabeth Douglas (1931), *Foundation Figurines and Offerings* (Berlin).
" (1952), "The Building of a Temple-Tower," *Revue d'Assyriologie* 46:65-74.
" (1952), "Foundation Rites for a New Temple," *Orientalia* 21:293-306.

Vernant, Jean-Pierre (1982), *The Origins of Greek Thought* (Ithaca).
" (1983), *Myth and Thought Among the Greeks* (London and Boston).

Versnel, H. S. (1970), *Triumphus: An Inquiry into the Origin, Development and Meaning of the Roman Triumph* (Leiden).

Wheatley, Paul (1971), *The Pivot of the Four Quarters: A Preliminary Enquiry into the Origins and Character of the Ancient Chinese City* (Edinburgh).

Yallop, David A. (1984), *In God's Name: An Investigation into the Murder of Pope John Paul I* (New York.)

Yoffee, Norman (1977), *The Economic Role of the Crown in the Old Babylonian Period* (Malibu).

Zaccagnini, Carlo (1983), "Patterns of Mobility among Ancient Near Eastern Craftsmen," *Journal of Near Eastern Studies* 42:2-64.
" (1986), "The Dilmun Standard and its Relationship with Indian and Near Eastern Weight Systems," *Iraq* 48:19-23.
" (1987), "Aspects of ceremonial exchange in the Near East during the late second millennium BC," in Michael Rowlands, Mogens Larsen and Kristian Kristiansen, eds., *Center and Periphery in the Ancient World* (Cambridge).

11

Entrepreneurs: From the Near Eastern Takeoff to the Roman Collapse*

A century ago economists could only speculate on the origins of enterprise. It seemed logical to assume that entrepreneurial individuals must have played a key role in archaic trade, motivated by what Adam Smith described as an instinct to "truck and barter." When a Mycenaean Greek site from 1200 BC was excavated and storerooms with accounting records found, the building accordingly was called "a merchant's house," not a public administrative center.[1]

There was little room for Max Weber's idea that a drive for social status might dominate economic motives. Materialist approaches to history both by Marxist and by business-oriented writers assumed that economic factors determined status and political power, not the other way around. The basic context for enterprise was deemed to consist of timeless constants: money, account-keeping to calculate gains and basic contractual formalities. To the extent that public institutions were recognized as economic actors, they were assumed to be an overhead, incurred at the expense of enterprise, not the means of promoting it. There was little idea of temples and palaces playing a catalytic role, much less a key one in production or as providing money and provisioning commercial ventures. There was even less thought of rulers regulating markets, cancelling personal debts and reversing land transfers as a way to enhance prosperity.

Translation of cuneiform records over the past century has changed these attitudes. A veritable explosion of colloquia over the past decade

---

* Originally published in David S. Landes, Joel Mokyr, and William J. Baumol, eds., *The Invention of Enterprise: Entrepreneurship from Ancient Mesopotamia to Modern Times* (Princeton University Press, Princeton, 2010):8-39, the work to which references below to "this volume" refer. It is used and republished in this collection with the permission of Princeton University Press; permission conveyed through Copyright Clearance Centre, Inc.

[1] I discuss the public and private role of merchants and enterprise in Hudson 1996a and 1996b.

has analyzed the emergence of enterprise in Mesopotamia and its neighbors (Dercksen 1999; Bongenaar 2000; Zaccagnini 2003; Manning and Morris 2005; and earlier, Archi 1984, in addition to the compendious *Civilizations of the Ancient Near East* [Sasson et al. 1995]). Our own working group, the International Scholars Conference on Ancient Near Eastern Economies, has held colloquia dealing with the public/private balance (Hudson and Levine 1996), the emergence of urban and rural land markets (Hudson and Levine 1999), debt practices and how societies handled the economic strains they caused (Hudson and Van De Mieroop 2002), account-keeping and the emergence of standardized prices and money (Hudson and Wunsch 2004). These conference volumes have been bolstered by many books and articles presenting a complex view of the emergence of commercial enterprise.

The vast supply of Near Eastern tablets and inscriptions dealing with economic affairs is being translated free of the past generation's ideological controversy over whether the economic organization of classical Greece was "ancient," "primitivist," and "anthropological" in character, as asserted by Karl Bücher, Karl Polanyi, and Moses Finley, or "modern," as asserted by Eduard Meyer and Mikhail Rostovtzeff. (The basic documents in the century-old debate are collected in Finley 1979. For a recent discussion see Manning and Morris 2005.) Half a century ago, Polanyi and Finley criticized "modernist" views of antiquity by claiming that its economies operated as part of a system more redistributive and bureaucratic than entrepreneurial. The quasi-Marxist theory of Oriental Despotism was even more extreme. But the past few decades of scholarship have seen the pendulum swing back away from such views, finding many innovative economic practices in the ancient world (Hudson 2005-6).

It is now recognized that most of the techniques that would become basic commercial practices in classical antiquity were developed already in the third millennium BC in the temples and palaces of the Bronze Age Near East – money, along with the uniform weights, measures and prices needed for account-keeping and annual reports (Hudson and Wunsch 2004), the charging of interest (Van De Mieroop 2005; Hudson and Van De Mieroop 2002), and profit-sharing arrangements between palaces, temples and private merchants, ranging from long-distance trade to leasing land, workshops, and retail beer-selling concessions (Renger 1984, 1994 and 2002). Assyriologists now apply the term *entrepreneur* broadly to Assyrian and Babylonian *tamkarum* "merchants" from early in the second millennium BC down to the Egibi and Murashu families of Babylonia in the 7th through 5th centuries BC, who created sophisticated commercial strategies to manage estates and provision the palace and its armed forces.

These practices initially were developed to produce an export surplus of textiles, metalwork, and other labor-intensive handicrafts to obtain the stone, metal, and other raw materials lacking in southern Mesopotamia (what is now Iraq). During the second millennium these commercial techniques diffused westward via Ugarit and Crete to Mycenaean Greece. After the long Dark Age that followed the collapse of Mycenae circa 1200 BC, seafaring merchants brought them to Greece and Italy, where they were adopted circa 750 BC in a context with fewer institutional checks and balances on debt, dependency, and economic polarization. Clientage came to be viewed as a natural state of affairs as economic attitudes changed from those in the Near East.

Wealthy Greek and Roman families controlled handicraft production, trade, and credit directly rather than coordinating these activities for temples and palaces. Yet classical antiquity's aristocratic attitude viewed commercial enterprise as demeaning and corrupting. The details of trade, enterprise and moneylending typically were left to outsiders or to slaves and other subordinates acting as on-the-spot managers, organizers, and middlemen for their aristocratic backers. Most enterprising individuals were drawn from the bottom ranks of the social scale, typified by the fictional but paradigmatic freedman Trimalchio in Petronius's comedy dating from the time of Augustus. "The greater a man's *dignitas*," D'Arms (1981:45) has pointed out, "the more likely that his involvement [in business] was indirect and discreet, camouflaged behind that of an undistinguished freedman, – client, partner, 'front man,' or 'friend,'" and leaving management of his affairs to slaves or other subordinates. When such lower-status individuals were able to accumulate fortunes of their own, they aspired to high status and prestige by sinking their money into land and obtaining public office. The freedman Trimalchio "immediately ceased to trade after amassing a fortune, [and] invests in land and henceforth talks and acts like a caricature of a Roman senator" (D'Arms 1981:15; see Dio Chrysostom, *Or.* 46.5).

Although we might expect Romans at the high end of the economic scale to have had enormous personal fortunes corresponding to the city-state's great riches (parasitic as these may have been), Heichelheim (1970 III:125) notes that its leading families spent beyond their means, running up catastrophic debts in their drive for status and power. This behavior "finds no analogy at the time of the Golden Age of Greece either among private individuals or among princes."

The history of enterprise in antiquity therefore falls naturally into two periods. First is the development of economic practices in Mesopotamia circa 3500-1200 BC. Second is the period of classical antiquity from circa 750 BC, by the end of which we find gain-seeking having shifted away from productive enterprise to land acquisition, usury, profiteering from political office, and extraction of foreign tribute by force. To begin the story of enterprise in this later classical epoch would be to ignore the fact that most commercial practices had a pedigree of thousands of years by the time Near Eastern traders brought them to the Mediterranean lands in the mid-8th century BC.

What led communities to develop a commercial ethic in the first place? Who were the beneficiaries, and how were the benefits shared? Why did this ethic, which seems so natural to us today, take so long to emerge in the ancient world, only to be overwhelmed by less economically productive, more corrosive social values? To answer these questions it is necessary to address the transition from interpersonal gift exchange to bulk trade at standardized market prices, that is, from "anthropological" to "economic" exchange and production.

Traditional sanctions against the entrepreneurial gain-seeking ethic

Trade extends back deep into the Paleolithic. Modern tribal experience and logic suggest that the earliest trade probably occurred via gift exchange, whose primary aim was to promote cohesion and reciprocity among the community's members, and peaceful relations among chiefs of neighboring tribes. Mauss's *The Gift* [1925] is the paradigmatic study along these lines. Anthropological studies have documented that the typical attitude in low-surplus communities living near subsistence levels is that self-seeking tends to achieve gains at the expense of others. That is why traditional social values impose sanctions against the accumulation of personal wealth. The economic surplus is so small that making a profit or extracting interest would push families into dependency on patrons or bondage to creditors. The basic aim of survival requires that communities save their citizenry from falling below the break-even level more than temporarily. In antiquity, for example, losing land rights meant losing one's status as a citizen, and hence one's military standing, leaving the community prone to conquest by outsiders.

While low-surplus economies usually did produce surpluses, archaic social mores dictated that they should be consumed, typically by public display and gift exchange, provisioning feasts at major rites of passage (entry into adulthood, marriage or funerals), or burial with the dead.

Status under such conditions is gained by giving away one's wealth, not hoarding or reinvesting it. It long remained most culturally acceptable to consume economic surpluses in public festivals, dedicate them to ancestors, and, in time, supply them to provision the construction of temples and other monumental structures. The entrepreneurial gain-seeking ethic was revolutionary. It was catalyzed by the gains being used visibly for the benefit of the community as a whole.

Concentration of the economic surplus at the top of the social pyramid

When tribal communities mobilize surpluses (usually as much by warfare as by trade), they tend to be concentrated in the chief's household, to be used, at least ostensibly, on behalf of the community at large. The ethic of mutual aid calls for chiefs to act in an open-handed way. And as part of their role as the community's "face" in its commercial or military relations with outsiders, the chief's "household" tends to absorb runaways, exiles and other unattached individuals.

Some surplus normally is needed for specialized nonagricultural production. The chief or leading families may administer a sanctified, corporately distinct cult charged with capital-intensive production such as metalsmithing. Such occupations often involve a particular class of workers, who need to be supplied with raw materials, and with their own self-support land or with food from the chief's household or from land leased out to tenants for rent, typically on a sharecropping basis. Such professional groups tend to institutionalize themselves on the model of families, but with an essentially public identity.

Profit-seeking "economic" exchange was so great a leap that initially it seems to have been conducted mainly in association with civic institutions. The first documented "households" to be economically managed were those of Mesopotamia's temples. To be sure, Lamberg-Karlovsky (1996:80-82) has traced their evolution out of what began as the chief's household from the sixth through the third millennium; they were followed by palaces that emerged from temple precincts circa 2800 BC (Adams 1981). These large institutional households developed a community-wide identity, especially as they absorbed dependent labor such as that of war widows and orphans, the blind and infirm taken out of their family environment on the land, and also slaves captured in raiding. It is in these institutions that the first standardized bulk production was organized to yield a commercial surplus.

Temples of enterprise

Southern Mesopotamia was in a uniquely resource-dependent position. Its land consisted of rich alluvial soil deposited by rivers over the millennia, but lacked copper, tin, lapis, and other stone, and even much hardwood. The region needed to obtain these materials from distant sites ranging from the Iranian plateau to central Anatolia. In the mid-fourth millennium BC the Sumerians created fortified outposts up the Euphrates to the north, but archaeologists have found that they were abandoned after a century or so. Military conquest was too expensive a means to obtain distant raw materials by force. Although Sumerian cities fought among themselves in the fourth, third, and even second millennia BC, acquisition of foreign materials in large quantity over long distances had to be organized on a reciprocal and voluntary basis with Anatolia and the Iranian plateau, while trade with the Indus Valley was conducted mainly on the island of Dilmun.

Peaceful trade meant enterprise, requiring southern Mesopotamia – Sumer – to have exports to offer. Because of the large quantitative scale involved, city temples and palaces played the dominant role as producers and suppliers of goods. Ships and overland caravans were outfitted and provided with textiles and other products to exchange for the raw materials lacking in the Sumerian core.

In recent years Assyriologists have reconstructed how this system worked, using as evidence royal inscriptions and the archives of palace officials and merchant-entrepreneurs. In contrast to imperial conquerors imposing tribute on defeated populations, city-temples and palaces did not levy taxes as such. They supported themselves by their own workshops, large herds of animals and means of transport, and by leasing out fields and workshops, much as Athens later would do with its Laurion silver mines. Their labor force produced textiles for export, and beer for domestic sale.

The absence of export or local sales documents suggests that the temples, palaces and local consigners advanced these commodities to merchants for later payment upon the return from a voyage, typically after a five-year period, or at harvest time for domestic sales for payment in crops. In time these merchants accumulated capital of their own, which they used along with that of private backers (typically their relatives). Most of their personal business archives have been excavated in temple or palace precincts and found along with public administrative records, indicating that there was no idea of conflict of interest with regard to their position in the temple or palace bureaucracy, which seems to have remained mainly in the hands of leading families. The major way to become an entrepreneur was to interface with these large institutions. That is what made Mesopotamian economies "mixed" rather than statist (run by bureaucracies such as the "temple state" postulated in the 1920s) or strictly "private enterprise," as assumed by the older generation of economic modernists.

The large institutions established relationships with well-placed individuals, whose title – Sumerian *damgar*, Babylonian *tamkarum* – usually is translated as "merchant" or, for Babylonian times, "entrepreneur." Applying Israel Kirzner's (1979:39) definition of the entrepreneur's role, Johannes Renger (2000:155) points out that it is a 17th-century French term denoting "a person who entered into a contractual relationship with the government for the performance of a service or the supply of goods. The price at which the contract was valued was fixed and the entrepreneurs bore the risks of profit and loss from the bargain."

An entrepreneur seeks economic gain either with his own money or, more often, with borrowed funds or by managing the assets of others (including public institutions) to make something over for himself by selling high, cutting expenses or creating a business innovation. In Babylonia, the palace leased out land and workshops at stipulated rents, and advanced textiles and other handicrafts to merchants engaged in long-distance trade. In the process of developing this enterprise, administrators and entrepreneurs created the managerial elements for large-scale production and market exchange, enabling them to squeeze out an economic surplus and reinvest it to obtain further gains.

Debt relationships

A tug of war existed between local magnates and the central palace, not unlike that between the barons and the kings of England in the 12th century of the modern era. An important role of palace rulers, for instance, was to prevent interest-bearing debt – and subsequent foreclosure, especially by palace revenue collectors – from stripping away the citizenry's basic means of self-support. Royal "clean slates" preserved economic solvency by annulling agrarian "barley" debts (but not commercial "silver" debts), reversing land forfeitures and freeing debt pledges from bondage. Indebted citizens could only lose their liberty and self-support lands temporarily.

Ancient historians found the logic for these policies to be based on recognition that the infantry was drawn from the citizen body composed of landowning males. Hammurabi's laws, for example, assigned charioteers their own self-support lands, kept free from foreclosure. To have left these men to become prey to creditors expropriating their land would have put Babylon in danger of conquest by outsiders.

The Near East thus managed to avert the debt problem that plagued classical antiquity. Although debt forced war widows and orphans into dependency and obliged the sick, infirm and others to pledge and then lose their land's crop rights to creditors at the top of the economic pyramid, such forfeitures were of merely temporary duration (*viz.*, the long tradition of Mesopotamian royal Clean Slate proclamations, echoed in the Jubilee Year of Leviticus 25). But they became permanent in Greece and Rome, reducing much of the population to the status of bondservants and unfree dependents.

This is primarily what distinguishes Greek and Roman oligarchies from the Near Eastern mixed economies. It proved much easier to cancel debts owed to the palace and its collectors in Mesopotamia than to annul debts owed to individual creditors acting on their own in classical times. (Even Roman emperors occasionally cancelled tax arrears in order to alleviate widespread debt distress – mainly by the wealthiest landowners and tax avoiders, to be sure.)

Debt was the lever that made land transferable in traditional societies, which usually had restrictions to prevent self-support land from being alienated outside of the family or clan. (Hudson and Levine 1999 gives examples.) By holding that the essence of private property is its ability to be sold or forfeited irreversibly, Roman law removed the archaic checks to foreclosure that prevented property from being concentrated in the hands of the few. This Roman concept of property is essentially creditor-oriented, and quickly became predatory. But as in the Near East, commercial law freed merchant entrepreneurs from debt liability in the case of shipwreck or piracy.

Documentation of early entrepreneurial activity

Our sources oblige us to rely almost exclusively on archives and inscriptions from Babylonia, Assyria and their neighboring lands for documentation regarding early economic organization. Little early primary data survive from Egypt, which remained much more commercially self-sufficient than other parts of the Near East, although it did undertake military incursions. We know from pictorial sources that there were markets, but according to Bleiberg (1995:1382-1383) the normal Egyptian state of affairs was a redistributive economy. The hints of entrepreneurial behavior are limited to "intermediate periods," transitions in which the pharaoh's power weakened and economic life became less centralized (as also occurred in Mesopotamia). "One recent exponent of the belief that there was a place for the private merchant in ancient Egypt is Morris Silver," comments Bleiberg. "Not surprisingly, the evidence that he adduces for private traders comes from the First Intermediate Period and the end of the Ramesside period, both times of weak or nonexistent central government. The existence of such traders is never attested in Egyptian sources from periods when the economic apparatus of the central government was functioning well."

No written records exist for the Indus Valley, although archaeological evidence shows that it traded with southern Mesopotamia via the island of Dilmun (modern Bahrain) in the third and second millennia BC. Phoenician society and its colonies to the west, in Carthage and Spain in the first millennium, are also undocumented. The syllabic record-keeping found in Crete and Mycenaean Greece from 1600 to 1200 BC pertains only to the collection and distribution of products, not enterprise as such.

The largest archives dealing with entrepreneurs are from Neo-Babylonian times (7th-6th centuries BC). Nothing remotely as sophisticated is available for Greece or Rome even for the brief period in which economic magnitudes are recorded. "Since it was a part of upper-class etiquette for a rich man to pretend that he was not really well-to-do," D'Arms (1981:154) points out, "the character and degree of senators' involvement in money-making ventures usually resist precise documentation." Andreau (1999:17) notes that "when Brutus's money was loaned to the people of Salamis in Cyprus through the intermediaries Scaptius and Matinius, these two were the sole official creditors. Until Brutus revealed his hand in the affair, neither the people of Salamis nor Cicero knew that the sums loaned belonged to him." We would not know either, if not for the political exposés, lawsuits and prosecutions that illuminate how fortunes were made in Greece and Rome. (Matters may not be so different today. Former New York attorney general Eliot Spitzer's prosecutions and reports by congressional committees on investigations have done more to describe corporate and banking practices than a generation of management textbooks has done.)

Economic details are available only for about two centuries of Roman history, circa 150 BC to AD 50. Business archives are lacking, as the focus is mainly military and political. After Augustus, MacMullen (1974:48) notes: "Among thousands of inscriptions that detail the gifts made by patrons to guilds, cities, or other groups, only a tiny number indicate where the donor got his money." For Greece, the window of economic visibility is several centuries earlier, but again details are limited, with lawsuits here too being major sources of information. In any event, it was the Near Eastern forerunners of Greece and Rome that provided the models and even the vocabulary of commerce and banking, contractual formalities and other preconditions for market exchange and enterprise.

Productive versus corrosive enterprise

In light of this *longue durée*, the problem for economic historians is to explain why commerce and enterprise yielded to a Dark Age. What stifled enterprise thousands of years after the Near Eastern takeoff? For a century the culprit was assumed to be state regulation. But it was the temples and palaces of Sumer and Babylonia that first introduced most basic commercial innovations, including the first formal prices and markets. The collapse of antiquity can be traced to creditor-landowning oligarchies capturing the state and blocking the checks and balances that had kept economies in the Near East from polarizing to so fatal an extent as occurred in the West between creditors and debtors, patrons and their clients, freedmen and slaves. The ascent of Rome saw laws become more creditor-oriented and property appropriations more irreversible, while the tax burden was shifted onto the lower orders. The effect was to exhaust the regions absorbed into antiquity's empires and deplete the home market.

Hereditary wealth tends to gravitate toward corrosive forms of enterprise, and Greek and Roman status and gain-seeking was more military than commercial. The privileged aristocrats who inherited economic and political status felt that acting to gain wealth directly by financial or commercial activity (especially retail trade with social inferiors) was déclassé, in contrast to military conquest and producing, consuming or distributing output on their own estates. The classical ideal was to be self-sufficient and independent on large landed estates, not to dirty one's hands by engaging in trade and moneylending. Much like sex in Victorian England, everyone seemed to be engaged in it (commerce and moneylending), but it did not add to one's prestige. In Greek and Roman antiquity prestige stemmed from autonomy, not commerce.

What is most important for society is the set of rules and social values that govern how enterprise creates wealth. The path does not always lead upward toward higher productivity, to say nothing of greater efficiency, social development or even survival. "Indeed," observes Baumol (1990:894), "at times the entrepreneur may even lead a parasitical existence that is actually damaging to the economy." In classical antiquity the three most lucrative areas of gain-seeking were tax farming, public building contracts, and provisioning the civic government, temples, and army. Building a fortune involved interfacing with the state under conditions where the surplus took the form of tribute, usury, land grabbing and profiteering from public administrative position. The domestic surplus, and ultimately the land itself, was obtained increasingly via interest-bearing debt (often via foreclosure or forced sale) and by conquest.

On an economy-wide scale the oligarchy stripped away much of the land from the community through debt foreclosure, reduced much of the population to bondage, and brought commerce and even the money economy to an end, leading to Western Europe's Dark Age. The oligarchic ethic preferred seizing wealth abroad to creating it at home. Along with tax farming in the provinces, public contracts (by forming corporations such as those of the publican tax collectors) and state provisioning, the major ways to make fortunes were by conquest, raiding and piracy, slave capture and slave dealing, moneylending and kindred activities more predatory than entrepreneurial. Gaining wealth by extracting it from others, especially by military means, was deemed to be as noble (if not more so) than doing so commercially, which was deemed to be exploitative but lacking the dimension of personal bravery.

Although entrepreneurs stood at the economy's fulcrum points – managing estates, organizing shipping and public construction, operating workshops and provisioning armies – they worked in an environment less and less conducive to such activities over the course of antiquity, not only because of the aristocratic disdain for commerce but also because of the increasing opprobrium attaching to the appearance of wealth. "When I was young it was safe and dignified to be a rich man," complained Isocrates in Athens during that city-state's struggles between democracy and oligarchy; "now one has to defend oneself against the charge of being rich as if it were the worst of crimes" (*Antidosis* 159-160, quoted in Humphreys 1978:297). It was preferable to become a leisurely *rentier*.

A shift occurred from the Bronze Age Near East to classical Greece and Rome from productive to unproductive enterprise. "If entrepreneurs are defined, simply, to be persons who are ingenious and creative in finding ways that add to their own wealth, power, and prestige," Baumol concludes (1990:897-898), "then it is to be expected that not all of them will be overly concerned with whether an activity that achieves these goals adds much or little to the social product or, for that matter, even whether it is an actual impediment to production (this notion goes back, at least, to Veblen 1904)."[2]

Rome's wealthiest families sought to make as many clients, debtors, and slaves as dependent as possible through force, usury and control of the land. This predatory *rentier* spirit led to the century-long Social War (133-29 BC) that saw the Republic polarize economically, paving the way for the subsequent empire to give way to serfdom. One looks in vain for the idea that profit-seeking enterprise might drive society forward to achieve higher levels of production and living standards. No major minds set about developing a policy for society or even the oligarchy as a class to get rich by economic growth and development of an internal market.

Some myths regarding the genesis of enterprise

If a colloquium on early entrepreneurs had been convened a century ago, most participants would have viewed traders as operating on their own, bartering at prices that settled at a market equilibrium established spontaneously in response to fluctuating supply and demand. According to the Austrian economist Carl Menger, money emerged as individuals and merchants involved in barter came to prefer silver and copper as convenient means of payment, stores of value, and standards by which to measure other prices. But instead of supporting this individualistic scenario for how commercial practices developed in the spheres of trade, money and credit, interest and pricing, history shows that they did not emerge spontaneously among individuals "trucking and bartering." Rather, money, credit, pricing and investment for the purpose of creating profits, charging interest, creating a property market and even a proto-bond market (for temple prebends) first emerged in the temples and palaces of Sumer and Babylonia.

From third-millennium Mesopotamia through classical antiquity the minting of precious metal of specified purity was done by temples, not private suppliers. The word *money* derives from Rome's Temple of Juno Moneta, where the city's coinage was minted in early times. Monetized silver was part of the Near Eastern pricing system developed by the large institutions to establish stable ratios for their fiscal account-keeping and forward planning. Major price ratios (including the rate of interest) were

---

[2] In fact, Livy, Diodorus, and Plutarch blamed the decline and fall of the Roman Republic on usury and related oligarchic greed, and on the use of political violence against populist leaders such as the Gracchi brothers, whose murder initiated Rome's Social War. See my *The Collapse of Antiquity* (2023) for a detailed discussion.

administered in round numbers for ease of calculation (Renger 2000 and 2002, and Hudson and Wunsch 2004).

Instead of deterring enterprise, these administered prices provided a stable context for it to flourish. The palace estimated a normal return for the fields and other properties it leased out, and left managers to make a profit – or suffer a loss when the weather was bad or other risks materialized. In such cases shortfalls became debts. However, when the losses became so great as to threaten this system, the palace let the agrarian arrears go, enabling entrepreneurial contractors with the palatial economy (including ale women) to start again with a clean slate (Renger 2002). The aim was to keep them in business, not to destroy them.

More flexible pricing seems to have occurred in the quay areas along the canals. Rather than a conflict existing between the large civic institutions administering prices and mercantile enterprise, there was a symbiotic relationship. Liverani (2005:53-54) points out that administered pricing by the temples and palaces vis-à-vis *tamkarum* merchants engaged in foreign trade "was limited to the starting move and the closing move: trade agents got silver and/or processed materials (that is, mainly metals and textiles) from the central agency and had to bring back after six months or a year the equivalent in exotic products or raw materials. The economic balance between central agency and trade agents could not but be regulated by fixed exchange values. But the merchants' activity once they left the palace was completely different: They could freely trade, playing on the different prices of the various items in various countries, even using their money in financial activities (such as loans) in the time span at their disposal, and making the maximum possible personal profit."

A century ago it was assumed that the state's economic role could only have taken the form of oppressive taxation and overregulation of markets, and hence would have thwarted commercial enterprise. That is how Rostovtzeff (1926) depicted the imperial Roman economy stifling the middle class. But Jones (1964) pointed out that this was how antiquity ended, not how it began. Merchants and entrepreneurs first emerged in conjunction with the temples and palaces of Mesopotamia. Rather than being despotic and economically oppressive, Mesopotamian institutions and religious values sanctioned the commercial takeoff that ended up being thwarted in Greece and Rome. Archaeology has confirmed that "modern" elements of enterprise were present and even dominant already in Mesopotamia in the third millennium BC, and that the institutional context was conducive to long-term growth. Commerce expanded and fortunes were made as populations grew and the material conditions of life rose. But what has surprised many observers is how much more successful, fluid and also more stable economic organization was as we move back in time.

Growing awareness that the character of gain-seeking became economically predatory has prompted a more sociological view of exchange and property in Greece and Rome (*e.g.*, the French structuralists, Kurke 1999 and von Reden 1995), and also a more "economic" post-Polanyian view of earlier Mesopotamia and its Near Eastern neighbors. Morris and Manning (2005) survey how the approach that long segregated Near Eastern from Mediterranean development has been replaced by a more integrated view (*e.g.*, Braudel 1972 and Hudson 1992), in tandem with a pan-regional approach to myth and religion (Burkert 1984 and West 1997) and art works (Kopcke and Takamaru 1992). The motto *ex oriente lux* now is seen to apply to commercial practices as well as to art, culture and religion.

For a century, Near Eastern development was deemed to lie outside the Western continuum, which was defined as starting with classical Greece circa 750 BC. But the origins of commercial practices are now seen to date from Mesopotamia's takeoff two thousand years before classical antiquity. However, what was indeed novel and "fresh" in the Mediterranean lands arose mainly from the fact that the Bronze Age world fell apart in the devastation that occurred circa 1200 BC. The commercial and debt practices that Syrian and Phoenician traders brought to the Aegean and southern Italy around the 8th century BC were adopted in smaller local contexts that lacked the large civic institutions found throughout the Near East. Trade and usury enriched chieftains much more than occurred in the Near East where temples or other public authority were set corporately apart to mediate the economic surplus, and especially to provide credit. Because the societies of classical antiquity emerged in this non-public and indeed oligarchic context, the idea of *Western* became synonymous with the private sector and individualism.

Some contrasts between enterprise in antiquity and today

A number of differences between antiquity's economic practices and those of the modern world should be borne in mind when considering the changing context for enterprise. Handicraft workshops were located on basically self-sufficient landed estates, including those of the large civic institutions. Such industry was self-financed rather than operating on credit, which was extended mainly for long-distance and bulk trade.

From Babylonian times down through late Republican Rome, commercial income tended to be invested in land. But there was not price speculation on credit until the late 1st century BC in Rome. Land was the major savings vehicle and sign of status. The largest estate owners shifted subsistence land to growing cash crops, headed by olive oil and wine in the Mediterranean, and dates in the Near East, harvested increasingly by slaves.

We do not find banking intermediaries lending out people's savings to entrepreneurial borrowers. Throughout the Near East, what have been called "banking families" such as the Egibi (described by Wunsch in this volume) are best thought of as general entrepreneurs. They did hold deposits and made loans, but they paid the same rate of interest to depositors as they charged for their loans (normally 20 percent annually). There was no margin for arbitrage, and no credit superstructure to magnify the supply of monetary metal on hand. (See the discussion in Hudson and Van De Mieroop 2002:345-347.) Promissory notes circulated only among closely knit groups of *tamkaru*, so a broad superstructure of credit was only incipient, and did not come to fruition until modern times with the development of fractional-reserve banking from the 17th century onward (see Wray 2004, especially the articles by Ingham and Gardiner). Most lending was for commercial trade ventures – in which the creditor shared in the risk as well as the gain – or took the form of predatory agrarian loans or claims for arrears of taxes or other fees owed to royal or imperial collectors. Down to modern times, small-scale personal debt was viewed as the first step toward forfeiting one's property, a danger to be entered into only unwillingly. The dominant ethic was to keep assets free of debt, especially land.

Moneylending in classical Greece was mainly in the hands of outsiders, foreigners such as Pasion in Athens. In Rome the elite left banking to low-status individuals headed by slaves or freedmen, ex-slaves who "confine[d] their activities to bridging loans and the provision of working capital," operating only "on the margins of trade and industry" (Jones 2006:245).

Throughout antiquity entrepreneurs tended not to specialize but to pursue a broad range of activities, organizing and managing voyages, fields, workshops, or other productive units. They rarely acted by themselves for just their own account but as part of a system. Traders and "merchants" tended to work via guilds, such as those organized by Assyrian traders early in the second millennium, and in the Syrian and Phoenician trade with Aegean and Mediterranean lands that was occurring by the 8th century BC. Wealthy "big men" such as Balmunamhe in Old Babylonian times, Assyrian traders in Asia Minor (Dercksen 1999:86), the Egibi and Murashu in Neo-Babylonia, Cato and other Romans spread their capital over numerous sectors – long-distance and local trade, provisioning the palace or temples with food and raw materials, leasing fields and workshops, moneylending and (often as an outgrowth) real estate.

As late as the 2nd century BC when we begin to pick up reports of the Roman *publicani*, they had not yet begun to specialize. Despite the fact that collecting taxes and other public revenue must have required a different set of skills from furnishing supplies to the army and other public agencies, most *publicani* acted opportunistically on an *ad hoc* basis. "What the companies provided was capital and top management, based on general business experience," observes Badian (1972:37), probably with a small permanent staff of assistants and subordinates. An entrepreneur might run a ceramic workshop, a metal workshop, or the like, as well as dealing in slaves or renting them out. Jones (1974:871) concludes: "The term *negotiator* was widely interpreted, including not only merchants, shopkeepers and craftsmen but moneylenders and prostitutes."

There was no such thing as patent protection or "intellectual property" rights, and little thought of what today would be called market development. Artistic styles and new techniques were copied freely. Finley (1973:147) cites the story, "repeated by a number of Roman writers, that a man – characteristically unnamed – invented unbreakable glass and demonstrated it to Tiberius in anticipation of a great reward. The emperor asked the inventor whether anyone shared his secret and was assured that there was no one else; whereupon his head was promptly removed, lest, said Tiberius, gold be reduced to the value of mud. ... neither the elder Pliny nor Petronius nor the historian Dio Cassius was troubled by the point that the inventor turned to the emperor for a reward, instead of turning to an investor for capital with which to put his invention into production."

Finley holds discouragement of an entrepreneurial ethic along these lines to be largely responsible for the fact that antiquity never embraced or even formulated the modern goal of achieving technological progress and economic growth. "What is missing in this picture," he concludes (1973:158), "is commercial or capitalist exploitation. The ancient economy had its own form of cheap labour and therefore did not exploit provinces in that way. Nor did it have excess capital seeking the more profitable investment outlets we associate with colonialism."

However, the most recent generation of economic historians has criticized Finley for being too extreme in doubting the existence of gain-seeking investment and "modern" economic motivation. There are many examples of Baumol's "productive enterprise," especially in the Near East. What remains accepted is that usury and slavery became increasingly predatory and corrosive practices, and that wars were fought mainly to strip the wealth of prosperous regions as booty to distribute at home.

Entrepreneurs, predators, and financiers

How many of these activities were truly entrepreneurial in the productive and innovative sense understood today? The key to defining productive entrepreneurs should be their contribution to generating an economic surplus, not merely appropriating it for themselves or, even worse, stripping the economy. War-making and piracy to seize booty and slaves were common predatory activities, and the largest fortunes known in classical antiquity were made by conquering or administering foreign lands and collecting taxes from defeated populations. So not all fortunes were amassed through enterprise, and only some managers were entrepreneurs.

Even when entrepreneurs played a nominally productive role in classical antiquity, they worked in a war-oriented environment. A major source of fortunes was provisioning of the army, mainly with food but also with manufactured goods. Frank (1933:291) notes that during 150-80 BC "we hear of only one man ... who gained wealth by manufacturing, and that was in public contracts for weapons during the Social War (Cicero, *in Pis.* 87-89)." On the retail level, Polanyi's paradigmatic example of free price-making markets was the small-scale food-sellers who followed Greek armies. Provisioning armies with food was indeed the main commercial activity, with the most economically aggressive being the public contractors who supplied Roman armies on the wholesale level. Contracts were set at auctions that became notoriously "fixed" by the 1st century BC.

Financial extraction is a different form of enterprise from industrial investment. Evolving largely as a byproduct of collecting public fees and revenues in Babylonia, moneylending grew from a side activity of the *tamkaru* to a major focus of the Roman *publicani*. Weber (1976:316) refers to Rome's publican companies as enterprises, but most writers today depict them as predatory. MacMullen (1974:51-52) notes the increasingly agrarian focus of moneylending, citing Rostovtzeff's calculation that Roman mortgage loans yielded "either fields foreclosed or interest in the neighborhood of 6 to 8 per cent. The rate compared favorably with the 6 per cent (at least in Italy) that one might reasonably hope for from money invested in agriculture." The effect was to divert capital to usury. "Why take a chance in trade?"

There may be a fine line demarcating an investor from an entrepreneur, but the latter certainly must play a more active managerial role than *rentiers* such as the Old Babylonian *naditu* heiresses investing their inheritance by making loans and buying revenue-yielding properties (although Yoffee 1995 refers to these women as entrepreneurs and some no doubt acted in this way). Cato's treatise on agriculture acknowledged that trade and usury were more lucrative than farming, but warned that commerce was risky and moneylending was considered immoral. Landowners needed managerial talent, but are not usually deemed entrepreneurs. A rental levy or property foreclosure is not profit earned in production, except to the extent that land use is upgraded (which did indeed occur, through date palms in the Near East to olive growing in Italy).

A key to whether engaging in a trade was entrepreneurial depends on the degree to which one worked either for oneself or as an agent or employee sharing directly in the profits of buying and selling. Furthermore, although self-employed craftsmen often doubled as sellers of their wares, they would not qualify as entrepreneurs unless they also acted as managers and organizers of a complex system of production and trade.

Humphreys (1978:153), however, points out a problem of deeming classical antiquity's craft workshops entrepreneurial:

> To run a workshop in an "entrepreneurial" spirit would have required supervision by the owner. Instead, the workshops of which we know details were managed by slaves or freedman, and the owner drew a fixed income from them. There was no interest in expansion. ... Demosthenes' father owned two workshops, one making beds and the other knives: there was no connection between them. Pasion's bank and shield-factory were equally unconnected and it is significant that while Pasion, an ex-slave, evidently devoted considerable energy and personal attention to the bank, his son Apollodorus (who received Athenian citizenship with his father) acquired three estates, preferred the shield-factory to the bank as his share of the inheritance, and devoted his energies to politics and the showy performance of liturgies, in the style of an Athenian gentleman. As metic traders and bankers became more important to the prosperity and food-supply of the city, the most successful of them were rewarded with citizen privileges, came under pressure for gifts and contributions to the *demos*, and tended to adopt the ethos of the rich citizens rather than encourage the latter to venture into new fields of investment.

There was a basic conflict between social ambition for high status and the aristocratic antipathy to engaging directly in business ventures. "Although Aristotle asserted that 'unnatural' *chrematistike* (money-making) knew no bounds," Humphreys concludes, "the general impression given by our sources is that the majority of Athenians were quite ready to give up the effort to make money as soon as they could afford a comfortable *rentier* existence, and that even the few who continued to expand their operations could not pass on the same spirit to their sons. The result was small-scale, disconnected business ventures, assessed by the security of their returns rather than their potentiality for expansion."

The most typical form of enterprise remained long-distance trade. Its organizational pattern changed little from the epoch when Mesopotamia's temples and palaces provided merchants with commodities or money. Drawing a parallel with the medieval Italian *commenda* and *compagnia*, as well as the Arabic *muqarada* practice, Larsen (1974:470) views such entrepreneurs as administering advances of money or inventories from their backers.

Opportunities for making money evolved as a byproduct of this mercantile role. In Old-Sumerian documents, Leemans (1950:11) notes, "*damkara* are only found as traders. But when private business began to flourish after the beginning of the Third Dynasty of Ur [2112-2004 BC], the *tamkarum* was the obvious person to assume the function of giver of credit." By the time of Hammurabi's Babylonian laws, in many cases "*tamkarum* cannot denote a traveling trader, but must be a money-lender." Leemans concludes (1950:22): "The development from merchant into banker [that is, a moneylender or investor backing voyages and similar partnerships] is a natural one, and there is no essential difference between these two professions – surely not in Babylonia where in principle no distinction was made between silver (money in modern terms) and other marketable stuffs. In a society whose commerce is little developed, trade is only carried on by merchants, who buy and sell. But when commerce increases, the business of a merchant assumes larger proportions."

As merchants rose to the position of being able to supply money to agents and subordinates, after the model of the early temples, these varied functions were telescoped into the word *tamkarum*. But none of them involved banking in the modern sense of the term. *Tamkarum* merchants did not lend out deposits, but worked with their own funds. By the same token, individuals who accumulated savings had to invest these personally or participate in partnerships. Although merchants formed guilds to coordinate their trading activities in foreign regions, there were no formal money managers outside of families.

Over time, financial backers gained ascendancy over on-the-spot traders, largely because trade was a risky and speculative business in which wrecks or piracy ate up much of the gain. By the Late Roman Empire, explains Jones (1964:867-868), "so much depended on an intimate knowledge of shippers and their ships [that it] did not appeal to the ordinary investor and was usually conducted by men, often retired sea captains, who specialised in the work." A specialization of functions developed, although nothing like the large trading companies found in England and Holland in the 17th century (for instance, the Russia Company, the East India Company, and so forth). "In maritime commerce a distinction must be drawn between the shipper (*navicularius*), the captain (*magister*) and the merchant (*mercator, negotiator*) or his agent. All these roles might be, and very commonly were, filled by one man, the owner of a vessel which he navigated himself and which he loaded with cargoes which he bought and sold. There were, however, shipowners who did not navigate their own ships."

Reflecting the disdain in which active participation in money-seeking commerce was held by antiquity's aristocratic ethic, most of the shippers engaged in Rome's maritime trade were foreigners or ex-slaves owning one or two small sailing vessels. Whether the shipper was wealthy or a petty tradesman, explains Jones (1964:868) he "rarely depended on his own capital, exclusively, preferring to raise nautical loans, which would partially cover him against loss by storm. For such loans, since the creditor stood the risk of losing his money if the ship were wrecked or the cargo jettisoned, the rate of interest was subject to no legal limit, until Justinian in 528 fixed the maximum at 12 per cent. per annum, as against 8 per cent. for ordinary commercial loans and 6 per cent. for private loans."

Undertaking risk does not in itself make an activity entrepreneurial. Nearly everyone was subject to risk, and to varying degrees, laws took a pragmatic approach in recognizing this fact. Cultivators and sharecroppers faced the possibility of drought, flooding, and military hostilities. In the Near East, rents and fees owed to the large institutions and other creditors were annulled in such circumstances. In the commercial sphere, when ships were lost at sea or caravans were robbed, commercial laws from Babylonia down through Roman times freed traveling merchants from the obligation to repay their backers.

The well-to-do backers accordingly spread their risk by taking partial investment shares in many ventures, much as Lloyd's insurance does in modern times. Plutarch describes Cato as "requir[ing] his borrowers to form a large company (*epi koinonia*)," summarizes D'Arms (1981:39), "and then when there were fifty partners, and as many ships for security, he took one share in the company himself and was represented by Quintio, a freedman of his, who accompanied his clients in all of their ventures. In this way his entire security was not imperiled, but only a small part of it, and his profits were large."

Plutarch describes Cato as anticipating what Weber would call the Protestant ethic. He was a stingy and self-abnegating man who did not enjoy the riches he made, refusing to buy expensive clothes or food for himself, preferring to drink the same lowly wine as his workmen, and turning out old and worn-out slaves when they no longer could do enough work to justify their support. In his public role he cut costs, opposed corruption, and increased the price that Rome received for farming out its taxes while minimizing the prices given out in public contracts. "To incline his son to be of his kind of temper, he used to tell him that it was not like a man, but rather like a widow to lessen an estate. But the strongest indication of Cato's avaricious humor was when he took the boldness to affirm that he was a most wonderful, nay, a godlike man, who left more behind him than he had received." The emphasis that Plutarch gives to his behavior suggests that such economic calculation was exceptional.

To sum up, entrepreneurs in antiquity either headed wealthy families or sought fortunes by managing other people's money, which typically was provided subject to a stipulated return. Regardless of the source of their capital, they coordinated a complex set of relationships whose institutional structure evolved throughout the second and first millennia BC.

Social status of merchants and entrepreneurs

In Babylonia after about 1800 BC, Renger explains (2000:155; see also 1984:64), the entrepreneurs to whom the palace leased fields, herds, and workshops tended to be "members of the elite or upper classes." The title of *damgar* or *tamkarum* merchant presupposed social status and connections to the palace or temple bureaucracy, administering franchises in "a form of economic management termed by F. R. Kraus as '*Palastgeschäft*.'" Some managers worked in the palace bureaucracy, but others worked entirely on their own account. Renger (2000:178) notes that the prominent Balmunamhe was a private *tamkarum* merchant, not a palace functionary. (Van De Mieroop 1987 surveys the archive recording his activities.)

By contrast, the absence of public entrepreneurial institutions and indeed, the less trade-oriented aristocratic ethic prevalent from Greece through Rome, led foreigners to play a leading commercial role throughout most of the Mediterranean. It was Syrian and Phoenician traders who brought Near Eastern commercial and economic practices to Greece and Italy around the 8th century BC, and by the end of the Roman Empire only Near Eastern traders were left, as commerce in the West shrank to a small scale. During the interim, the westward shift of antiquity's military and political center was associated with a lower status for commercial enterprise, mainly because its association with aliens and low-status individuals deterred high-status individuals from taking a direct role. Apart from the Near Easterners, slaves and freedmen played the leading commercial role in Greece and Rome. Humphreys (1978:148) describes them as becoming "foremen, managers of shops and workshops, captains of trading vessels and bailiffs of estates; slaves acquired legal capacity in lawsuits concerning banking and trade; they increasingly often lived and worked independently, paying a fixed sum to their masters and accumulating surplus earnings, if they could, toward the purchase of their freedom; ... in banking, where success depended heavily on experience and goodwill, a slave could rise to citizenship and the highest level of wealth," gaining status by acting as a philanthropist or public official.

Commenting on the link between the scale of business and social prestige, Cicero expressed the prevalent attitude of his time (*De Officiis* I:150-151): "Public opinion divides the trades and professions into the liberal and the vulgar. We condemn the odious occupation of the collector of customs and the usurer, and the base and menial work of unskilled laborers; for the very wages the laborer receives are a badge of slavery. Equally contemptible is the business of the retail dealer; for he cannot succeed unless he is dishonest, and dishonesty is the most shameful thing in the world. The work of the mechanic is also degrading; there is nothing noble about a workshop. The least respectable of all trades are those which minister to pleasure." He seems to be representative of his time and place in explaining that "business on a small scale is despicable; but if it is extensive and imports commodities in large quantities from all over the world and distributes them honestly, it is not so very discreditable; nay, if the merchant, satiated, or rather, satisfied, with the fortune he has made, retires from the harbor and steps into an estate, as once he returned to harbor from the sea, he deserves, I think, the highest respect. But of all the sources of wealth, farming is the best, the most able, the most profitable, the most noble." By farming Cicero, of course, meant being a *rentier* living off a landed estate.

It helped to be born rich and inherit land. When one was rich enough to purchase a governorship, it was reputable and almost a source of pride to squeeze as much as one could out of the provinces. In modern terms, the Roman ethic preferred asset stripping and hoarding over more economically productive modes of gain-seeking.

This oligarchic value system went hand in hand with highly stratified Roman commercial roles with respect to nationality and political and economic status. Entrepreneurs played a subordinate role, as the aristocracy preferred dealing with high finance on the public plane and involving itself with commerce only as *rentiers*. Emphasizing the linkage between landownership and the financing of commerce, Weber (1976: 316) points out that the publican companies "were the largest capitalist enterprises in Antiquity. ... Participation in these enterprises was limited to men with vast capital holdings in slaves and cash. They also needed to have extensive landed possessions, preferably with Italic status (which was privileged and therefore at an economic advantage), since they had to offer land as security when bidding for contracts. This last condition, by which only land enjoying full privileges under Roman land law could be offered as security, had the effect of giving the capitalist class in the Roman state a distinctively national character. It was much more so than had any similar class been in the Near East. Under the Ptolemies, for example, the publicans seem to have been mainly foreigners, and in Greece the smaller states actually encouraged foreign capitalists to make bids in order to have more competition."

What made Rome unusual, continues Weber (1976:317), was that despite the fact that "exclusion of aristocrats from direct involvement in industry was common throughout Antiquity," in Rome "this exclusion was extended to include tax farming and shipping; a senator might possess ships only of a capacity just sufficient to transport the products of his own estates. As a result, senators could gain wealth only from political office, from the rents paid by their tenants, from mortgages assumed through the agency of freedmen (though this was forbidden, it was commonly done as early as Cato), and from indirect investment in commerce and shipping. On the other side was the class of capitalists [the publican class of equestrian knights], the men who participated directly in capitalist enterprise. They were excluded from the Senate. ... From the time of Gaius Gracchus they formed a legally constituted order," detested for profiteering at society's expense.

The public context in which entrepreneurs operated

In southern Mesopotamia entrepreneurs are mostly documented first as emerging in some relationship with the palaces and temples, although no doubt there was interpersonal trade and production on a small local scale, weaving and making clothing and other personal needs on the land. But by the time Assyria developed trade relations with Asia Minor in the 19th century BC, private merchants had come to play a much larger role than in the south, in Sumer and Babylonia. Larsen (1974:469) describes the Assyrian trade as "venturing, *i.e.* all shipments were sent abroad without the sender being guaranteed a certain price for them in advance." He adds: "The economically decisive element in the Assyrian society is not found on the 'state level,' even though the role played by the temples is still somewhat obscure. Instead, the trade is clearly organized via a great number of large kinship-based groups, called 'houses,' which we may provisionally describe as 'firms.'" Mercantile guilds functioned as trade associations representing merchants vis-à-vis local authorities, reducing the risks involved by creating an "underlying pattern of permanent representation, partnerships, and 'factories.'"

Moving westward from the Near East to the Mediterranean we find more predatory and corrosive economic strategies as society became more "individualistic," that is, oligarchic. Yet even in Rome, where the links between positive commercial enterprise and the state were looser than elsewhere (Weber 1976:316), the most successful entrepreneurial path was to work in conjunction with public institutions. Contracts for public works and services have been traced back to the 4th century BC, first to provide supplies for religious rituals, public building, and similar civic projects, and then for the operation of public enterprises (from fields to mines and workshops) and collection of public fees and revenues. Provisioning the army soon became the largest category of contracts, along with collecting taxes from defeated lands.

Lacking a permanent public or royal bureaucracy such as characterized the Near Eastern mixed economies, Rome's government needed private suppliers for services it could not perform itself and relied on private individuals to collect its taxes and administer its domains. Rome's absence of civic oversight and even significant taxation of business enabled businessmen to profiteer at public expense. "The publican's chief profits came from the *ultro tributa* (contracts for goods and services, especially army supplies)," summarizes Badian (1972:24). In view of the scale involved, even a small rate of profit could produce a large fortune. But Rome's financial knights were most notorious for their predatory behavior. Livy (45.18.4) complained famously that "where there was a *publicanus*, there was no effective public law and no freedom for the subjects." Describing how publican tax collectors enslaved debtors, selling many in the market on Delos, Badian (1972:33) cites the report of Diodorus (5.38) regarding Spain's fabulously rich iron and silver mines, where publican managers "literally worked [slaves] to death as quickly as possible, to produce the maximum of profit in the shortest possible time." The resulting economic polarization was aggravated as mines passed into private hands during the Republic, many into those of Crassus (Frank 1933:374).

A comparison of classical antiquity's leading families with the Forbes lists of today's richest individuals in many countries shows a common basis of well-placed families taking control of the land, mineral rights, and other enterprises from the state, and leasing them for a stipulated rent to be paid to the civic authority. State monopolies for salt, mining, and even the postal service were farmed out down through medieval European times. In due course rent-seeking individuals took direct possession of these assets, especially in lands that were conquered. In Egypt, Johnson (1946:v) finds: "The Romans apparently surrendered the Ptolemaic monopolies to private enterprise, and Alexandria developed as one of the most important centres of trade and industry in the empire." The Romans themselves sought not so much to gain via workshops and industry (Frank 1933:291) as to profiteer from the state and the provinces it conquered. The time frame of merchants and financial *rentiers* always has been notoriously short – and it was shortened further as debt bondage, asset stripping, and economic polarization dried up domestic markets.

Financing enterprise

Many economic historians (*e.g.*, Andreau 1999:151, and earlier Humphreys 1978:151, and Larsen 1974:470) have cited the terms of commercial lending in Babylonian times as prototypes not only for classical antiquity but for the Italian *commenda* loans of medieval Europe. Such loans combined interest-bearing debt with a profit-sharing partnership agreement. And often the senior partner was the palace or a temple – or in classical times, the relevant civic authority.

Hammurabi's laws spell out how creditors shared in the debtor's risk under such contracts. Paragraphs 98-107 prescribe what seems to have been the typical Babylonian arrangements governing trade. Merchants were to split their profit with their backers, keeping strict books recording their activities. Paragraph 100 explains the normal procedure: "If a merchant gives silver to a trading agent for conducting business transactions and sends him off on a business trip ... [and] if he should realize [a profit] where he went, he shall calculate the total interest, per transaction and time elapsed, on as much silver as he took, and he shall satisfy his merchant" (translation Roth 1995). If he reports no profit, he must give his backer(s) double the original advance (para. 101). If he makes a loss, he still has to return the original capital sum (para. 102). However, paragraph 103 stipulates that he shall be free of debt if he is robbed or if a ship sinks and its cargo is lost. But a merchant is liable for triple damages if witnesses claim he has testified falsely about how much he has been advanced (para. 106).

Most commercial loans throughout antiquity took the form of such shipping loans. They paid a high return: 20 percent in the Near East, the standard fractional interest rate, plus a share of the trading profits perhaps reflecting the risk that the ship might not reach port safely. In Roman times we still find rules that the merchant's debt was cancelled if his ship was lost at sea or raided by pirates or if a caravan was robbed. This gave such borrowing the character of marine insurance to the shipper, while limiting such backing to experienced professionals down through Roman times.

Veenhof (1999:55) describes the drive for financial gain by Assyrian caravans bringing "tin and woollen textiles into Anatolia in order to convert them, directly or indirectly, into silver, which was invariably shipped back to Assur. After necessary payments had been made (expenses, taxes, debts, interest, dividend), much of what remained was again used for commercial purposes, either directly, by contributing to or equipping a new caravan, or indirectly, by investing it in a firm or issuing a loan to a trader." This trade developed such modern credit innovations as "promissory notes which do not mention the creditor by name, but refer to him as *tamkarum*, 'the merchant/creditor.' In a few cases such notes add at the end the phrase 'the bearer of this tablet is *tamkarum*.' This clause suggests the possibility of a transfer of debt-notes and of ceding claims, which would make it a precursor of later 'bearer cheques'" (Veenhof 1999:83).

Most agrarian debts were owed to royal collectors of rents, fees and other debts, or to managers of public enterprises (including "ale women" who sold beer apparently advanced by the temples or palaces). Royal clean slates alleviated the risk that agrarian debtors might not be able to pay their debts as a result of natural disaster or warfare. Hammurabi's laws prescribed that if lands were flooded, the cultivator was freed from the obligation to pay rent. Annulling these debts also cancelled those which royal agents and leaseholders owed to the palace. In times of weak rulers, it seems that these individuals were able to keep the rents and other fees in any event.

With respect to the situation in classical antiquity, Finley (1973:141) cited three characteristics making the Greek and Roman economies pre-modern. First was the absence of productive loans – a view that subsequent economic historians have found extreme, especially when the spread of Near Eastern models is recognized. Second, was the fact that although "there was endless moneylending among both Greeks and Romans ... all lenders were rigidly bound by the actual amount of cash on hand; there was not, in other words, any machinery for the *creation of credit* through negotiable instruments. ... In Greek law sales were not legal and binding until the sale price had been paid in full; credit sales took the form of fictitious loans." Finally, most loans were short-term, mainly to finance voyages or overland trading expeditions.

There has been a tendency to assume that what Finley was describing must have been the "primitive" case from the outset. But as noted above, these generalities do not apply to the Near East, especially to the complex financial arrangements found in Neo-Babylonian practice. The Egibi archive in particular stands in sharp contrast to the view by Finley's generation of economic historians of classical Greece and Rome, who found almost no productive lending for tangible capital investment. The Egibi took out antichretic loans – that is, advances where the collateral that secured the loan generated the interest being charged. This is the same strategy used by many real estate investors today, as expressed in the motto, "Rent is for paying interest." The family also pledged urban property (the "House of the Crown Prince") to obtain a commercial line of credit. Finally, their partnerships sometimes extended over more than one generation, as described by Wunsch in this volume.

The inability of historians of Greece and Rome to find anything so sophisticated makes the classical economies appear as the end-result of decay into more rudimentary financial arrangements. As Finley (1973:108) famously noted in the most extreme statement of this view:

> There was no clear conception of the distinction between capital costs and labor costs, no planned ploughing back of profits, no long-term loans for productive purposes. The import in this context of the short-term loan (like the short-term tenancy) cannot be exaggerated. From one end of antiquity to another, one can easily count the known examples of borrowing on property for purposes of purchase or improvement. The

mortgage was a disaster ("mortgaging the old homestead"), a short-term personal loan designed to "cover deficiencies in the supply of necessities occasioned generally by some emergency which has made unexpected demands upon the resources of the borrower," not a deliberate device for raising money at a low rate in order to invest at a higher rate, [which is] the main function of the modern business mortgage.

Andreau (1999:147-148) finds a few scattered examples of Roman businessmen borrowing to tide their operations over or making delayed payment of a final balance owed to buy a business. However, he sums up: "Did Roman financiers direct most of their efforts towards economic life in order to create an effective instrument for investments? Did any financial establishments specialize in the promotion of productive loans? The answer to both questions must definitely be no."

One deterrent was the fact that most Greek and Roman trading enterprises were organized as partnerships, as would characterize most trading companies throughout Europe down to the 17th century. (Corporations were created only for large public projects such as major building construction or tax collecting.) "Every partner was held liable for the full amount of any debt and ... the partnership came to an end at the death of any partner," Frank explains (1940:217). "Under such strict limitations large business enterprises were not apt to prosper." Walbank (1969:48) likewise cites the absence of permanent joint-stock corporations as discouraging enterprise: "Because of the risks entailed, it was always costly to raise capital for a trading venture." Roman law did recognize that the large sums involved in public building projects required corporate organization, and on much the same logic the *publicani* knights also were empowered to organize companies to conduct public enterprise (including tax farming), above all that associated with military provisioning and other imperial spending. (Nicollet 1966 and Badian 1972 describe these activities.) However, notes Frank (1933:350), "Roman law persisted in discouraging joint stock companies with limited liability in business not directly serving the state," and "firms dealing in state contracts were given business for only five-year terms." (See also D'Arms 1981:41).[3]

---

[3] The commercial activities for which corporations could be organized remained limited to state projects, including the exploitation of subsoil resources in the public domain. "At some point," notes Jones (2006:208), "the *societas vectigalis* was granted a form of corporate entity, according to the jurist Gaius in the second century (*Digest* 3.4.1): 'Partners in tax farming, gold mines, silver mines, and saltworks are allowed to form corporations. ... Those permitted to form a corporate body consisting of a *collegiium* or partnership ... have the right, on the pattern of the state (*ad exemplum rei publicae*),

Also limiting the potential takeoff was the absence of paper credit. There was no public debt to manage. Budget deficits prompted the Roman emperors to adulterate the coinage, not to monetize their spending by creating public credit as national treasuries and central banks do today.

These institutional constraints limited the buildup of capital reserves in mercantile undertakings and gave them an ad hoc character. The result, summarizes Frank (1940:28), was that "partnerships based on the full liability of each member could hardly grow to great size." Under the Empire, "We hear of no bankers of importance. … In the houses of the nobles the old custom still prevailed of trusting financial matters to personal slaves and freedmen, so that there was little room for investment banking; and in Rome's economic structure there was no place for corporation banking." This custom "led to business success not being held in any esteem … the only occupations befitting senators were agriculture, and civil or military office. Lucrative business in shipping, industry, and banking rested almost entirely in the hands of foreigners and freedmen. And to such people social position did not come, whatever the scale of their profits."

Freedmen played a key role in Roman enterprise and became some of Rome's most successful entrepreneurs when elite families provided them with a *peculium*, observes David Jones (2006:244-245), but this "did not produce a 'middle class' of businessmen." After getting their start, "non-economic values held sway." The sole upward mobility that ex-slaves enjoyed was through aping the landed aristocracy as best they could. "Trimalchio made a seamless transition from trading in mixed cargoes ('wine, bacon, beans, perfumes and slaves') to settling down on a country estate and providing finance for another generation of ex-slave entrepreneurs." This simply emulated what the philosopher Seneca "described [as] the characteristics of the 'fortunate man': a handsome family, a fine house, plenty of land under cultivation and plenty of money out on loan (*familiam formosam habet et domum pulchram, multum serit, multum fenerat*). Elsewhere he says that the rich man 'has gold furniture … a large book of loans (*magnus kalendarii liber*) [and] plenty of suburban property.'" (Seneca, *Epist.* 41.7; 87.7, cited in Jones 2006:173.) It was land and money out on loan that made up Seneca's own wealth.

---

to have common property, a common treasury and an attorney or legal counsel through whom, as in a state, what should be transacted and done in common is transacted and done.'"

Describing the freedmen who became bankers in Puteoli, the grain and export emporium on the Bay of Naples 170 miles south of Rome, Jones (2006:165) finds: "The business of the Sulpicii was built around the provision of small, short-term secured loans. There is no evidence in the Murecine archive to suggest that the Sulpicii or their depositors made medium- or long-term loans for capital projects such as the construction of ships, buildings or workshops. Nor is there any sign that the Sulpicii or their depositors lent money for high-risk, high-reward maritime ventures. Furthermore the bank operated on a local basis." Their loan market was local, despite the fact that they took in deposits and lent cash to members of the imperial household. "There is no suggestion that the acquisition of additional funds by the elite furthered, or could have furthered, the expansion of trade and industry," he concludes (2006:174). "It was taken for granted by Roman commentators and their audiences that the Roman elite took no interest in commercial activities and did not consider investment in trade and industry as an appropriate use of their capital." It was a rather thoughtless extractive spirit with little concept of economic growth. This explains a feature of ancient enterprise noted by Baumol: the failure to commercialize technology, which began only in medieval times.

Entrepreneurs, debt and commercial abuse, and shifting property relations

"Stretching the envelope" of what is deemed legal and ethical always has been most pronounced in the financial sphere. It was debt foreclosure that first turned family self-support land into absentee-owned property. Plutarch's melodramatic depiction of a Spartan father disinheriting his son and bequeathing his land to a creditor acquaintance finds its counterpart over a thousand years earlier in Babylonia. To circumvent the traditional sanctions that prevented (and indeed, protected) citizens from alienating their subsistence land outside of their families, Babylonian creditors (and also those of Nuzi to the northwest) hit upon the tactic of getting their debtors to adopt them as "sons" and hence legitimate heirs to their land in payment for debt. These "fake adoptions" enabled creditors to start monopolizing the land, disenfranchising citizens and hence the community's fighting force.

The laws of Hammurabi (1750 BC) and his dynasty's "economic order" (*misharum* or *andurarum*) proclamations, culminating in that of Ammisaduqa (1648 BC), sought to preserve stability and a strong military capability by annulling agrarian and personal debts, preventing creditors from reducing citizens permanently to debt bondage. No such society-wide laws of this type are found in Greece or Rome. Without "divine rulership" or other central authority to check narrow self-interest, Rome in particular became harshly creditor-oriented and oligarchic.

Retail trade always has been notorious for cheating, and crooked practices such as using false weights and measures are attested as rife throughout antiquity, from Babylonian "wisdom literature" down through biblical proverbs. But what is most noteworthy in classical times is vast large-scale fraud. The earliest description of the Roman *publicani* appears in a Senate prosecution. When the Treasury was strapped during Rome's war with Carthage, suppliers obtained a government agreement to insure all supplies once they were loaded onto ships. Two eminent Etrurian contractors, T. Pomponious and M. Postumius, loaded "worthless goods on board unseaworthy ships and [claimed] the insurance sum for army supplies when the ships sank." Badian (1972:17-18) remarks that: "The incident ... shows the *publicani*, on practically their first explicit appearance in our record, already organized as an extra-legal pressure group, already putting private profit above the public interest, and willing to defend a member of their class, no matter how bad his case." Cicero's surviving defense pleadings show the *publicani* continuing to stick together in a tacit compact of mutual support. There thus was little peer pressure to behave better – and if anything, mutual support for the most rapacious practices.[4]

Rome's major attempt to prevent commercial abuses occurred in 133 BC, when Gaius Gracchus established a system of checks and balances whereby the Senate and the *publicani* knights were to act as mutual checks by prosecuting each other's misdeeds. But instead of the *publicani* financial class turning into the "jury" class to adjudicate on Senators acting as provincial administrators, the knights colluded with the administrators for mutual gain. The case of Verres in Sicily showed how crooked governors and businessmen made corrupt deals together. Cicero depicted him as a bad apple, and a time-honored strategy of businessmen has been to single out an individual as a scapegoat to be punished conspicuously so that the others can go about their business as usual. Verres became the sacrificial lamb, immortalized by Cicero's eloquent *Verrines* speeches.

But the system itself had gone bad, culminating in the excesses of Brutus, Caesar, and other patricians looting Rome's provinces by levying extortionate taxes and tribute and then charging exorbitant interest on payment arrears. Badian (1972:107) describes publican com-

---

[4] I discuss the *publicani* and their abuses in *The Collapse of Antiquity* (2023).

panies forming a cartel that "must have included the whole upper order of society and of the State, except for a few traditional aristocrats." The money was spent mainly on buying domestic Roman political support, as public administration and the right to loot ended up being a lucrative source of wealth – the antithesis of productive enterprise. It was said that a provincial governor "had to make three fortunes during his year's administration, one to pay his debts, another on which to retire, and a third to bribe the jurors in the inevitable trial for extortion" (Walbank 1969:7). The Senate proved too weak and indifferent to stop such abuses. And inasmuch as the richest sources of loot were the most productive regions, the effect was to strip their capital and stifle economic growth wherever the Empire reached.

From commercial entrepreneurship to oligarchy

What is widely described as the individualistic spirit of Greece and Rome was primarily a military and increasingly oligarchic ethic of status and prestige. It relied on conquest and moneylending as the main sources of gain, disdaining profit-seeking commerce. The Theognid poetry of Greece in the 7th and 6th centuries BC reflects the conservative aristocratic ethic:

> ... this city is still a city, but truly the people are different.
> Those who, in the past, knew neither justice nor laws
> but wore out the goatskins which covered their sides
> and grazed like deer on the outskirts of the city,
> now these men are the nobles (*agathoi*) ... and
> those who before were of the nobility (*esthloi*) now
> they are inferiors (*deiloi*).
> — Theognis (53-58, in Figueira and Nagy 1985:16)

Commerce seemed akin to money-grubbing, a violation of the aristocratic ethic reflected in Aristotle's attitude finding "natural" self-sufficient householding more socially acceptable than commerce (*kapelike*). Humphreys (1978:144) finds this spirit reflected in "the Theban law that anyone who had traded in the market within the last ten years could not hold political office [and] in the hostility against traders as foreigners callously exploiting the hardship of others which flared up in Athens when corn prices rose. A type of interaction in which each party was expected to consider only his own immediate economic advantage was a flagrant contradiction of every conception of social life: the man who lived by such transactions could only be an 'outsider.'" The irony is that a major factor stifling the Greco-Roman economic takeoff was the aristocratic disdain for enterprise, productive as well as predatory.

The Romans are credited with a genius for organization, but they devoted it mainly to organizing their army. The city's historians described its founders, Romulus and Remus, as feral children nurtured by a wolf, establishing a city of refuge between its two hills to attract exiles, refugees, and criminals who in due course became the basis of its citizen army. By the 6th century BC the city had built substantial defensive walls and the largest temple in Italy. The preconditions for a commercial takeoff were present, but a patrician oligarchy gained dominance through usury and land acquisition, with little thought that reducing much of the population to bondage would destroy the home market needed to grow.

Roman affluence – literally a "flowing in" – stemmed largely from slave capture and booty hunting, usury, and tribute from defeated realms. Military to the end, as Frank (1933:399) summarized, "the larger fortunes during the last fifty corrupt years of the Republic [80-30 BC] came, not from business, but from military returns, from dealing in confiscated goods, and from various abuses of power. To these sources are traceable the wealth of Lucullus, Caesar, Pompey, and Crassus, who were the richest Romans of the period."

In today's economic terminology this was classic rent-seeking behavior. Instead of having a commercial strategy, "The aristocracy that directed Roman policy during the Republic was almost wholly agrarian-militaristic," Frank concluded (1940:295). "Clearly, it was not less moved by an economic drive, by self-seeking, and by greed than the commercial societies of today. But the gain sought was of a different kind. The trade and commerce of the Mediterranean were then largely controlled by old seafaring peoples with whom the Roman nobles, wedded to agriculture, could not compete with success, or by ex-slaves accustomed to trade, who had no influence in shaping the politics of government. By the Augustan day the important men of the state had placed their investments in provincial real estate and mortgages, not in industry or commerce."

The decline of enterprise

"Before Caesar's death Rome was probably the financial center of the Roman world," remarks Frank (1933:350). "Yet no dominating banking firm grew up." Andreau (1999:137) attributes this striking fact to the shortcomings of the oligarchy. Most moneylending was predatory.

Rome's *publicani* lent abroad to appropriate the wealth of others, not to finance enterprise. "The generation that came to maturity under the Julio-Claudian emperors provides one of the best examples known to history of an upstart aristocracy that abused the benefits of prosperity," Frank (1940:29) sums up. Without much productive investment from the 2nd century BC onward, Rome could consume only by taking booty from foreign lands – tribute and usury from Asia Minor, Spanish mine output (dug out largely by slaves), and the looting of Egypt that continued long after the tribute demands of Mark Antony and Caesar.

Replacing the *publicani* knights with an imperial bureaucracy hardly helped matters. By the time of Septimius Severus (AD 193-211), regional armies were fighting among themselves for the Roman throne, plunging the Empire into economic as well as military instability. "With the exception of a few military 'houses' who still succeeded in recouping their fortunes abroad, few families managed to remain in the wealthiest group for long," writes Humphreys (1978:146). Rostovtzeff (1926:399) quotes the *History* by Herodian (7.3.3-6) (AD 180-250): "Every day one could see the wealthiest men of yesterday beggars today. Such was the greed of the tyranny which used the pretext that it needed a constant supply of money to pay the soldiers." The resulting military state stifled enterprise while shifting the tax burden onto the lower orders, paving the way for the Dark Age to come.

Instead of policies like Near Eastern Clean Slates to restore a balance between debt and liberty by freeing bondservants and other unfree labor and redistributing land throughout the Roman Empire, Diocletian (284-305) tried to save matters by imposing price controls and a "totalitarian economics" (Frank 1940:303). Herodian reports that earlier, "When Maximinus [235-238], after reducing most of the distinguished houses to penury, found that the spoils were few and paltry and by no means sufficient for his purposes, he attacked public property. All the money belonging to the cities that was collected for the victualling of the populace or for distribution among them, or was devoted to theaters or to religious festivals, he diverted to his own use; and the votive offerings set up in the temples, the statues of the gods, the tributes to heroes, all the adornments of the public buildings, everything that served to beautify the cities, even the metal out of which money could be coined, all were melted down."

"Commerce was at a standstill, and consequently industry was much reduced," concludes Broughton (1948:912) in describing the 3rd and 4th centuries AD; "all fortunes dependent upon loans, notes, mortgages, and such forms of investment were practically wiped out. Those dependent upon real estate, urban and nonurban, although reduced in number and amount by imperial collections and confiscations, probably retained some proportion of their value but for a time provided no income at all, or only a small one in kind. A tendency in the country to revert to a form of feudalism was an almost inevitable result. Thus the reign of Gallienus [253-268] brought to a climax all the miseries of the century," with him debasing the silver content of the coinage from about 15 percent to less than 2 percent in the final eight years of his rule.

By the Late Roman Empire industry ended much as it had begun, concentrated in public-sector potteries, mints, textile production, iron foundries, and armor workshops to supply the army's needs. "For some time," summarizes Walbank (1969:80), "the State (or Emperor) had been the largest landowner; now it became the largest owner of mines and quarries and the greatest industrialist." But in the Empire's shrinking economy these state enterprises could only afford to pay their workers in kind, and ended up tying them to their professions on a hereditary basis.

Fortunes dried up as the economy was stripped of money. Most of it flowed eastward, increasingly to India. Handicrafts and industry moved from the cities to the villages and self-sufficient country estates, partly to escape the fiscally predatory militarized state. And "[by] making everything on the spot," explains Walbank (1969:56-57), "the late Roman precursor of the feudal baron would eliminate the most costly item in his bill of expenses," transportation. Large estates became "the symbol of the decline of urban civilization, and both the result of the general decay and a factor in hastening it ... each estate, in proportion as it became self-sufficing, meant so many more individuals subtracted from the classical economic system, so many less potential consumers for those commodities which still circulated in the old markets."

The largest landowners were able to obtain exemption from imperial taxes, shifting the fiscal burden onto mercantile activity (Hudson 1997). "Influential people could wangle immunity either as individuals or as a class," summarizes MacMullen (1988:42): "'registrars of the municipalities through collusion are transferring the burden of the taxes of *potentiores* to *inferiores*,' Constantine angrily declares in 313; or again, in 384, the entire body of senators in Thrace and Macedonia are excused from paying anything at all on their lands."

The Empire had expanded by economically slashing and burning an ever-widening area, stripping populations of their potential to serve as a market. It took four centuries to exhaust the supply of booty and slaves. Rome's richest province, Asia Minor, failed by the end of the 3rd

century, while the temples spent their resources on charity under permanent emergency conditions (Broughton 1938:912). Piracy became prevalent again, and almost the only documented building was for walls to protect against robbers. The best that can be said is that in the West the epoch of Roman conquest was ended by the barbarian invasions. The northerners always were there, of course, but the imperial economy had become too weak to resist.

Conclusion

> Past events make us pay particular attention to the future, if we really make thorough enquiry in each case into the past.
> – Polybius (XII 25e, 6)

Mesopotamia's lack of basic raw materials prompted even military rulers such as Sargon of Akkad to boast that they had extended long-distance commerce. By contrast, classical antiquity's aristocracies sought local self-sufficiency (supplemented by foreign booty and tribute, to be sure). This became the condition into which the western Roman Empire sank as economic life retreated to landed estates, while prosperity lasted longer in Egypt and the eastern half of the Roman Empire ruled from Constantinople.

The fact that Near Easterners were the first to develop the basic repertory of business practices poses the question of what is distinctly Western. Classical Greece and Rome have long been depicted as representing a fresh start, in contrast to the allegedly stagnant Near Eastern economies. Yet the Near East enjoyed superior prosperity from the beginning to the end of antiquity, as well as better economic balance and stability. What has long been viewed as a fresh spirit of individualism in the West turns out to be a product of the breakdown following the devastation that swept the eastern Mediterranean circa 1200 BC. The ensuing half-millennium brought a free-for-all that never developed an ethic of steering gain-seeking along productive rather than predatory and extractive lines.

When Syrian and Phoenician merchants organized Mediterranean trade in the 8th century BC, they brought standardized weights and measures, money, a financial vocabulary, and interest-bearing debt to Greek and Italian communities. Local chieftains applied these practices in a smaller, more localized context that lacked the checks and balances found in the Near East to save economies from polarizing between creditors and debtors. There were numerous one-off debt cancellations under the 7th- and 6th-century tyrants, and Solon's *seisachtheia* in 594 BC, but Greece and Rome never developed a tradition of annulling debts to prevent creditors from foreclosing on the land and reducing much of the citizenry to debt bondage. Just the opposite: Greece and Rome measured success by the ability of creditors to achieve social status through landownership with its patronage power over tenants and clients. There was no attempt to justify wealth and property by attributing it to the labor expended by its owners. Land was obtained by inheritance or through foreclosure on the impecunious, or taken from the public domain by military conquest or insider dealing. Bondage became harsher and more inexorable, with more than a quarter of the Roman population falling into servitude by the 4th century AD, increasingly on large slave-stocked estates.

Rome's economic history provides a leading example of Arnold Toynbee's conclusion in *A Study of History* that the cause of imperial collapse invariably is "suicidal statecraft." It also illustrates the contrast that Baumol has drawn between productive and unproductive enterprise, with its foreign relations *in particular* aimed at extorting tribute and indebting local populations. The short time frame of Roman imperial administrators did not allow replenishment of the resources stripped from the provinces. And instead of promoting domestic market demand at home, Rome let debt service and taxes siphon off purchasing power and dry up commercial enterprise, and debased the coinage in a futile attempt to deal with the fiscal crisis that culminated in feudalism.

In these respects classical antiquity must be viewed as an unsuccessful mode of exploitation. Nobody voiced a program of raising general living standards, labor productivity or technology by developing a home market. Charity by the wealthy seemed the best that could be hoped for. It remained for John Locke and other Enlightenment political economists to justify property morally by the labor that went into its acquisition (an idea that, Locke acknowledged, applied only on the small scale of self-sufficient holdings). But for this labor theory of property value to apply, the political and fiscal context for enterprise had to be transformed.

And indeed, a new world did emerge out of Rome's collapse into a Dark Age. The transition from slave labor via serfdom to free labor transformed the social character of enterprise. Commerce began to revive with the Arab and Moorish trade across southern Europe to Spain. In 1204 the looting of Constantinople by the Crusaders, financed by the Venetians as a paying venture for a quarter of the loot, drew vast sums of monetary bullion into western Europe. It was enough to provide the basis for an expansion of credit. The Schoolmen permitted loopholes to the Christian ban on usury for bankers to charge interest in the form of *agio* on foreign payments, mainly to finance trade – along with royal war debts.

It was in the late medieval period, and more so during the Renaissance and Enlightenment, that economic gain-seeking took the form of expanding production. Trade became the means of obtaining the monetary metals, and credit came to be monetized on the basis of national treasuries and central banks. Bankruptcy laws became more humanitarian and debtor-oriented, at least until quite recently.

But the history of antiquity shows that evolution is not inevitably carried upward by economic or technological potential automatically realizing itself. Entrepreneurs have obtained surpluses through the ages, but often in ways that injure society as a whole. Predatory loans mounting up to strip capital, and economies living in the short run by asset stripping, are universal deterrents to long-term investment.[5] Many vestiges of the *rentier* ethic that culminated in the post-Roman feudal period are still with us, weighing on the present like a dead hand (*lit. mort-gage*). Much as classical antiquity plowed its commercial gains and extraction of interest into the land, many enterprises today find land (along with financial speculation and corporate takeovers) more attractive than new capital formation.

Modern observers have criticized Rome's legal framework for not replacing commercial partnerships with permanent limited-liability joint-stock companies. Trading profits had to be paid out each time a partner died or a new one joined, and often at the end of each voyage. But today's stock-market raiders appear to be reverting to the short-term perspective that historians have blamed for blocking Rome's economic takeoff. The economic environment that most effectively contributes to

---

[5] This dynamic was recognized already at the takeoff of the practice of charging interest in Sumer in the third millennium BC, in the Hymn to Shamash, the Akkadian god of justice (lines 103-106):

103 What happens to the loan shark who invests his resources at the (highest) interest rate?
104 He will lose his purse just as he tries to get the most out of it.
105 But he who invests in the long term will convert one measure of silver into three.
106 He pleases Shamash and will enrich his life.
(in Buccellati 2024:194)

The basic tension between financial claims on the economy and wealth created by direct long-term investment (which today expresses itself in the distinction between finance capitalism and industrial capitalism) was thus recognized five thousand years ago. But it was not a contrast drawn by Church canon law when distinguishing "good" interest from "bad" usury. Recognition of it lay too far in the future ... and in the past.

prosperity is one that induces entrepreneurs to gain by investing in new means of production, not by rent-seeking, redistributive property expropriation, debt foreclosure and insider dealing. Successful enterprise helps economies grow by contributing to output, or adding to efficiency by innovations that minimize costs, not by generating a proliferation of debt and property claims.

The moral is that the race is not always to the strong nor economic victory to the most productive. The economic course of civilization has not always been upward, as historians who focus more on technology than on the institutions of credit and property tend to imply. That is the main lesson taught by a review of the history of enterprise, positive and negative, over the course of antiquity.

Bibliography

Andreau, Jean (1999), *Banking and Business in the Roman World*, translated by Janet Lloyd (Cambridge, Cambridge University Press).

Andreau, Jean, P. Briant, and R. Descat, eds. (1994), *Économie antique: Les échanges des l'Antiquité, le rôle de l'État* (Saint-Bertrand-de-Comminges: Musée archéologique départemental).

Archi, Alfonso, ed. (1984), *Circulation of Goods in Non-palatial Context in the Ancient Near East* (Rome, Edizioni dell'Ateneo).

Badian, Ernst (1972), *Publicans and Sinners: Private Enterprise in the Service of the Roman Republic* (Ithaca, NY, Cornell University Press).

Baumol, William J. (1990), "Entrepreneurship: Productive, Unproductive and Destructive," *Journal of Political Economy* 98:893-921.

Bleiberg, Edward (1995), "The Economy of Ancient Egypt," in Sasson 1995:1373-1386.

Bongenaar, A. C. V. M., ed. (2000), *Interdependency of Institutions and Private Entrepreneurs: Proceedings of the Second MOS Symposium (Leiden 1998)* (Istanbul, Nederlands Historisch-Archaeologisch Instituut te Istanbul; Leiden, Nederlands Instituut voor het Nabije Oosten).

Broughton, T. R. S. (1938), "Roman Asia Minor," in Frank 1938.

Buccellati, Giorgio (2024), *"When on High the Heavens...": Mesopotamian Religion and Spirituality with Reference to the Biblical World* (London, Routledge).

Burkert, Walter (1992), *The Orientalizing Revolution: Near Eastern Influence on Greek Culture in the Early Archaic Age*, translated by Walter Burkert and Margaret E. Pinder (Cambridge, Harvard University Press).

Calhoun, George M. (1965), *The Business Life of Ancient Athens* (Rome).

Cartledge, Paul, Edward E. Cohen, and Lin Foxhall, eds. (2001), *Money, Labour, and Land: Approaches to the Economics of Ancient Greece* (London, Routledge).

Casson, Lionel (1984), *Ancient Trade and Society* (Detroit, Wayne State University Press).

Charpin, Dominique (1982), "Marchands du Palais et Marchands du Temple à la Fin de la Ire Dynastie de Babylone," *Journal Asiatique* 270:25-65.

Cohen, Edward E. (1992), *Athenian Economy and Society: A Banking Perspective* (Princeton, Princeton University Press).

D'Arms, John. (1981), *Commerce and Social Standing in Ancient Rome* (Cambridge, Harvard University Press).

Dercksen, J. G., ed. (1999), *Trade and Finance in Ancient Mesopotamia: Proceedings of the First MOS Symposium (Leiden 1997)* (Istanbul, Nederlands Historisch-Archaeologisch Instituut te Istanbul; Leiden, Nederlands Instituut voor het Nabije Oosten).

Diakanoff, Igor M., ed. (1991), *Early Antiquity*, translated by Alexander Kirjanov (Chicago, University of Chicago Press).
" (1992), "The Structure of Near Eastern Society before the Middle of the 2nd Millennium BC," *Oikumene* 3:7-100.

Figueira, Thomas J., and Gregory Nagy, eds. (1985), *Theognis of Megara: Poetry and the Polis* (Baltimore, Johns Hopkins University Press).

Finley, Moses (1973), *The Ancient Economy* (Berkeley and Los Angeles, University of California Press).
" ed. (1979), *The Bucher-Meyer Controversy* (New York, Arno Press).

Frank, Tenney, ed. (1933), *An Economic Survey of Ancient Rome. Vol. 1, Rome and Italy of the Republic* (Baltimore, Johns Hopkins Press).
" ed. (1938), *An Economic Survey of Ancient Rome. Vol. 4, Roman Africa, Syria, Greece, and Asia* (Baltimore, Johns Hopkins Press).

" ed. (1940), *An Economic Survey of Ancient Rome. Vol. 5, Rome and Italy of the Empire* (Baltimore, Johns Hopkins Press).

Frankfort, Henri (1951), *Kingship and the Gods: A Study of Ancient Near Eastern Religion as the Integration of Society and Nature* (Chicago, University of Chicago Press).

Garnsey, Peter, Keith Hopkins, and C. R. Whittaker, eds. (1983), *Trade in the Ancient Economy* (Berkeley and Los Angeles, University of California Press).

Gress, David (1998), *From Plato to NATO: The Idea of the West and Its Opponents* (New York, Free Press).

Heichelheim, Fritz (1958-70), *An Ancient Economic History: From the Palaeolithic Age to the Migrations of the Germanic, Slavic, and Arabic Nations*, 3 vols. (rev. ed., Leiden, A.W. Sijthoff).

Hudson, Michael (1992), "Did the Phoenicians Introduce the Idea of Interest to Greece and Italy – And If So, When?" in Kopcke and Tokumaru 1992:128-143.
" (1996a), "The Dynamics of Privatization, from the Bronze Age to the Present," in Hudson and Levine 1996:33-72.
" (1996b), "Privatization in History and Today: A Survey of the Unresolved Controversies," in Hudson and Levine 1996:1-32.
" (1998), "Land Monopolization, Fiscal Crises and Clean Slate 'Jubilee' Proclamations in Antiquity," in Robert C. Hunt and Antonio Gilman, eds., *Property in Economic Context* (Lanham, MD, University Press of America):139-169.
" (2000), "How Interest Rates Were Set, 2500 BC-1000 AD: *Máš, tokos* and *fænus* as Metaphors for Interest Accruals," *Journal of the Economic and Social History of the Orient* 43:132-161.
" (2005-6), Review of *Autour de Polanyi: Vocabularies, théories et modalities des échanges*, eds. Ph. Chancier, F. Joannès, P. Rouillard, and A. Tenu (Paris, De Boccard, 2005) and *The Ancient Economy: Evidence and Models*, eds. J. G. Manning and Ian Morris (Stanford, Stanford University Press, 2005), *Archiv für Orientforschung* 51:405-411.

Hudson, Michael, and Baruch A. Levine, eds. (1996), *Privatization in the Ancient Near East and Classical World* (Cambridge, MA, Peabody Museum of Archaeology and Ethnology).

" eds. (2000), *Urbanization and Land Ownership in the Ancient Near East* (Cambridge, MA, Peabody Museum of Archaeology and Ethnology).

Hudson, Michael, and Marc Van De Mieroop, eds. (2002), *Debt and Economic Renewal in the Ancient Near East* (Bethesda, MD, CDL Press).

Hudson, Michael, and Cornelia Wunsch, eds. (2004), *Creating Economic Order: Record-Keeping, Standardization, and the Development of Accounting in the Ancient Near East* (Bethesda, MD, CDL Press; repr. Dresden, ISLET 2023).

Humphreys, S. C. (1978), *Anthropology and the Greeks* (London, Routledge and Kegan Paul).

Joannès, Francis (1995), "Private Commerce and Banking in Achaemenid Babylon," in Sasson:1475-1486.

Johnson, Allan Chester (1936), *Roman Egypt to the Reign of Diocletian* (Baltimore, Johns Hopkins Press).

Jones, A. H. M. (1964), *The Later Roman Empire, 284-610: A Social, Economic, and Administrative Survey* (Norman, University of Oklahoma Press).

Jones, David (2006), *The Bankers of Puteoli: Finance, Trade, and Industry in the Roman World* (London, Tempus).

Kirzner, Israel M. (1979), *Perception, Opportunity, and Profit: Studies in the Theory of Entrepreneurship* (Chicago, University of Chicago Press).

Kopcke, Günter, and Isabelle Tokumaru, eds. (1992), *Greece between East and West: 10th-8th Centuries BC* (Mainz, Verlag Philipp von Zabern).

Kurke, Leslie (1999), *Coins, Bodies, Games, and Gold: The Politics of Meaning in Archaic Greece* (Princeton, Princeton University Press).

Lamberg-Karlovsky, Carl (1996), "The Archaeological Evidence for International Commerce: Private and/or Public Enterprise in Mesopotamia," in Hudson and Levine 1996:73-108.

Lambert, Maurice (1960), "La naissance de la bureaucratie," *Revue Historique* 224:1-26.

Larsen, Mogens Trolle (1974), "The Old Assyrian Colonies in Anatolia," *Journal of the American Oriental Society* 94:468-475.

Latouche, Robert (1961), *The Birth of Western Economy: Economic Aspects of the Dark Ages*, translated by E. M. Wilkinson (London, Methuen).

Leemans, W. F. (1950), *The Old-Babylonian Merchant: His Business and His Social Position* (Leiden, E. J. Brill).

Liverani, Mario (2005), "The Near East: The Bronze Age," in Manning and Morris 2005:47-57.

MacMullen, Ramsay (1974), *Roman Social Relations, 50 BC to AD 284* (New Haven, Yale University Press).
" (1988), *Corruption and the Decline of Rome* (New Haven, Yale University Press).

Manning, J. G., and Ian Morris, eds. (2005), *The Ancient Economy: Evidence and Models* (Stanford, Stanford University Press).

Nicolet, Claude (1966), *L'Ordre équestre a l'Epoque républicaine* (Paris, E. de Boccard).

Parkins, Helen, and Christopher Smith, eds. (1998), *Trade, Traders, and the Ancient City* (London, Routledge).

Postgate, J. N. (1992), *Early Mesopotamia: Society and Economy at the Dawn of History* (London, Routledge).

Renger, Johannes (1984), "Patterns of Non-institutional Trade and Non-commercial Exchange in Ancient Mesopotamia at the Beginning of the Second Millennium B.C," in Archi 1984.
" (1994), "On Economic Structures in Ancient Mesopotamia," *Orientalia* n.s. 63:157-208.
" (2000), "Das Palastgeschäft in der altbabylonischen Zeit," in Bongenaar 2000:153-183.
" (2002), "Royal Edicts of the Babylonian Period – Structural Background," in Hudson and Van De Mieroop 2002:139-162.

Rostovtzeff, Mikhail (1926), *The Social and Economic History of the Roman Empire* (Oxford, Clarendon Press).

Roth, Martha T. (1995), *Law Collections from Mesopotamia and Asia Minor* (Atlanta, Scholars Press).

Sasson, Jack, editor in chief (1995), *Civilizations of the Ancient Near East* (Peabody, MA, Hendrickson).

Scheidel, Walter, and Sitta von Reden, eds. (2002), *The Ancient Economy* (Edinburgh, Edinburgh University Press).

Scott, William Robert (1912), *The Constitution and Finance of English, Scottish, and Irish Joint-Stock Companies to* 1720, 3 vols. (Cambridge, Cambridge University Press).

Stolper, Matthew (1985), *Entrepreneurs and Empire: The Murašû Archive, the Murašû Firm, and Persian Rule in Babylonia* (Leiden, Nederlands Historisch-Archaeologisch Instituut te Istanbul).

Van De Mieroop, Marc (1987), "The Archive of Balmunamhe," *Archiv für Orientforschung* 34:1-29.
" (1992), *Society and Enterprise in Old Babylonian Ur* (Berlin, D. Reimer).
" (2005), "The Invention of Interest," in William N. Goetzmann and K. Geert Rouwenhorst, eds., *The Origins of Value: The Financial Innovations That Created Modern Capital Markets* (Oxford, Oxford University Press):17-30.

Veblen, Thorstein (1904), *The Theory of Business Enterprise* (New York, Scribner).

Veenhof, Klass R. (1972), *Aspects of Old Assyrian Trade and Its Terminology* (Leiden, E. J. Brill).
" (1997), "'Modern' Features of Old Assyrian Trade," *Journal of the Economic and Social History of the Orient* 40:336-366.
" (1999), "Silver and Credit in Old Assyrian Trade," in Dercksen 1999:55-83.

von Reden, Sitta (1995), *Exchange in Ancient Greece* (London, Duckworth).

Walbank, F. W. (1969), *The Awful Revolution: The Decline of the Roman Empire in the West* (Liverpool, Liverpool University Press).

Weber, Max (1976), *The Agrarian Sociology of Ancient Civilizations*, translated by R. I. Frank (London, NLB).

West, M. L. (1997), *The East Face of Helicon: West Asiatic Elements in Greek Poetry and Myth* (Oxford, Clarendon Press).

Wray, Randall, ed. (2004), *Credit and State Theories of Money: The Contributions of A. Mitchell Innes* (Cheltenham, UK, Edward Elgar).

Yoffee, Norman (1995), "The Economy of Ancient Western Asia," in Sasson 1995:1387-1400.

Zaccagnini, Carlo, ed. (2003), *Mercanti et Politica nel Mondo Antico* (Rome, "L'Erma" di Bretschneider).

12

Money and Land as Public Utilities

The economic takeoff of Bronze Age Mesopotamia ca. 3500-1200 BC put in place the basic building blocks of civilization's economic organization – what today is called a market, shaped by land tenure, standardized weights and measures, money and interest accruals, the organization of labor services and fiscal obligations to the palaces, temples and community.

Fiscal needs and proto-taxation created land tenure. Land was allocated and corvée labor obligations stipulated for its holders to work on public construction projects and serve in the army. These obligations were the original land rent, that in time came to be payable in crop-value equivalents. Land held by the palace and temples was rented out to sharecroppers to provide food for their work force.

Large-scale handicraft production and other specialized labor in the palace and temples needed forward planning and resource allocation. That required account-keeping, which in turn required volumetric measures for crops and the distribution of raw materials on a calendrical basis, and weights for the metals and raw materials obtained in foreign trade. What today is thought of as a monetary system became the organizing principle to denominate credit and exchange during the crop year, and to pay debts and other obligations at harvest time.

Grain was used to denominate official prices for domestic transactions with the palace and temples, and silver was used in the sphere of foreign trade and among merchants. These measures of domestic and foreign monetary usage were given value by their use for transactions with the palatial economy, and were assigned fixed equivalencies with each other to produce a bimonetary grain-and-silver system. (A shekel of silver was equal to "bushel" of barley.)

Long before money and land could become "commodities" as vehicles for their owners to seek personal gain without concern for how this affected the overall economy, they had to be organized as what today would be called public utilities. Interest rates were administered both for domestic agrarian debts denominated in barley and mercantile debts in silver. Most credit was run up during the course of the crop year, in anticipation of being able to be paid out of normal harvests, but with safeguards to cancel the obligations if the harvest failed. There was no thought of a private-sector "market" setting interest rates to reflect shifts in profit opportunities, productivity, risk, or the supply and demand of money and credit.

The first means of obtaining rural labor for hire was by making loans to be "worked off" as debt service. This tended to be at the expense of the palatial economy's claims for labor, so rulers sought to prevent labor from being appropriated in this way. The Mesopotamian idea of economic order called for maintaining stability of the land-based economy's basic relationships by proclaiming Clean Slates when new rulers took the throne, and as military or economic conditions required. This subordination of the debt and financial system to the "real" economy thus was quite different from modern financial dynamics, which have taken on an independent "free" life of their own, decontextualized from government writedowns. Money is treated as a commodity, and specifically as an investment vehicle as "property," independent of public checks on the purely mathematical self-expansion path of interest-bearing credit.

The Near Eastern protection of debtors reflected the fact that the Bronze Age was an epoch of labor shortage. Flight to new land was an ever-present option. Just as nomadic chieftains maintained solidarity by an ethic of mutual aid, it was in the interest of palace rulers in more settled territories to limit the power of creditors or "big men" to appropriate the labor service, crop yields and land of indebted cultivators at the palace's expense. Cancelling agrarian debts, liberating debtors from bondage and restoring self-support land maintained the supply of corvée labor and service in the military. From the palace's vantage point, labor itself was a public utility – that is, the liberty of labor from debt to private creditors so that it could serve its public functions to the palatial economy.

How Western economies disembedded land tenure, money and personal liberty

Classical Greece and Italy decontextualized the archaic administration of land, credit and labor. By the 8th century BC, when Near Eastern traders brought interest-bearing debt westward, lands were filling up. Without a tradition of palace rulers cancelling agrarian debts, local chieftains and powerful families used credit as a lever to reduce much of the population to clientage and quasi-serfdom. Their autocracy was ended by reformer-"tyrants" emerging in Greece and some Aegean islands in the 7th and 6th centuries to exile the most offensive elites, cancel debts and redistribute land.

Athenian elites averted a total revolution by appointing Solon as archon in 594 BC. He cancelled the debts that bound cultivators to the land but did not redistribute it. His successors promoted civic building projects and introduced political reforms that catalyzed the drive for democracy. But rising prosperity empowered creditor oligarchies to block democratic reform throughout Greece, fearing that this would lead to a new redistribution of land and annulment of debts, emulating the policy of the earlier tyrants.

Pro-creditor policies were the main reason why Rome's economy polarized and lost its resilience. Its harsh legal principles favoring creditors became its legacy to Europe, and remain the distinguishing feature of the West's economic ideology. Yet in contrast to Rome's own historians, today's free-market historiography euphemizes classical antiquity's oligarchies as democratic, while portraying Near Eastern kingship as Oriental Despotism. But Mesopotamian "divine kingship" aimed at economic objectives similar to those of modern social democracy, seeking to "protect the weak from the strong" by preventing a creditor oligarchy from taking control of government and law-making through the practice of regular Clean Slates.

These acts never became a civic tradition in the West, despite cries for similar economic renewal down through the very end of the Roman Republic when Caesar was assassinated in 44 BC. Western civilization has not prevented financial oligarchies from arising and enacting policies that impoverish much of the population. The idea of writing down debts to keep them within the ability to be paid today is viewed as autocratic, much as attempts to do so in ancient Greece and Rome were disparaged as leading to tyranny or kingship.

Civilization could not have begun with a policy of giving private creditors the power to permanently deprive cultivators of their self-support land and liberty. Populations threatened with debt bondage would have run away to join other communities, to find employment as mercenaries or to back a new leader to liberate them. Such flight also occurred from oppressive Italian autocracies to Rome. That is how its legendary kings (753-509 BC) are said to have built up their city and its army, by offering land to fugitives from neighboring towns. But the protective rule of Rome's kings ended in 509 BC when the last king was overthrown by an oligarchic coup that concentrated political control in the hands of the wealthiest landowning families. The 5th century BC saw repeated "secessions of the plebs," but the land was filling up and there were no more promising territories to which to emigrate.

The five centuries of the Roman Republic (509-27 BC) resisted reform. The public budget was mainly military, minimized social spending, and was administered corruptly by publican tax collectors and provincial governors drawn from the Roman elite. Monopolizing the land and reducing small landholders to clientage, the oligarchy used violence and assassinated reformers who demanded debt relief and land reform, culminating in the destruction of Catiline's army in 62 BC and the murder of Julius Caesar in 44 BC.

Classical antiquity's overwhelming power of creditors marked a great divide separating the West from the earlier Near Eastern takeoff. The path to today's world started by finance, land and labor being commodified and mobilized for private profit. This privatization of authority over finance, land and the conditions of labor has left nominal political democracy unable to protect economies from a rising debt overhead and deepening concentration of land and other property ownership reducing the status of labor to one of peonage.

Modern economic ideology's contrast to Near Eastern rulership

The most critical economic issue confronting any society is how it treats debt dynamics, land tenure and tax policy. Will governments protect the economy's overall viability by subordinating financial and property interests to the common weal, or will these interests break free from regulation and taxes to impose creditor and other *rentier* claims at society's expense?

Only a strong government can regulate economies in the public interest. The ability to prevent *rentier* oligarchies from emerging turns out to be the key distinction between "kingship" (or modern socialism) and "free market" economies. What is euphemized as the "individualism" inherited from classical antiquity and applauded in modern times as expressed in political democracy has meant in practice allowing the public domain, land and basic infrastructure to pass into the hands of a creditor class, and failure to bring financial dynamics under control to protect the population and even governments themselves from deepening indebtedness.

As Aristotle noted, democracies evolve into oligarchies as the wealthiest families gain control of government and write new laws to consolidate their power. If the West's genesis is viewed as starting with classical Greece and Rome, it must be acknowledged that antiquity's great transition lay in replacing kingship not with democracy but with oligarchy enacting a pro-creditor legal philosophy permitting creditors to draw wealth into their own hands irreversibly. What was lost was the economic balance and long-term economic viability that Near Eastern rulers were able to maintain by proclaiming Clean Slates.

The ethic of mutual aid that typically has led low-surplus economies to deter letting personal gains be obtained selfishly at the expense of society at large found an echo in antiquity's Stoic and ultimately Christian disparagement of gain-seeking, wealth addiction and money-lust ("love of silver"), leading the Church to declare the charging of interest to be sinful. But today's "greed is good" individualism ("private vices, public benefits," as Bernard Mandeville's 1714 *Fable of the Bees* put it) is held to be the driver of material progress. Western "free markets" are following a fiscal and financial dynamic similar to that which led to the decline and fall of Rome, leaving creditors "free" to indebt economies and monopolize their wealth. This freedom for *rentiers* is juxtaposed to autocracy, defined to mean strong government forward planning with an ability to check creditors and the overgrowth of debt and financial wealth. Frederick Hayek's idea of freedom was to accuse any public regulation and government planning of leading society down the road to serfdom, not as saving economies *from* it.

Today's legal principles follow those of Rome in upholding the sanctity of an exponentially increasing debt burden. This policy is rationalized by the rhetoric of individualism and "free markets," a euphemism for letting financial wealth remove money, land, basic infrastructure and labor from their public context, without concern for how this polarizes the distribution of income and wealth. Today's mainstream ideology defines liberty and free markets to mean freedom *from* public regulatory authority, leaving the economy "free" for the power of *rentier* wealth to shape markets and politics to serve creditor and other *rentier* interests without government regulatory constraint.

The rationale for weak government regulation of finance and debt is the fantasy that economic downturns – typically resulting from rising indebtedness and interest rates – are self-curing by automatic stabilizers. Since the mid-20th century this "free market" ideology has held that credit markets left to themselves will work automatically to maintain social balance and viability, and that economies can adjust to any volume of debt with a presumably fair distribution of income and wealth. If that assumption were correct there would be no need for governments to intervene to save economies from being increasingly indebted and rent-burdened.

The problem is that the market's "adjustment" is achieved by transferring more and more income and property from debtors to creditors as the expanding volume of debt mounts up more rapidly than the ability of debtors to pay. Yet economists typically project national income as growing at an exponential trend rate, without recognizing that the debt overhead tends to expand faster, so that an increasing proportion of personal and business income must be paid as debt service instead of being available for spending on goods and services.[1] The resulting debt deflation leads to austerity as the economy polarizes and the power of the creditor oligarchy increases.

Are Western oligarchies a long detour of civilization?

Bronze Age rulers had no free-market advisors to argue against managing the money and credit system as a public utility. Rulers recognized the ever-present tendency for economies to be destabilized by debt when floods or drought, war, disease or personal misfortune prevented cultivators from paying the debts that accrued during the crop year. But modern economic ideology, like Rome's pro-creditor legal philosophy, insists on the "security of contracts," above all for debt liabilities. Today's economic orthodoxy rejects acknowledging that the exponential dynamics of debt leads to oligarchy if governments do not intervene to write down debts.

Neoliberal policy deems deregulation and privatization to be synonymous with democracy, human rights and prosperity. Francis Fukuyama helped popularize the belief that this convergence is an inherent evolutionary dynamic of history. Liberalism advises governments to stand aside and not regulate ("interfere with") the free market. In practice that means leaving economic planning in the hands of financial centers, whose business plan is to make money by establishing financial claims and rent-extraction privileges (literally "private law") on society at large.

Oligarchies through the ages have demonized public oversight so as to privatize the land's economic rent by predatory wealth-seeking taking land and credit out of the social and fiscal context in which it originally emerged in archaic economies. Modern economies are polarizing as their debt burden transfers income and property from debtors to the finan-

---

[1] Thomas Piketty's *Capital in the 21ˢᵗ Century* is a welcome exception, explaining today's widening economic inequality by his formula $r > g$: the rate of return to capital (r) exceeds that of economic growth (g). He does not, however, suggest the Mesopotamian solution of debt cancellation.

cial sector, while other *rentiers* extract economic rent through privatized infrastructure, natural resources and other monopolies. Banks lobby to protect such rent extraction, seeing that most land rent today is paid as interest. Creditors now end up with more rent than the tax collector.

So we are brought back to how deregulation of credit and the ensuing monopolization of land and other wealth led to ancient Greece's "oligarchized democracies" and the creditor-landowning oligarchy that destroyed Rome. Its own historians blamed the destruction of the Republic on Rome's oligarchy monopolizing the land, and opposing debt relief and land redistribution, leading to economic polarization and austerity that prevented Rome from creating prosperity from within. Its collapse was a forerunner of the economic polarization caused by modern pro-creditor laws that produce the same effect of concentrating property and control of government in financial hands.

The Bronze Age's management of credit and debt shows that there is an alternative to the "sanctity of debt." Near Eastern rulers recognized that economic resilience requires treating the monetary, banking and credit system as a public utility, along with land. The Western path was for private-creditor power to lead to oligarchy dismantling public authority and impoverishing society. Avoiding that dynamic was the great achievement of the Near Eastern economic takeoff and its tradition of Clean Slates.

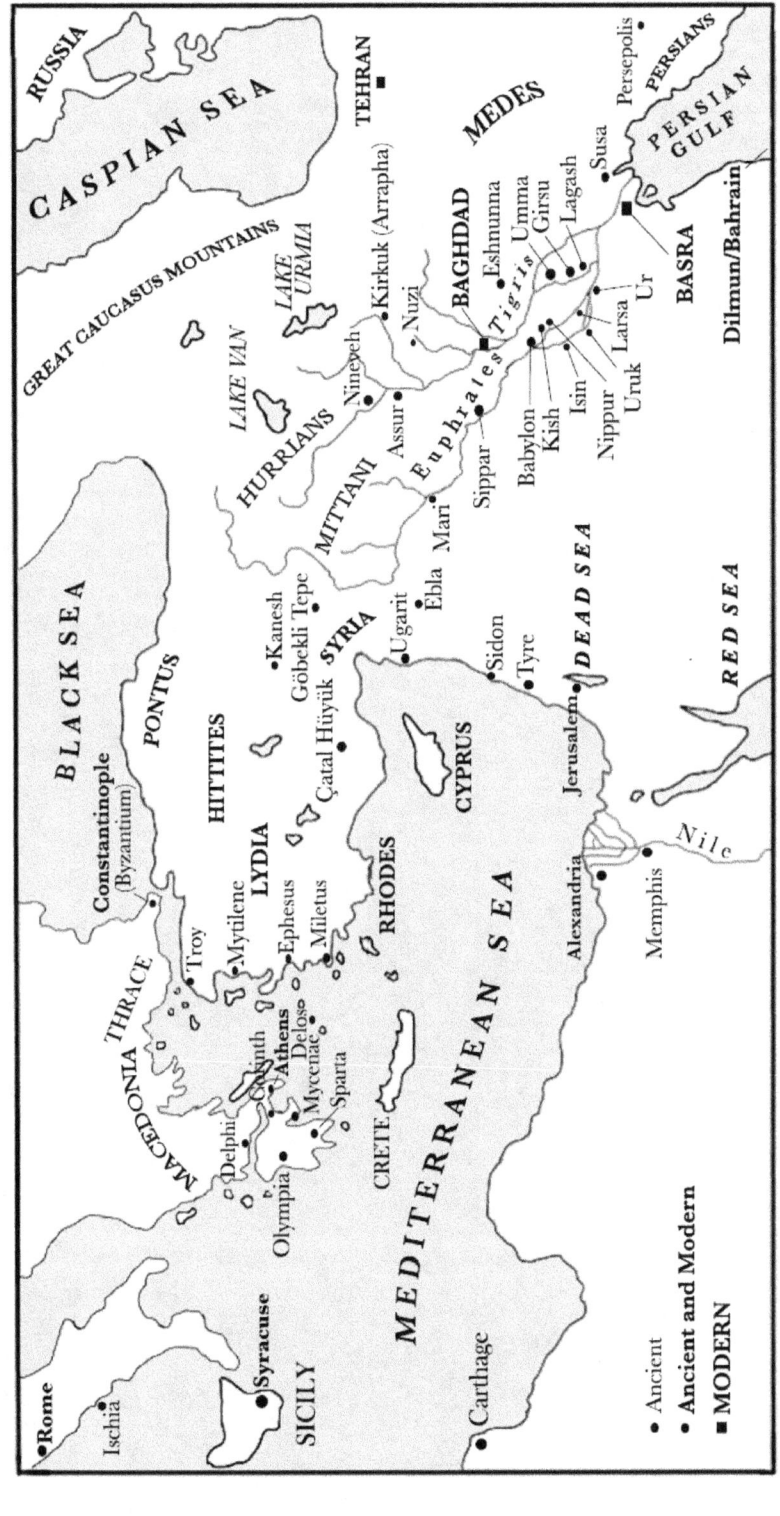

Subject Index

A

account-keeping 5, 9-10, Ch. 1 (esp. 20-2, 29), 84-6, 103, 142, 148-9, 150-1
    Near Eastern institutional origins 9-10, 19-22, 130-1, 150-1, 153, 223, 225, 228, 249-50, 295
    & inception of writing 182-3
agio 64-5, 133, 171-2, 285-6
agrarian debt & usury iii, 31, 33, 36, 97-9, 110-2, 120-5, 153-4, 160-1, 295-6
    origins 120-2
    consequences of 198-200
    arising from accrued arrears (not monetary loans) iii, 19, 34, 86-7, 97, 121, 160, 274
    denominated in barley 120-1, 160
    due at harvest 19, 87, 103, 122, 157, 160, 188
    rate *see* interest rates
    & land tenure 122-3, 160-1, 163-4, Ch. 5 (esp. 198-9)
    as means to obtain labor 153-4, 198, 296
    as unproductive credit 34, 108, 110, 132-3, 171
    annulled by Clean Slates iii, 6-7, 11, 24, 31, 34, 87, 93, 112, 119, **123-9, 147**, 161, 163-4, 255, 261, 274-5, 278, 296
    in Greece & Rome 36-7, 108, 110, 131, 265
    see also debt; usury
agriculture
    Neolithic – agricultural revolution 1, 208-9
    & urbanization 213, 221-3

B

banking & bankers 62-6, 263-7
    Mesopotamia 34, 263-7
        Egibi family 34, 62, 121, 250-1, 263-4, 275
        Murashu firm 62, 250-1, 264
    classical antiquity 15, 62-3, 99, 239-40, 263, 266, 277-8, 281-2
        aristocratic disdain for 263, 281
        public banks 62
    privatization of 26, 62, 64-6
    Western European revival of 64-5, 133, 169, 171-2, 285-6
    modern 53
        19th century 172
        German vs. British 74
        commercial banking 26-7, 38, 173-4, 200
        rent paid as interest to 157-60, 174, 179, 197, 200, 301
        offshore banking centers 235-7, 240-1
    fractional-reserve banking 263
    as a public utility 301
    see also debt; FIRE; money-changers; moneylending; *publicani*; usury
barter *see* money
Bronze Age Mesopotamia/Near East
    economic takeoff iii, 9-10, 254-5, 261-2, 295
    palatial-temple economies 19-24
    innovation of basic economic practices 1-6, 9-14, 19-20, 148, 150-1, 216-7
        see also "Near Eastern institutional origins/innovation" under account-keeping; enterprise & entrepreneurs; exchange; interest; labor; land & land tenure; markets; money; weights & measures
    see also Clean Slates
Byzantine Empire (Byzantium) 64, 112, 162, 169-71, 179, 193-6
    interest rates 94-5, 109

C

calendar – calendrical observation & cosmology 14, Ch. 9
    calend/*calendarium* 108
    & Neolithic agriculture 207-9
    & Paleolithic & later social organization 208-12
    & cognitive development 209-11
    & development of arithmetic, mathematics & predictive sciences 209-10, 223, 228-9
    & development of symbolic notation 228
    calendrical basis of weights, measures & interest rates 22, 85-7, 102-4, 109, 151, 207, 211, 295
        & food & resource distribution 207, 295
    calendrical timing of debt payment 107-9, 207, 209, 211
    & ritual/ceremonial gatherings 14, 142-3, 207-8, 223, 229
    calendrical political/tribal divisions 211-2
    & urbanization 142-3, 207-8, 211-2, 219
        calendrical orientation of early ceremonial sites & cities 208
    & birth cycle metaphors 105-8
    & ceremonial-community based labor 142-3
    Neolithic calendars 207
    Near Eastern shift from lunar to solar calendars 22, 85-6, 102-3, 211
        administrative managerial calendar 150-1
    silver's cosmological association with the moon & lunar calendar 50, 81
    calendrical fractions & musical scale 210
capital 33, 79-80, 95-101, 107, 264
charity 169, 284-5
Christianity
    on interest/usury 133, 171, 285-6, 299
    & wealth & landownership 59, 168-9, 195-6
    see also Crusades; Jubilee Year; Knights Templar & Hospitaller
cities *see* urbanization
classes
    smallholders, landless peasant-tenants & landlords 199
    managerial class 5, 143, 148, 222
    rentier class 172-4, 187, 197-8, 298-9
    ancient working class 151-4
    modern middle class 173-4
    Roman military concept of class 142
Clean Slates iii-iv, 2, 5-9, **11**, 15, 24, 36-7, 64, 87-9, 93, 111-2, **Ch. 5**, 147, 154, 157, 163-4, 179-83, 198-9, 255-6, 296-7, 301
    terminology (amargi, *andurarum, misharum, kittum, shudutu, deror*) 6, 124-7, 131, 180-1
    logic of (preserving corvée labor, military service & fiscal revenue) **5-7**, 15, 36, 64, 87, **123-4**, **128-9**, 147, 154, 191-2, 255-6
    cancelling agrarian not commercial debts 24, 34, 87, 123, 132-3, 147, 161, 163, 181, 255
    restoring self-support land 2, 5, 119, 123, 131, 157, **163-4**, **179-83**, 189-92, 198-9, 255-6, 296
        not townhouses 163, 181, 218
    liberating bondservants 2, 6, 119, 124-31 (*passim*), 147, 151, 154, 163, 190-2 198-9, 296
    based on distinction between productive & unproductive credit 34, 132-4, 171
    cosmological dimension 129-30
    as restorations of order 6, 9, 24, 55, 119, 123-6, 129-30, 180-2
    & circular time 129-30, 133
    & freedom & liberty 6-7, 124-7, 183
    & economic/social resilience 5-9, 299
    & resistance to oligarchy 19, 64,

157, 179, 198, 301
  primarily cancelling debts owed to palace & its collectors iii, 36, 124, 256, 274-5
  creditor stratagems to circumvent 188-92
  declining frequency of 112
  not transmitted to classical Greece & Italy iv, 11, 34-7, **130-2**, 154, 163-5, 192-3, 198, 256, 284-5, 296-9
  in Byzantium 64, 170-1, 193-5
  modern historiography of 124-8
  anachronistic creditor-oriented views of 96-7, 127-9
  & modern ideology & opposition to 15, 88-9, 298-300
  Hammurabi
    misharum proclamations 6-7, 130, 147, 163, 189, 278
    laws annulling debt 7, 124, 161, 274-5, 278
    laws liberating bondsmen 112, 190
  Ammisaduqa's edict 24, 86, 188-90, 278
  see also debt cancellation; debt dynamics; Jubilee Year
coinage 10, 29-30, 35-6, Ch. 2
  numismatics 24, 49, 75
  as state money 49, 57-9, 75
  as creation of law 24-5, 49, 55, 75
    nomisma (coinage) 24, 55-6, 75
  civic-temple origins 10, 49-52, 57-9
    not issued by individuals 53, 57
    transition from temple to civic coinage 57-8, 62-3
  public fiscal origins & role 35, 49-51, 63
  fiscal value derived from acceptability for paying taxes & fees 63, 75
  coinage as public debt to temples 59
  role of temples
    as mints striking coins 10, 14, 29, 50-3, 57, 59, 81
    lending treasure to city-states to strike coins 52, 59
  functions of coinage
    to standardize fiscal payments 54
      to pay taxes, fees & fines 35, 49
      to pay militaries/mercenaries 29, 35, 49, 59, 82
    to finance credit transactions 35
    for trade (esp. at public festivals & games) 35, 54-7
  economic & social impact of coinage 10, 29-30, 36, 49-50, 53-6
  pre-dated by metallic money (weighted metal) 29-31, 36, 49
  cosmology & religious character of early coinage 50-1, 56-8, 81
  introduction by democratic reformers & tyrants 53-5
  & democratizing money 55-6
  increasing military character of coinage 56
  Near Eastern antecedents 29-30
  Greece & Asia Minor 10, 35-6, 49-59
    Aegina (silver stater) 35, 51
    Argos 51, 54
    Athenian (silver "owls") 36, 54-5
      gold coinage 82
    Corinth 35, 54
    Lydian (electrum stater) 54, 75
    Sparta (iron-money *pelanors*) 54, 63, 75
  Rome 49, 51, 63-4, 81, 166, 260
    silver coinage 29, 51, 166
    gold coinage 29, 82, 166
    debasement of coinage 35-6, 63-5, 277, 283, 285
    & inflation 63
    deterioration into commodity (barter) quasi money 49,

63-4
Middle Ages 49-50, 65
Russian 104
see also money
collateral 91-2, 98-9, 187, 275
 livestock 79, 98-9
 persons 99, 187
 land 60, 99, 183, 187, 190
colonies & colonization
 trade colonies 84, 217, 226, 232, 236
 classical antiquity 164, 167
commerce *see* enterprise & entrepreneurs; trade
commercial debt 110-1, 120
 denominated in silver 81, 103, 120
  "silver debt" 23
   also payable in barley 23, 77, 84-6
 & financing long-distance trade 2-3, 14, 32, 81, 93-4, 160-1
 as productive credit 34, 64-5, 132-3, 171
 not cancelled by Clean Slates 24, 34, 132-3, 147, 163, 181, 232, 255
 forgiven if merchandise lost 120, 124, 268, 274
 rate *see* interest rates
 see also debt; enterprise & entrepreneurs; interest
conspicuous consumption 225
corporations 225, 243, 259, 276-7
credit
 archaic exchange & economies operated on credit (not barter) 1, 19, 37-8, 58-9, **72, 86-8**, 120-2, 157, 160-1
  provided by large institutions 27-8, 36, 262
 money as means of settling credit transactions 35
 secularization of – transition from temple to civic credit 57-63
 public creation of 38, 65-6, 277
 privatization of 15, 26, 36-8, 62-6, 87-9, 296-301

productive vs. unproductive credit 34, 64-5, 108, 110, 132-3, 171
see also debt; money
creditors *see* banks & banking; debt; debt dynamics; moneylending; oligarchy; *rentier*
Crusades 64, 169, 171, 195-6, 285
culture, music & art 107, 208-10, 262
 naturalistic art 221, 223, 228-9

D

damgar 269, 255
Dark Ages
 Greek Dark Age 132, 164, 192, 251
 Western Europe 258-9, 282, 285
debt *see* interest-bearing debt; agrarian debt; commercial debt; debt dynamics; debt bondage; debt cancellation; debt & land crises; interest; interest rates; credit
 money's initial role as a medium to pay debts iii, 25, 72, 84-8, 160-1
 terminology (sin, *Schuld*) 52, 73
  see also interest, archaic birth words
 debt-collection procedures 4-5, 74
debt dynamics 120, 132, 197-200, 296-301
 & oligarchic power iv, 7, 53, 163
 as major polarizing & destabilizing force 7-8, 11, 36-7, 53, 72, 93, 112, 154, 163
 debt as means of obtaining labor 151-4, 161, 198-9, 296
 debt as lever to privatize & concentrate land tenure 12, 157-8, 163-4, 171, 179-83, 187-93, **197-200**, 278
 & Rome's decline & fall 2, 8, 134, 199-200, 258-60, 285, 297-301
debt bondage & slavery 120, 151-4, 198-200
 Near Eastern 122-3, 151-4, 157, 180, 190
  liberty from *see* Clean Slates
 Egypt 151

classical antiquity 9, 53, 55, 151-2, 154, 157-8, 164, 256, 259, 285
debt cancellation
 Near Eastern *see* Clean Slates; Jubilee Year
 Egypt 128-9, 132, 192
 Hittite 91
 classical antiquity by tyrants/reformers 10-11, 53-5, 125, 132, 164-5, 284-5, 297
debt & land crises & revolts
 classical antiquity 36, 54-5, 132, 134, 164-9, 192-3, 284-5, 296-8
 Byzantium 170-1, 193-5
democracy 15, 297-301 (*passim*)
 vs. oligarchy & kingship iv-v, 15, 174, 297-9
 Western nominal political democracy 15, 298
 as euphemism for oligarchy 297
 & neoliberal policy 300
 Greek democratic reforms 10, 53-7, 297
 coinage & democratization 53-7
 democratization of land tenure 158, 172-4

E

economic ideology
 & economic origin scenarios 4, 26-7, 37-9, 65-6, 71-2, 77, 87-9, 158-60
 modern economic ideology vs. Near Eastern rulership 7-9, 37-8, 298-301
 classical economics (rent theory) 158, 172-4
  anti-classical 173-4
 Austrian 10, 25, 58-9, 64, 260
 neoliberal – free market 2, 4, 7-9, 15, 26, 32, 71, 83, 88-9, 124, 133, 173-4, 297-301
  contrasted to Near Eastern idea of freedom 183
 pro-creditor ideology 37-9, 65-6, 87-9, 102, 127-8

 idealizing selfishness – "greed is good" individualism 1-2, 299
 New Institutional Economics 28, 65, 84, 89
 security of contracts & sanctity of debt iv, 2, 11, 15, 37-9, 87-9, 183, 198, 299-301
 see also historiography
economic polarization
 debt as major polarizing force iv, 2, 7-8, 11, 15, 36-7, 72, 93, 112, 154, 163, 299-300
 Near Eastern minimization by Clean Slates iv, 2, 7-9, 11, 15, 36-8, 72, 93, 163, 198
 classical antiquity 2, 8, 9, 11, 36-7, 63, 72, 112, 158, 166-7, 238, 260, 273, 297, 301
  irreversibility of 131, 133-4
 modern West 7-8, 15, 89, 134, 154-5, 300-1
economic rent 172-4, 300-1
 see also interest; land rent; *rentier*; value
empire & imperialism
 empire building (classical antiquity) 219
 Near Eastern 146
enterprise & entrepreneurs 14-5, Ch. 11
 entrepreneur defined 255, 259-60, 265-6, 269
 entrepreneurial gain-seeking ethic 252-3, 264-5
  traditional sanctions against 252-3
  role of temples in legitimizing 215, 238, 253, 261
 Near Eastern institutional origins 1, 9, 14, 19-20, 148-50, 223-6, 242, **249-55**, 260-2, 284
  catalytic role of large institutions 249-51, 260-2
  handicraft workshops 1, 14, 84, **148-50**, 153, 215-8, **223-6**, 254
  temples of enterprise 253-5

administered prices 260-1
    & imperative to trade 148, 251, 254, 284
    & debt management 255-6
    increasing private character 184
    see also temples; trade; palaces; Clean Slates
Near Eastern merchants-entrepreneurs (*damgar; tamkarum*) 148, 153, 250-1, 254-5, 261, 263-5, 267, 269, 272, 274
    interface & symbiotic relationship with large institutions 148, 153, 182, 215, 220-1, 224-6, 254-5, 261, 272
    & moneylending/credit 153, 191, 263-5, 267, 274
enterprise in Egypt 256-7
enterprise in classical antiquity 251-2, 258-86
    shift from productive to unproductive enterprise: extractive rent-seeking 252, 258-60, 262, 265-7, 279-86
    state/public interface 259, 272-3
    individualistic, oligarchic *rentier* ethic 258-60, 269-73, 279-81, 298
    aristocratic disdain for enterprise 251, 258-9, 267-71 (*passim*), 277-8, 280-1
    conducted by outsiders – foreigners, slaves & freedmen 15, 251, 263, 266, 268-71, 277-8
    war-oriented entrepreneurship 265
    organization as partnerships vs. corporations 276-7, 286
    decline & collapse of 258-60, 281-6
    see also publicani
documentation of early enterprise 249-50, 254, 256-8
myths about genesis of enterprise 260-2
    & drive for social status 249
    status of merchants & entrepreneurs 269-71, 277
    productive vs. corrosive, parasitic enterprise 258-60, 265-9, 286-7
        & hereditary wealth 258
        entrepreneurs vs. predators 265-9
        see also moneylending; piracy; *publicani*; *rentier*; usury
    financing ancient enterprise 273-278
        commercial lending 273-4
        promissory notes 263, 274
        antichretic loans 275
        classical antiquity's financing limitations 275-8
            absence of public credit 277
    contrasts with modern enterprise 262-5
    commercial/debt abuses & fraud 278-80
    failure to commercialize technology 278
    mercantile trade guilds 263-4, 267, 272
exchange
    anthropological (gift exchange) 3, 73, 76, 91-2, 252-3
        vs. interest 3, 73, 91-2, 120
        ritual exchange centers 14, 142, 207-8, 215, 217, 220
    transition from anthropological to profit-seeking economic exchange 252-5
    Near Eastern institutional innovation of elements for market exchange 1-2, 9, 150-1, 258, 295-6
    archaic exchange conducted on credit (not barter) *see* credit
    Rome's "barter" exchange 37, 49
    Polanyi's 3 stages of exchange (reciprocity, redistributive, market) 25, 76, 225
    see also markets; trade

F

festivals, ceremonies, games & fairs
    & trade, markets & coinage 14, 49, 54-5, 57, 59, 215, 233, 236
    & consumption of economic surplus 75, 253
    occasion for Clean Slates 129-30
    New Year 86, 91, 129-30
    Egyptian *sed* festivals 91, 234

FIRE (Finance, Insurance & Real Estate) sector 173-4

foreclosure 3, 61, 91-2, 120, 154
    & land privatization & concentration 163, 171, 179, 187-8, 199, 259, 278, 285

G

greed *see* wealth addiction

H

hierarchy 6, 224-5

historiography
    of money's origins 10, 26-7, 37-9, 87-9
    of origins of interest 37-9
    of Clean Slates 124-8
    of land tenure origins 158-60
    see also economic ideology

I

Ice Age 14, 107, 142-3, Ch. 9, 213, 215, 219-20
    art 107, 208, 229

inflation 24, 63, 65, 88
    asset-price inflation 158, 160

interest Chs. 1, 3 & 4
    Near Eastern institutional origins 2-3, 11, 14, Ch. 1 (esp. 19, 32-4, 37-8), Ch. 3 (esp. 79-81), Ch. 4 (esp. 91-5, 102-4, 111), 120-2, 250, 260, 295
        origins in commercial sphere as means of financing long-distance trade 2-3, 14, 32, 38, 80, 93-4, 104, 111, 120
    origins of agrarian interest (advancing land to cultivators or managers) 32, 38, 96-7, 120-2
    individualistic productivity theories of 32-4, 71, 79-80, 92-102
        shortcomings & lack of evidence 32-4, 79-80, 92-3, 95-9
        pastoral origin theory not supported by archaic birth words 79-80, 92-4, 97-102
    anthropological perspectives 3-4, 72-4
        gift-exchange 3, 73, 91-2
        injury compensation (wergild) 3-5, 20, 73-4, 91
    archaic birth words (*máš, tokos, faenus*) as metaphors for interest being born 32, 79, Ch. 4 (esp. 92-4, 100-2, 104-9, 111)
    antichretic interest 79, 98-9, 161, 275
    as payment for time 106-7
    as unnatural, sterile & metaphor of homosexuality 108, 110
    & concept of cutting 103-4
    Aristotle on 79, 108, 110
    Aristophanes on debt payment 109
    interest cf. usury 34, 64-5, 109, 133, 285-6
    denunciation & bans on *see* usury
    politics & historiography of interest origin theories 37-9
    see also usury

interest-bearing debt
    origins *see* interest, Near Eastern institutional origins
    innovation accompanied by Clean Slates 2, 11, 93, 111-2, Ch. 5 (esp. 119, 123-4, 132-4), 180
    transmission to Greece & Italy 4, 11, 34, 108
        without Clean Slates 131-2, 284-5, 296-7
    exponential growth at compound

interest iv, 132, 173-4, 299-300
polarizing dynamics *see* debt
dynamics
calendrical timing of payment
107-9, 207
formal nature of 91-2, 120
see also debt
interest rates
   setting of 11, Ch. 4
      set by local unit-fraction for
      ease of calculation 11, 22,
      32, 34, 37, 86, 94-5, 102-3,
      108-9, 111
         calendrical basis 85-6,
         102-3, 109, 151, 207, 211
         adoption of practice in
         Greece & Italy 11, 32, 34,
         94-5, 103, 108-9, 111
   administered, not based on productivity, profitability, risk 11, 32-4, 37, 86, 94-9, 127-8, 260-1, 295-6
   not based on supply & demand 95, 99, 127, 295-6
   stability of traditional administered rates 32-3, 37, 64, 86, 92-7, 99
   long-term decline in rates 92, 94-5, 111, 127
   uneconomic interest rates 93, 110-11
   in Mesopotamia
      commercial "silver" rate 3, 6, 11, 22-3, 32, 34, 86, **92-5**, 99, 102-3, 111, 120, 151, 211
      agrarian rate (based on sharecropping rental rate) 11, 34, 93, 96-7, 111, 121-2, 127
      petty usury 85
   in classical antiquity 11, 34, 92, 94-5, 99, 103, 108-9, 111, 211, 265
   in Byzantium 95, 109, 194
interest-free *eranos* loans 4, 92
Intermediate Periods 146-7, 161, 256-7

J

Jubilee Year (Leviticus 25) iii, 124, 130-1, 147, 163, 180, 256
   deror 124, 131, 180
   prosbul clause 96, 189-90

K

kingship
   Bronze Age "divine" kingship vs. "free market" economies 15, 297-301
   classical antiquity's great transition – replacing kingship with oligarchy 154, 298-9
   modern aristocratic kingship 192
   "kingship" as oligarchic invective 297
Knights Templar & Hospitaller 64, 110, 171, 195

L

labor 4-6, 12-3, Ch. 6
   Near Eastern institutional innovation of labor obligations 1, 12-3, Ch. 6
      organization of labor as a public utility iv, 12, Ch. 6, 296
      communal-institutional origins of labor mobilization & organization 12-3, 141-3, 148-50, 152-3
      & fiscal system – labor as primordial "tax" obligation 12-3, 142-4
      & land tenure – land allocated in proportion to obligation to provide corvée labor & military service 5, 12-3, 141-4, 157-8
      managerial innovation to organize & provision labor 4-6, 142, 150-1, 153
   specialization of labor
      individualistic speculation 77-8
      in Near Eastern temples &

palaces 1, 4, 27, 78, 222, 224, 230
   & urbanization 221-2, 224
ceremonial community-based labor 142-3
corvée labor 5, 12, 142-6, 152-3
   & feasts 144-6, 152
   & communal identity 145
   & political/cultural integration 146
   producing social value not exchange value 142, 152
military service 5, 12, 142-4, 154, 157
Bronze Age commodity-producing labor 148-50, 218
   centered in temple & palace workshops 78, 148, 150, 153, 218, 224
   specialized skilled craft labor 148, 150, 153, 224
   dependent labor – widows, orphans, blind & infirm 1, 84, 148, 162, 181, 215, 218, 253
   aim to produce a monetary surplus 148
managerial class 5, 143, 148, 222
merchants *see* enterprise & entrepreneurs
labor services through interest charges & debt bondage 122-3, 151, 153-4, 161, 296
tension between palace & local authority/creditors over labor 146-7, 153-4
debt cancellation to preserve corvée labor & military service *see* Clean Slates
labor-for-hire 122-3, 146, 150, 153, 296
piecework 150, 153
unfreedom of archaic labor 151-2
local abuse of labor 146-7, 153-4
labor conditions & remuneration 149, 152-3

labor supply contractors 146-7
"time-factored" divisions of labor & skill 208-9
Bronze Age labor shortage 5, 12-3, 144, 152, 227
labor in classical antiquity 151-2, 154
professional craft work guilds 57, 216, 222, 224, 226
see also debt bondage & slavery; slaves & slavery
land & land tenure 12-3, Chs. 6, 7 & 8
   Near Eastern fiscal origins of land-tenure: self-support land allotted with corvée labor & military service obligations 12-13, 142-4, 157-8, 160-1, 179-80
   individualistic origins myth 12, 158-60
      Locke – labor theory of property 12, 144, 159-60, 285
   Engels's monopolization theory 12-3
   as a public utility iv, 5, 12, 187, 295, 301
   Near Eastern land-tenure
      social-communal basis of 12, 179-80, 182-3
      absence of words for "property" 160, 184
      & freedom & liberty 183
      self-support land 161, 180-1
      palace & temple lands 162, 181, 185-7
      sharecropping land 121-2, 162, 181, 225, 242, 295
      military land tenure 162
      townhouses 163, 181, 184, 218, 220
      alienation restrictions 161-3, 180-4, 187-92
         protection against permanent alienation of self-support land *see* Clean Slates
         creditor avoidance

stratagems 188-92
fictive-adoption stratagem 161, 190-1, 198-9, 278
increasing private character of 183-92, 218
    privatization of crop revenue 184-7
privatization of property immune from Clean Slates 218
Greek land tenure 164-5
Roman land tenure 165-9
    latifundia 159, 166-7, 199-200
Byzantine land tenure 170-1, 193-6
land privatization, financialization & monopolization 12-3, 157-8, 184-200, 218
    role of debt – as lever to privatize & concentrate 12, 157-8, 161, 163-4, 171, 179-83, 187-93, 197-200, 278
        foreclosure turning land from natural right into *rentier* property 187-8
    acquisition of land & temple property by Near Eastern rulers & warlords 162, 181, 185-7
    townhouses 163, 181, 218
    privatization of temple offices – prebend income 184-7
    in classical antiquity 164-9, 192-3, 198-200
    in Byzantium 170-1, 193-6
    in Medieval Europe 171-2, 195
    in modern world 154, 173-4, 197-8
    private property vs. commons 182-3
absentee land ownership & landlords
    Near Eastern temples & palaces (first permanent absentee landlords) 162, 181, 184, 225, 242
    Near Eastern creditors (officials & merchants) 179, 182-4, 187-9, 199, 278
    in classical antiquity 158-9, 164-9, 197-9
    in Byzantium & medieval world 12, 159, 169-72, 193-6
    in modern world 12, 160, 172-4, 197
land boundary markers 60, 164, 226-8
oligarchic drive to avoid land's fiscal obligations 154-5, 179, 187-8, 197-9
nationalization of land 158, 172
land rent 158-60, 172-4
    classical definition 172
    taxation of *see* taxation
    paid as interest to bankers 157-60, 174, 179, 197, 200, 301
large institutions *see* palace; temples
    & public/private dichotomy iv, 213
law
    laws of Eshnunna 24, 85, 99, 153
    Hammurabi's laws *see* Hammurabi
    Horemheb & Nauri decrees 146-7
    common law 4, 13, 73-4, 161, 217-8, 235, 242
    general society-wide law vs. trade entrepot institutional law 218, 230-1, 234-6, 242-3
    Greek – *nomos* (law) 24, 49, 55, 75
    Western pro-creditor legal philosophy 2, 9, 36-8, 88, 134, 198, 256, 297-301
liberty & freedom (amargi, *andurarum*, *deror*) 6-7, 124-7, 154, 183
    vs. oligarchic concepts of 8, 134, 165, 174, 299
    see also Clean Slates

M

markets

Near Eastern institutional innovation of iii, 1-2, 150-1, 258, 295-6
individualistic theories of 72, 77-8
markets & prices outside palatial-temple sector 23-4, 103
in antiquity generally 29-30, 51
classical antiquity's depletion of 128, 154, 219, 258, 273, 281-5
& coinage 49, 54-7
& temples 83, 214-5, 260
& public games & festivals 54, 57, 233
land markets 162-3, 170, 183-4, 198-9
stock market in shares of temple prebend revenue 84, 187
slave markets 239-41, 273
see also exchange; enterprise & entrepreneurs; trade
merchants *see* enterprise & entrepreneurs
money
  Near Eastern institutional origins in fiscal & credit arrangements not barter iii, 6, 9-10, Ch. 1 (esp. 19-24), Ch. 3 (esp. 71-2, 81-8), 249-50, 260-1, 295-6
    as medium to denominate & pay debts to temples & palaces 9-10, 20, 25, 54, 72, 84-8, 160-1
    Mesopotamia's grain-silver bimonetary system 6, 9-10, 20-4, 84-6, 102-3, 160-1, 295
    & account-keeping 9-10, 20-2
    & administered prices 6, 21-4, 76-7, 84-6, 150-1, 260-1
    & calendrically based rationing 22, 85-6, 102-3, 150-1, 207
  in classical antiquity 10, 34-7, Ch. 2 (*passim*)
    Rome's collapse into barter – commodity quasi-money 13, 35-7, 49, 63-4, 88
  stages of monetary development (credit-money-barter) 27, 37, 63-4, 87-8

monetary origin theories 10, 24-9, Ch. 3
  State Theory (chartalism) 24-7, 37-8, 63, 74-7, 81-2
    as creation of law 24-5, 49, 55, 75, 81
    as state money 49, 57-9, 74-5
    value based on acceptance by civic institutions for paying taxes & other fees 10, 20, 23, 25, 63, 75, 81-2
    & fiat money 25-6, 54
  barter (commodity) theory 10, 25-8, 31, 58-9, 71-2, 77-8, 84, 87-8, 260
    Menger 10, 25, 28, 58, 260
    failings & lack of evidence 1, 26-9, 31, 37-8, 50, 58-9, 71-2, 80-4, 87-8, 141-2, 260
    money as a veil 71-2
    money as a commodity 25-7, 31, 72, 88, 296
    metallism 25-6, 50, 63, 66, 74, 78
  pastoral/agricultural-capital theories 32-4, 79-80, 95-102
  anthropological & philological perspectives 2-4, 20-1, 72-4
    gift-exchange 73
    injury compensation (wergild) 20, 73-4
    food money 20-1, 33, 75, 96, 100
  politics & historiography of monetary origin scenarios 10, 26-7, 37-9, 88-9
functions of money
  unit of account (measure of value) 20-2, 76-7, 81-2, 84-5
  means of payment
    of taxes, fees & other

debts to civic institutions 20, 25, 35, 38, 49, 54, 63, 81-2, 85, 87-8, 160-1, 197
for enterprise & trade 20, 81-2
denominating debts & payments 10, 52, 55, 63, 78, 81-2, 295
store of value (capital) 25-6, 76, 79, 82
monetary role of temples
mints issuing metallic money 10, 14, 29, **50-3**, 59, 83, 225, 260
overseeing weights & measures 20, 83, 225
as creditors 30, 52, 59-63, 81, 242
grain as money 9-10, 20-4, 30, 85
weighed metal as money 10, 29-30, 36, 49-50
silver as money 9-10, 20-4, 29-31, 80-6, 260-1
monetary role of silver 30-1, 81-2
commercial use 20-3, 30-1, 81-2, 120
as dominant monetary medium 22, 83
& ceremonial & cosmological associations 30, 50, 81-2
gold as money 22-3, 82
jewelry as money 29, 31
coinage as *see* coinage
sources of monetary metal 286
Near East (trade) 30-1, 81-2, 84
classical antiquity (military conquest & Laurion mine) 35-6, 55-6, 59, 108, 254
money & public oversight of weights & measures 28-9, 75
Near Eastern monetary units
shekel 11, 20, 22, 84, 86, 103
mina 11, 22, 86, 103

bushel (gur) 20, 22, 24, 84, 86, 103
sila 24, 149
shekel-bushel equivalence 6, 9, 20, 22, 84, 86, 103, 161, 295
money & prices 21-4, 76-7, 84-6
administered prices (price equivalency schedules) 3, 6, 20-5, 76-7, 84-6, 150-1, 260-1
& money supply 23-4, 86
money as a public utility 31, 295-6, 300-1
privatization of money creation 15, 26, 63-6, 87
government money creation 25, 38, 65-6, 277, 286
public vs. private creation & control of money 10, 15, 25-6, 37-8, 65-6, 74, 88-9, 300-1
monetary terminology
chremata (money) 55
chrematistike (money-making) 267
money, mint *monere, monera, moneta* 29, 51, 81, 260
nomisma (money/coinage) 24, 55, 75
money-changers 36, 51, 62, 110, 171
moneylending
in Near East (origins as side activity of *tamkarum* merchants) 265, 267
in classical antiquity 15, 251, 258-9, 263-6, 275, 280-2
see also agrarian debt & usury; banking & bankers; interest-bearing debt; *publicani*; usury
mutual aid ethic 4-5, 13, 163, 179, 253, 296, 299
Western inversion of 15, 134

N

Neolithic 1, 12, 19, 33, 96, Ch. 9 (*passim*)

& bequest to Bronze Age 143
& labor organization 142-3
notational systems
    Paleolithic-Ice Age "time-factored" notation 207-10
        evolution into arithmetic 209-10
    Sumerian 104-7, 228
    Mesopotamian sexagesimal system of fractions 5, 11, 22, 85-6, 102-3, 106-7, 109, 151, 211, 229
    Greek decimal system 11, 94, 103, 108-9
    Roman duodecimal system 11, 34, 94, 103, 109, 211

O

oligarchy 297-301
    conflict between government & oligarchic power 157-8, 170, 174, 198
        oligarchic dynamics 198-200
    Bronze Age resistance to 7-9, 19, 133, 157, 198, 256, 297-9
        proto-oligarchies 163, 179, 187-92
    in classical antiquity iv-v, 8-12, 36-7, 63-4, 132-4, 163-70, 296-301
        replacement of kingship & Clean Slates by oligarchies iv, 129, 154, 157-8, 192-3, 198-9, 217, 256, 279, 298-9
        individualistic oligarchic ethic 270-2, 280
        oligarchy & enterprise 258-60, 279-84
    in Byzantium 64, 170-1, 194-6
    vs. democracy & kingship iv-v; 15, 174, 297-9
    opposition to public oversight, regulation & reform 174, 197, 299-300
    & land tenure 174
    see also Western Civilization
Oriental Despotism 141, 250, 297

P

palaces
    corporately distinct institutions set apart from the community iv, 213, 217-8, 238, 242, 262
    emergence from temple precincts 78, 253
    relations with temples 185-7, 218
    roles of 1-6, 9-10, 14
    management/control of treasuries, silver, gold, textiles & luxuries 30, 81-2
    & innovation of economic practices *see* "Near Eastern institutional origins/innovation" under account-keeping; enterprise & entrepreneurs; exchange; interest; labor; land & land tenure; markets; money; weights & measures
    enterprises, production & workshops 1, 19, 148-50, 153, 218, 224, 254-5
    as creditors 3, 14, 36, 81
    as landholders 84, 162, 185, 188, 225-8
    as landlords 120-2, 127, 162, 181, 225, 261, 269
    & specialization of labor 4, 221, 224
    & urbanization 216-8, 220-6 (*passim*), 238
    & social stratification 222, 224-5
    & development of writing 223, 228
    see also large institutions; temples
Paleolithic Ch. 9 (*passim*), 223, 252
partnerships 243, 267-9, 273, 275-7, 286
peasants 199
    in Byzantium 170-1, 193-5
    see also serfs & serfdom; smallholders
philanthropy 81, 270
    see also charity; conspicuous consumption
piracy/pirates 108, 239-41, 256, 259,

265, 274, 284
privatization
    of credit/money *see* credit; money; banking & bankers
    of land *see* land & land tenure
    of enterprise 153, 225
    of state monopolies 197, 200, 273, 301
    & asset stripping/corrosive activity 182
    & neoliberal policy 300-1
production
    Mesopotamian institutional large-scale commodity production 14, 148-9, 216-7, 224-6, 253-5
        vs. public infrastructure construction 148
        labor as scarcest factor of production 5, 12-3, 144, 152, 227
    in classical antiquity 151-2, 251, 259-60, 283
        smaller in scale & complexity 53, 130-1, 217, 224
public regulation 298-301
    Bronze Age regulatory oversight 2, 7, 15, 28-9, 216, 260-1
        see also Clean Slates; interest rates; money; weights & measures
    creditor-*rentier* opposition to 2, 7-10, 15, 26, 59, 65, 71-2, 89, 133, 158, 174, 299-301
public utilities iv, 5, 12, 31, 187, 242-3, 295-6, 300-1
publicani 168, 276
    & predatory enterprise 259, 264-6, 271-3, 298
    & moneylending 265, 281-2
    corruption & fraud 279-80, 298

R

reciprocity 5, 73-6 (*passim*), 252
reformers
    classical antiquity 10-1, 13, 36, 53-6, 132, 164-5, 174, 284-5, 296-8
    19th-century 158, 172-3
    see also tyrants
religion & gods
    religious attitudes to debt 199
    & monetary origins & coinage 20-1, 50-1, 57-8, 81
    religious tax exemptions 169, 195-6
    Adad 124, 161
    Aphrodite 51
    Apollo 51, 60-1, 238-40
    Astarte 51
    Athena 52
    Enki 218
    Enlil 7, 84
    Ishtar 126
    Mars 56
    Minerva 52
    Shamash 286
    Zeus 56
    see also Christianity
rentier 187, 197-8, 266, 273
    rentier oligarchies iv, 6, 173-5, 298-301
    in classical antiquity 258-60, 267, 270-3, 281, 286
    naditu heiresses 110, 150, 266
    see also economic rent; oligarchy; *publicani*
resilience 1-2, 5

S

serfs & serfdom
    & debt dynamics 10, 198-200, 296
    Rome's collapse into 36, 63, 200, 260, 285
    Byzantium 194-5
    see also peasants; smallholders
sharecropping
    Near East 96-7, 120-2, 162, 181, 225, 295
    classical antiquity 63, 199
silver *see* money, silver as money
    hacksilver 29, 36, 72
slaves & slavery

Near East & Egypt 6, 103, 126, 149, 151, 181, 218, 253
classical antiquity 60, 151-2, 166-7, 259-60, 200, 259, 263-6 (*passim*), 281, 283, 285
Delian slave trade 238-41, 273
slaves as bankers & entrepreneurs 4, 15, 251, 263, 266, 270, 277
as collateral pledged for debt 99, 122, 198
see also debt-bondage & slavery
smallholders
    self-support land tenure 161, 183
    maintenance by Clean Slates 6-7, 36, 64, 163-4, 170-1, 191, 193-4, 198-9
    expropriation of iv, 12, 63, 133, 158, 164, 179, 193, 198-9
socialism 169, 173, 298
standardization 5-6

T

tamkarum 23, 153, 182, 191, 225, 250, 255, 261-9 (*passim*), 274
taxation
    labor obligations attaching to Near Eastern land tenure (the primordial proto-tax) 12-3, 143-4, 160, 179-80
        land-tenure basis 5, 12-3, 141-4, 160, 162, 295
        & Clean Slate fiscal rationale *see* Clean Slates (esp. 64)
    other proto-taxes 100-2, 185
    land taxation 157-8, 172-4,
        rentier opposition 15, 173-4, 197, 301
        see also land, oligarchic drive to avoid land's fiscal obligations
    oligarchic resistance to 13, 49, 63-4, 154, 161, 165-74, 187-8, 193-9
        tax shift to lower classes 132, 179, 199, 258, 282-3
        offshore tax-avoidance centers 235-7, 240-2
    Church tax exemptions 169, 195-6
    modern tax exemptions 197
    & urbanization & Bronze Age trade entrepots 221, 232, 242-3
    taxes on foreign trade 232
    taxes as giving value to money 10, 20, 23, 25, 63, 75, 81-2
    Near East 102, 146, 162, 216, 254
    classical antiquity 35-6, 74
        Roman tax farming 259, 271-3, 276, 279
        tax burden 169, 258, 261, 283, 285
        tax remissions 132, 256
        Rome's fiscal collapse 13, 35-6, 49, 63-4, 193
    Byzantine 193-6
temples
    evolution out of seasonal ceremonial gathering centers 242
    Near Eastern temples as administrative nodes organizing & conducting enterprise/industry, sponsoring trade & governing external contacts 1, 14-5, **215-8**, 222-6, 231, 238, 242-3, 253-5
        temples of enterprise 253-5
        handicraft workshops 1, 14, 19, 84, **148-50**, 153, 215-8, **223-6**, 254
        organizing & sponsoring trade 1-3, 14, 84, 215, 217, 219-20, 223, 226, 250
        sponsoring markets 215
    & origins of enterprise *see* enterprise, Near Eastern institutional origins (esp. 215-8, 249-51, 253-5, 260-2)
        evolution of commercial functions out of role as ritual centers & gathering places 213-20
        legitimizing entrepreneurial gain-seeking 215, 238, 253
    as corporately distinct institutions

set apart from the community iv, 27, 213, 215, 217-8, 225, 238, 242, 262
as public utilities 242-3
& innovation of economic practices *see* "Near Eastern institutional origins/innovation" under account-keeping; enterprise & entrepreneurs; exchange; interest; labor; land & land tenure; markets; money; weights & measures
as mints issuing metallic money 10, 14, 29, **50-3**, 57-9, 83, 225, 260
as treasuries & storehouses 51-2, 57-8, 60-1, 216, 222, 225, 242
    looting of 35, 56, 59
    war as source of temple treasure 35, 108
as creditors 3, 14, 30, 52, 59-62, 81, 242
sanctifying the context in which money & debt relationships evolved 59-60
overseeing (& sanctifying) weights & measures 14, 20, 29, 49, 83, 225, 242
temple lands 162, 181, 185-7
as landlords 162, 181, 184, 225, 242, 250
& specialization of labor 1, 27, 148-50, 222, 224
registering land sales 60
preserving mortgage & debt records 60
regulatory functions & law 216
as sanctuaries 215-6, 234
civic authority over Greek temples 57-9
& urbanization *see* urbanization, central role of temples
& origins of monumental architecture 227-8
& development of writing & arithmetic 228-9
Temple of Apollo (Delos) 52, 60-2, 238-41

    archive of 60-1
Temple of Apollo (Delphi) 52, 60
Temple of Artemis (Ephesus) 52, 59
Temple of Athena (Athens) 58, 146
Temple of Bel 60
Temple of Hera (Argos) 51
Inanna Temple (Nippur) 184, 186
Temple (Jewish) 51
Temple of Juno Moneta 29, 51, 81, 166, 260
Temple of Minerva 52, 58
Nanna Temple 187
time (circular vs. linear) Ch. 5 (*passim*)
    circular time 129-30, 133, 198
    linear progress 133-4, 198
timocracy 74
trade
    Mesopotamia's need to trade 1-2, 19, 93, 148, 213, 217, 224, 251, 254, 284
    long-distance (foreign) trade 2-3, 14, 19-20, 32, 38, 84, 153, 254-5, 257, 261-76 (*passim*), 281, 295
        conducted using silver 22-3, 30-1, 82, 120
        using gold 82
    trade entrepots 214-5, 230-43
        ports of trade 214-5
    temple organizing & sponsoring of 1-3, 14, 84, 215, 217, 219-20, 223, 226, 250
    financing of 62-5, 132-3, 160, 171-2, 273-8, 285-6
        interest as means of financing long-distance trade 2-3, 32, 38, 93-4
    & urbanization 219-26 (*passim*), 230-3, 242-3
        cities as planned response to need to trade 213, 217
    in classical antiquity 56, 238-41, 262-86 (*passim*)
        aristocratic ethic against 15, 251, 258, 267-71, 278, 280
    & coinage 35, 49, 56, 59
    & risk 120, 266, 268-9, 272-6

(*passim*)
    trade at public festivals & games 14, 49, 54, 57
    & transmission of Near Eastern economic practices 3-4, 34, 51, 53, 252, 262, 270, 284, 296
    local trade 19, 264, 272
    retail trade 56, 86, 265, 279
    see also enterprise & entrepreneurs; exchange; markets
tribute 65, 232, 242, 254
    in classical antiquity 35, 42, 52, 63, 82, 219, 252, 259, 279, 281-5
tyrants 10-1, 53-6
    as reformers 10, 13, 36, 53-6, 164
        introducing coinage 53-6
        debt cancellation & land reform 10, 53-4, 164, 284, 297
    "tyrant" as oligarchic invective 10-1, 53

U

urban revolution 221
    & agricultural revolution 1, 213, 221, 223
urbanization 14, Chs. 9 & 10
    urbs/urban 222
    primary urban sites 220
    genesis of urban centers & cities – evolution out of ritual & sanctified functions
        as gathering places & sacred ritual centers 14, 142-3, 213-23 (*passim*), 229-30, 242
        as sanctified commercial meeting places 214-7, 230-3, 237-8, 242
        as cosmopolitan neutral zones 213-4, 230-3, 237-8
    physical orientation & cosmological symbolism of archaic cities 14, 214, 227-8
        calendrical orientation & shaping of urban centers 207-8, 212
    geographic location of archaic cities 214, 224
    central role of temples 213-30
        as forerunners of cities 219-22
        as earliest city centers 14, 214-5, 222-3, 231
        as administrative nodes organizing & conducting enterprise/industry & sponsoring trade & governing external contacts 14-5, 215-8, 222-6, 231, 238, 242-3, 253-5
        as sanctuaries 215-6, 234
    urban cosmology 14, Ch. 9 (*passim*), 214, 219-23, 228, 230, 243
    characteristics of Near Eastern urbanization & cities 217-9, 220-30
        commercial & industrial role 213-5
        as planned response to need for external relations & trade 213, 217-8
        as sanctified neutral public spaces 14, 213-7, 230-3, 237-8, 242
        military concerns 218-9
    Childe's ten characteristics of urbanization 220-30
        as reflected in Bronze Age temples 222-30
        effect of material factors 213, 221-2, 230
    Bronze Age Near Eastern cities
        as temple & palace enclaves serving specialized functions 223
        contrasted to centers of government 213-9 (*passim*), 230-2, 237, 242-3
        contrasted to modern states 216-8, 242-3
        multiethnic multilingual character 222, 227, 230-5
    Near Eastern entrepot cities 214,

230-8, 242
    trade-commercial entrepots 214, 230-3, 236-8, 242
        ports of trade 214-5
    not governing or military centers 230-1, 237, 242
    as gateways 234-6
    sacred status 236-8
    geographic location (island entrepots) 230-2, 236-8, 242
    parallels with modern offshore banking centers 235-8
        classical Delos as a prototype of modern Panama 238-41
cities of refuge 215-6, 233-4, 237, 281
urbanization & cities of classical antiquity 213, 217-9, 227, 230-1, 238-41
    & militarization & empire building 218-9
    shift from amphictyonic/ritual centers to classical political capitals 217-9, 230-1
    privatization of 218
amphictyonic sites 14, 214, 219, 237
towns 213-4, 221, 223-4, 231, 243
    walled fortifications 213-4
    townhouses 163, 181, 184, 218, 220
development of states 218, 242-3
    development of Western state 217
    counter-states 240
usufruct 98-102, 181, 187, 198
usury 4, 82, 109-10, 120-5, 153-4, 198-200
    vs. mutual aid 4
    agrarian usury *see* agrarian debt & usury
    cf. interest 34, 64-5, 109, 133, 285-6
    as unnatural, sterile & metaphor of homosexuality 110
    denunciations of 110, 121, 132-3, 270, 299
    banning of 125, 171, 193, 285-6
    & classical enterprise 252, 259-60, 262-3, 265-6, 281-2
    see also banking & bankers; interest; interest-bearing debt; moneylending

V

value
    social value vs. exchange value 152
    real cost value vs. market price 172
    see also economic rent

W

warfare/military
    & debt dynamics 196-200 (*passim*)
    & logic of Clean Slates 123-4, 128-9, 179-80, 192
    military service
        as a primordial "tax" obligation 5, 12, 142-4, 157-8, 160
        & land tenure 5, 12, 157-8, 160-2, 170-1, 179-80, 187, 193-4
    & spread of coinage 29, 56, 59
    conquest as source of monetary metal & public revenue 35-6, 56, 59, 82, 108
    temple credit-financing of 29-30, 52, 59, 76, 82
    medieval financing of 64-5, 285-6
    private financing of 65, 166
    as source of labor (slaves) 151, 200, 218, 265
    mercenaries 29-31, 35, 59, 171, 199
        path for dispossessed debtors & fugitives 37, 123, 134, 151, 297
    Mesopotamian payment of soldiers in silver 31, 82
    & urbanization 218-9, 230, 242-3
    Near Eastern 254
        Destruction of Nippur 186
        Lagash & Umma 148
    classical antiquity's military gain-seeking & status 258-9, 280-2

Roman warfare 165-9, 200, 265, 298
    war-oriented entrepreneurship 265, 279
Peloponnesian War 30, 59-60, 62
Punic Wars 29, 59, 81, 166, 279
sack of Rome 134
sack of Constantinople 59, 64, 171, 196, 285
modern wars & financial conquests 200

wealth
    polarization of *see* economic polarization
    hereditary wealth 12, 169, 258-9
    mostly in form of rent-yielding assets 197

wealth addiction (money-lust) 14, 199, 299
    modern celebration of 1-2, 8, 299
    cf. Bronze Age ethics 1, 7, 13, 225

weights & measures
    Near Eastern institutional origins 1, 9-10, 78, 85-6, 102-3, 150-1, 183, 250, 295
    calendrical basis 85-6, 102-3, 151, 207, 211
    transmission to Mediterranean world 34, 51, 284
    & money 22, 28-9, 49-50, 75, 83, 101-2
    false weights & measures 28-9, 83, 279
    need for public oversight 28-9, 83
    temple oversight 14, 20, 29, 49, 83, 225, 242
    carat/*keration* 34

wergild 3-5, 20, 73-4, 91

Western civilization, democracies & economies 15, 284-6, Ch. 12
    Near Eastern origins of Western economic practices iii, 9-15, 262, 284, 295
    decontextualizing land tenure, credit & labor iv, 130-1, 192, 262, 284-5, 296-8
    see also Clean Slates, not transmitted to classical Greece & Italy

Western as synonymous with private sector & individualism 165, 262, 284, 298-9
    individualistic-oligarchic spirit 8, 15, 165, 272, 280
    privatization of credit as a distinguishing feature 65
    sanctity of debt: pro-creditor legal philosophy (as distinguishing ideological feature) iv, 2, 9, 11, 15, 36-8, 87-9, 134, 183, 198-9, 256, 258, 297-301
    creditor-*rentier* oligarchy as Western civilization's defining economic feature iv-v, 15, 154, 165, 197-200, 296-301
    Western oligarchies as a detour of civilization 15, 300-1
    & economic polarization 89, 134, 301
    & linear progress 8, 133-4, 198

writing – Near Eastern institutional origins 150, 182-3, 221, 223, 228, 235

Name Index – People(s)

A

Abraham of Ur 233
Adam, Cain & Abel 215, 233
Alexander the Great 35, 56, 238
Alexius I 196
Ammisaduqa
    Edict of 24, 86, 130, 188-90, 278
Amorites 147, 186, 190
Amos 28
Anacharsis 77
Andreau, Jean 257, 273, 276, 281
Antony, Mark 168, 282
Appian 167-8
Arabs 196, 267, 285
Archi, Alfonso 121, 225-6, 250
Aristophanes 109
Aristotle
    on democracy & oligarchy iv-v, 298
    on money & coinage 24-5, 49, 55, 75, 77-8, 81
    on interest 79, 108, 110
    on money-making & commerce 267, 280
Arsaces 62
Assurbanipal 85
Athenaeus 77
Augustus (Octavian) 168, 241

B

Badian, Ernst 264, 272-3, 276, 279-80
Balkan, Kemal 126, 180
Balmunamhe 263-4, 269
Balmuth, Miriam 29-30
Bardas Phocas 194-5
Bardas Sclerus 194-5
Barton, George 125
Basil I 170, 193-4
Basil II 171, 194-6
Baumol, William J. 258-60, 265, 278, 285
Benveniste, Emile 79-80, 97, 100

Berle, Adolph 186
Berriman, A. E. 34
Bleiberg, Edward 256-7
Bocchoris 128, 192
Boeckh, August 58
Böhm-Bawerk, Eugen von 32, 93, 98
Bongenaar, A. C. V. M. 20, 250
Bottéro, Jean 123, 127, 180
Broughton, T. R. S. 60, 62-3, 282-4
Brutus, Marcus Junius 168, 257, 279
Buccellati, Giorgio 7, 286
Bücher, Karl 250

C

Caesar, Julius 105, 112, 168, 279, 281-2, 297-8
Capitolinus, M. Manlius 166
Cassius, Dio 264
Cassius, Gaius 168
Catiline, L. Sergius 298
Cato the Elder 264, 266, 268-9, 271
Charpin, Dominique 123, 125-6, 128, 162, 180, 186-7, 189
Childe, V. Gordon 220-30
Cicero 151-2, 193, 257, 265, 270, 279
Clark, John Bates 173
Cleisthenes 212, 226
Cleomenes III 165
Comnenos Dynasty 171, 196
Constantine 95, 283
Constantine VII 170
Crassus 168, 273, 281
Cripps, Eric L. 21-2
Curtius, Ernst 51, 57-8
Cypselids of Corinth 164

D

Dante 110
De Callataÿ, François 56
Defoe, Daniel 13
Deimel, Anton 125

Demosthenes 266
Diakonoff, Igor M. 96, 105, 123, 126, 180, 188
Dilke, O. A. W. 105
Diocletian (emperor) 282
Diodorus Siculus 128-9, 134, 192, 260, 273
Diodotus Tryphon 239
Dionysius of Halicarnassus 165

E

Egibi family 34, 62, 121, 250-1, 263-4, 275
Eliade, Mircea 81, 129
Engels, Frederick 12-3
Englund, Robert 21-2
Eniggal 148-9
Enmetena 119, 124-5, 147
Etruscans 231

F

Finkelstein, J. J. 123, 128, 180, 189
Finley, Moses 21, 230, 250, 264, 275-6
Foster, Benjamin 85, 96-7, 127-8
Frank, Tenney 265, 273, 276-7, 281-2
Furius, Lucius 165-6

G

Gaius (2nd century jurist) 276
Gallienus 283
Gelb, Ignace J. 99, 102, 214, 218, 224
Genucius, Gnaeus 165
George, Henry 173
Germans 3, 232
Gilgamesh 223
Goelet, Ogden 144, 146-7, 150-1
Goodhart, Charles 20, 26, 74
Gracchi (Gaius & Tiberius Grachus) 132, 167, 260, 271, 279
Graeber, David 27
Greirson, Philip 20
Gudea 119, 125, 130, 229

H

Hammurabi 7
    laws of 242
        monetary convertibility 23, 85
        weights & measures 28
        interest rates 99, 103
        institutional professionals 224
        debt annulment (for floods, drought) 6-7, 124, 161, 274-5, 278
        liberating bondsmen 112, 190
        restrictions on land alienation 162-3, 188, 191, 255-6
        & financing enterprise 273-4
    misharum proclamations 6, 130, 147, 189, 278
        & land tenure 162, 185
        dynasty of 7, 147, 186, 278
Hannibal 59, 166
Hardin, Garrett 182
Hayek, Fredrick 299
Head, Barclay 50-1, 56-8
Hectataeus of Miletus 35
Heichelheim, Fritz 33, 60, 62, 79-80, 96-8, 251
Hernici 165
Herodian 282
Hicks, John 76
Hillel (Rabbi) 96, 128, 189
Hippias of Athens 54
Hocart, Arthur 50, 71, 81-2
Homer 146, 232
Howgego, C. J. 57
Humphrey, Caroline 27
Humphreys, Sarah 152, 214-5, 266-7, 270, 273, 280, 282
Hurrians 147

I

Iddin-Dagan 186
Ilushuma 126
Innes, Alfred Mitchell 25
Ishme-Dagan 186
Isocrates 259

Israelites 28-9, 215, 233-4
Italians 166-8, 239, 241

J
Jebb, R. C. 58, 61
Jews 29, 51-2, 63, 96, 128, 171-2, 233
Jones, A. H. M. 261, 263-4, 268
Jones, David 276-8
Joshua 234
Jursa, Michael 131-2, 149-50
Justinian 95, 109-10, 112, 268

K
Kashtiliashu 189
Kassites 82
Keynes, John Maynard 74, 76-7
Kirzner, Israel 255
Knapp, Georg Friedrich 20, 25, 74-5, 77, 81
Kraay, Colin M. 35, 54, 57
Kramer, Samuel 125, 218
Kraus, Fritz R. 123, 125, 180, 269
Kurke, Leslie 54-6, 262
Kwakiutl 3, 73
Kypselos of Corinth 53-4

L
Lamberg-Karlovsky, Carl C. v, 142-3, 207, 237-8, 253
Lambert, Maurice 22, 103, 125, 148-9, 180
Larsen, J. A. O 53, 60-1
Larsen, Mogens 126, 226, 232, 267, 272-3
Latins 165
Laum, Bernard 20, 75-6, 100
Leemans, Wilhelmus F. 93, 96-7, 226, 267
Lehner, Mark 145, 152
Leo VI 170, 194
Levine, Baruch v, 131, 180, 234
Lewy, Julius 126, 189
Lieberman, Stephen 125
Livy 134, 165-6, 260, 273
Locke, John 12, 144, 159-60, 172, 183, 285

Lu-Bau 191
Lucullus 281
Lugalanda 148, 185
Lycurgus 54, 164

M
MacMullen, Ramsay 257, 265, 283
Mandeville, Bernard 299
Manishtushu (stele of) 162, 181, 226
Manlius, Gaius (consul 474 BC) 165-6
Mann, Thomas 89
Marius, Gaius 167
Marshak, Alexander 14, 107, 142-3, Ch. 9, 229
Marx, Karl 77
Matinius 257
Mauss, Marcel 3, 73, 252
Maximinus (emperor) 282
Means, Gardner 186
Menger, Carl 10, 25, 28, 58, 260
Meyer, Eduard 250
Micah 29
Middleton, J. Henry 58-60
Mill, John Stuart 172
Moors 285
Morgan, Lewis Henry 226-7
Moses 29, 227, 233-4
Murashu 62, 250-1, 264

N
Nelson, Benjamin 4
Nicephoros Phokas 195
Noriega, Manuel 241
Normans 12, 196
North, Douglass 28, 89, 183

O
Ober, Josiah 28
Octavian *see* Augustus
Oppenheim, Leo 30, 76, 224, 226, 242

P
Pasion 263, 266
Peisistratids of Athens 54-5
Periander of Corinth 54

Petronius 251, 264
Phaecians 232
Pheidon of Argos 51, 53-4
Philip IV (the Fair) 65, 110
Phocians 59
Phoenicians 3, 56, 110, 231-2, 240, 257, 263
    transmission of commercial practices 34, 53, 108, 262, 270, 284
Piketty, Thomas 300
Pittakos of Mytilene 54
Pliny the Elder 159, 264
Plutarch 54, 59, 106, 134, 260, 268-9, 278
Polanyi, Karl 25, 76, 214-5, 250, 265
Polybius 284
Polyckrates of Samos 54
Pompey 281
Pomponious, T. 279
Postgate, J. N. 126, 131, 180
Postumius, Marcus 279
Powell, Marvin A. 28, 30-1, 83, 102-3
Ptolemies 271
Ptolemy 238
Pythagoreans 106, 210

R

Renger, Johannes 20, 25, 76, 93, 99, 122, 149-50, 152-3, 250, 255, 261, 269
Ricardo, David 172
Richardson, Seth 145
Romanos I Lekapenos 170, 194-5
Romanos II Porphyrogenitus 170
Romulus & Remus 227, 233, 281
Roscher, Wilhelm 92, 98
Rostovtzeff, Mikhail 240, 250, 261, 265, 282

S

Sahlins, Marshall 91
Salvian 169
Samuelson, Paul 27, 72, 89
San Nicolo 60
Sargon of Akkad 183, 185, 227, 230, 284

Sargon II 131
Scaptius, Marcus 257
Scheidel, Walter 149
Schneider 96
Schorr, M. 125
Schumpeter, Joseph 8
Scipio Africanus 166
Seidenberg, A. 106 f
Seleucids 239
Seneca the Younger 158-9, 277
Sennecherib 30
Severus, Septimius 282
Shu-Sin 186
Shulgi 147
Silver, Morris 257
Smith, Adam 25, 88, 124, 141, 172, 249
Snodgrass 228
Solon 53, 55, 125, 132, 164, 284, 297
Speiser, Ephraim 127
Spitzer, Eliot 257
Spurius Cassius 165
Steinkeller, Piotr v, 79, 93, 96, 100-3, 121-3, 144-6, 149, 152
Stieglitz, Robert R. 106-7
Stone, Elizabeth 161, 184-7, 191
Strabo 62, 239
Strepsiades 109
Sulla, L. Cornelius 59, 167-8
Sulpicii 278
Syrians 3, 263
    transmission of commercial practices 34, 53, 108, 262, 270, 284

T

Tacitus 3
Tacticus 129
Tarn, W. W. 240
Thatcher, Margaret 7
Theognis of Megara 280
Thucydides 62
Thureau-Dangin, Francois 124-5
Tiberius 264
Toynbee, Arnold 166, 170, 193-4, 226, 285
Trimalchio 251, 277

Tudhaliya IV 91
Turks 196

U

Ur-Lumma 191
Ur-Nammu 147
Urukagina of Lagash 28, 100-1, 119, 124-6, 147, 185

V

Van De Mieroop, Marc v, 21, 121-2, 250, 263, 269
Veblen, Thorstein 141, 145, 259-60
Veenhof, Klass R. 23, 274
Verres 279
Virgil 159
von Reden, Sitta 55-6, 262

W

Walbank, F. W. 276, 280, 283
Weber, Max 249, 265, 269, 271-2
Westbrook, Raymond 91, 126
Wray, Randall 25, 27, 56, 74, 263
Wunsch, Cornelia v, 34, 62, 87, 121, 263, 275

Y

Yallop, David A. 236
Yoffee, Norman 185, 225, 266
Yoruba 220

Z

Zimri-Lim 189

Name Index – Places

A

Aegean 3, 131, 158, 192, 238-41, 262-3, 297
Aegina 35, 51
Africa 106
    North Africa 166-9
Akkad
    Akkadian terminology
        Clean Slates (*andurarum, misharum, kittum*) 124-7, 131, 180
        interest (*máš*) 32, 111, 133
        proprietor (*bēlum*) 160, 184
        urbanization *(alu)* 223
    cities 230
Alexandria 273
Anatolia 3, 84, 142, 171, 254, 274
Antioch 60
Argos 51, 54
Asia Minor
    money & coinage 10, 35, 49, 53, 62
    temples 60, 62
    trade 226, 264, 272
    & urbanization 213-4, 231-2
    & Rome 167, 239, 241, 282-4
    see also Anatolia; Çatal Hüyük; Göbekli Tepe; Kanesh;
Assur 126, 214, 274
Assyria 256
    money/coinage antecedents 29-30, 82
    foreign trade 3, 22-3, 82, 226, 232, 263-4, 272, 274
    Clean Slates (*andurarum*) 126-7, 131-2
Athens 52-62 (*passim*), 226
    money/coinage 36, 54-5
        melting statues to coin 30, 76, 82
        Laurion silver mines 35, 55, 254
    debt crises & cancellation 125, 132, 134, 164, 297
    labor 151, 199
    markets & market regulation 29, 55
    enterprise 259, 263, 266-7, 280
    & empire 219, 238
    political units 212, 221, 226
    Piraeus 232
Avebury 142

B

Babylonia
    temple-palatial innovation of basic economic practices 4-6, 19-24, 84-5, 216-8, 258, 260
    Clean Slates (*misharum*) 6-7, 23-4, 55, Ch. 5 (esp. 119, 125-33), 147, 163, 180-1, 234, 255-6, 278-9
    & metallic money & temples 83-5
    polarization 112
    banking & lending 62-3, 265-7, 273-5
    account-keeping 142, 150-1
    labor organization 142-6, 149-54
    land tenure 157, 171, 180-91 (*passim*), 278
    tax exemptions 195
    social stratification 224-5, 269
    linkage to Indus civilization via Dilmun 235, 237-8, 257
    entrepreneurs 122, 250-1, 255-8, 263-9, 272
    restitution fines 73
Bahamas 235
Bermuda 235
Bithynia 240
Branchidae 35
Britain 12, 172-3, 236
    see also Avebury; England; Stonehenge

British West Indies (Cayman Islands) 235-6
Bulgaria 195

C

Campania 166, 168
Canada (Kwakiutl) 3, 73
Cappadocia 84, 171
Carthage 56, 82, 166, 239, 257, 279
Çatal Hüyük 213-4, 231, 236-7
China 220, 235
Cilicia 239-41
Cnidus 52
Constantinople 59, 64, 193-6, 284-5
    see also Byzantine Empire
Corinth 35-6, 52-4, 62, 134, 164, 239
    coinage 35, 53-4
    games 233, 236
Cornwall 232
Crete 91, 108, 251, 257
Cyprus 257

D

Delos 214
    temple of 52, 60-2, 238-41
    as free-enterprise entrepot 62, 110, 226, 238-41, 273
    & Delian League 52
    Delian games 57
Delphi 214, 236
    temple of 52, 59-61
    & organizing trade 226
    Pythian games 57, 233, 236
Dilmun (Bahrain) 232, 235, 237-8, 257
Dura 60

E

Edessa 60
Egypt 1
    economic bifurcation 30
    redistributive economy 256-7
    account-keeping 20, 142
    labor 27, 141-52 (*passim*), 239
    land tenure 157-8, 160-1
    debt 91, 104
    debt cancellations 128-9, 132, 192
    entrepreneurial activity 30, 256-7, 273
    trade 56, 226, 231
        Nile Delta entrepot 231, 237
    urbanization 220, 226-7
    sed festivals 91, 234
    decimal system 11, 108, 229
    pyramids 141, 145, 152
    number anthropomorphism 106
    calendar 102
    Intermediate Periods 146, 161, 256-7
    & Rome 273, 282, 284
England 146, 153, 171-3, 192, 255, 268
    see also Britain
Ephesus 52, 59
Eshnunna 24, 85, 99, 153
Ethiopia 192
Etruria 110, 168
Euphrates River 23, 190, 254
Europe
    Ice Age 220, 229
    archaic/tribal 3, 5
    medieval 14, 58-9, 64-5, 110, 171-2, 195-6, 215, 224, 232, 236, 273, 276, 285-6
    eurozone 26

F

France 65, 110

G

Gadir 232
Gaul 166, 169
Genoa 196
Germany 74, 232
Göbekli Tepe 142-3
Gotland 232
Greece
    Mycenaean 21, 53, 91, 108, 142, 147, 192, 227, 249, 251, 257
        Linear B 21, 108, 147
    see also Athens; Corinth; Delos; Delphi; Sparta

H

Hana 189
Helgoland 232
Hittite kingdom 91
Holland 268
Hong Kong 232, 235-6

I

Illyricum 109
India 50, 224, 283
    Indus civilization 91, 220, 224, 235, 237, 254, 257
Ionia 35
Iran
    Iranian plateau 84, 226, 254
    Iranian shore 235, 237
Iraq 251
Ireland 173
Ischia/Pithekoussai 231-2, 237
Isin 23, 186
Isthmus 35, 164
    Isthmian games 57, 233, 236

J

Jamaica 236
Jericho 214
Jerusalem 60, 63
Judah 131

K

Kanesh 226, 232
Korea 148

L

Lagash 30, 119, 124, 126, 148-9, 185
Lebanon 235
Levant 163, 193, 239
Liberia 235-6
Lydia 54, 75

M

Macao 235
Macedonia 166, 283
Mari 189
Mesopotamia *see* Akkad; Assyria; Babylonia; Euphrates River; Lagash; Nippur; Sumer; Tigris River; Ur; Uruk
    ecological imperative to trade 148, 213, 216, 251, 254, 284
Miletus 35
Motya 232
Mytilene 54

N

Nemea (games) 233, 236
Netherlands Antilles (Curacao) 235
Nile 231
Nippur 62, 84, 184, 186, 191, 237, 242
Nuzi 190, 278

O

Øland 232
Olympia 57, 60, 233, 236
Ortygia 232

P

Panama 235-6, 240-1
Peloponnese 51, 57
Persia 52, 62, 238
Peru (Incan) 224
Phoenicia 56
    see also Phoenicians
Piraeus 232
Pontus 241
Puteoli 278

R

Rhodes 239
Rome 239, 241
    origins 13, 152, 230, 233, 281, 297
    fiscal collapse & monetary deterioration 13, 35-7, 49, 63-4, 87-8, 154, 193, 277, 281-3
    economic polarization & collapse 8-9, 37, 132, 134, 154, 157-9, 193, 198-200, 219, 258-60, 281-5, 297-301
    enterprise Ch. 11 (*passim*, esp. 263-87)

    decline of enterprise 281-7
oligarchy 8-11, 154, 164-9, 174, 198, 271, 279-82, 297-301
pro-creditor legal philosophy iv, 2, 9, 11, 15, 36-8, 88, 134, 183, 198, 256, 258, 297-301
money *see* coinage; money
land tenure 165-9
land & debt crisis 164-9, 174
increasing servile labor 151-2
civil/Social War 132, 167, 260
militarism *see* warfare/military
empire & imperialism 219, 279-85
    Roman Empire 63-4, 284
    Roman Republic 63, 260, 281, 297-8, 301
Russia 208-9
    Russian rouble/coins 103-4
Ru'ush eg-Gibal 232

S

Salamis 257
Samos 54
Scilly Isles 232
Sepphoris 60
Sicily 279, 169, 232
Sicyon 52
Sidon 51
Singapore 235
Spain 257, 273, 282, 285
Sparta
    debt crises & reforms 36, 53-4, 134, 164-5, 226, 278
    rejecting commerce & silver money 53-4
    iron money 53-4, 63, 75
    Peloponnesian War 60, 82
    Peloponnesian League 52, 57
    empire building 219
Stonehenge 142-3
Sumer
    temple-palatial innovation of basic economic practices 3-6, 19-24, 84-5, 216-8, 258, 260
    Sumer's temples – first centers of enterprise 14, 216-8, 254-5
    palace management of monetary metals & luxuries 30, 81-2
    invention of interest 2-3, 32, 91, 111
        birth metaphors for 32, 94, 100-7, 111
    setting of interest rates 92-5, 102-4, 111
    interest-bearing debt 120
    Clean Slates (amargi) 6, 24, Ch. 5 (esp. 119, 123-7, 130, 133), 147
    earliest written records 120, 142
    notational systems 104-7
    account-keeping 78, 142
    labor organization 142, 148-9
    land tenure 180-2
    trade & enterprise 2-3, 14, 32, 148-50, 272
        damgar merchants 255, 267, 269
    linkage to Indus civilization via Dilmun 235, 237-8, 254, 257
    urbanization 14, 217-8, 223
    & empire building 146, 219
    see also Lagash; Nippur; Umma; Ur; Uruk
Syracuse 59, 232
Syria 63, 226, 239
    see also Syrians; Tell Abyad; Ugarit

T

Tal-i-Bakun 143
Tell Abyad 143
Thebes 52
Thrace 109, 283
Tigris River 24, 214
Türkiye 239

U

Ugarit 30, 251
Umbria 168
Umma 30-1, 148-9
United States 24, 125, 158, 173-4, 197, 235-6, 241

Ur 23, 82, 186-7
    Ur III period 24, 85, 93, 96, 99, 102, 104, 107, 111, 122, 146, 149-50, 186, 267
Uruk 150, 217, 223
    Uruk expansion 84, 226
    Eanna district 217

V

Vatican 236
Venice 64, 196, 285

www.ingramcontent.com/pod-product-compliance
Lightning Source LLC
LaVergne TN
LVHW060135080526
838202LV00050B/4116